C000100697

Covenant Theology

From Adam to Christ

Containing

A Discourse of the Covenants
that God made with men before the Law.
Wherein, the *Covenant of Circumcision*
is more largely handled, and the invalidity of
the plea for paedobaptism taken from thence discovered.

By Nehemiah Coxe

And

An Exposition of Hebrews 8:6-13.
Wherein, the nature and differences between
the Old and New Covenants is discovered.

By John Owen

Edited by Ronald D. Miller, James M. Renihan
and Francisco Orozco

Reformed Baptist Academic Press
Palmdale, CA

Copyright © 2005 Reformed Baptist Academic Press. All rights reserved. The copyright does not apply to the material by Coxe and Owen.

Requests for information should be sent to:

Reformed Baptist Academic Press
37104 Bridgeport Ct.
Palmdale, CA 93550
rbap@sbclgobal.net
www.rbap.net

No part of this publication may be reproduced, stored in a retrieval system, or transmitted in any way by any means, electronic, mechanical, photocopy, recording, or otherwise, without the prior permission of Reformed Baptist Academic Press except as provided by USA copyright law.

Printed in the United States of America.

ISBN 0-9760039-3-7

In spiritually healthier times Covenant Theology was more readily appreciated and less misunderstood than it is today. With the outright rejection of covenantalism by some Baptists and the heretical overextension of it by some Presbyterians, we can use as much help as we can get from our Protestant heritage. This volume brings together wonderful insights from two faithful church leaders of an earlier generation with helpful analyses from competent teachers of today. The result is a valuable resource for students, academics, and pastors.

Thomas K. Ascol, Ph.D.
Pastor, Grace Baptist Church, Cape Coral, FL
Editor, Founders Journal

....

It is strange that Nehemiah Coxe's *A Discourse of the Covenants* has not been reprinted since it first appeared in the 17th century, for some of our Calvinistic Baptist forebears—men like John Sutcliff of Olney—appeared to have deeply appreciated it. Be this as it may, this fresh edition is extremely welcome: it clearly demonstrates that 17th century Calvinistic Baptists like Coxe—and his modern descendants in this century—are *fully* part of that stream of Reformed theology that has come down from the Reformation work of men like Huldreich Zwingli, John Calvin, Heinrich Bullinger, and Théodore de Bèze. More times than I can count—and personally I find it so frustrating—I have heard Reformed theology defined in such a way that it excludes those who hold to believer's baptism. This valuable work will help set the record straight.

Michael A.G. Haykin, Th.D.
Principal, Toronto Baptist Seminary,
Toronto, Ontario

....

Nehemiah Coxe's work on the covenant is an important piece of writing by a significant seventeenth century Particular Baptist theologian. Its republication is long overdue. As a bonus the reader has Coxe himself rescued from obscurity in a well-researched introduction by Dr. James M. Renihan. Since Coxe referred his readers to John Owen's treatment of the nature and differences between the Old and New Covenants, Owen's exposition of Hebrews 8:6-13 is included. Both Coxe and Owen have been lightly and sensitively edited with explanatory notes. The essay by Richard C. Barcellos places Owen's teaching on the covenant firmly within the wider Reformed consensus. The book as a whole has modern practical application. It shows that Reformed Baptists do have a consistent and well argued doctrine of the covenant. It also shows that the seventeenth century Particular Baptist fathers, while emphasizing the newness of the new covenant, argued that the Decalogue remains a rule of life for the believer. This work is an important resource for twenty-first century Reformed Baptists.

Robert W. Oliver, Ph.D.
Pastor, Old Baptist Church Bradford on Avon, UK
Lecturer in Church History/Historical Theology, London Theological Seminary
Lecturer in Church History Nonconformity, The John Owen Centre, London
Guest lecturer, Westminster Theological Seminary, London

....

In most of the material that has been reprinted over the last half-century, Covenant Theology has been presented as if it necessarily implied the doctrine and practice of infant baptism. We could fill much space here simply listing the books that have taken this position. Many of us, however, have been unconvinced of this stipulation, believing that it is an unnecessary consequence of theological reasoning. We believe that it is very possible, even requisite, to formulate an exegetically based Covenant Theology that upholds the centrality and continuity of God's plan of redemption through the ages without falling into the deduction that infant baptism must attend that doctrine.

Sadly, there have been few works available that have wrestled with these issues at a profound exegetical and theological level. The books written from a paedobaptist perspective are often dismissive of the credobaptist (i.e., believer's baptism) point of view, and those defending believer's baptism have often failed to give sufficient effort to presenting a full-blown covenantal system. The end result is that paedobaptists have seldom, if ever, considered the possibility of a covenantal credobaptist position, and many Baptists are simply ignorant of the centrality of the covenant and its usefulness in defending their own beliefs. This book is an attempt to begin to rectify this deficiency.

James M. Renihan, Ph.D.
Escondido Reformed Baptist Church, Escondido, CA
Dean, Institute of Reformed Baptist Studies
Westminster Theological Seminary in California, Escondido, CA

....

Table of Contents

PART II: John Owen

APPENDICES

INDICES

Introduction:

Why is this reprint important?

James M. Renihan

In the decades since 1950, the Christian reader has had the privilege of access to a whole host of reprinted works. The majority of these books have been of incalculable blessing to the Church of Jesus Christ, helping believers to understand the great historic doctrines of the faith. Under the hand of God, and with His blessing, the revival of interest in the Reformed faith must be, too a large degree, credited to the widespread availability of these theological masterpieces. As the truth has been disseminated, lives have been changed and churches have been ordered to the glory of God according to the Scriptures.

In the richness of treasure deposited in the past, other valuable pieces of theological literature remain to be rediscovered. Even though half a century of reprinting has passed, presses continue to issue vital documents drawn from the rich store of Reformation and Post-Reformation writings, and the treasury is still stocked with books worthy of attention. Some deserve translation into English in order to increase their accessibility, while others simply wait for the resources necessary to bring them to the Christian public. It is a great pleasure to make one step forward in this process through the publication of the present volume.

As men confessionally committed to the Reformed faith, the modern editors of this work believe that it fills a very important niche in the explication of that system of theology. We believe that the structure of Scripture is properly defined by what has been designated as Covenant Theology—to grasp this fact is to grasp the central architecture of the entire Bible. Its divine author has revealed himself to men by way of covenant, and calls us to see that this is the most foundational means of understanding the full picture presented on its holy pages.

In most of the material that has been reprinted over the last half-century, Covenant Theology has been presented as if it necessarily implied the doctrine and practice of infant baptism. We could fill much space here simply listing the books that have taken this position. Many of us, however, have been unconvinced of this stipulation, believing that it is an unnecessary consequence of theological reasoning. We believe that it is very possible, even requisite, to formulate an exegetically based Covenant Theology that upholds the centrality and continuity of God's plan of redemption through the ages without falling into the deduction that infant baptism must attend that doctrine.

Sadly, there have been few works available that have wrestled with these issues at a profound exegetical and theological level. The books written from a paedobaptist perspective are often dismissive of the credobaptist (i.e., believer's baptism) point of view, and those defending believer's baptism have often failed to give sufficient effort to presenting a full-blown covenantal system. The end result is that paedobaptists have seldom, if ever, considered the possibility of a covenantal credobaptist position, and many Baptists are simply ignorant of the centrality of the covenant and its usefulness in defending their own beliefs.

This book is an attempt to begin to rectify this deficiency. In the seventeenth century, covenantal defenses of believer's baptism were the rule rather than the exception, and the work by Nehemiah Coxe reprinted here stands out as an excellent example. Coxe lived in a day when the best exegetes and theologians, Baptist and paedobaptist, explained and defended Covenant Theology, and he joined with them in presenting his views of the historical covenants. Recognizing the covenants as the structure of redemptive revelation and history, he progressively offers an exposition of each of God's covenantal dealings with men prior to the law. In doing this, he is able to demonstrate that Baptists share with their other Reformed friends a commitment to this historical and progressive revelation of God's grace to men. This is vitally important, and has been the source of surprise and blessing to paedobaptists who have discovered this point. They realize that confessional Reformed Baptists are not closet dispensationalists, but full-blown adherents to Covenant Theology.

We have chosen to include John Owen's comments on Hebrews 8:6-13 alongside Coxe's work, for several important reasons. We know, of course, that Owen was a life-long paedobaptist, and briefly defends that view in his other writings. We do not intend, in any way, to imply that Owen would have endorsed Coxe's (or our) objections to the paedobaptist position. Nevertheless, it has seemed good to incorporate his views into this work. The reader will notice that Coxe, in the preface to his *Discourse*, indicates that he was preparing materials for a subsequent volume to be written on the Mosaic Covenant and the New Covenant, but was "happily prevented" by the publication of Owen's volume on Hebrews chapter 8. So far as the Baptist Nehemiah Coxe was concerned, John Owen's work on this part of Hebrews clearly articulated the things that Coxe himself would have said (and he recognized that Owen said them better as well). This does not imply that Coxe endorsed every jot and tittle of Owen's work, but simply indicates the massive agreement between the two. Owen, for his own part, exegetically demonstrates that the New Covenant is profoundly different from the Old — It is characteristically *new*. For Coxe (it must be remembered that he is the most likely candidate to have served as editor of the Second London Confession of 1677/1689 [2nd LCF]), and confessional Reformed Baptists who agree with his theology, Owen's emphasis on the newness of the New Covenant is a helpful step forward in the discussion.

In our own day, there have been some who have floated the notion that Owen's emphasis on newness is tantamount to the perspective developed by some Baptists who adhere to the so-called *New Covenant Theology*. Nothing could be further from the truth, and it is hoped that the combination of these works will rectify the situation. Owen was one of the principal architects of the Covenant Theology articulated in the 1658 Savoy Declaration of Faith, and Coxe's relationship to the 2nd LCF, a document closely based on Savoy, is apparent. In both cases, these men, committed to the doctrines presented in those Confessions, saw no contradiction between their formulations of Covenant Theology and the full range of doctrines expressed in their Confessions. This is especially apparent in their views of the abiding validity of the Moral Law, summarized in the Ten Commandments. For both of them, the progressive nature of the historical covenants and the newness of the New Covenant was no barrier to the recognition of an abiding continuity. There is covenantal unity, even while there is covenantal diversity.

Since this issue is so vital, we have included as an appendix an essay written by Richard Barcellos entitled "John Owen and New Covenant: Owen on the Old and New Covenants and the Functions of the Decalogue in Redemptive History in Historical and Contemporary Perspective." In this essay, Pastor Barcellos thoroughly demonstrates that there is no basis in reality, fact, or fancy to assert that Owen's view of the covenants was anything but soundly orthodox, consonant with the confessional documents and bears no essential resemblance to the emerging views of the so-called *New Covenant Theology*. It is our hope that this essay will not only put the nail in the coffin (so to speak), but bury it six feet under the ground. It is tempting to enlist Owen's name and reputation in support of one's position—in this case, said effort is shown to be a failure. The juxtaposition of Coxe, Owen, and Barcellos' appendix make this crystal clear.

It is our hope that this volume will serve several purposes. On the one hand, we wish to strengthen the hands of the pastors of confessional

Reformed Baptist churches by providing them with this excellent material defending their theology. On the other hand, we hope that this work will move forward the process by which our paedobaptist friends recognize that we are very serious about Covenant Theology. We are truly convinced that it is the structure of the Bible. Further, we hope that some of those who have been tempted to stray from the Confessional paths into novel ideas might read and return to a commitment to this marvelous system, drawn forth from the pages of Holy Scripture. May the Lord bless this effort for His glory and the good of the Church. Amen.

James M. Renihan, Escondido, California, February 2004

PART I

Nehemiah Coxe

An Excellent and Judicious Divine:

Nehemiah Coxe

James M. Renihan

In God's providence, many of His saints have lived and died without recognition or historical acclaim. The book of Hebrews, in chapter 11, summarizes the lives of believers from all ages who faithfully endured, looking not for earthly fame but for the promised reward, shared with the people of God through all of the ages. Only the Last Day will reveal the fullness of God's workings among His elect. We are thankful for the historical record given to us, providing noble testimonies of those who demonstrated that the life of faith is the essence of godliness. Many are famous, most are obscure. Such is the case with Nehemiah Coxe. Perhaps the chief editor of the most famous Baptist Confession ever, his name is unrecognized by the majority of his theological heirs. Even the published editions of the 2nd LCF, when listing the names of the subscribers, make no mention of him. It is a pleasure to bring some attention to the work of God through this devoted servant of Jesus Christ.

The story of his life must begin with his father, Benjamin Coxe. Probably the son of a Church of England clergyman,[1] Benjamin matriculated at Christ Church, Oxford, in April 1609, when he was 14 years old. He received the Bachelor of Arts degree from Broadgates Hall, Oxford in June 1613, and his Master of Arts degree in June, 1617.[2] He was appointed rector of the western village Sampford Paverel, but at this point in his career his doctrinal convictions are unclear. W.T. Whitley notes that the high Presbyterian Thomas Edwards "twitted" Coxe "for having been zealous concerning Laud's innovations."[3] Whatever the

---

[1] It is popularly reported that Benjamin Coxe was the son of a bishop of the Church of England, often said to have been Richard Cox. In an unsigned biographical article, W.T. Whitley demonstrated that this could not be true. All of Bishop Cox's children were born by 1568, and he died in 1581. Benjamin was not born until 1595. See (W.T. Whitley) *"Benjamin Cox," Transactions of the Baptist Historical Society* 6 (1918-1919): 50. It may be that he was the *grandson* of Bishop Cox.

[2] Joseph Foster, ed., *Alumni Oxoniensis*, Volume I.—Early Series (Nendeln, Liechtenstein: Kraus Reprint Limited, 1968), 340.

[3] Whitley, *Benjamin Cox*, 50. Edwards, in a listing of several leading "Sectaries" of the 1640s speaks of "One Master *Cox* who came out of *Devonshire*, an Innovator, and great time-server in the Bishops time, that against the will of the Bishop of *Exeter*,

truth of this allegation, by 1642 Coxe was defending a position not far from that of the Baptists in his pamphlet *A Thesis or Position Concerning The Administering and Receiving Of The Lord's Supper Cleared and Confirmed*. The thesis of his argument is thus: "He who administers the Lord's Supper to one who is a fornicator, or covetous, or an idolater, or a railer, or a drunkard, or an extortioner, does therein commit a very grievous and hateful sin. The children of God must have no fellowship at all with this sin, but reprove it."[4] Clearly, Coxe was moving toward a Baptist view of the sacraments. It is only a small step from guarding the holiness of the Lord's Table to admitting only believers to baptism. Whitley says it well: "Once a man sets to work in earnest to limit communion to real believers, he is likely to be challenged about confirmation and infant baptism."[5] This seems to have been the case, for by 1643 Benjamin was in Coventry, and was confronted by Richard Baxter to debate the topic of infant baptism.[6] His presence there ensued in imprisonment for an undetermined but apparently brief period of time, according to Baxter because "he would not promise to leave the City and come no more."[7] In 1645, he was invited to participate in a debate with, among others, Edmund Calamy, on the same topic in London, but it was forbidden by the Lord Mayor.[8]

Doctor *Hall* his Diocesan, brought in Innovations into his Parish Church, (as some godly people that came out of those parts have informed me) who hath put out a Pamphlet, called, *A Declaration concerning the publike Dispute which should have been in the publike meeting house of Aldermanbury, the third of* December *concerning* Infants Baptism." Thomas Edwards, *Gangraena: Or A Catalogue and Discovery of many of the Errors, Heresies, Blasphemies and pernicious Practices of the Sectaries of this time* (London: Ralph Smith, 1646), The Third Edition, Part 1, 38 (2nd pagination), emphasis his. Throughout this biographical sketch, I have retained the archaic and often irregular spelling, punctuation and capitalization of the original documents.

[4] *A Thesis or Position Concerning The Administering and Receiving Of The Lord's Supper Cleared and Confirmed* by B. C. Preacher of God's Word, 1642, 1. No place of publication or publisher/printer is provided. Coxe signed his name at the end of the pamphlet.

[5] Whitley, *Benjamin Cox*, 51.

[6] Thomas Crosby, *History of the English Baptists* (London, 1738), 1:354.

[7] Richard Baxter, *Plain Scripture Proof of Infants Church-membership and Baptism* (London: 1656 4th Edition), unnumbered page 4 of *"The True History of the Conception and Nativity of this Treatise."*

[8] The Baptist side of the intended debate has been recorded in the previously mentioned *A Declaration Concerning the Publike Dispute which should have been held in the Publike Meeting House of Alderman-Bury, the 3d of this instant Moneth of*

The association with London Baptists is of great significance, for it demonstrates the growing prominence of Benjamin Coxe. When Daniel Featley attacked seven points of the theology of the *1644 London Confession*, the churches issuing the Confession revised it to satisfy Featley's objections. The new edition was published in 1646, signed by among others, Benjamin Coxe as a representative of one of the London churches. In addition, he published, probably on his own, an *Appendix* to the Confession, seeking to further explain some of the positions held by the subscribers. Coxe believed that reasonable men would read and understand that the Baptists were highly orthodox in their views, and perhaps would as a result be granted a measure of toleration. His optimistic expectations were not fulfilled. Murray Tolmie tells the story well:

> On 29 January 1646, Samuel Richardson and Benjamin Cox stood outside the door of the House of Commons to hand copies of the second edition of the *Confession* of the seven churches to Members as they entered the House. It had been revised with great care. . . . Care had been taken to have the pamphlet duly licensed by John Downham. The House of Commons proved unsympathetic; it sent the Serjeant-at-arms to seize the pamphlets and to bring Richardson and Cox to the bar of the House, and it ordered the Stationers' Company to suppress the *Confession*.[9]

Toleration was still far away. In 1646, Coxe printed a small work, written during his time of imprisonment in Coventry, entitled *Some Mistaken Scriptures Sincerely Explained*,[10] an effort to undo the ill effects of Arminianism spreading throughout the land. He visited the same subject in a "Letter to the Reader" published in the same year as a preface to John Spilsbury's *God's Ordinance, The Saints Priviledge*.[11]

December, Concerning Infants-Baptisme (London, 1645) with the names *Benjamin Coxe, Hanserd Knollys,* and *William Kiffen* prominently printed on the title page.

[9] Murray Tolmie, *The Triumph of the Saints* (Cambridge: Cambridge University Press, 1977), 63-64. Tolmie cites the *Journal of the House of Commons*, iv:420-421 as a source for this information.

[10] Benjamin Coxe, *Some Mistaken Scriptures Sincerely Explained in Answer to one infected with some Pelagian Errours* (London: Tho. Paine, 1646).

[11] John Spilsbury, *God's Ordinance, The Saints Priviledge* (London: M. Simmons, 1646). For biographical information on Spilsbury, see James M. Renihan, "*John Spilsbury (1593-c1662/1668)* in Michael A.G. Haykin, ed., *The British Particular Baptists 1638-1910* (Springfield, MO: Particular Baptist Press, 1998), 1:21-37.

Coxe enlarged some portions of the second part of this treatise, which handled matters related to the Calvinistic doctrine of Particular Redemption.

Two years later, Coxe was apparently in Bedford. B.R. White states that "the London Presbyterians insisted in September [1648] that a letter be sent to the authorities in Bedford reporting Cox's 'heterodox' opinions—presumably his opposition to Infant Baptism."[12] Until 1653 he seems to have maintained a low profile, but appears in that year as a representative of the Kensworth, Bedfordshire church at a meeting of the Abingdon Association.[13] For the next seven years, his name appears regularly and prominently in the Association minutes. By this time Benjamin would have been about 65 years old. Crosby reports that at the Act of Uniformity in 1662 Coxe conformed to the Church of England, soon to repent and return to the Baptist fold,[14] but provides no corroborating evidence. Since he had only recently written a forceful argument against the propriety of Baptist ministers receiving pay from the government,[15] one would think that the story of his conformity is highly unlikely. While his death year is not known, it was most probably around 1664.

Two matters of consequence need to be mentioned before moving forward. The first has to do with Benjamin Coxe's advocacy of closed-membership principles. In the decades following the appearance of the Particular Baptist churches, several positions on the relationship between baptism and church membership may be noted. For some, believer's baptism was a *sine qua non* of church membership; others promoted it and resisted paedobaptism, but allowed individuals to join who had scruples over the need for what they considered to be rebaptism (thinking that their baptism as infants was sufficient). A third position argued that baptism was a personal matter, and was thus irrelevant to membership in the church. Coxe, the London Baptists who issued the *1644/46 London Confession*, and the Abingdon Association churches all held firmly to the first position. The second is represented by churches like the one in

---

[12] B.R. White, *Cox, Benjamin (1595-c. 1664)* in Richard L. Greaves and Robert Zaller, *Biographical Dictionary of British Radicals in the Seventeenth Century* (Brighton: The Harvester Press, 1982), 1:184.

[13] B.R. White, *Association Records of the Particular Baptists of England, Wales and Ireland to 1660* (London: The Baptist Historical Society, 1971-74), 3:129.

[14] Crosby, *HEB*, 1:354.

[15] Written in early 1658 and now accessible as an appendix in White, *Association Records*, 1:43-50.

Broadmead, Bristol, and individuals such as Henry Jessey.[16] The last view was the conviction and practice of John Bunyan and the Bedford church where he ministered. Benjamin Coxe vocally advocated the necessity of believer's baptism for membership, and this advocacy seems to have been a legacy imparted to his son. It will take on importance in the early stage of Nehemiah's ministry.

The second matter deserving note is the close relationship sustained by the Petty France church in London to the Abingdon Association churches in general, and to the Kensworth church in particular. In 1656, the Abingdon churches were struggling with matters relating to the choice and installation (ordination) of officers in the church. They determined to seek assistance, and sent a letter to the Petty France church asking for advice. The London congregation replied in a lengthy epistle, explaining their own practice.[17] Evidently, this large assembly was held in esteem by the associated churches. Perhaps the reason for this is to be found in the relationship between Benjamin Coxe, Edward Harrison, Petty France and Kensworth. When Coxe signed the 1646 edition of the *London Confession*, he did so as a representative of the church that would come to be known through its meeting place in Petty France. Edward Harrison, who joined this church in 1651, and was its pastor by 1657, came to London from Kensworth, having served as vicar of the parish church there. He abandoned paedobaptism by 1645, and may have been (after the Civil War), the founder of the Kensworth church.[18] Throughout the history of these churches, there seems to have been regular communication.[19] The significance of this relationship will be noted below.

In the words of W.T. Whitley, "instead of the fathers come up the sons."[20] Nehemiah Coxe was the son of Benjamin Coxe. We know almost nothing of his birth and childhood, except to presume that it was

---

[16] For Jessey, see B.R. White, *"Henry Jessey in the Great Rebellion"* in R. Buck Knox, *Reformation, Conformity and Dissent: Essays in Honour of Geoffrey Nuttal* (London: Epworth Press, 1977), 132-153.

[17] White, *ARPB*, 3:168-172.

[18] W.T. Whitley, *The Baptists of London 1612-1928* (London: The Kingsgate Press, n.d.), 105; Whitley, *Edward Harrison of Petty France* in *The Baptist Quarterly*, 7:214.

[19] See the *Petty France Church Book* held at the Guildhall Library in London and H.G. Tibbutt, *Some Early Nonconformist Church Books* (Bedford: Bedfordshire Historical Record Society, 1972). The Kensworth Church Book is transcribed on pages 10-18.

[20] Whitley, *Benjamin Coxe*, 58.

spent in Bedfordshire with his father. His first known appearance in the historical record is on 14 May 1669, when he joined the open-membership Bedford Church made famous by John Bunyan.[21] Though still relatively young (as we shall see below), he must have risen in the esteem of the congregation, as his name is signed, along with three other men, to a letter written on 21 March 1671 from the Bedford Church to one of its wandering members. William Whitbread had joined the assembly, but had stopped attending and participating in the activities of the church. To make matters worse, he was found to have frequented public worship services in the Church of England. To the Bedford congregants, this was a serious breach of propriety, as the following letter indicates:

> Bro Whitbread
> We your brethren the congregation of Christ, to which you as yet stand related, having formerly admonished you by our epistles, for severall high miscarriages, and that of long continuance; had hoped that God might have blessed you with unfeigned repentance for the same. But considering that you have added more wickedness to your former transgressions so long continued in, in that now of late you have in ye face of the Canaanites that dwell in the land, presented your person, at that superstitious, and idolatrous worship, that with force and cruelty is maintained in opposition to the true worship, and worshippers of God, to whom long since you have joyned yourself; we cannot but feare, your former repentance was feigned; but also for your adding this last above all, as a wickedness that may not be borne with by us, least we also be guilty of your transgressions. And we further tell you, that our uprightness in this matter may appeare to all the Churches, if you respond not, we shall further put forth that power, that is committed to us, by Christ for your edification; even to withdraw from you as a person not fit to be companyed with, that now you may be ashamed, and saved in ye day of the Lord.
> Written by the appointment of the congregation, and by the same ordered to be sent to you, by the hand of these brethren. As we whose names are here underwritten as witnesses.[22]

One senses the profound distaste the suffering saints of Bedford had towards their persecutors. To make common ground with them was

---

[21] *The Church Book of Bunyan Meeting* (London: J.M. Dent Facsimile Reprint, 1928), 27.
[22] *Church Book of Bunyan Meeting*, 43-44.

utterly unacceptable. At the same meeting, Coxe was appointed, along with another man, to bring notice of the church's act of withdrawal from one more member, Richard Deane. In both cases, the participation of this young man indicates some sense of the esteem in which he was held by the church. These two matters were of the utmost importance for the discipline of the local assembly.

In June of the same year, Nehemiah signed, this time alongside John Bunyan, a further letter written by the church. It was addressed to Sister Tilney, a woman of the congregation who had moved to London and desired to join a church pastored by her son-in-law, Mr. Blakey.[23] It is a fascinating letter, expressing deep affection for this woman who was well loved in the church, but still unwilling to release her to the care of this church, because it was unknown to them. They suggest that she consider several options, among them getting a "commendatory epistle" from "Bro. Owen, Bro. Coakain, Bro. Palmer or Bro. Griffith, confirming the faith and principles of the person, and people whom you mention."[24] This is the famous Dr. John Owen.[25] On 12 July the church met again, and Coxe reported to the congregation that William Whitbread had "confessed his guilt for the miscarriages charged upon him" and gave hopeful indication "of the furtherance of repentance in him."[26] At the same meeting, the records state that the "same brethren" (i.e., Coxe and his companion) reported the results of two other disciplinary visits upon which they had been deputed. By all accounts, the Bedford church was willing to entrust serious matters to this young man. His name continues to appear signed to the official correspondence of the church.

---

[23] He is possibly to be identified as Nicholas Blakie, minister of a Scots Church in London. See Walter Wilson, *The History and Antiquities of Dissenting Churches and Meeting Houses* (London: For the Author, 1808), 2:460-467.

[24] *Church Book of Bunyan Meeting*, 46.

[25] The connection between Bunyan and these men is mentioned in Christopher Hill, *A Turbulent, Seditious, and Factious People: John Bunyan and His Church* (Oxford: Oxford University Press, 1988), 149. "Brother Coakain" is George Cokayne (1620-1691), a London Independent minister born in and with many ties to Bedfordshire; "Bro. Palmer" is Anthony Palmer (1616-1679), a London Independent minister; and "Bro. Griffith" is George Griffith (1619-1702), a London Independent minister. It is fascinating to note that none of these approved assemblies were Baptist churches. See Greaves and Zaller, *BDBR*, *s.v.* *"Cokayne, George," "Palmer, Anthony"* and *"Griffith, (or Griffiths), George."*

[26] *Church Book of Bunyan Meeting*, 46, 47.

In December 1671, Nehemiah Coxe's stature in the church took another step forward. On the 21st of that month, John Bunyan was formally called to "pastorall office, or eldership" in the church. The minutes state that at "the same time; and after the same manner, ye church did solemnely aproove of the gifts of, and called to the work of the ministery" seven men, among whom was Nehemiah, "for the furtherance of the work of God, and carrying on hereof, in the meetings usually maintained by this congregation, as occasion and opportunity shall by providence be ministred to them." This was not a full and free call to exercise gifts, as the minutes immediately state that the church

> did further determine, that if any new place offer it self, or another people that we have not full knowledge of, or communion with, shall desire that any of these brethren should come to them, to be helpful to them, by the word, and doctrine, that then such brother so desired, shall first present the thing to ye congregation, who after due consideration will determine thereof: and according as they shall determine, so shall such brother act and doe.[27]

The distinctions in these words need to be noted. These men were called to be "ministers," or "gifted brethren," but not elders. They acted in subordination to the will of, and at the disposal of, the church as a whole. The strict rules circumscribing their activity demonstrate the sobriety with which the church treated the action. Public ministry of any kind was a high and holy calling, and could not be treated lightly.

The responsibility of such recognition brought with it not only opportunities for public ministry and leadership, but for theological reflection as well. On 25 June 1672, the church "ordered that a brief confession of faith be drawn up by the elders and gifted brethren of the Congregation." Sadly, there is no record of the finished product. On 29 July, the records state that "the matter heretofore propounded concerning a drawing up of a brief Confession of faith etc., was omitted, by reason of bro: Bunyans absence."[28] There seems to be no further mention of such a Confession in the church minutes. It is known, however, that Bunyan published, in 1672, his *A Confession of My Faith, and a reason*

---

[27] Ibid., 51. These men are explicitly called "gifted brethren" in the notation for 25 June 1672, see p. 52.

[28] Ibid., 52-53.

of My Practice.[29] One wonders if there is a connection between these things.

In the late Spring of 1673, one of the Bedford church's daughter assemblies made an important request: "it was desired by the church at Hitchin that this congregation would give up to them our Bro Nehemiah Coxe in order to the exercise of the office of an elder or pastor with them: The which the congregation concluded to take in to consideration."[30] Several items of note are present in this minute. Among the Independent and Baptist churches, it was believed that membership must precede a call to pastoral office. Churches generally did not approach a man directly and ask him to accept a call to serve in their midst, though certainly this would have been done informally. The only proper procedure was to address the church in which the desired man was a member, and ask them to release him for the purpose of taking on the new ministry. For this reason, the Hitchin church addressed themselves to the Bedford people for permission to proceed.[31] This implies that Coxe had exercised some form of ministry among the Hitchin people, most probably in the fulfillment of the work of a gifted brother as noted above. Interestingly, the Bedford congregation did not immediately accede to the inquiry, but only took it under advisement. The records do not indicate whether the request was ever granted; almost certainly it was not.

Just less than a year later, in May 1674, Coxe, apparently still a member of the Bedford church, faced censure for certain undefined "miscarriages." The note in the record book is as follows:

Our Bro: Nehemiah Coxe did publickly make an acknowledgement of several miscarridges by him committed and declared his repentance for the same; and because he had bin faulty in such things heretofore therefore it was desired by som of the Bre that the form of his submission should be presented to us in writing, which also accordingly was, and was as followeth. Whereas several words and

---

[29] See George Offer, ed., *The Whole Works of John Bunyan* (Grand Rapids: Baker Book House, 1977), 2:593-601; W.T. Whitley, *A Baptist Bibliography* (Hildesheim: Georg Olms Verlag, 1984 reprint), 1:99.

[30] *Church Book of Bunyan Meeting*, 54.

[31] Ibid. This was the standard procedure followed between the churches. A fascinating account of protracted discussions between two churches on this matter may be found in E. B. Underhill, ed., *The Records of A Church of Christ meeting in Broadmead, Bristol, 1640-87* (London: J. Haddon, 1847), 108-160; 380-384.

practices have been uttered and performed by me, that might justly be
censured to have a tendency to make rents and divisions in the
congregation, I do declare myself unfeignedly sorry and repentant for
the same. Ne. Coxe."[32]

One wonders just what these miscarriages may have been. Thomas
Armitage surmises that since "it related to some point of faith or practice
about which there were differences of opinion in the body, and as he was
a stout Baptist, they, most likely, had reference to some Baptist
differences." T.E. Dowley suggests a similar solution: it may be that
Coxe's "words and practices" were related to the issue of open or closed
membership, so hotly debated at the time.[33] Benjamin Coxe clearly
advocated a closed membership position in his published writings, while
the Bedford church, and especially Bunyan, resisted such a notion with
great vigor.[34] Could Nehemiah have been advocating such opinions,
which the Bedford people would view as having "a tendency to make
rents and divisions in the congregation?" Is the fact that he "had bin
faulty in such things" previously an indication that this was the nature of
the problem? It would seem that this solution is very likely. His
appearance at the closed membership Petty France church so soon after
this could help to explain the situation.

Walter Wilson records an interesting anecdote from this period of
Coxe's life:

> On a blank leaf, at the beginning of his [i.e., Coxe's] Discourse of the
> Covenants, in the possession of Mr. Sutcliff, the following anecdote is
> recorded in manuscript. 'The author lived at Cranfield, where he
> followed the business of a cordwainer, and during his residence there,
> was imprisoned for preaching the gospel. When he came upon his trial
> at Bedford assizes, he first pleaded in Greek, and then in Hebrew; upon
> which the judge calling for the indictment, wherein he was styled,

---

[32] *Church Book of Bunyan Meeting*, 54.

[33] Thomas Armitage, *A History of the Baptists* (Watertown, WI: Baptist Heritage
Press, 1988 reprint), 2:524; T.E. Dowley, "*A London Congregation during the Great
Persecution*" in *The Baptist Quarterly* (Jan. 1978), XXVII, no. 5, 238.

[34] Benjamin Cox "An Appendix to a Confession of Faith" reprinted with *A
Confession of Faith of Seven Congregations of Churches in London, Which are
Commonly (but unjustly) Called Anabaptists* (Rochester, NY: Backus Book Publishers,
1981), 32, 33; John Bunyan, "A Confession of My Faith, and a Reason of My Practice"
in *Works*. Bunyan published two other works on the subject, "Differences in Judgment
about Water Baptism no Bar to Communion" and "Peaceable Principles and True".

Nehemiah Cox, cordwainer, expressed his surprise, and declared, that none could answer him. And upon Mr. Cox arguing, that it was but fair he should plead in what language he pleased, he was dismissed.'—Mr. Sutcliffe says, he has various times heard the above anecdote repeated in conversation, in the town and neighbourhood of Bedford, and particularly with this addition, that the judge should say to the counsellors, 'Well, the cordwainer has wound you all up, gentlemen.'[35]

From this note it would seem that Coxe, though highly intelligent, supported himself as a cordwainer, or shoemaker.

Fifteen months after the censure incident, on 21 September 1675, the following note was entered into the Petty France (London) Church Minute Book: "bro Collins & Bro. Coxe were solemnly ordained pastors or elders in this church."[36] It is probably safe to assume, based on the normal processes involved in calling pastors to churches, that these two men had been examined by the church and had passed some kind of trial period. In any case, they became co-elders on that day. William Collins is said to have had a thorough University training followed by a tour of the European continent. He remained as pastor of the church until his death on 30 October 1702. In a funeral sermon preached by John Piggott, a fortnight after Collins' death, mention is made of the encouraging "offers he had to join the National Church, which he judiciously refus'd; for twas Conscience, not Humour, that made him a Dissenter."[37]

---

[35] Wilson, *History and Antiquities*, 2:186-187. Wilson provides this footnote: "Mr. Sutcliff's Appendix to Dr. Ryland's Sermon, on the Death of the Rev. Joshua Symonds, p. 53-4." Christopher Hill confirms Coxe's imprisonment for preaching, citing E. Stockdale, "*A Study of Bedford Prison, 1660-1877*," in *Publications of the Bedfordshire Historical Record Society*, 56 (1977), 14-16, 70-71, as his source. See Hill, *A Turbulent... People*, 122. Later in the same work, Hill states that in 1669 Coxe "was accused of saying 'the Church of England as it now stands is an Antichristian church." Hill, 145, citing M. Mullett, "*The Internal Politics of Bedford, 1660-1688*" in *Publications of the Bedfordshire Historical Record Society* 59 (1980), 4, 5, 37. Such a statement would be perfectly consistent with the view held by many dissenters of the day.

[36] *Petty France Church Book, 1675-1727*, 1. The book may be viewed at The Guildhall Library, London. The Bedford Church Book does not record the dismissal of Coxe from membership, but this is probably an oversight. There are only a few brief entries for 1675.

[37] John Piggott, "*A Funeral Sermon Occasioned by the Death of the reverend Mr. William Collins, Late Minister of the Gospel in London, Who died the 30th of October, 1702,*" in *Eleven Sermons Preach'd upon Several Occasions, by the Late Reverend Mr. John Piggott, Minister of the Gospel* (London: John Darby, 1714), 241-286. The esteem in which he was held by his fellow ministers may be noted in the fact that he was requested by the 1693 General Assembly to draw up a Catechism, and on the strength of

Together with Coxe, Collins was to have a place of important leadership
from their London base in the Petty France Church. The Coxe father and
son duo had thus come full circle. The church of which the father had
been a part in the 1640s, and which maintained a strong Bedfordshire
connection in the 1650s and 1660s, became the home of the son in the
1670s.

Coxe was a qualified physician,[38] skilled in Latin, Greek and
Hebrew, and a discerning theologian. When the West Country evangelist
Thomas Collier[39] began to deviate from the Calvinistic Orthodoxy of the
London Churches, the elders in London asked Coxe to participate with
them in attempts to recover him and/or refute his doctrine. Collier was a
man of prominence and importance. Sent out by William Kiffin's
Devonshire Square, London, Church in the 1640s, he was the most
influential leader among the Particular Baptists in the west. His work was
so effective that he aroused the attention of Thomas Edwards, who wrote
in his work *Gangraena* (1646) that Collier was "the first that sowed the
seeds of Anabaptism" in the west.[40] For forty years he labored tirelessly
to plant and build churches. By the 1650s, there were evidences of
theological drift, and by the mid 1670s, he openly repudiated the
Calvinism of the London churches. Such actions could not be tolerated or
ignored.

Nehemiah participated in the theological recovery/refutation process
in two ways. In 1676, he accompanied a delegation that traveled west to
confront Collier. The Broadmead Records describe the situation:

> 5 Elders and brethren . . . were coming down from London, to visit a
> Neighbouring Church in ye Country about 15 miles off near Bradford
> or Trowbridge, to settle some disorder there; as ye Pastor thereof, T. C.,
> holding forth some unsound Doctrine, or New Notions, Contrary to ye

---

this Joseph Ivimey asserts "it is probable that the Baptist Catechism was complied by Mr.
Collins, though it has by some means of other been called Keach's Catechism." Joseph
Ivimey, *A History of the English Baptists* (London: B. J. Holdsworth, 1823), 2:397.

[38] Walter Wilson designates him as "Nehemiah Coxe, D.D." There is, however, no
evidence that he was ever granted the Doctor of Divinity degree. More likely this is a
mistake, made by conflating his medical career with his theological career. Unaware of
his medical practice, and reading of Dr. Nehemiah Coxe, one might assume that the
respected theologian had received the accepted theological doctorate of the day. Walter
Wilson, *History and Antiquities*, 2:185.

[39] On Collier see B.R. White, *"Thomas Collier and Gangraena Edwards"* in *The
Baptist Quarterly* xxiv:3 (July, 1971), 99-110.

[40] Edwards, *Gangraena*, Third Part, 29, 40-41.

generall reception of Sound and *Orthodox* Men. Ye names of ye London Brethren were, Br. Kiffin, Br. Deane, Br. Fitten, Br. Cox, and Br. Moreton.[41]

The visit by this delegation was unsuccessful, Collier persisting in his deviant doctrinal views.

As a result of the failure of the visit to accomplish its goals, Coxe was enlisted to expose and reply in print to Collier's views. He did this in his 1677 work *Vindiciae Veritatis, or a Confutation of the Heresies and Gross Errours Asserted by Thomas Collier*. In a brief epistle at the beginning of the work, the older and more well-known London leaders address the issue of Coxe's "inferiority in years," stating that he did not write the book out of a sense of personal ability, but at their request, because "we did judge him meet and of ability for the work" and because his responsibilities at the time provided him with the opportunity to answer Collier's errors. They say of this work, "we hope, we may truly say, without particular respect to his Person, he hath behaved himself with that modesty of Spirit, joined with that fulness and clearness of answer and strength of argument, that we comfortably conceive (by God's blessing) it may prove a good and soveraign Antidote against the poison."[42] Even as a relatively young man, these experienced leaders saw unusual skill and ability, so much so that they were willing to entrust Nehemiah with this grave responsibility. The product is a powerful expression of Reformed doctrine, well-stating the case against Collier and expounding the doctrines of Calvinistic orthodoxy held by the majority of the churches and ministers.

Collier's prominence forced the Particular Baptist leaders to take determined actions to prevent both the spread of his views, and the possibility of another round of theological guilt by association. They may well have feared that their opponents would tar them with the same broad

---

[41] Roger Hayden, ed., *The Records of a Church of Christ in Bristol, 1640-1687* (Bristol: Bristol Record Society, 1974), 185. The Broadmead church hoped that the men might be able to make the further journey to visit their assembly and ordain their pastor, Thomas Hardcastle. The London men refused, citing pressing personal reasons to return to London.

[42] Nehemiah Coxe, *Vindiciae Veritatis, or a Confutation of the Heresies and Gross Errours asserted By Thomas Collier in his Additional Word to his Body of Divinity* (London: Nath. Ponder: 1677), unnumbered pages 1 and 2. The letter is signed by William Kiffin, Daniel Dyke, Joseph Maisters, James Fitton, Henry Forty and William Collins. This is an impressive roster of capable and qualified men.

brush used to delineate Collier's errors. Some have suggested that there
may be a relationship between this situation and the appearance of the
Second London Baptist Confession in 1677.[43] This proposal is very
compelling. In any case, the most important Confession in Baptist history
appeared in that year. The first known reference to the document is found
in the manuscript minute book of the Petty France Church. On 26 August
1677, this note was entered: "It was agreed that a Confession of faith,
wth the Appendix thereto having bene read & considered by the Bre:
should be published."[44] Joseph Ivimey, the English Baptist historian of
the early nineteenth century took this to imply that the Confession
originated in the Petty France Church,[45] very likely an accurate
supposition. This would, of course, mean that Nehemiah Coxe and
William Collins are the most likely candidates to have served as editors
of the document. In the absence of any other theory, and based on the
circumstantial evidence available to us, this is a strong possibility.[46]
Since Coxe was already at the forefront of theological articulation,

---

[43] Robert Oliver, *"Baptist Confession Making, 1644 and 1689"* an unpublished
manuscript delivered to the Strict Baptist Historical Society, March 1989, 13-14; Michael
A.G. Haykin, *Kiffin, Knollys and Keach* (Leeds: Reformation Today Trust, 1996), 68.

[44] *Petty France Church Minute Book*, 5.

[45] Joseph Ivimey, *HEB*, 3:332. Ivimey writes, "It should seem . . . that this
confession was prepared for the purpose of expressing the faith of that particular church,
but was adopted by upwards of one hundred churches at the General Assembly in 1689."
At another place in the same volume, he baldly asserts that Coxe and Collins "wrote the
Confession of Faith adopted by the General Assembly, in 1689." 3:260.

[46] There are some literary indications that Coxe and Collins were its authors. In E.B.
Underhill's *Confessions of Faith and Other Public Documents Illustrative of the Baptist
Churches of England in the 17th Century* (London: The Hanserd Knollys Society, 1854),
172, a noteworthy "advertisement" is prefaced to the reprint of the Second London
Confession. It indicates that William Collins and Benjamin Keach, from 1668-1704 an
elder of the Southwark, Horselydown Church owned the proprietary rights to these two
documents, the Confession and the Catechism. This would tend to indicate that they had
some stake, as holders of the "property, right and title" to them, in the authorship, or
editing of the two. Keach could not have been the original editor of the Confession. It
incorporates several statements from the *1644 London Baptist Confession*, and Keach
stated in 1692 that he had not seen that document until just prior to the General Assembly
held in London during that year. Although he could not have been responsible for the
appearance of the Confession, he has been frequently identified with the Catechism. It is
possible that he owned the "property, right and title" to it, and that Collins owned the
"property, right and title" to the Confession as its original editor. Both Collins and Keach
died by 1704, thus the advertisement must have been appended to an earlier edition of the
Confession. Since Nehemiah Coxe died in 1689, the absence of his name does not
militate against the notion that he was co-editor of the Confession with Collins.

having been chosen as the spokesman for the London churches in their controversy with Collier, he would be a natural choice for this task; he had been assigned to a similar labor while a minister of the Bedford church.

The Petty France Church was large and prominent in London. As one of the original seven churches, it had an historical stature, and this was increased as the membership of the church grew larger. The records of the congregation indicate a flourishing assembly: from 1675 to 1688/89, there seem to have been more than 530 people in membership. The church was involved in all of the normal activities associated with church life, adding members, marriages, baptisms (the record for 24 December 1676 states that two women were accepted for baptism but "the administration of the ordinance to them was deferd a while, because by reason of the extremity of ye present frost, we could not now come at ye water"),[47] and church discipline. Nehemiah Coxe figures prominently in the records, not only internally, but also as a frequently chosen representative of the assembly in their involvement with the Associations of Churches in London and Hertfordshire. The vigor of this church is amazing, especially when one remembers that life in London, as in Bedford, was not easy. The fires of persecution flared against the Petty France Church, so much so that at times they could not assemble in their meeting place.[48] Nonetheless, they pressed on with the work to which they were called.

Coxe and Collins turned their attention to many issues outside of their own church. In 1675, they both signed, along with eleven other men, a letter to Andrew Gifford[49] of the Pithay Church in Bristol, arguing that it was the duty of all men to pray. Apparently, Gifford had come into the acquaintance of some Hyper-Calvinists who argued that since unconverted men could not perform any good deeds accompanying salvation, they were under no obligation to pray and worship God. He asked the London pastors to weigh in on the subject, and this letter was

---

[47] *Petty France Church Book*, 3.

[48] See T.E. Dowley, "*A London Congregation during the Great Persecution*" for details of some of the incidents known to have taken place. The Petty France records contain statements such as "our meeting being disturbed on the Lord's Daye . . . in regard of the uncertainty of our obtaining conveniencye of meeting as formerly by reason of the present persecution & our exclusion fro(m) Pett: Fr: . . ." *Petty France Church Book*, 20-21.

[49] On Gifford (1641-1721), see Ivimey, *HEB*, 1:412-415; 2:541-552.

the result.[50] In 1680, along with William Kiffin, Hanserd Knollys,[51] John Harris[52] and Daniel Dyke,[53] Coxe signed an introduction to John Russel's narrative about the struggles of the fledgling Baptist church in Boston, New England. They assert that the Boston Baptists "have declared their perfect agreement with us both in matters of Faith and Worship, as set down in our late Confession," and argue that it is exceedingly strange that Christians who hold the same essential doctrines, differing only in the point of the subjects of baptism, should be persecuted by those who are so close to them.[54] They were likewise active in assisting other churches. In addition to the Collier matter, Coxe and Daniel Dyke (co-elder with William Kiffin at Devonshire Square, London) ordained Andrew Gifford to his pastoral position in Bristol in 1677.[55]

In 1681, during a period of persecution, Coxe published *A Sermon Preached at the Ordination of an Elder and Deacons in a Baptized Congregation in London.*[56] This is a helpful summary of the roles and responsibilities of elders and deacons. The service is the first known public ordination in a dissenting congregation after the Restoration. Also in 1681, Coxe published the work reprinted here, *A Discourse of the Covenants that God made with Men before the Law.* Coxe's contemporary C.M. du Veil in his 1685 Commentary on Acts, gave high encomiums to the author and the book, calling him "that great divine, eminent for all manner of learning," and asserting that "by most weighty and solid arguments has demonstrated in his excellent discourse of the covenants that God made with men before the law" that "by baptism and circumcision two covenants altogether differing, were to be sealed; of which the one was with those who by the law of nature were born of the

---

[50] The full text of the letter may be found in Ivimey, *HEB*, 1:417-420.

[51] Helpful biographical information on Kiffin and Knowles may be found in Haykin, *Kiffin, Knollys and Keach*.

[52] Harris's ministry is briefly summarized in Ivimey, *HEB*, 3:498.

[53] For Dyke (1617-1688), see A.G. Matthews, *Calamy Revised* (Oxford: Clarendon Press, 1988 reissue), 176; Ivimey, *HEB*, 2:328-330. He was the nephew of the famous puritan Daniel Dyke, author of *Michael and the Dragon, or Christ Tempted and Satan foyled* (London: 1635).

[54] The text of the preface is in Nathan Wood, *The History of the First Baptist Church of Boston* (New York, NY: Arno Press, 1980 facsimile reprint of 1899 edition), 149-151.

[55] Hayden, *Records of a Church of Christ*, 191.

[56] See Nehemiah Coxe, "A Sermon Preached at the Ordination of an Elder and Deacons in a Baptized Congregation in England," *Reformed Baptist Theological Review*, Volume I, Number 1 (January 2004), 133-156.

seed of Abraham; the other with those who by the gift of faith, like Abraham, were spiritually re-born."[57] Du Veil's words are echoed by those of John Piggott, who called Coxe an "excellent and judicious divine."[58]

The last known published writing by Coxe was *A Believers Triumph over Death, exemplified in a relation of the last hours of Dr. Andrew Rivet.* This seems to have been a translation from Latin of a French original, describing the life of this Frenchman who fled to Holland for the sake of religious freedom.[59] The tradition of his being a physician is strong. In an unsigned note in the Baptist Quarterly, we are told "By Sloane MS 656 we learn that he was hon. F.R.C.P., and that 'Institutiones Medica' was dedicated to him by G. Needham."[60] The *British Museum General Catalogue of Printed Books* lists a book published in 1684 by Nehemiah Cox under the title *Disputatio medica inauguralis de arthride.*[61] There is no known record of medical training, nor why he was made an honorary Fellow of the Royal College of Physicians. One can only surmise that a certain level of skill was present in his practice, and a good reputation must have developed from it.

What about his domestic life? There is very little information. The same note mentioned in the previous paragraph says that he "married

---

[57] C.M. Du Veil, *A Commentary on the Acts of the Apostles* (London: The Hanserd Knollys Society, 1851 reprint), 70. Du Veil himself is an interesting character. Born a Jew, he successively became a Roman Catholic, an Anglican, and a Particular Baptist. See W.T. Whitley, "*Charles-Marie, de Veil*" in *The Baptist Quarterly* 8, no. 8 (Oct. 1937): 444-446. Du Veil's *Commentary on Acts* was originally published in 1685.

[58] John Piggott, *Eleven Sermons Preach'd upon Special Occasions* (London: John Darby, 1714), 190.

[59] Erasmus Middleton, *Biographica Evangelica* (London: R. Denham, 1804), 3:205-353.

[60] *The Baptist Quarterly*, 4:275.

[61] *British Museum General Catalogue of Printed Books* (London: The Trustees of the British Museum, 1966), 45:364. The title roughly translates to "A First Medical Discussion on Arthritis." The publication data listed in the catalogue is "*Typis Appelarianis: Ultrajecti,* 1684. A fascinating incident is recorded by W.T. Whitley: "[Nehemiah Coxe] had the opportunity of heaping coals of fire on the aged head of Richard Baxter, who was being dragged off to prison in 1683 when Cox met the party and certified that Baxter was too ill to endure a jail." Whitley, *Benjamin Coxe*, 59. There is, however, strong reason to believe that Whitley was incorrect, and that Nehemiah Coxe was not the participant in this event. In Baxter's autobiography, the name of the physician is given as *Thomas Coxe*. Richard Baxter, *The Autobiography of Richard Baxter, being The Reliquiae Baxterianae,* abridged from the folio of 1696, (London: J.M. Dent, 1931), 251.

Margaret, second daughter of Edmund and Margaret Portman."[62] On 26 January, 1688/89, a Margaret Cox was received into membership by the Petty France Church, but there is no certainty that this was Nehemiah's wife. Several years earlier (1679), a "Sister Cox" was admonished for lack of attendance and going off "to follow the Quaquers."[63] There is no evidence that she was related to Nehemiah. We do know that he had a son, for soon after his death, the Petty France minutes state, "There was a meeting of the Brethren at Bro. Lock's where it was agreed that somethings should be raised by subscription for ye maintaining Br. Cox's son and yt the congregation should bee moved in it."[64]

Nehemiah Coxe died on 5 May 1689, and was buried in the tomb of his in-laws at Bunhill Fields, London. Since his death preceded the General Assembly by four months, his name has not been recorded among those who participated in that meeting, or who subscribed the Confession of Faith. It is strangely ironic that one who seems to have been so closely associated with its origin has been forgotten through these circumstances. May the publication of the present work restore to our memories the name and work of a noble witness to the truths of Scripture.

Finis[65]

---

[62] *The Baptist Quarterly*, 4:275.

[63] *Petty France Church Book*, 10.

[64] Ibid., 26.

[65] Many thanks to Mr. Ronald D. Miller for his help in collecting source material for this biographical sketch.

A

DISCOURSE

OF THE
Covenants

That God made with men before the Law.

Wherein,

The *Covenant of Circumcision* is more largely handled,
and the Invalidity of the
Plea for Paedobaptism taken
from there discovered.

By *NEHEMIAH COXE.*

"Search the Scriptures" John 5:39

Printed by J. D. and are to be sold by
Nathaniel Ponder
at the Peacock in the *Poultry*; and *Benjamin Alsop*
at the Angel and Bible in the *Poultry*, 1681.[1]

---

[1] [From this same location in London, Ponder also sold books for John Owen and John Bunyan, most notably the first editions of both parts of *The Pilgrim's Progress* in 1678 and 1684, and *The Life and Death of Mr. Badman* in 1680. Likewise, Alsop in his London shop sold the first edition of Bunyan's *The Holy War* in 1682.]

Editor's Introduction

A word concerning the editor's method is in order. Coxe's work could not merely be set in new type and reprinted – his seventeenth century vocabulary and style are too removed from the contemporary reader for that approach to be edifying. In addition, Coxe references many items no longer obvious to us, although they were readily understood by his educated readers. So this edition is not a precise duplication of his text; instead, the work has been annotated and editorially revised using the following grammatical and stylistic guidelines.

1. Spelling and word usage: update, for example, "knowledg" to "knowledge", "&" to "and", "Fœderal" to "federal", and "hath" to "has." Incidental archaic words are modernized according to definitions from the Oxford English Dictionary. Technical theological terms such as "restipulation" are retained with an explanation added in a footnote.
2. Capitals: removed from non-proper nouns. It was a standard printing convention in the seventeenth century to capitalize the first letter of nouns and some other important words in a text.
3. Italics: removed italicized text except when it is a Latin or Greek quote or in accordance with modern style.
4. Punctuation: removed excess commas and replaced sentence-ending colons and semicolons with periods.
5. Footnotes: Coxe's original footnotes are all included. The editor's footnotes are placed in square brackets ([…]). Obvious typesetting and printing errors are corrected and footnoted.
6. Word and paragraph divisions: lengthy sentences and paragraphs are broken up. Words in a sentence are sometimes rearranged for better clarity.
7. Titles and headings: Coxe prefaced each chapter with an outline. These have been summarized and used as section headings. The original section numbering and sub-points have been retained as an aid to clarity.

A precise transcription of the original text is available by request from the editor.

I would like to thank Dr. James M. Renihan and Mr. David Goodwin for their unflagging support. J. Mark Sugars, Ph.D., has my deep appreciation for translating and referencing most of the Latin quotes.

Ronald D. Miller
Heritage Baptist Church
3585 Thruston Dermont Road
Owensboro, KY 42303

The Preface to the Reader

The usefulness of all divine truth revealed in the Holy Scriptures and the great importance of what particularly concerns those federal[1] transactions which are the subject of the following treatise are my defense for an essay to discover the mind of God in them.

As for that part of the discourse which is most controversial concerning the covenant of circumcision, I have been further engaged in it on occasion of Mr. Whiston's treatises[2] about baptism, especially his last entitled *Infant Baptism Plainly Proved*. For observing the main hinge of the controversy about the right subjects of baptism to turn on Genesis 17, I concluded the only way to clear this great point must be to make a diligent search after that account which the Scripture gives us of the nature and ends of the covenant recorded there. I have declined handling these things in a polemical way and therefore have not undertaken to return a particular answer to everything that has been asserted in opposition to my sentiments. Yet I hope the thoughtful reader may observe such attention paid to what has been urged against those principles on which I proceed, as will excuse me from the charge of crudely reasserting those things that have been already answered or refuted, without giving any new enforcement to them, or endeavoring to

---

[1] [A synonym for covenant. "*Fœdus*," from which "federal" derives, was the standard Latin term used in 16th and 17th century Reformed theology to describe the relationships imposed by God on man for his obedience and salvation – the *fœdus operum* (covenant of works) and *fœdus gratiæ* (covenant of grace). Coxe's use of their English equivalents, his quotations from the day's leading federal theologies (written in Latin by men such as Cocceius), and the substance of his discourse display his thorough acquaintance and identification with covenant theology. See Richard A. Muller, *Dictionary of Latin and Greek Theological Terms* (Grand Rapids: Baker Book House, 1985), 119-122, 217.]

[2] [Joseph Whiston (d. 1690) wrote at least four treatises defending infant baptism to which Coxe refers, including: *Infant Baptism from Heaven* (1670); *An Answer to Mr. Danvers* (1675); *An Essay to Revive the Primitive Doctrine and Practice of Infant Baptism* (1676); and *Infant Baptism Plainly Proved* (1678). The last title contained an "epistle to the pious and learned among the anti-paedobaptists, especially the authors of the late confession of their faith." Coxe, likely a co-author of the *London Baptist Confession of 1677* (hereafter 2nd LCF), was thus directly addressed, and replied in the present work in 1681. Whiston responded the following year in *A Brief Discourse concerning Man's Natural Proneness to, and Tenaciousness of Errour*, in which he adds "some arguments to prove, that the covenant entered with Abraham, Genesis 17:7, is the covenant of grace," opposing one of Coxe's main points in this work.]

remove the ground and occasion of those mistakes which I suppose in others.

I refer myself to the Holy Scriptures for the trial of what is written and sincerely desire that nothing may pass for truth but on their testimony. If I sometimes walk in an untrodden path, it is not from any fondness of novelty but in pursuit of that light which they afford me. Perhaps seeing that these seemingly new things are, for the most part, deduced from a plain record of matters of fact, they may on second thought gain an assent to their truth sooner than opinions arising from more intricate speculation.

That notion (which is often supposed in this discourse) that the old covenant and the new differ in substance and not only in the manner of their administration, certainly requires a larger and more particular handling to free it from those prejudices and difficulties that have been cast on it by many worthy persons who are otherwise minded. Accordingly, I designed to give a further account of it in a discourse of the covenant made with Israel in the wilderness and the state of the church under the law. But when I had finished this and provided some materials also for what was to follow, I found my labor for the clearing and asserting of that point happily prevented by the coming out of Dr. Owen's third volume on Hebrews.[3] There it is discussed at length and the objections that seem to lie against it are fully answered, especially in the exposition of the eighth chapter. I now refer my reader there for satisfaction about it which he will find commensurate to what might be expected from so great and learned a person.

The publication of this little tract was long delayed, in part, by those perplexities which the restless plots of the papists[4] have caused in their bold attempts to overwhelm us with the worst of miseries. I thought this would scarcely give opportunity for considering what might be offered in

---

[3] [John Owen, *Commentary on Hebrews*, vol. VI, (Edinburgh: Banner of Truth Trust, 1991), 3-177. The original work was published in four folio volumes from 1668 to 1684 for Nathaniel Ponder. The referenced volume appeared in 1680.]

[4] [A reference to the years 1678 to 1681 in which "the scoundrel Titus Oates" alleged a popish plot to murder King Charles II and install his Roman Catholic brother, James, Duke of York, as King. This led to parliamentary crises and a general societal upheaval which evidently held up publishing this reply to Whiston's 1678 work. Oates was the son of a Baptist evangelist and although disowned by the Baptists was nonetheless linked to them. For the effects of this on the London Baptists, see B.R. White, *The English Baptists of the 17th Century* (Didcot: The Baptist Historical Society, 1996), 126-128.]

this kind. But the delay was partly from my own aversion to anything that looks like the taking up of any controversy with those that love the Lord Jesus[5] and sincerely espouse the Protestant interest, though differing in principle and practice from me in some controverted point. There is nothing that my soul more longs for on earth than to see an entire and hearty union of all that fear God and hold the Head, however differing in their sentiments about some things of lesser moment. Together with these things, a sense of insufficiency to perform my undertaking with the desired advantage to truth had its share in the delay. However, after I had weighed all the circumstances, I was satisfied that no man is provoked by me in any indecent reflection or any occasion is given to uncharitable and unchristian contention. My hope that what is offered here may inform some and give others occasion for more accurate thoughts in a further systematic inquiry of the truths pointed at, prevailed with me at length to cast this my mite into the public treasury.

I will only add this: that on the whole, my aim has been to speak the truth in love and to take my notions from the Scriptures, not grafting any preconceived opinions of my own onto them. Where the evidence of truth appears, let it not be refused because it is offered in a mean dress and presented under the disadvantage of a rude and unpolished style. But consider instead the reason of what is said and with the noble Bereans search the Scriptures to see whether these things be so or not. And the Lord give you understanding in all things.

N. C.

---

[5] [Coxe's irenic spirit is evident throughout the language of the work and stands in marked contrast to the temper displayed in many of the period's treatises.]

Chapter One

Covenant Relationships to God in General

A General Introduction

§. 1. The great interest of man's present peace and eternal happiness is most closely concerned in religion. And all true religion since the fall of man must be taught by divine revelation which God by diverse parts and after a diverse manner[1] has given out to his church. He caused this light gradually to increase until the whole mystery of his grace was perfectly revealed in and by Jesus Christ in whom are hid all the treasures of wisdom and knowledge. God, whose works were all known by him from the beginning, has in all ages disposed and ordered the revelation of his will to men, his transactions with them, and all the works of his holy providence toward them, with reference to the fullness of time,[2] and the gathering of all things to a head in Christ Jesus. So in all our search after the mind of God in the Holy Scriptures we are to manage our inquiries with reference to Christ. Therefore the best interpreter of the Old Testament is the Holy Spirit speaking to us in the new. There we have the clearest light of the knowledge of the glory of God shining on us in the face of Jesus Christ, by unveiling those counsels of love and grace that were hidden from former ages and generations

Nevertheless the greater light of the New Testament does in no way abate the usefulness of the Old; rather it obliges us all the more to a humble and diligent study of it. This is (as for so many reasons, so also for this one) because the mystery of the gospel cannot be thoroughly apprehended by us without some good understanding of the economy of the law and also of the state of things before the law. The mutual respect

---

[1] Hebrews 1:1, 2. Πολυμερῶς, *Deus non semel olim omnia, sed particulatim, deinde etiam diversis modis sus notitiam ac cultum declaravit per prophetas, quo propius dies imminibat, eo clariorem lucem Edentes.* Bez. [Hebrews 1:1, 2. "In diverse ways." God did not ever declare everything at one time, but rather in piecemeal fashion; then too in diverse ways He declared the knowledge and worship of Himself through the prophets, who gave forth a brighter light, the nearer His day loomed. Theodore Beza, 1519-1605, assisted, then succeeded Calvin in Geneva.]

[2] *Deus in omnibus Actionibus prisci seculi, semper ob oculos habebat tempora Massia,* Grot. [God, in all his actions of the earlier period, always had before His eyes the times of the Messiah. The author is Hugo Grotius, 1583-1645, famous Dutch legal and theological writer.]

and dependence of the Old and New Testaments are such that neither can be understood apart or without the other, nor can an entire system of truth as it is in Jesus be collected except from both.

So it must be acknowledged that it is of great use and concern for us to be well acquainted with those transactions of God with men and his dispensations toward them that are recorded in the sacred history of the first ages of the world and the church of God in it. In this inquiry I will engage myself as far as those times reach that preceded the giving of the law by Moses and no further. In the performance of this (to avoid tediousness in repeating what has been handled by others at length and fully made clear) I will for the most part confine myself to brief observations on the records of these things, as left to us in the Holy Scriptures. I will chiefly insist only on such passages that I conceive have not been so fully spoken to by others or at least not handled in the method and order which seem to me best suited to the nature of the things treated of, and so most apt to convey a clear notion of them to our minds.

God's Covenant Proposed to Men and their Response

§. 2. Seeing that those transactions of God with men which we will meet in this inquiry are of a federal nature, it will be required first that something be said about covenant relationships to God in general.

The original words by which the making, striking, or entering into covenant are signified, with their various uses and application to particular cases and occasions, have been fully explained by many.[3] Therefore passing by that, it will be enough for our present purpose to

---

[3] *Vid.* Coeceii *de fœdere* ca. I. & Rivet. In *Genesis Exerc.* 53. [See chapter 1 of Johannes Cocceius *On the Covenant* and Andrew Rivet, *Commentary on Genesis*, 53. These refer to the following Latin works: Johannes Cocceius, *Summa Doctrinæ de Fœdere et Testamento Dei*, (Batavia: Elsevier, 1654), the continental theologian's (1603-1669) famous study on the covenants; and Andrew Rivet, *Commentary on Genesis*, the French theologian's (1572-1651) critical work. Rivet was apparently a favorite of Coxe's. He not only quotes him several times in this book but in 1682 published *The Believer's Triumph over Death*, an account of Rivet's last days, "to comfort Christians against fear." For an account of Rivet's life see Thomas M'Crie, *Miscellaneous Writings* (Edinburgh: John Johnstone, 1841), 113-143.]

remind you that a covenant is to be considered either simply as proposed by God or as man enters into it by restipulation.[4]

1. Whatever is transacted in a federal way between God and men, God has the first hand in it. As Christ said to his disciples in another case, they had not chosen him but he had chosen them. So we may say that man has not at any time entered into covenant with God but God has entered into covenant with man. It only belongs to his sovereign majesty and is the fruit of his infinite goodness to propose, as well as his wisdom to choose and order, the terms of a covenant relationship between himself and his creatures. Therefore the covenant that he has made with men is frequently in Scripture said to be the Lord's covenant, as in Psalm 25:14, Isaiah 56:4, 6, and other places.

2. Nevertheless, a covenant relationship to God and interest in him does not immediately result from the proposal of a covenant and terms of a covenant relationship to man. But it is by restipulation that man actually enters into covenant with God and becomes an interested party in the covenant. It is a mutual consent of the parties in covenant that states[5] and completes a covenant relationship. And this is called an avouching of the Lord to be their God by consent to the terms of a covenant proposed to them (Deuteronomy 26:16-18); a subscribing with the hand to the Lord (Isaiah 44:5); and taking hold of his covenant (Isaiah 56:4, 6). The formal notion of a covenant entered or made includes mutual engagement.

3. Yet there can be no covenant of mutual benefits between God and men as there may be between one man and another. For all creatures necessarily depend on and have both their being and well-being from the bounty of their Creator. There is nothing that they have not received from him and therefore the most perfect of them can render nothing to

---

[4] [The *Oxford English Dictionary* indicates this rare word carries the sense "to promise or engage in return; a counter-engagement." It cites an occurrence from Thomas Adams' commentary on 2 Peter 2:9 to make the point: "If he covenant with us, 'I will be your God'; we must restipulate, 'Then we will rest upon you'." "Restipulation" appears to have a technical use in covenant theology closely related to the *fœdus dipleuron* (the two-sided covenant) which describes "the relationship of God and man together in covenant, and particularly the free acceptance on the part of man of the promise of God and of the obedience required by the covenant" (Muller, *Dictionary*, 120, 122). The same covenant viewed as the declaration and imposition of God's will toward man is the *fœdus monopleuron* (the one-sided covenant). These standard Protestant covenant theological terms are clearly behind Coxe's thinking in this section.]

[5] [To instate or establish in the covenant.]

him but what is due by the law of their creation. None can be profitable to God[6] though he that is righteous may be so both to himself and his neighbor. And therefore none can oblige God or make him their debtor unless he condescends to oblige himself by covenant or promise.

The General Notion of a Covenant and its Inferences

§. 3. The general notion of any covenant of God with men, considered on the part of God or as proposed by him, may be conceived of as "A declaration of his sovereign pleasure concerning the benefits he will bestow on them, the communion they will have with him, and the way and means by which this will be enjoyed by them."[7]

For the better understanding of what I intend by this general description, I will briefly propose some particulars that are either included in it or are the immediate and necessary consequents of it.

1. It implies a free and sovereign act of the divine will exerted in condescending love and goodness. It is not from any necessity of nature that God enters into covenant with men but of his own good pleasure. Such a privilege and nearness to God as is included in covenant interest cannot immediately result from the relationship which they have to God as reasonable creatures, though upright and in a perfect state. For the Lord does not owe to man the good promised in any covenant he makes with him previously; but his first right in it is freely given to him by the promise of the covenant.

2. The notion of a covenant adds assurance to that of a promise, since it implies a special bond of favor and friendship which belongs to federal-interest and relation. For a covenant is the foundation of a special relationship between the parties involved in it. The kind and benefit of this relationship is determined by the covenant itself and its nature, promises, and end.

3. The immediate and direct end therefore, of God's entering into covenant with man at any time (so far as concerns man himself) is the advancing and bettering of his state. God never made a covenant with

---

[6] Job 35:7, 8; Romans 11:35, 36.

[7] *Est enim Dei Fœdus nihil aliud quam divina declaratio de ratione percipiendi amoris Dei, & unicne, ac communione ipsius potiendi.* Cocceius *de Fœd.* [For the covenant of God is nothing other than a divine declaration concerning a method of perceiving the love of God, and achieving union and communion with Him. Cocceius, *On the Covenant.*]

Not sure about pt 3, does God find fault with the covenant or Mankind?

man in which his goodness to him was not abundantly manifest. Yes, such is his infinite bounty that he has proposed no lower end to his covenant transactions with men than to bring them into a blessed state in the eternal enjoyment of himself. And therefore, when one covenant (through the weakness of man in his lapsed state) has been found weak and unprofitable as to this great end of a covenant because insufficient to accomplish it, God finds fault, abolishes it, and introduces another in which full provision is made for the perfect salvation of those that have interest in it (Hebrews 8:7, 8).

4. The kindness and condescending love of God in entering into covenant with man strengthens that bond of love and obedience to God that he is under by the law of his creation by adding a new obligation to it. So the sin of man in breaking covenant with God rises higher, and is accompanied with greater aggravations, than the bare transgression of a law, if no such covenant relationship had been added to it.

5. Therefore, the revelation of the counsel of God's will in a covenant proposed to man is so far from excluding a restipulation on his part, that it renders it a necessary duty on him. This case is not like federal transactions between equals where one is at liberty to refuse the covenant offered by the other party. But the sense of our infinite distance from God as creatures, and the dependence we necessarily have on him, and the duty we owe to him by the unalterable law of our creation, (as well as our own advantage and profit), obliges us to accept with holy fear and thankfulness both the benefits he offers to us and the terms on which they are offered in his covenant. We must diligently perform what he commands and directs us to for the ends proposed in the covenant.

6. Yet this restipulation (and consequently, the way and manner of obtaining covenant blessings, as well as the right by which we claim them) necessarily varies according to the different nature and terms of those covenants that God at any time makes with men. If the covenant be of works, the restipulation must be by doing the things required in it, even by fulfilling its condition in a perfect obedience to its law. Suitably, the reward is of debt according the terms of such a covenant. (Do not understand it of debt absolutely but of debt by compact.[8]) But if it be a covenant of free and sovereign grace, the restipulation required is a humble receiving or hearty believing of those gratuitous promises on

---

[8] [Synonym for covenant in this work.]

which the covenant is established. Accordingly, the reward or covenant blessing is immediately and eminently of grace.

7. Therefore the good and glory of any covenant that God makes with men, whether it be considered absolutely or in comparison with another covenant, is to be measured chiefly by its promises and terms. If one covenant is established on better promises (i.e., either promising a more excellent good or in a more excellent way) than another, it is from there denominated and for that reason to be esteemed a better covenant than the other (Hebrews 8:6).

God has Always Dealt with Men by Way of Covenant

§. 4. Together with these things, it may not be unseasonable in this place to further observe that the holy and wise God has always dealt with the children of men in a way of covenant. The display of infinite goodness has always accompanied the discovery of his infinite glory in his dealing with men. Thus he has not acted toward them to the utmost right of his sovereignty and dominion over them. Had he done so, there never would have been any reward of future blessedness assigned and made due to their obedience, as there has been by covenant. Nor would they have been brought into any nearer relationship to God than that which resulted from their creation by him. But the great God has not so kept his distance from man but he has condescended to come to terms with him. And as he has required obedience in some things beyond the immediate dictates of the law of nature by positive[9] institutions, so he has been pleased also to oblige himself, beyond the debt of a creator, by the promise of a bountiful reward.

So it follows that all the worship and obedience that God has required and accepted from the children of men have been on covenant terms. Their ability or moral capacity to walk well-pleasing before him has also been given to them, or worked in them, in accordance with the ends of their covenant relationship. Therefore this ability must be the inseparable addition, not of the bare proposal of a covenant to them, but

---

[9] [Coxe uses "positive" in contrast to "natural" in regard to law. Natural (moral) laws are rooted in the nature of God and his creation and so are necessary and eternal. Positive (ceremonial) laws are binding because God, the lawgiver, freely chooses to require them temporarily. But they are not native to man's constitution (Romans 2:14-15) and so, like the rule given to Adam not to eat from the tree of the knowledge of good and evil, must be overtly revealed to him.]

of that covenant interest in which they have been stated.[10] From this are several consequences.

1. Once people have fallen under the guilt of breaching the covenant, they are by their own failure utterly disabled from yielding any acceptable obedience to God on the terms of that covenant which they have violated. Their interest in that covenant relationship is forfeited and lost by them. They remain under the penal sanction of the covenant but are utterly deprived of strength to answer the ends of that covenant, and have wholly lost their right in its reward.

2. If they are without strength with respect to the condition and end of that covenant which they once had an interest in and principles suited to, then are they so much more without strength, while they remain in their lapsed state, with respect to the terms of another covenant more excellent and mysterious, and wholly supernatural in its doctrine and terms.

3. Therefore, spiritual strength and ability to please God cannot in any way be restored to them except by a new covenant interest and that new creation which is its adjunct.

God's Covenant Always Transacted with a Representative Head

§. 5. This is also worthy to be noted by us: that when God has made covenants, in which either mankind in general or some select number of men in particular have been involved, it has pleased him first to transact with some public person, head, or representative for all others that should be involved in them. So it was in the covenant of creation which God made with Adam in his upright state and with all mankind in him. And the same is to be observed in the Noahic covenant as also in the covenants made with Abraham considered either as the father of believers or of the Israelite nation. In the interest of a spiritual relationship to him, believers claim the blessings of the covenant of grace that was made with him. And in the interest of a natural relationship to him, his offspring according to the flesh claimed the rights and privileges of that covenant of peculiarity which was first made with him as the head of that separate people. But more eminently, the covenant of grace is established in Christ as its head. All its promises were first given to him

---

[10] [To instate or establish in the covenant.]

and in him they are all yes and amen. It is by union to him that believers obtain a new covenant interest and from him they derive a new life, grace, and strength to answer the ends of the new covenant.

General Directions to Rightly Understand
Covenant Transactions

§. 6. Now it is evident from what has already been said, that all federal transactions of God with men flow only from his good pleasure and the counsel of his will. So on that ground it is certainly to be concluded that our knowledge and understanding of them must wholly depend on divine revelation. No one can pretend acquaintance with the secret of God except as he has been pleased to reveal it in his word. This light must guide all our inquiries after it. Our sentiments in things of this nature must be strictly governed by this rule, seeing the nature of them is such as transcends the common principles of reason or natural light. This is so since they owe their origin to the free acts of the divine will and wisdom, which are unaccountable until revealed by God himself. Therefore it becomes us to captivate all our thoughts of them to the obedience of faith, knowing that learning and strength of parts (though of excellent use in their place) not guided by Scripture light in these inquiries can only form an ingenious error and lose a man in the labyrinth of his own imagination and uncertain guesses. The simple advantage of those aids (in this case trusted to and stretched beyond their limit) can reach no further than to enable him *cum ratione errare*[11] and so to wander from truth in a path seemingly more smooth but no less dangerous than others light upon.

In these things lies the spring of most mistakes and corruptions of doctrine and practice in matters of religion. Men easily find out and agree in the true dictates of the law of nature but in things pertaining to the covenants of God, how varied are their sentiments! Yes, many great, learned, and good men have been divided in their judgments about some things of great importance to the faith and edification of the church though not absolutely necessary to her being. One error admitted about the nature of God's federal transactions with men strangely perplexes the whole system or body of divinity and entangles our interpretation of innumerable texts of Scripture. By this means jars and contentions have

---

[11] [To err with reason.]

been perpetuated in the church to the great grief and hindrance of all, the offence of the weak, and the greater scandal of the blind world. All this has often occurred through the lack of a due and humble attention to that revelation of truth which God has given us in the holy Scriptures, and endeavoring to collect the mind of God from there without a preconceived judgment,[12] and a careful avoiding of the undue mixture or confusion of things natural with those that are purely of a federal nature.

The covenant of God is his secret and only he can make us know it. And yet our faith, practice, comfort, and holiness are closely concerned in a good acquaintance with it; so we need no other motive to a diligent and humble search of the Scriptures for the right informing of our judgment about it. Nor do we need any other caution against attributing too much to our own wisdom or abilities. Rather we must manage all our inquiries with earnest prayer to God for that Holy Spirit of light and truth, who only can lead us into all this truth and bring us to a clear acquaintance of the mind of God concerning it.

---

[12] [Coxe parenthetically notes, "which is a greater occasion of those mistakes than men are generally aware of."]

Chapter Two

God's Transactions with Adam
The Importance of this Study

§. 1. In the former chapter I briefly touched on some things of a more general nature which I thought were necessary to set out in order to handle the particulars which follow. Now my work is to consider the first state of man, an account of which is to be taken from the state of Adam in whom the world of mankind was epitomized. We are all most closely concerned in the transactions of God with him and the relationship he had to God with their events and outcome. The right understanding of these things is not only necessary but lies at the very foundation of all useful knowledge of ourselves and of the mind of God in all the revelations of his will and counsel to the children of men which he has made in following ages, either before or in the law of Moses or by the word of the gospel. Their ignorance of these is apparently the reason for the blindness and miserable mistakes of the wisest heathen philosophers in a thousand other things of the greatest importance. If a man misses the right account of this, he is certainly bewildered in all further searching for that truth which most concerns him to know. Therefore it is necessary for us to observe with all diligence what the Holy Spirit has left on record for our instruction in this matter. This discourse may be referred to these three heads:

1. The condition of Adam before he sinned.
2. His sin and its immediate effects.
3. How God dealt with him in his fallen state.

I will discuss each only very briefly.

Man's Original State and the Law

§. 2. Concerning the condition of man before his fall we may observe these things.

First, God made him a reasonable creature and endued him with original righteousness, which was a perfection necessary to enable him to answer the end of his creation. Eminently in this respect he is said to be created in the image of God (Genesis 1:26, 27) and to be made upright (Ecclesiastes 7:29). This uprightness or rectitude of nature consisted in the perfect harmony of his soul with that law of God which he was made under and subjected to.

1. This was an eternal law and an invariable rule of righteousness by which those things that are agreeable to the holiness and rectitude of the divine nature were required and whatever is contrary to it was prohibited. This law was only internal and subjective to Adam, being communicated to him with his reasonable nature[1] and written in his heart, so that he needed no external revelation to perfect his knowledge of it. And therefore in the history of his creation there is no other account given of it but what is comprised in this (and which is twice repeated) that he was made in the image of God. The apostle teaches us this consists in righteousness and true holiness (Ephesians 4:24). The sum of this law was afterward given in ten words on Mount Sinai and yet more briefly by Christ who reduced it to two great commands respecting our duty both to God and our neighbor (Matthew 22:37-40).[2] And this as a law and rule of righteousness is in its own nature immutable and invariable, as is the nature and will of God himself whose holiness is stamped on it and represented by it.

2. It pleased the sovereign Majesty of Heaven to add to this eternal law a positive precept in which he charged man not to eat of the fruit of one tree in the midst of the garden of Eden. This tree was called the tree of the knowledge of good and evil (Genesis 2:16, 17; 3:3). The eating of this fruit was not a thing evil in itself but was made so by divine

---

[1] *Jus naturale est dictamen rectæ rationis, judicantis actut alicus, ex ejus convenientia vel disconvenientia cum ipsa natura rationalis, inesse moralem turpitudinem, aut necessitatem moralem, & consequienter ab Authore Naturæ, ipso Deo, talem aitem aut Vetari aut Treoisi.* Grot. This, as a late philosopher expresses it, was *Nota Artificis operi suo impressa.* And of some dictates of the law of nature (as I remember) Cicero says, that with respect to them, *facti non docti, imbuti, non instructi, sui mios.* [Natural law is the dictate of right reason, which judges from its convenience or inconvenience with rational nature itself that there is in some act moral turpitude, or moral necessity, and by the Author of nature, God Himself. Hugo Grotius. This, as a late philosopher expresses it, was the "mark of the Craftsman stamped on His work." And of some dictates of the law of nature (as I remember) Cicero says that with respect to them, "We were made, not taught; imbued, not instructed." The "late philosopher" referred to is Rene Descartes writing in *Meditatio* III.38. Cicero's words are from his *Orator ad M. Brutum* 49.165.]

[2] [This paragraph closely follows the *Baptist Catechism*, questions 13, 45-47, (*Westminster Shorter Catechism*, questions 10, 40-42) and the 2nd LCF, 19:1-2.]

prohibition. So it was necessary that the will of God concerning this should be expressly signified and declared to man. Otherwise by the light of nature he would have been no more directed to abstain from the fruit of this tree than of any other in the garden; indeed, he would not have been under any bond of duty to it. But the command being once given out, this positive law had its foundations surely laid in the law of nature. For it is an infallible dictate "that it is a most righteous and reasonable thing that man should obey God, and that the will of the creature should ever be subject to the will of the Creator."[3] Therefore the heart of an upright man could not but naturally close with and submit to the will of God by whatever means made known to him. There can be no transgression of a positive precept without the violation of that eternal law that is written in his heart.

Secondly, this law was guarded by a sanction in the threatening of death for its transgression (Genesis 2:17). This commination[4] is delivered in terms denoting the utmost misery that can befall a reasonable creature and the highest certainty of its befalling him in the case of his transgression: "In the day you eat of it", says the Lord, "in dying you will die." This sanction belonged not only to the positive precept to which it was expressly annexed, but also to the law of nature; the demerit for transgressing this law is known to man by the same light as the law itself is known to him. This is made good by the experience of mankind even in their fallen state, who do not only find some remaining notions in themselves of the difference of good and evil, and some sense of their duty to embrace the one and eschew the other, but also have a consciousness of punishment due to the transgression of these dictates of their reason. These notions are connatural[5] to them and therefore are to be observed both in those that have not and in those that have the light of a written law to guide them (Romans 1:32; 2:15). If this is so with fallen man regarding the law itself, then its sanction was also perfectly and distinctly known to Adam in his upright state. His conscience was pure and his mind irradiated with a clear light, being perfectly free from those dark fumes of sensual lust with which the reason and judgment of his lapsed offspring is darkened and perverted.

Thirdly, Adam was not only under a commination of death in case of disobedience, but also had the promise of an eternal reward on condition

---

[3] [This is an unknown reference.]

[4] [A curse or formal denunciation, especially a threatening of divine vengeance.]

[5] [Innate.]

of his perfect obedience to these laws. If he had fulfilled this condition, the reward would have been due to him by virtue of this compact into which God was pleased to condescend for the encouraging of man's obedience and the manifestation of his own bounty and goodness.

The Promise of a Reward Proved

§. 3. Now that such a promise of reward was given to Adam, and indeed implied in the commination of death in case of disobedience, may be concluded from the following.

1. The state and capacity in which God set him. This state was a trial in a way to eternal happiness under a law of works and an exercise of obedience which we cannot conceive of except for the purpose of some reward and highest end. This was proposed to him and was attainable by him.

2. The natural inclination of men. They expect a reward of future blessedness for their obedience to the law of God and to stand before him on the terms of a covenant of works. This necessarily arises from man's relationship to God at first in such a covenant (which included the promise of such a reward) and the knowledge of these covenant terms communicated to him, together with the law of his creation.

3. The sacramental use of that tree in the midst of the garden of Eden. This was called the tree of life because it was instituted by God for a sign and pledge of that eternal life which Adam would have obtained by his own personal and perfect obedience to the law of God if he had continued in it. That this tree was appointed by God for such a use and end is collected from the following:

a. The allusion that Christ makes to it in the New Testament (Revelation 2:7). There he promises an eternal reward to him who overcomes in these words, "I will give him to eat of the tree of life, which is in the midst of the paradise of God." The reason for this is taken from God's appointment of this tree to be an assurance of eternal life to Adam on the terms and condition of a covenant of works, and the analogy of that reward which Christ gives to his faithful ones in the terms of another covenant. This analogy consists in the general nature of the promised eternal reward though there is not an identity or perfect agreement in its degree or particular kind. I will not pretend to exactly determine the mode or degree of that blessedness which was set before Adam by the covenant made with him, whether it was a confirmation in his present state (which was very happy) or a translation to a better state when the course of his obedience in this was run out. However, it seems reasonable to conclude that it was in some respects short of that glory we are called to by Jesus Christ. But they both agree in the notion of an eternal, and in its kind, perfect happiness; therefore, the one is expressed by those terms that relate to a former assurance of the other.

b. The method of God's dealing with Adam in reference to this tree after he had sinned against him and the reason assigned for it by God himself. You may read an account of the whole in Genesis 3 from verse 22 to the end of the chapter where it says in part, "Lest he put forth his hand, and take also of the tree of life, and eat, and live forever." We are not to suppose that Adam could indeed have obtained eternal life by eating of the fruit of that tree after he had sinned against God. But the whole scheme of that discourse is ironical.[6] I take the foregoing words,[7] "Behold the man is become like one of us," to be a holy upbraiding of the folly of man in aspiring to such a state by the breach of God's law on the credit of the devil's suggestion. So I take these words also to intimate a further delusion that fallen man was in danger of. He entertained an opinion (that vain man is on any pretence ready to nourish in himself) of his yet being capable of recovering his forfeited happiness this way, or by any other work of his own. The words teach us what was the use and end for which this tree was first designed, as well as that Adam was not ignorant of these. Yet now he was to be taught the utter impossibility of obtaining life by a broken covenant through the guarding and prohibiting of all access to that tree by the cherubim's flaming sword that turned every way to keep the way of the tree of life.

c. This also must not be forgotten: that as Moses' law in some way included the covenant of creation and served for a memorial of it (on which account all mankind was involved in its curse), it had not only the sanction of a curse awfully denounced against the disobedient, but also a promise of the reward of life to the obedient. Now as the law of Moses was the same in moral precept with the law of creation, so the reward in this respect proposed was not a new reward, but the same that by compact had been due to Adam, in the case of his perfect obedience.

---

[6] [Having the nature of irony; meaning the opposite of what is expressed.]

[7] *En divinitatem promissam!* [Behold, the promised divinity! Almost as if to say, "Look at the divinity promised to us, but lost by Adam's sin!"]

The Reward and Punishment of the Law

§. 4. From what has been said it is apparent that Adam was set in his way but not actually brought to his eternal rest in the state in which he was created. He was capable of and made for a greater degree of happiness than he immediately enjoyed. This was set before him as the reward of his obedience by that covenant in which he was to walk with God. Of this reward set before him, these things are further to be observed.

1. Although the law of his creation was attended both with a promise of reward and a threatening of punishment, yet the reason of both is not the same nor necessary in the same way. For the reward is of mere sovereign bounty and goodness. It therefore might have been either less or more, as it pleased God, or not proposed at all without any injury being done. But the threatened punishment is a debt to justice and results immediately from the nature of sin with reference to God without the intervention of any compact. It is due to the transgression of a divine law as such, and therefore still due to every transgression of it, even by those that are already cut off from any hope of reward by a former breach of the covenant. And as it may not be more than the offence deserves without injury to man, so neither may it be less, without a diminution of the glory of justice, by the strict rule of which it is always measured. So that death which was threatened in the curse is in a strict and proper sense the wages of sin (Romans 6:23).

2. In the history of this transaction, as left on record by the Holy Spirit for our instruction, we have a more particular and express mention made of the threatened curse than of the promised reward. So we have a more distinct notion of the curse conveyed to our minds than of the promise, although we have reason to think both were known to Adam with equal clearness. This may be because it is more important for us to be thoroughly humbled under a sense of the present misery of mankind in their lapsed state, than to curiously inquire after the particular mode or degree of that blessedness which was once proposed but can never be obtained by us in the interest of that covenant which first gave man a right to it.

Adam a Public Person

§ 5. In this transaction of God with Adam, he is not to be considered in a private capacity or as one concerned for himself alone. Rather, God treated him as the common root and representative of all mankind who were to spring from him according to the ordinary course of nature[8] and were then reckoned to be in him both as a natural and federal root. Therefore in his standing all mankind stood, and in his fall,[9] they all sinned and fell in him. "For by the disobedience of one many were made sinners" (Romans 5:19). And in this respect he is said to be the type (and Christ the antitype) or figure of him that was to come. Because as Adam's sin is imputed to all that were in him, and so judgment to condemnation comes on all that were represented by him, so also the obedience of Christ is imputed to all that are in him, and the free gift redounds on them to the justification of life by virtue of their union to and communion with him.

God's Transaction with Adam a Covenant

§. 6. From these things it is evident that God dealt with Adam not only on terms of a law but by way of covenant. This transaction with him was of a federal nature although it is not in Scripture explicitly called a covenant. Yet it has the explicit nature of a covenant and there is no reason for niceties about terms where the thing itself is sufficiently revealed to us. There is no explicit mention of a covenant of grace before Abraham's time and yet the thing is certain and clearly revealed in Scripture, namely, that all who were saved before his time were interested in such a covenant and saved only by its grace. The evidence of Adam's covenant relationship to God may briefly be summed up as follows:

1. It is probable that God set him not only under the necessary law of his creation but added to it a positive law. This may be observed to be an adjunct of a covenant transaction in all his later dealings with men.

2. But it is certainly concluded from that promise of reward and the assurance that was given to Adam which he could never have obtained except by God condescending to deal with him by terms of a covenant.[10]

3. It could only be on the account of such a covenant that Adam's posterity should be involved as they were in his standing or falling. Let the first be denied and the latter is altogether unaccountable. For had he only been under a law to God, his sin would have remained on himself. It

---

[8] [*Baptist Catechism*, question 19; (*Westminster Shorter Catechism*, question 16).]

[9] *Nos omnes eramus ille unus homo.* [We all were that one man.]

[10] [This entire section closely follows the 2nd LCF, chapters 6, 7, and 19.]

could not have redounded on the whole world of mankind by a just imputation as it now does, any more than the sin of any particular person can now be imputed to another man that is not actually guilty of it – at least the sins of immediate parents to their children.

In this lies the mystery of the first transaction of God with man and of his relationship to God founded on it. This did not result immediately from the law of his creation but from the disposition of a covenant according to the free, sovereign, and wise counsel of God's will. Therefore, although the law of creation is easily understood by men (and there is little controversy about it among those that are not degenerate from all principles of reason and humanity), yet the covenant of creation,[11] the interest of Adam's posterity with him in it, and the guilt of original sin returning on them by it, are not owned by the majority of mankind. Nor can they be understood except by the light of divine revelation. Nor is the heart of man humbled to a due acknowledgment of them by a clear and deep conviction except by a work of the Holy Spirit. As long as men measure this counsel of God by their own narrow and dark reason and refuse to submit their sentiments concerning it to the revelation of his sovereign pleasure, unaccountable will, and wisdom they must necessarily fall into grievous mistakes and fill the world with fruitless contentions through their darkening of counsel by words without knowledge.

The General Nature of the Covenant with Adam

§. 7. As to the terms and condition of this covenant that God made with Adam and all mankind in him, it was a covenant of works. With respect to immediate privilege and relationship it was a covenant of friendship. With regard to the promised reward it was a covenant of rich bounty and goodness. But it did not include or intimate the least iota of pardoning mercy. While its law was perfectly observed it raised man within a degree of the blessed angels. But the breach of that law inevitably brought him under that curse which sank him to the society of apostate devils and left him under a misery like theirs.

---

[11] [The *Fœdus naturae* or *naturale* (the covenant of nature or natural covenant) was another name used by Protestant federal theologians for the *fœdus operum* (the covenant of works) that emphasizes the original pre-fall integrity of man and his capacity to obey the covenant stipulations. Coxe here calls this the covenant of creation. (Muller, *Dictionary*, 122.)]

Under this covenant man was left to the freedom of his own will.[12] It was in his own power and choice either to obey and be eternally happy, or to sin and so expose himself to eternal misery. He was not so confirmed in grace that he could not sin and die, but he was endowed with that power and rectitude of nature that he might not have sinned nor ever died. Though he did not have a *non posse peccare*[13] and so a *non posse mori*;[14] yet he had a *posse non peccare*[15] and so a *posse non mori*.[16] He was a perfect though mutable creature and had every possible advantage of moral persuasion to make him constant in his obedience. He could not be without a clear conviction of the greatest obligation to this both in point of duty and in gratitude toward his Creator and covenant God. He had present happiness and future hope in the way of his duty and fair warning of the misery that sin would bring on him in the proclamation of that curse which was the sanction of the law given to him. And yet when the time of trial comes all this does not prevail against the temptation; but his mutability becomes the original of that Original Sin by which he, and in him the world of mankind, were ruined and made miserable.

The Sin of our First Parents

§. 8. The next thing to be inquired into is the sin of our first parents and their resulting state and condition.

As to the first, their transgression was actually completed by eating of the fruit of the tree of the knowledge of good and evil concerning which the Lord had commanded them that they should not eat (Genesis 3:6). With respect to this let it be observed:

1. That it was by the breach of a positive law that mankind was lost. This was the door through which sin and all the consequent miseries invaded and by their entrance ruined this lower world.

2. Since man fell by the transgression of this positive precept, his breach of covenant with God was much more conspicuous because this precept belonged not immediately and necessarily to the law of his

---

[12] [Quoted from the *Baptist Catechism*, question 16; (*Westminster Shorter Catechism*, question 13).]

[13] [Inability to sin.]

[14] [Inability to die.]

[15] [Ability to not sin.]

[16] [Ability to not die.]

creation, but was superadded to it as a special term and condition of his covenant relationship.

3. The breach of this positive law supposes and necessarily infers a violation of the eternal law of his creation. This transgression was a total apostasy from God and in it all conceivable wickedness was included, even "the lust of the flesh, the lust of the eyes, and the pride of life" (1 John 2:16). All the villainies that to this day have been or ever will be perpetrated in the world are its genuine fruit and on a strict search its aggravations will be found to be uncountable.

The State and Condition of Fallen Man

§. 9. Next to be inquired into is the state and condition of fallen man. This was most miserable and dreadful. For having broken covenant with God after this manner by a wicked and willful transgression of his holy law:

1. He thereby utterly forfeited and lost all covenant interest in God. He could no longer claim a right in, or hope for, that reward which was promised on condition of his perfect obedience to the law of that covenant which God had made with him. Instead, he immediately fell under guilt, being by the sentence of his own conscience bound over to punishment under the just wrath of the Almighty. And therefore he dreaded nothing more than the approach of God to him (Genesis 3:8-10).

2. He not only forfeited his right but also his present relationship to God by this sin. Moreover, he was by this means rendered incapable of true happiness, inasmuch as he was now apostatized from a covenant of friendship to a state of enmity against God and alienation from him, which is the necessary adjunct of wickedness. He fell under the dominion of sin and that image of God in which he was created was in a manner wholly defaced. He sinned and fell short of the glory of God (Romans 3:23). And now instead of that original righteousness with which he was first beautified, there was nothing to be found in him but abominable filthiness and horrid deformity. His mind was covered over, even possessed with hellish darkness. Hatred of God reigned in his heart and his affections were no longer subject to right reason but became vile and rebellious. It is evident that in this state he must be utterly incapable of communion with God and of the enjoyment of him in whom alone the true happiness of a reasonable creature consists.

3. The curse of the law in its utmost rigor and prime intention was immediately and only due to him. Nothing less than its utmost execution was every moment to be expected by him; and that was death, even the worst of deaths, eternal death, which is "an everlasting punishment of soul and body under the wrathful vengeance of a provoked Deity."[17]

That this was the prime intention of the threatening might be clearly demonstrated by many reasons but for now I will content myself with the mention of only two.

1. This punishment will be inflicted on many of the ungodly posterity of Adam who have been guilty of no other transgression but against the light and law of nature. Such were those wicked heathen that Paul speaks of[18] who, though they never had the written law or knew of any repeated promulgation[19] of it, (and therefore we may conclude they were much more unlikely to be acquainted with the new covenant and its terms) yet being a law to themselves were liable to this punishment for the transgression of this law. Now this punishment must be the fruit of that curse which is the sanction of that law which they were under, and which was transgressed by them, which was the law of creation, even the same law that Adam was made under. And if the law is the same, the same penalty was incurred by its transgression. And if they are liable to eternal death for the transgression of this law there is no rational doubt that Adam was also.

2. If the just demerit and wages of sin was contained in the threatening (as no doubt it was) it could be no less than an eternal punishment that was threatened. For if that is not the desert[20] of every sin, it cannot be due to any sin. The reason why the punishment of any sin is eternal is so that the penalty inflicted on the sinner may be adequate to the offence. The punishment has an infinity in its eternity, because the fault is infinitely aggravated, and that can only be in regard of its object. There is nothing that can be an infinite aggravation of sin but its being committed against a God of infinite greatness, glory, and goodness. And this aggravation attends every sin, as it is sin against God, and though other circumstances may increase the provocation and so intend the degree of the sinner's pain, yet none but this can reach infinity. The punishment therefore due to Adam for sin against God

---

[17] [The *Heidelberg Catechism*, question 11.]

[18] Romans 1:20; 2:6-16.

[19] [Putting into effect a law by formal public announcement.]

[20] [Something that is deserved or merited, in this case a punishment.]

could be no other or no less than eternal death, which is that intended in the sanction of the law given to him.

3. The whole creation of this visible world became liable to destruction with fallen man as an inheritance forfeited by his treason against the supreme majesty. By the sin of man the frame of earth and the heavens made for his service and delight was loosed, and their foundations so shaken as would have issued in an utter ruin had not Christ interposed and upheld their pillars (Psalm 75:3 with Hebrews 1:3). If the curse had been immediately executed in its rigor with these desolations following, there was a hell prepared ready for man. For suppose, I pray you, all the lights of heaven to be put out, the whole order, symmetry, and beauty of the creation to be destroyed, and all reduced to a chaos of confusion and horrid darkness about man, and the burning wrath of God kindled on him, now cast into the jaws of eternal despair and tormented by a worm that never dies. Think, I say of this, and you will hardly be able to conceive of a state more dreadful and dismal than the one on which man stood at the very brink.

4. In this condition man was altogether helpless and without strength, being utterly disabled to stand before God on terms of a covenant of works, and incapable to bring himself on other terms. For he was not able to move one step toward a reconciliation with God or the ransoming of himself out of these miseries. The door of repentance was not opened to him by the covenant of creation, or if it had, there was now in him neither power nor will to enter in there. He was utterly disabled from obeying God acceptably on any terms until made a new creature. Therefore it was impossible that this now broken covenant should be renewed with him or any of his posterity for the same ends and in the same manner as it was first made with upright man. Nor could any covenant ever again be immediately struck with him or them in which fallen man should have been the first and immediate covenanter with God for himself as Adam was in his state of integrity.

God's Mercy to Fallen Man

§. 10. Inexpressibly miserable was the state of fallen man. Let us now see how the boundless mercy of God was revealed to him when he was lost in this way and miserably ruined by his own sin. And to better understand what is to follow, I will premise two things which are necessary to be kept in our eye.

1. The infinitely wise and gracious God, who from eternity foresaw the fall of man, also had from eternity a gracious purpose in himself according to the counsel of his own will, to redeem and save a remnant of lost mankind from their lapsed and fallen state,[21] and by his all-powerful grace, through the merits of Christ, to recover them from misery to the inheritance of a kingdom and glory far greater than that set before Adam in his integrity. And these eternal counsels that were hid with himself were transacted in a way of covenant between the Father and the Son, even in a covenant of redemption,[22] now revealed in the Scriptures of truth.[23] To this covenant belong all the promises of the Father to the Mediator, and the restipulatory engagements of the Redeemer about the salvation of sinners and the way and method of its accomplishment. With respect to these counsels the Son of God is said to be the Father's delight, and himself also to have his delight in the habitable world when the highest part of its dust was formed[24] (Proverbs 8:22-31). In this context the mutual acquiescence both of the Father and the Son, in this admirable contrivance of infinite grace and wisdom, is not obscurely set out.

2. In pursuing this covenant of redemption and the suretyship of Christ taken in it upon the fall of man, the government of the world was actually put into the hands of the Son of God, the designed Mediator, who interposed himself for the prevention of its present and utter ruin. By him were all future transactions managed for the good of man, and all discoveries of grace and mercy were made to the children of men in him and by him. All things in heaven and earth were brought into an order subservient to the ends of the new creation and the redemption of lost man to be accomplished in the fullness of time by the Son of God incarnate. Fallen man could have no more to do with God, nor God with him in a way of kindness, except in a mediator.[25]

---

[21] 2 Timothy 1:9-10; Titus 1:1-2.

[22] [This is the *pactum salutis* (the covenant of redemption), "in Reformed federalism, the pretemporal, intratrinitarian agreement of the Father and the Son concerning the covenant of grace" (*fœdus gratiæ*). (See Muller, *Dictionary*, 217.)]

[23] [2nd LCF 7:3.]

[24] [The original reads "when the head of the dust thereof was formed." See Proverbs 8:26, 31.]

[25] [2nd LCF 7:3d expanded.]

A Promise of Redemption in a Treaty

§. 11. It was from this design of love and mercy that when the Lord God came to fallen man in the garden in the cool of the day, and found him filled with horror and shame in the consciousness of his own guilt, he did not execute the rigor of the law on him. Instead he held a treaty with him which issued in a discovery of grace. By this a door of hope was opened to him in the laying of a new foundation for his acceptance with God and walking well pleasing before him.

1. For in the sentence passed on the serpent (which principally involved the Devil whose instrument he had been in tempting man, and who probably was made to abide in his possession of the serpent until he had received this doom, Genesis 3:15) there was couched a blessed promise of redemption and salvation to man. This was to be worked out by the Son of God made of a woman, and so her seed, and man was to receive the promised salvation by faith and to hope in it. In this implied promise was laid the first foundation of the church after the fall of man which was to be raised up out of the ruins of the Devil's kingdom by the destruction of his work by Jesus Christ (1 John 3:8).

2. In this commination of the serpent there is not only implied a promise of raising up a Savior of the seed of the woman, and sending him into the world for the breaking of the serpent's head, (that is, the perfect conquest of Satan and the utter ruining of his kingdom) but also of propagating and preserving a church in the world that should be heirs of that salvation. These would maintain a spiritual war with Satan and his kingdom which on their part would end in perfect conquest and victory. While Satan is nibbling at their heel, the God of Peace would bruise him under their feet and make them to be more than conquerors through him that loved them. For the seed of the woman is to be understood collectively of Christ and his members (as the seed of the serpent includes all wicked men) though it has a principal reference to Christ personally, who alone has obtained the victory over the infernal power and destroyed the works of the Devil. But although this was done by himself alone, yet it was not only for himself but for his body the church, of which every true believer is a member and will certainly obtain victory through the faith of his name. Against this church the gates of hell can never prevail but it will always be in the world as long as the world continues. This was the case ever since the first promise, though the church was maligned and persecuted by the Devil and wicked men,

as appears early in the instance of Cain and Abel (Genesis 4 compared with 1 John 3:12). And something of this nature is intimated in the name of Seth and the reason given by Eve of her imposing that name (Genesis 4:25).

3. Following this there was an immediate restraint and modification of the curse in the sentence pronounced on Adam and Eve (Genesis 3:16-19). Although they and their offspring were necessarily subjected to many evils and miseries while they lived, and dissolution by a temporal death at last, yet they were not immediately laid under a sentence of eternal death which was the punishment they had deserved. And concerning this sentence we may further observe:

4. That the promise of breaking the serpent's head which was revealed to our first parents did not give them a deliverance from all misery but only an exemption from eternal death. Despite this promise and all that Christ has now done for its full accomplishment, it is the will of God that all men, believers as well as others, will in this world be exercised with miseries and remain subject to temporal death, or dissolution of the body into dust.

5. The corruptibility of man, all the miseries he is subject to while he lives, and temporal death at last are the fruits of sin and of the curse due to it, since they are natural evils or punishments. But they are not the only fruit or result of the curse, nor the full wages of sin. Since they are evil they flow from the curse, but being only temporal their evil is limited and thus modified by mercy or at least compassionate goodness. The positing of temporal death clearly proves that sin is in the world. But this limitation of death also proves that there is mercy reserved for some and that those who do not obtain mercy must be brought to a reckoning afterward because the fruit of their doings has not fully been repaid to them in this world.

6. And so none of these evils are incapable of a change as to their penal nature, including the change of that man's state on whom they come. For though they fall as so many drops of wrath that foretell a dreadful storm coming on the wicked, yet they[26] are all sanctified to a

---

[26] *De prima igitur Corporis Morte, dici potest quod bonis bona sit, malis mala, secunda vero sine dubio sicut nullorum bonorum est, ita nulli bona.* Aug. *De Civit. Dei Lib. 13. Cap.2.* [Consequently, we may say of the first death, that of the body, that it is good for those who are good and evil for those who are evil. But as for the second death, just as it happens to no one who is good, so doubtless it is good for no one. For this translation see Augustine, *The City of God Against the Pagans*, IV, Book 13, Chapter 2 (Cambridge, MA: Harvard University Press, 1966), 138-139.]

believer and turned into real blessings. But the utmost execution of the curse is not capable of this change for eternal punishment can never be turned into a blessing for any.

Since there is reason to suppose that God not only promised a redeemer to Adam before he pronounced this sentence but also gave him faith in the promise, then it came immediately on him as a fatherly chastisement and not as a fruit of unpacified anger.

It is also true on the other side that the goodness and forbearance of God is, through the wickedness of man, turned into a judgment on the ungodly and impenitent who abuse the day of his patience to the treasuring up of wrath against the day of wrath and revelation of the righteous judgment of God (Romans 2:5). Both temporal mercies and temporal evils are wholly subservient to the design of God's glory in the future and eternal state of man. And we may conclude there would have been no such thing as temporal death if there had not been a day of patience.

It is more than probable that at the same time or immediately after, God instituted those bloody sacrifices that were offered to him from then on and accepted by him when offered in faith. This was for the further instruction of man in the general notion of the way of his redemption by the promised seed and for the help and confirmation of his faith in the promise. Even the coats of skin which the Lord made and by which he clothed Adam and Eve, then confounded with the shame of their own nakedness, seem to be designed by God not only for a natural but also a spiritual use. They were for their instruction concerning that imputed righteousness in which they must now stand before him and without which they could find no acceptance with him. Especially if these coats were made of the skins of those beasts that Adam was then directed to offer in sacrifice to God (as some conjecture they were), we can hardly imagine less to be intended. For no doubt with the institution of sacrifices something of the use and end of them was revealed to Adam.

It must also be noted that although the covenant of grace was revealed this far to Adam, yet we see in all this there was no formal and express covenant transaction with him. Even less was the covenant of grace established with him as a public person or representative of any kind. But as he obtained interest for himself alone by his own faith in the grace of God revealed in this way, so must those of his posterity that are saved. Therefore the corruption of fallen Adam and the guilt of his fall were derived from him to all his offspring because they were in him as a public person and federal root when he fell. Yet they cannot derive from him any interest in his renewed state or in the grace or holiness of it, since with respect to this God dealt with him only as a private person. And the good of the promise now given out was no more entrusted with him than with his posterity or any of them in particular.

The State and Condition of Adam's Posterity

§. 12. The state and condition that the world of Adam's posterity is now in, is as follows.

1. They are all born in Original Sin, in the fallen image of the first Adam, and so are under a broken covenant being by nature children of wrath, unholy, and without strength.

2. Yet they are necessarily under the obligation of a law to obey, worship, and serve their Creator though they have no covenant interest in him. For it is impossible and implies a contradiction that reasonable creatures should be brought into the world and not be subject to the law of their Creator or that eternal death should not be due to the breach of that law by them. The law of creation binds when the covenant of creation is broken. Though the transgression of man has forfeited his interest in the one, yet it cannot dissolve the obligation of the other.

3. Yet, the world is set under a general reprieve and the full execution of the deserved curse is delayed until the day of judgment. Until that time the children of men are under a dispensation of goodness and sparing mercy. So they are in a remote capacity or possibility of obtaining salvation by Christ where it pleases God to send the gospel, the dispensation of which is made effectual for the salvation of all the elect, who are in this way gathered into the kingdom of Christ.

4. The Lord Christ has undertaken in the close of his mediatorial kingdom, when all his sheep are brought into his fold, (for whose sake alone the day of his patience is lengthened out to the world) to raise all mankind again in an incorruptible state, prepared for that eternal duration to which they were designed in their first creation. Then he will glorify with himself all those for whom he has satisfied the justice of God, born the curse of the law, and worked out everlasting righteousness, who have been also called by his grace to a participation of these benefits through faith. Others he will deliver up by a righteous sentence to the full execution of the curse on them in its utmost rigor which until then was suspended for the ends stated before.

Chapter Three

God's Covenant with Noah

A New Relationship Established

§. 1. From the first dawning of the blessed light of God's grace to poor sinners faintly displayed[1] in the promise intimated in Genesis 3:15, the redeemed of the Lord were brought into a new relation to God, in and by Christ the promised seed, through faith in him as revealed in that promise. Their obedience and religious service were stated[2] and accepted by God on a new foundation of pardoning mercy and forgiveness through the Redeemer (Psalm 130:4). They were no longer on terms of personal and perfect obedience or doing of a law, but on terms of faith or believing a gratuitous promise which wholly changed the order of their acceptance with God. For by the covenant of creation, the work of obedience was to maintain the relation and secure the acceptance of the person with God. But by the covenant of grace and redemption, the relationship and previous acceptance of the person in Christ was the reason of the good acceptance of all their sincere though imperfect obedience which now sprang from faith. And so it is said in Hebrews 11:4, "God had respect to Abel and his offering;" first to the person and then to his work. This order and way of salvation in its general nature always was and must be the same and invariable in all ages and under all different dispensations of God toward his church.

God's Revealed Word is Men's Rule of Faith

§. 2. Since holy men then lived by faith, so it follows they had the object of faith with them, that is, the revelation of God's counsel by his word. Though the word was not written until Moses' time, yet the church was never without God's oracles. In those days they were made known to it by those ways and means that the infinite wisdom and goodness of God chose. This we have seen in the first promise and in the institution of sacrifices which could not have been offered in faith as Abel's was, if God had not commanded and appointed them. It also appears that God

---

[1] [The original reads "being broken up".]
[2] [To instate or establish in the covenant.]

had given them some particular directions concerning which beasts they might offer in sacrifice and which not, for in Noah's time the distinction of clean and unclean beasts is mentioned as a thing well known (see Genesis 7:2, 3 and 8:20). To this we may add that at least some of the names of Seth's line were imposed by a spirit of prophecy, that Enoch was a prophet, and that Noah was a preacher of righteousness. All these infer a revelation of the mind of God and of his counsels made at that time to the church, distinct from the light and law of nature and transcending all their dictates; although it must be granted that this light did not shine on them with the same clearness as it did on later ages.

Enoch

§. 3. In addition, there is the extraordinary dispensation of God's providence toward Enoch who by faith walked with God and then was translated to the heavenly inheritance without being made subject to the common lot of mankind in dissolution by temporal death. This was not only a singular favor to himself, but was also an eminent discovery to the rest of the believers of that age that the right of adoption and the claim of an inheritance in light by faith was restored to them in the promised seed. This greatly tended to encourage their faith and hope in the expectation of a glorious state for soul and body to be enjoyed in a blessed immortality and eternal life hereafter. They had this earnest in the present enjoyment of one member of that body to which they were all united (Compare Genesis 4:24 and Hebrews 11:5.).

The very time when this was done casts some further light on its spiritual[3] meaning. Enoch was the seventh from Adam and this septenary number is famous in Scripture for its spiritual signification of that perfect rest or Sabbath that Christ should bring his church to. So Matthew counts the genealogy of Christ by septenary generations. Again, the translation of Enoch happened soon after the death of Adam, the first whose natural death is mentioned in Scripture. Enoch in the seventh generation was translated that he should not see death. As they had seen the fruit of the curse exemplified in Adam's death so they saw that life which the promise gives exemplified in Enoch's translation. He is the one who walked with God before he was translated or, as the apostle gives it, had this testimony, "that he pleased God".[4] Indeed the Hebrew phrase used in

---

[3] [The original reads "mystical".]
[4] [Hebrews 11:5.]

Genesis 5:22 not only signifies integrity and eminent holiness in a private capacity but also (as the learned Ainsworth[5] notes on the place) is often used for a pleasing administration of office before God. In this respect he was a special figure of Christ, and his translation prefigured Christ's entering into heaven as a forerunner for us.

For three hundred years the church had enjoyed his ministry and seven patriarchs were left alive as witnesses of his translation so that the whole number of the sons of God had the benefit and comfort of instruction from it. He prophesied of the destruction of wicked men and summed up his prophecy in the name he gave to his son Methuselah. It may be interpreted, "they die by a dart" or "he dies and then is the dart" (i.e., the dart of divine vengeance in punishing the ungodly) or "he dies and then it is sent." This was almost one thousand years before the flood but was exactly fulfilled in the issue, for Methuselah died only about the space of one month before the flood came. This prophecy is more fully set down by Jude in verse 15 (which may be taken as a divine paraphrase on this prophetic name like Daniel's interpretation of the writing on the wall) and applied analogically[6] to the sinners of his time. This first judgment was a type of future judgments on wicked men, especially of the destruction of the Jewish state by the fire of God's wrath for their rejecting of Christ. Each of these was a *præludium*[7] of the general judgment of the world, so the threatening of this first judgment to the ungodly then living was also a denouncing of judgment against all ungodly sinners in future times.

The General Propagation of the Church

§. 4. In these ages of the church it was generally propagated in that line through which the blood of the promised seed ran. Yet we do not find any such wall of partition set up between one family and another; any that desired might freely associate themselves and join with the true worshippers of God.[8] It is even possible that some of the line and race of

---

[5] [This reference is to Henry Ainsworth, *Annotations on the Pentateuch and Psalms*. The Puritan Ainsworth, 1571-1622(?), was a noted Hebrew scholar whose two-volume work was recently reprinted by Soli Deo Gloria, Morgan, PA.]

[6] [Analogously; by analogy.]

[7] [Prelude.]

[8] *Potuit fieri ut quidam privati Homines ex generatione Cain, Instinctu divino, se ad Adam conjunxerint, & salvati sint.* Luther in Genesis [But so it was possible for some of his (Cain's) descendents, by the prompting of the Holy Spirit, to be saved. Comments on

cursed Cain did so. On the other hand, it is more than probable that others of the children of Adam, besides Cain, revolted with him from all true religion and holiness and joined issue[9] in an open contempt of God and rebellion against him. However, the nature and necessity of religious worship and the obedience that was due to God in it, obliged his servants to keep themselves distinct and separate from the rest of the world. While they did so, the general defection of mankind was prevented. But toward the completion of the old world, all things declined and grew worse and worse (Genesis 6:5, 12, 13). The violence and corruption of mankind abounded and even the sons of God were taken with the bait of sensual delights. Those who had formerly kept up a pure and distinct communion for the solemn worship of God by calling on his name (and so also had his name called on them, Genesis 4:26, being denominated the sons of God) now lost the sense of religion and broke the bounds of their just separation and mingled themselves with the daughters of men (Genesis 6:24). These were the women of Cain's offspring, or of confederacy with his seed, by whose beauty they were entangled while they regarded the gratifying of their lust more than the true ends of marriage. Being entangled like this they were also drawn into a partnership with them in their abominations to such a degree that when the time of the flood came the pure worship of God was maintained only in the family of Noah, who found grace in the sight of God (Genesis 6:1-11). He was preserved in the ark so that by him and his sons the desolate earth might be again replenished with inhabitants after the foundation of the wicked had been destroyed with a flood (Job 22:16).

The Ark as a Type

§. 5. Now in the dealings of God with Noah there are some things that call for our diligent attention. These carry to a further degree of light the

---

Genesis 4:10-12 from Martin Luther, *Commentary on Genesis: A New Translation by Theodore Mueller, volume 1* (Grand Rapids: Zondervan Publishing House, 1958), 105-106. Similar sentiments are also found on p. 108, "No doubt, some of his (Cain's) offspring turned to the true church, and so were saved;" and page 113, "These, then, were Cain's children and heirs, and, no doubt, they were persons of great wisdom and high station. I believe that some of them were saved by God's special grace, but the great majority hated and persecuted the true church most severely."]

[9] [To "join issue" is a legal phrase meaning to take up the opposite side of a case or a contrary view on a question. See the *Oxford English Dictionary*.]

discovery of grace and redemption by Christ and so further establish the church in its expectation.

After being warned, Noah built the ark by God's special direction for the saving of himself and his house, which were eight souls (1 Peter 3:20). This afforded them all a temporal deliverance from the deluge of waters by which God in his wrath swept away a disobedient world. It was also useful in its typical reference for their further instruction about the redemption of man from the floods of divine vengeance to be poured out later in eternal wrath on the world of unbelievers. For this is to be observed concerning the state of the church before Christ came in the flesh: that as the gospel was preached to them by types and dark shadows, so this kind of instruction was afforded them not only by the stated ordinances of ceremonial worship, but also by many extraordinary works of providence. These were so ordered by divine wisdom that they might bear a typical relationship to and be an apt representation of spiritual things. This may be observed in many instances in the history of Abraham and his offspring, the children of Israel. On this account the manna they ate in the wilderness is called spiritual meat; the water of the rock which they drank, spiritual drink; and the rock, Christ (1 Corinthians 10:3, 4). And yet we read of no special ordination or appointment of these things to such an end except what they had from the order and voice of providence, together with the peculiar circumstances of the people involved in them. Under this consideration is Noah's ark. It was either a type of Christ (like the ark in the Jewish sanctuary) or of the church viewed as being guarded with his salvation, which in the end comes near to the same thing.

This type is rendered more vivid by the form of the structure which God commanded and also the unusual use of one term in the directions given for securing the preservation of those who were to enter into the ark.

1. The form in which the ark was built, in the proportion of its dimensions, comes nearest to that of the body of a man. For it was in length three hundred cubits, in breadth fifty, and in height thirty, so that in figure it was shaped like a coffin. There was a resemblance of burial in entering into it and of a resurrection in coming out of it. In this respect the apostle Peter makes baptism to be the antitype to the ark (1 Peter[10] 3:19, 20). Thus the ark was an extraordinary sacrament, or prefiguring,

---

[10] [The original reads "Eph".]

of the church's redemption and salvation by the death and resurrection of Christ and of her union and communion with him that died and rose again, so as to enjoy all the benefits of his death and resurrection.

2. In the directions given for the building of the ark, Noah is commanded to pitch it with pitch both within and without (Genesis 6:14). The words in the Hebrew are *capharta baccopher*. The first sense of the verb (כפר) is to cover. By metaphor it signifies to expiate or make atonement because as things covered are hidden from sight, so expiated sin is blotted out and remembered no more against the sinner. The noun *copher* is never used in the same sense in all the Bible for the Hebrews have other words that properly signify such kind of stuff as was now to be made use of (see Exodus 2:3). But in the law it is often used for the covering of or propitiation for sin. So these terms seem to be especially adapted by the Holy Spirit to the typical reference of the ark which was to prefigure the salvation of the church through the expiation of sin and atonement made by the death of Christ. In the merit of his blood is her only defense against the swelling waters of divine wrath and the curse of the law under which the whole world of unbelievers must inevitably perish.

Though we have no reason to think that these things could then be apprehended so distinctly and clearly as we now see them by the light of the New Testament, yet have we good ground to believe that some general knowledge of them was conveyed to the minds of the faithful in the time of this type and by means of it. This informs us how Noah became an heir of the righteousness of faith by building the ark and entering into it (Hebrews 11:7). These were not the only proof of his obedience through which the truth of his faith was manifested, but additionally his faith reached and in some degree apprehended the spiritual use of the ark which he was building. While his hands were busied in this external work, and his life secured by his living in it, his faith was exercised about that spiritual and eternal salvation that was shadowed and typically represented by it.

God Establishes his Covenant with Noah

§. 6. On Noah's entrance into the ark and at his coming out, we find mention made of God's establishing his covenant with him (see Genesis 6:18 and 9:11). This is the first place and occasion of the explicit mention of a covenant in the Scriptures. Therefore we are more obliged to a serious inquiry after the true nature and import of this covenant. We will collect some observations on it according as things are presented in the order of their narration by Moses.

Only let this be premised: that though God's establishment of a covenant with Noah is mentioned at two separate times in the texts just referred to, they are not two different covenants that are mentioned but one and the same covenant in substance. The benefits of it are first expressed more generally and then more particularly.

In Genesis 6:18 God speaks to Noah as follows: "But with you I will establish my covenant and you will come into the ark." God's making of a covenant is the establishment of it because his promise is a full and sufficient assurance that he will perform what is engaged for in it to the end. The benefit immediately promised is the preservation of Noah and all who were with him in the ark. The restipulation required of him was a believing resignation of himself to God in an obedient use of those means of safety which he had ordained.

At first view this seems to convey no more than an outward and temporal favor. But if diligently looked into, we will discern a great deal more in it.

1. In this benefit of Noah's covenant there was not only a temporal salvation secured to him and his house but what is more, his eternal salvation. The salvation of the whole church was included in it and wholly depended on it since the promised seed which should break the serpent's head was not yet brought into the world. Therefore, if all mankind had now been destroyed, that first and great promise (which was a revelation of the sum of the covenant of redemption) would have failed, and so the whole covenant to which it belonged would have been evacuated and made of no effect. With respect to this as well as to its certainty in itself, the federal promise given here to Noah is aptly said to be an establishing of God's covenant with Noah since this covenant was made with him in pursuit of that gracious design of man's redemption revealed before. Since this was never suspended on the worthiness of man, so God by covenant assures Noah that its accomplishment should never be prevented by his wickedness.

2. Add to this the typical reference of the ark and you will discern that the covenant of eternal salvation by Christ was implied and darkly shadowed under this covenant, even as the promise of the heavenly inheritance to believers was afterwards couched in the promise of Canaan to Abraham and his seed.

The Noahic Covenant Developed

§. 7. What happened after Noah came out of the ark, you have recorded in Genesis 8 from verse 20 to the end of the chapter and in chapter 9. In this history you may observe:

1. That before there was any further transaction of God with Noah, he offered a sacrifice to the Lord in which the Lord smelled a sweet savor or a savor of rest (Genesis 8:21). This phrase of smelling a sweet savor signifies the acceptance of his offering. And this savor arose from the typical relationship of this offering to the sacrifice of Christ (compare Ephesians 5:2) and the faith of him that sacrificed which was through it directed to the same object. And this is to inform us that all which follows was transacted in the[11] interest of this sacrifice and is in some way to be referred to its ends. From this passage you may look back to Genesis 5:29 and you will find the reason for Lamech giving the name of Noah[12] to his son.

2. The blessings of Noah's covenant are first conceived in a gracious purpose of God's heart. The Lord said in his heart, "I will not again curse."[13] This is later put into the promises of the covenant which God engaged himself to bestow (Genesis 9:8, 9) and is reckoned equivalent to an oath in Isaiah 54:9, "I have sworn that the waters of Noah should no more go over the earth."

3. The particular benefits and blessings given to mankind by this covenant were: fruitfulness for the replenishing of the earth; dominion over the creatures and the free use of them for food; and assurance that the judgment which they had now escaped should not be repeated. This was given even though later generations were likely to prove as wicked as those that had gone before them seeing that the same root and spring of corruption remained in them (Genesis 8:21). And the rainbow was appointed to be the visible sign and token of this covenant (Genesis 9:12-17).

I am content to have briefly pointed at these things. But further we have to note:

1. The dispensation of goodness and forbearance which the world was set under by the first promise was now ratified by a solemn

---

[11] Christ's mediation and sacrifice is the cause of God's forbearance toward the world.

[12] And he called his name Noah, saying, This will comfort us, etc.

[13] [Genesis 8:21.]

covenant. It also ensured the successive generation of mankind for the production of the promised seed both personally and collectively considered.[14] And this assurance raised the faith of the church one degree higher than it had before attained.

2. This covenant also had its spiritual use to the faithful in foreshadowing the covenant of grace by Christ and its ratification in the blood of his sacrifice. By this we are saved from the curse and restored to a sanctified right in creature comforts and the hope of eternal life. The sovereignty of God's goodness and the absoluteness of his promise are exhibited in this covenant as a singular encouragement to the faith of the church in reference to the promise of that grace that reigns in the new covenant (Isaiah 54:9). And the token of this covenant is made the emblem of the steadfastness and eternal memorial of the other[15] (Revelation 4:3) so that in the typical reference of this covenant, the light of divine grace and mercy dawned on the church with more clearness than earlier.

3. This covenant is said to be made with Noah and his sons and their seed after them for perpetual generations. The terms are parallel to those we meet in chapter seventeen in the covenant made with Abraham for his seed in their generations. And yet here two things are evident:

a. Future generations to the end of the world are as much involved in this covenant as their immediate offspring with whom it was first made. They have equal claim with them to its blessings without any consideration of their immediate parents.

b. Although the grace of the new covenant was spiritually held out in this covenant with Noah (which was struck with him for all his posterity) yet the grace and blessing were not by this means bestowed on all mankind.[16] They surely all have an interest in that covenant that signified, and in some ways included, spiritual blessings but those blessings do not pertain to all who have their signs. Instead they remain the peculiar right of those who by faith receive them, "who are born not of blood, nor of the will of the flesh, nor of the will of man, but of God" (John 1:13).

---

[14] That is, the Messiah, and his members.

[15] The rainbow about the throne notes God's regard to his covenant in the government of the world. All the administration of providence is bounded by his faithfulness.

[16] The same may be said of the promises of typical blessings to Abraham's carnal seed and their interest in them.

Blessing and Curse to Noah's Sons

§. 8. In the following part of this history (Genesis 9:25 and following) we may observe the following points.

1. The curse of Ham on his son Canaan prepared the way for the blessing of Shem in his posterity by Abraham, for it was by the execution of this curse that the Canaanites were afterwards disinherited and Israel planted in their place. Concerning this prophetic curse on Canaan and blessing on Shem, you may read what is later noted by Moses (Deuteronomy 32:8). It is also worthy of our notice that the seal of Israel's covenant, by virtue of which they inherited the land of Canaan, kept alive the remembrance of Ham's wickedness and was a perpetual warning to them not to degenerate into his steps. He was condemned to servitude for looking on the nakedness of his father and they were circumcised in the foreskin of their flesh.

2. In the blessing of Shem special regard is paid to the Messiah whose coming into the world was now limited to the line of Shem. Therefore in his blessing is the spring of Japheth's blessing also. Shem is the first of whom it is expressly said that the Lord was his God. And by the Lord God of Shem is intended Christ who is over all, God blessed for ever, whose name is here celebrated by Noah as the only hope and salvation of the church.

3. The blessing of Japheth in the interest of Shem's blessing signifies not only his personal interest in the Messiah who was to come from Shem, but also the calling of the Gentiles from his posterity to be joint heirs with the Jews in the blessings of the new covenant. His dwelling in the tents of Shem intimates also the succession of the Gentile church to the church of the Jews, who were to be disinherited of all covenant interest for their rejection of the Messiah. In that passage "God will persuade[17] Japheth,"[18] there is an allusion to his name and the calling of the Gentile church is prophesied in similar terms (Hosea 2:14, 15).

Babel and the Confusion of Tongues

§. 9. Some time after these things, about the fourth generation, we find that according to the blessing of God on Noah and his sons (Genesis 9:1)

---

[17] יפת [Japheth means "he will persuade".]
[18] [Genesis 9:27.]

there was a very great increase of men in the world. As they increased they evidently drew on themselves the same charge that was laid on the old world, namely, that the imagination of their heart was evil from their youth. For in the days of Peleg[19] there was a very general conspiracy and rebellion against God managed by the children of men at Babel. Pursuing this they began to build a tower there (Genesis 11:1-9). And it is very probable that Nimrod the mighty hunter was one chief doer in the business (for a defection from the true religion and tyrannical oppression usually go hand in hand).[20] But their rebellious enterprise was interrupted by the confusion[21] of languages that God brought on them. Here the Hebrew tongue which had been universal remained in its purity only with the family of Heber and such other of the patriarchs and holy men then living who had not joined themselves with these workers of iniquity in their cursed design. On this occasion Heber has a special honor put on him which you may see in Genesis 10:21. There Shem is in a peculiar manner said to be the father of all the children of Heber. And Abraham with his posterity, the heirs of Shem's blessing, are from him designated "Hebrews".

The Evils in the Confusion of Language

§. 10. Now by this confusion of languages the children of men fell under a greater evil than we might possibly be aware of at first thought. For it not only frustrated their present design, it also rendered the means of their civil conversation difficult for the future and made the attainment of all natural knowledge full of labor and travail. But far more important are the following evils.

1. It was virtually a kind of excommunication from the church then in being (who retained the Hebrew tongue although it was from this time unintelligible to the greatest part of the world).

2. In the later dispensation of God toward the Hebrews, this diversity of their language from that of the rest of the world was like the addition of a natural fortification to that wall of separation by which the nations

---

[19] Genesis 10:25.

[20] [This political comment, indeed, the publication of this book, was a display of real courage for a London Baptist pastor in 1681. These were days of persecution and Coxe's Petty France Church was disrupted numerous times before the Glorious Revolution of 1688 provided significant relief.]

[21] This gave the name to the place Babel signifying confusion.

were excluded from the privileges of the church. They were left destitute of that blessing which of all others was the greatest Israel had: the oracles of God (Romans 3:1, 2) which were committed to them in the Hebrew tongue. Consequently, for many ages they remained strangers to the covenant of promise (Ephesians 2:12), living in the darkest cloud of ignorance and idolatry, and so without hope and without God in the world. And this dismal effect of the present judgment remained on them generally until the times of restitution and refreshing, even until the last days in which God would persuade Japheth and bring him into the tents of Shem. Then a door was opened for the breaking up of light to the Gentiles by the gift of tongues at Jerusalem by which the apostles and prophets of the New Testament were enabled to preach the gospel to all nations in their own tongue. Thus the salvation of God in Zion became a light to the Gentiles whose darkness was originally brought on them by the confusion of tongues at Babel.

3. Neither did the judgment of God on this evil generation stop here; for their days were also shortened and cut in half in anger for their sin. For you may observe in the genealogy (Genesis 11) that as none which were born after the flood attained to the years of those that lived before it, so most plainly the ordinary age of man was again shortened from the time of this defection at Babel so that none of the generations after Heber attained to more than about half the number of his years.

Chapter Four

The Covenant of Grace Revealed to Abraham

God Specially Honors Abraham by this Covenant

§. 1. The next signal advance that was made of the discovery of God's grace to men was in Abraham's time by the federal transactions of God with him. By these he was brought into such a relationship to God and the whole church as was in some respects peculiar to himself and never was the lot of any other of the children of men either before or since his time. In this respect Abraham may be considered a type of Christ who is eminently the Head and Prince of the new covenant. Because of that special grace and favor that the Lord bestowed on him in his transactions with him he is called the friend of God. The covenant is said to be mercy to Abraham and truth to Jacob (Micah 7:20). This intimates that the beginning of it with Abraham was of mere grace and mercy, though once made with him, the truth and faithfulness of God was engaged to make it good to its succeeding heirs. The covenant of grace made with Abraham was not the same for substance that had been more darkly revealed in the ages before, but it pleased God to transact it with him as he had not done with any before him. It may be noted also that Abraham is the first man in the world to whom God is said to have appeared or been seen (Acts 7:2 with Genesis 12).

Abraham's History and Apparent Incapacity

§. 2. This Abraham was of the posterity of Shem, descended from him in the tenth generation, and chosen of God from among all his numerous offspring to be in a special manner the heir of his blessing (Genesis 11). Yet we are not to imagine that Abraham and his family were the only people that God had in the world in his days. For although there was then a very great defection of the world from God and his true worship, yet was it not universal as in Noah's time. There were many alive that truly feared God and were accepted with him besides Abraham and those immediately depending on him. For even Shem lived till Abraham was 150 years old and Arphaxad lived till he was 88, which was thirteen years after that covenant was confirmed with him, mentioned in Genesis 12. Salah lived until Abraham was 118 years of age, which was about nineteen years after the covenant of circumcision was given to him. And Heber lived after his death until Jacob was about nineteen years old for he had the longest life of all who were born after the flood. There is no doubt that these patriarchs, worshiped and served the true God along with their houses and others joining with them under their leadership. Yet it pleased the Lord to single out Abraham, call him to his foot, and make him a head of all future covenants with men. This was done despite a bar lying in the way of his entering into any such relation at the time of his calling. This bar was impossible to remove except by omnipotent grace and power on both a moral and physical account.

1. On a moral account: Abraham was not a person eminent for holiness and religion. When God called him to inherit Shem's blessing, he was not better or more deserving than any of the rest of his posterity. Instead, he was swimming down the stream of a wicked world, having degenerated from the religion and piety of his ancestors to false worship and idolatry (Joshua 24:2, 3). Therefore it is not without reason that the prophet in Ezekiel 16:3 upbraids the people of Israel with the charge that their father was an Amorite and their mother a Hittite. He said this not properly but metaphorically because even they had been involved in the guilt of the same apostasy from God as these nations before the Lord graciously called them out of it.

2. On a natural account: for Sarah the wife of Abraham was barren and noted to be so before God called him (Genesis 11:30). Yet the blessing of Shem must have been lost, the hope of the church perished, and all covenant transactions with Abraham proved of no effect, if he had not had seed. By virtue of God's covenant to be established with him, the Messiah (in regard to the flesh) was to come of him. Yet all this was no impediment or obstruction in the way of him who quickens the dead and calls the things that are not as though they were (Romans 4:17).

Abraham's Double Role in the Covenant

§. 3. There is one more thing in particular to be premised to the consideration of God's covenant transactions with Abraham which is most clearly stated in the New Testament.

With respect to them, Abraham is to be considered in a double capacity: he is the father of all true believers and the father and root of the Israelite nation. God entered into covenant with him for both of these seeds and since they are formally distinguished from one another, their covenant interest must necessarily be different and fall under a distinct consideration. The blessings appropriate to either must be conveyed in a way agreeable to their peculiar and respective covenant interest. And these things may not be confounded without a manifest hazard to the most important articles in the Christian religion. The mutual reference of all God's covenant transactions with Abraham and God's dispensation toward the church for some ages following was such that it required a present intermixture of the promises, and an involving of spiritual blessings in the shade of temporal, and of a spiritual seed in a natural. This I suppose is more evident than to admit denial. The Scripture does not speak of any other relationship of Abraham in the covenants made with him. Neither can we prove by this that any of the covenants given to him were transacted with him simply under the notion, or in the relationship of, an ordinary believing parent or head of a particular household.

To better understand these things it is necessary that with due attention both to the history of the Old Testament and the light of the New, we humbly inquire concerning:

1. The covenant of grace as made with Abraham.
2. The covenant made with him for his natural offspring.
3. Their mutual relationship and dependence on one another.

The Covenant of Grace Revealed to Abraham

§. 4. First, it is plainly declared that God revealed the covenant of grace to Abraham, the general nature of that covenant, and the seed involved in it. I will here transcribe at length that account which the Holy Spirit gives of it in Galatians 3:6-9, 16, 17.

> Verse 6. Even as Abraham believed God, and it was accounted to him for righteousness. 7. Know therefore that they which are of faith, the same are the children of Abraham. 8. And the Scripture, foreseeing that God would justify the heathen through faith, preached before the gospel to Abraham, saying, In you will all nations be blessed. 9. So then they which be of faith, are blessed with faithful Abraham.
>
> 16. Now to Abraham and his seed were the promises made. He says not, And to seeds, as of many; but as of one, and to your seed, which is Christ. 17. And this I say, that the covenant that was confirmed before of God in Christ, the law, which was four hundred

and thirty years after, cannot disannul, that it should make the promise of none effect.

These words contain the whole of what I intend in this discourse. I will briefly collect their sum in some observations on them to my present purpose.

The Timing of the Covenant and its Inferences

§. 5. First, that the gospel was preached to Abraham and the covenant of grace revealed to him, is asserted in such full terms in this context that no one can rationally doubt it. Furthermore, in verse 17 we have the time of God's establishing this covenant with him exactly noted. The text says it was 430 years before the giving of the law on Mount Sinai (Galatians 3:17). Now the law was given a very short time after the children of Israel came out of Egypt. From the giving of the first promise to Abraham, which we have recorded in Genesis 12:2, 3, to that very night in which the children of Israel were brought out of their Egyptian bondage, is the computation of these years made. This will be evident to anyone who will diligently compare the chronology of those times with the express testimony of Moses (Exodus 12:41). And it came to pass at the end of the 430 years (even the self same day) that all the hosts of the Lord went out from the land of Egypt. From the time of the first promise to the end of Israel's sojourning in Egypt was 430 years, though their abode in Egypt was not near so long. From this we collect:

1. That in the transaction of God with Abraham recorded in Genesis 12 he solemnly confirmed his covenant with him, although Moses does not make express mention of the term covenant until another occasion in Genesis 15:18. For the promise mentioned there is asserted by the apostle to be the covenant confirmed of God in Christ to Abraham.

2. Israel's merciful redemption out of Egypt was in some respect to be referred to this covenant as its spring, although it was not immediately and in its own nature a new covenant blessing to all who partook in it. All the dealings of God with them as a select and peculiar people in covenant with himself were subservient to the great ends of this covenant with Abraham. Therefore none of them may be interpreted to the prejudice or disannulling of those promises in which the gospel was preached to Abraham.

3. By the computation of Moses (Exodus 12) it appears that the promise we are speaking of was given to Abraham on the 15th day of the month Abib. This was the first month according to the religious account[1] of the Jews, on which day Israel, a typical church, obtained a typical redemption in the interest of a typical Passover. And on that same day Christ, our true Passover, was sacrificed for us on the cross, obtained eternal redemption, and by confirming the covenant of grace with his own blood, passed all its promises into an unalterable testament.[2]

All Spiritual Blessings Included in the Covenant

§. 6. Secondly, the sum and substance of all spiritual and eternal blessings was included in the covenant and promise given to Abraham (Genesis 12) in these words: "I will bless you, and you will be a blessing." The grace and blessings of the new covenant were given and ensured to Abraham for himself. What is more, this honor was conferred on him that he should be a head of covenant blessings as the father of all true believers. No less is intended in those words "you will be a blessing." They certainly suppose that he should be blessed but the promise does not terminate in himself, but also conveys blessedness to many others through a relationship to him as his children. This is more fully expressed in what follows, "In you will all nations be blessed." This general promise does not intend that every individual person in every nation should at any time be blessed in Abraham. Rather, it means that his blessing should not be confined to any one nation, excluding others, and that all in every nation that were blessed would be so by virtue of the covenant now made with Abraham and in a relationship to him as their father. This was the gospel preached to Abraham and a promise of the justification of the heathen through faith (Galatians 3:8). In the interest of this blessing of Abraham they receive the promise of the Spirit as being his seed (verse 14). And this promise of a believing seed which would with him inherit the blessings of the covenant of grace, was further confirmed to Abraham a considerable time after this (Genesis 15 compared with Romans 4:3, 18).

---

[1] [Calendar.]
[2] The covenant of grace is to be considered by us a testamentary covenant. Compare Hebrews 7:22 with chapter 9:16.

This Covenant Confirmed in Christ

§. 7. Thirdly, this covenant was made with Abraham in and through Jesus Christ. It is not Abraham but Christ that is its first head. In and by him all the promises of it are ratified as he was the surety of the covenant (Hebrews 7:22) and in him they are all "Yes" and "Amen" (2 Corinthians 1:20). It is from him that all the grace of the covenant is derived on poor sinners through faith in his name. The apostle asserts this most clearly (Galatians 3:17) and argues it from the form of the promises made to Abraham (verse 16), "to Abraham and his seed were the promises made; he says not to seeds, as of many; but as of one, and to your seed, which is Christ."

The scope of the apostle's discourse teaches us that the promises referred to are those relating to the justification and salvation of poor sinners. These promises include that grace by which the Gentiles are called to inherit eternal life. Some refer this principally to Genesis 17:7. It will readily be granted that some of those promises that ultimately respect the spiritual seed and spiritual blessings are sometimes given to Abraham under the cover of those terms that have an immediate respect to his natural seed and temporal blessings as types of the other. When they are so, the promise still runs to his seed in the singular number. The Holy Spirit here teaches us to be on set purpose to gather up our thoughts to Christ alone as the spring and root of Abraham's blessing when we consider the spiritual import of such promises. But this being allowed, that the apostle has the form of that promise in view, we cannot from there conclude that the promise is made to Abraham's seed both natural and spiritual in one and the same sense. But only this much will fairly follow from it: that the apostle argues from the carnal seed as typical to the spiritual seed as typified by it. In so arguing he makes special use of the terms in which the promise is made as purposely fitted to its typical respect or spiritual sense. Similarly, the prohibition of breaking a bone of the paschal lamb, which was a type of Christ, is applied by John to Christ himself who was typified by it (John 19:36 with Exodus 12:46).

Nevertheless, I conceive the apostle here has a direct and special view to that promise found in Genesis 22:18,[3] "In your seed will all the families of the earth be blessed." This runs directly parallel both in terms and sense with the promise given to Abraham in Genesis 12:3 which was

---

[3] This promise is particularly cited by Peter as a summary of the covenant of grace made with Abraham, Acts 3:25.

pleaded by him earlier (Galatians 3:18). This promise was given out in the repetition and confirmation of the covenant made before with him on the occasion of Abraham's offering up Isaac in which the death and sacrifice of Jesus Christ was prefigured in a most lively manner. It clearly holds out this much: that as all nations should be blessed in a relationship to Abraham as his children, so that blessing should be derived to them through interest in Christ, his promised seed, by the efficacy of his mediation in the interest of that sacrifice and offering of a sweet smelling savor (Ephesians 5:2) that he should make to God in the fullness of time. And if it be objected that the promise there is made of or concerning Abraham's seed and not to his seed, let it be minded that all the promises made of this seed (namely, Christ) in one respect, may be said to be made to this seed in another, because they are originally established in the everlasting covenant of redemption that was between the Father and him.

Some[4] interpret this text in Galatians spiritually of Christ because of the order of the words. The promise, they say, is made first to Abraham and then to his seed. Therefore it is such a seed as comes to have a right in the promise second to Abraham and as his child; and also because the apostle's scope is to prove that the Gentiles are justified by faith as Abraham was. But I would rather apply them to Christ as personally considered. For the seed to whom the promise is made is the same as the one in whom all the nations of the earth are blessed (Genesis 22:18). Now although all believers, being the seed of Abraham, are blessed with faithful Abraham, yet they are not that seed in whom all nations are blessed. Rather, it is the nations who are blessed in this seed. And in the very next verse the covenant is said to be established of εἰς Χριστὸν[5] in or to Christ, who is the same seed spoken of in the preceding verse. Now the covenant is confirmed in Christ personally, not in Christ spiritually. Hence Pareus concludes it is to be understood "*indiviue de uno Christo, ex quo omnis spiritualis Benedictio in fideles diffluit.*"[6] But this also is to

---

[4] See Strong, *Of the Covenant*, p. 126. [The reference is to William Strong, *A Discourse of the Two Covenants* (London: Francis Tyton, 1678), a work concerned with the covenant of works and of grace.]

[5] [The "next verse" referred to is Galatians 3:17, which in most Greek manuscripts includes εἰς Χριστὸν, although some do not.]

[6] [Individually concerning the One, Christ, from whom every spiritual blessing flows down on the faithful. The quote is from David Pareus, 1548-1622, Reformed commentator and Professor of Theology at Heidelberg, in his *Commentary on Galatians* referencing 3:16-17.]

be observed: that Christ is given for a covenant of the people (Isaiah 42:6). Therefore the covenant is established in him and with him for all believers, who by union with him become that one seed of Abraham to whom the blessing of his covenant belongs. So in this sense it as strongly concludes for justification only by faith in Christ, as in the other.

As for the order of the words, it should not seem strange that Abraham is first mentioned and then his seed, Christ. For beside the promises chiefly intended, the first says "in you" and what is given afterward says "in your seed" will all nations be blessed (which is the order the apostle observes). It should also be considered that Abraham was really the father of Christ according to the flesh and by covenant appointed to be as David was also. And yet Christ is not only the offspring, but also the root of both Abraham and David. Although the mercies of the covenant are called the sure mercies of David because of the covenant which God made with him, yet they are all originally from Christ in one respect, though mediately by Christ in another, since they flow from a covenant first made with David, which was to be later ratified and fulfilled in Christ, the son of David.[7] And perhaps it is on the account of the covenants made with Abraham and David concerning this matter that in Matthew 1:1 they are so peculiarly mentioned in the genealogy of Christ as recorded by that evangelist.

Abraham a Root of Covenant Blessings and Parent to Believers

§. 8. Fourthly, this covenant was made with Abraham as a root of covenant blessings and the common parent to all true believers. Indeed, Abraham himself obtained the grace of this covenant by Christ, his seed, and so came into it secondhand with respect to the Son of God who is the Prince of the covenant. But with respect to us, the covenant was first given to Abraham and we are brought into it in the interest of a relationship to him as children, which also is by faith in Jesus Christ. This special honor God put on Abraham by the manner of his entering

---

[7] *Duorum maxime Filius dicitur Christus Abrahœ & David, quoniam istis sapius, ac desertius, quam cœteris, est promissus,* Lud. Viv. [It is of two men most of all that Christ is called the Son: Abraham and David, since he was promised to them more often, and more clearly, than to others. Joannis Ludovici Vivis Valentini is the Latin name of the Spanish humanist scholar and student of Erasmus, Juan Luis Vives, 1492-1540, of Valencia, Spain. In 1522 he published a commentary on Augustine's *City of God* from which this quote probably came.]

into covenant with him, that from then on, no people should be taken into covenant with himself except as his seed. This is evident as to Israel after the flesh in the Old Testament, that their covenant interest was derived from Abraham. And it appears just as plainly concerning the spiritual seed and Israel of God in the New Testament that Abraham is their father (Romans 4) and all true believers are blessed in him as his seed (Galatians 3:8, 29 with Genesis 12:3). By that promise in Genesis, Abraham was ordained and constituted by God to be the father of the faithful, as has been already dealt with. So it is that their enjoying of Paradise is called a resting in Abraham's bosom (Luke 16) because as they have their entrance into a state of grace, so also they are brought into the kingdom of glory and made to possess heaven as his children. They are also said to sit down with Abraham in the kingdom of heaven (Matthew 8:11).

The Way of Salvation by Faith in Christ in this Covenant

§. 9. Fifthly, the last thing I will note is the eternal settlement of the way of salvation according to the character of this covenant which is by faith in Christ. This is a covenant that conveys the grace of life to poor sinners by a free and gracious promise which admits of no other restipulation in order to covenant interest except believing. It is of faith because it is of grace (Romans 4:16) and this way is the only way of life. There is but one covenant of spiritual and eternal blessing in Christ Jesus, founded in the eternal decree and counsel of God's love and grace, which is now revealed to Abraham. There is but one seed, which is of true believers in union with Christ, promised to him as the heirs of this covenant and the grace given by it. In this manner the way of their justification and acceptance with God is determined; not by a natural descent from Abraham or any external privilege appended to it but by a walking in the footsteps of Abraham's faith (Romans 4:13). He is made the exemplar of justification to all in future ages for whose perpetual instruction this is recorded, that he "believed God and it was accounted to him for righteousness."[8] Therefore the substance of the promise now given to Abraham could never be altered, nor in any way evacuated or superseded by any future dispensation that the church was brought under. But whatever law or covenant was afterwards given to them, must

---

[8] [Romans 4:3.]

necessarily lie subservient to it and be directed toward the ushering in of the perfection of that dispensation of grace which was unalterably fixed by it (Galatians 3:17). It was the everlasting gospel that was now preached to Abraham, which was afterwards to break into view with the fullest glory and luster in the days of the Messiah, when the Lord performed his mercy to Abraham and remembered his holy covenant (Luke 1:72 and following).

The Promise Given before Circumcision

§. 10. I will now close this chapter with some corollaries deduced from the things already cleared and then proceed in the method before propounded.

1. This covenant of grace, of which we have been speaking and which the Holy Spirit in the New Testament has so remarkably pointed out to us, by which Abraham was made the father of the faithful and all believers according to it were to be considered as a seed that God would give to him, was confirmed and ratified by a sure promise to Abraham. This was a considerable time (about twenty five years) before the covenant of circumcision was given to him. The covenant of grace then had no outward sign or seal annexed to it. Indeed, that which has been lately affirmed, that the covenant of grace always had an outward sign or seal added to it, is so wide a mistake that on the contrary it may be affirmed that although the efficacy of its grace reached believers in all ages yet it was not filled up with ordinances of worship proper and peculiar to itself until the times of reformation. Nor was there until then any outward sign or token immediately belonging to it. For had it been, so this sign or token, like the covenant itself, would have remained without change and not vanished away with the other shadows of the Mosaic economy.

2. The promise made to Abraham gives the seed, as well as the blessing of that seed, to him. Believers are the children of promise, later typified by Isaac, being begotten to God of his own will by the efficacy and grace of his free promise and in its virtue. Yes, the seed is first supposed in the promise and then the blessing of that seed is promised, which being of grace, is made sure to all of them (Romans 4:16). As the blessing is spiritual so also is the seed; nor can it be extended further than to that seed which is its promised subject.

3. The sum of all gospel blessings is comprised in this promise. Therefore it will follow that the proper heirs of this blessing of Abraham have a right (not only in some, but) in all the promises of the new covenant. This is true not in a limited sense, suspended on uncertain conditions, but in a full sense and secured by the infinite grace, wisdom, power, and faithfulness of God. Accordingly, they are in time made good to them all. And this will be more manifest if we consider that all the blessings of this covenant redound on believers by means of their union and communion with the Lord Jesus Christ, who is both the Head and Root of the new covenant, and the Fountain from which all its blessings are derived to us. Since these blessings were entirely purchased by him, so are they entirely applied to all that are in him and to none other.

Therefore, I conceive the limiting of a new covenant interest to the grant of an external and temporary privilege only, to be utterly inconsistent with the promises of the covenant itself (such as these: Isaiah 54:13; 59:21; Jeremiah 31:33, 34; Ezekiel 36:26, 27 with Hebrews 8 and many others of like import). Neither will these texts admit of another notion lately insisted on for the commendation of paedobaptism, namely:

"That the infant seed of believers, during their infancy, have all of them a certain and definite interest in the covenant of grace by virtue of which they are completely justified before God from the guilt of original sin, both *originans* and *originatum*.[9] And yet when they come to years of discretion they may, (yea must) by their actual closing with or refusing the terms of the covenant, either obtain the continuation and confirmation of their covenant interest, or be utterly and finally cut off from it and so perish eternally in their ignorance of God and rebellion against him."[10]

As the promises of the covenant will not admit of any such partial interest, neither can this opinion co-exist with the analogy of faith in other respects. For either the stain of original sin in these infants is purged and the dominion of concupiscence in them is destroyed when their guilt is pardoned, or it is not. If it is, then the case of these infants in

---

[9] [Originating and originated. Original sin has two aspects: *peccatum originale originans*, originating original sin, which is Adam's act of disobedience itself; and *peccatum originale originatum*, originated original sin, which is the stain or defect in the individual's nature which is transmitted to him at his conception.]

[10] [This is an unknown reference but is probably from Whiston's *Infant Baptism Plainly Proved*.]

point of perseverance is the same with that of adult persons who are under grace by their actual faith. Then a final apostasy from the grace of the new covenant must be allowed possible to befall the one as well as the other, notwithstanding all the provisions of the covenant and engagement of God in it to make the promise sure to all the seed. But this the author will not admit. He may say that their guilt is pardoned but their natures are not renewed, nor the power of original corruption destroyed so that sin will not have dominion over them. It will then be replied that despite their supposed pardon, they remain an unclean thing, and so are incapable of admission into the kingdom of glory. But the truth is that none are at any time justified before God except those whom Christ has loved and washed from their sins in his own blood (Revelation 1:5). None are washed by him but those that are in him as the second Adam. It is by union to him as the root of the new covenant that the free gift comes on them to the justification of life.[11] And none can have union to him but by the indwelling of his Holy Spirit. Wherever the Spirit of God applies the blood of Christ for the remission of sins he does it also for the purging of the conscience from dead works to serve the living God. As certainly as any derive a new covenant right from Christ for pardon, they also receive a vital influence from him for the renovation of their natures and conforming their souls to his own image. And therefore to assert that the grace of Christ is applied to some for the remission of sins only, or that the guilt of any sin can be pardoned to any person and yet that sin retain its dominion over him, is (so far as I can discern) both unscriptural and incoherent with the doctrine that is according to godliness.

4. In conclusion, it is plain that a believer's claim to the blessings of the new covenant is in the interest of Abraham's seed and by virtue of the promises given to him relating to such a seed, and not as coordinate[12] with him in covenant interest. Each is not made by this covenant the father of a blessed seed as Abraham was the father of the faithful. Neither can they claim the promise for themselves and their seed according to the substance of Abraham's covenant and as he might. Instead, they must rest in a relationship to him as children and so receive his blessing, that is, the blessing promised to him for his seed and that by their own faith and for themselves alone. Because they are Abraham's seed, believers are blessed with faithful Abraham. And if we be Christ's, then are we Abraham's seed, and heirs according to the promise (Galatians 3:29).

---

[11] Romans 5:14 and following.
[12] [Equal in importance, rank, or degree.]

Chapter Five

The Covenant of Circumcision (I)

The Promises to Abraham for his Natural Offspring

§. 1. The method laid down before leads us in the next place to inquire after the promises given to Abraham for his natural offspring, and their assurance which God was pleased to give him by covenant transactions. As before, I will diligently review the history that Moses wrote of these things by the inspiration of the Holy Spirit and compare the promises made to the records of their accomplishment in other parts of holy Writ. In this way I will endeavor to collect from these their true import and extent with the proper nature and ends of that covenant to which they belong in a special manner.

Only this I will premise to the whole: that these promises were not all made to Abraham at one time nor was their covenant perfected by one transaction. Instead, they were given out in several parts and by degrees until at last the whole charter of privileges and blessings granted to the natural offspring of Abraham was fairly drawn, and the covenant of them sealed by circumcision. This will immediately appear in the historical account we will give of these things. And some regard to this may also be noted in the progression of Stephen's discourse when he gives a recapitulation of them (Acts 7:5-8).

Abraham Called out of Ur

§. 2. In Genesis 12:2 the God of glory[1] first appeared to Abraham and called him out from his own country, kindred, and father's house. Besides the promise of spiritual blessings that was given to him, both for himself and his spiritual seed, he also had the promise of a numerous offspring which would descend from him by natural means. No less can be intended in the words, "I will make of you a great nation" than this: you will be the father of a great nation which will spring and issue from your loins. Such is the plain sense of the similar words to Moses (Numbers 14:12). Abraham embraced this promise with the others by faith. To the eye of reason there was no present likelihood of its

---

[1] [Acts 7:2.]

accomplishment, seeing at this time he had no child (the lack of which he also makes complaint a considerable time after this, Genesis 15:2, 3) and his wife Sarah was barren. Yet esteeming him who had given these promises faithful and able to make good his word, he embraced them. On the call of God[2] he forsook all that before was dear to him and went out not knowing where he went (Hebrews 11:8). For it does not appear that the land of Canaan was mentioned to him at his first calling, but rather an absolute resignation of himself to divine goodness and conduct was required of him. He knew no more than that he must travel from his own to another country which was to a land that God would show to him, though as yet he did not know what or where it was. Therefore, though we read in Genesis 11:32 that he went from Ur of the Chaldees into the land of Canaan, I conceive those words should be taken as an historical anticipation and not a relationship of what fell within Abraham's knowledge and intention when he first undertook his journey. His peregrination[3] was in the counsel of God determined toward the land of Canaan. By a divine conduct he was brought there, though he did not know the place designed, at least not until he came nearer to Haran, where the Lord gave him a second call after the death of Terah to proceed in his journey to the land of Canaan.[4]

Abraham's Journeys and Renewed Promises

§. 3. When Abraham came into the land of Canaan to the place of Shechem on the plain of Moreh (the progeny of cursed Canaan then being the inhabitants of the country) the Lord appeared to him again.

---

[2] *Cus non magis est dulce proprium tugurium quam palatia Peregrina? & Voluntaria Casa, quam digesta Pratoria? Cus non est duram illos conscios natalium Parites, dulois illa Limena arg; amabilem larem, quem & parentum memoria, & ipsius infantia Rudimenta commendant – Inter hoc ergo tam bianda tem dulcia, quacum omni fuerant difficultate rilinguenda; Exs, ait, de texa? Quis hoc sin fides?* August. [To whom is his own little hut not more pleasant than foreign palaces? And a house of his own choice, than scattered estates? For whom is it not a hard thing, to leave behind those walls that witnessed one's birth, those sweet thresholds and kindly hearth, which both the memory of parents and the first experiences of infancy itself commend... Therefore in the midst of these things so pleasant and so sweet, which must have been left with the greatest difficulty, "Go out," He says, "from your land." Who would be glad to hear this, without the power of faith? Augustine.]

[3] Vid. Riveti *exercitationes in locum*. [See this passage in Rivet's *Commentary on Genesis*. Peregrination means to travel from place to place.]

[4] Genesis 12:4-5

Here he gave him a full and express promise of that land[5] (which for pleasantness and fertility was the glory of all lands) for an inheritance to his seed. There he first built an altar to the Lord so that by worshiping him he might testify of his gratitude for the promise so freely given to him, and also receive a ratification of it in the blood of his accepted sacrifice. Soon after this a famine drove Abraham into Egypt. There Sarah's chastity was endangered by the Egyptian king,[6] but the Lord's rebuke to him delivered his servant from that affliction and by his good providence he was again brought back in peace to the land of Canaan. All this time Lot, the son of Abraham's brother, was with him. But now their substance was increased and some contention happened between their servants. So Abraham, to take up the present controversy and prevent more of the same, made a proposal for them to part from one another which was accepted by Lot (Genesis 13). When Lot was separated from Abraham, the Lord again renewed and confirmed the promise of the land of Canaan to him and the great increase of his seed that would possess it. He did this with a special command to Abraham to walk through its length and breadth in order to survey it and take possession of it by faith, for as yet he was a stranger and had no inheritance in it, not even so much to set his foot on (Acts 7).

How the Promise of Canaan was Made Good to Abraham

§. 4. In the promise renewed in this manner, there are two things that require some further explanation.

First, the conveyance of this inheritance is directly made first to Abraham and then to his seed. "All the land which you see, to you I will give it, and to your seed" (Genesis 13:15). Now it is evident that Abraham had no possession in it all his days except that of a burial place which he purchased afterwards with money paid to its full value (Genesis 23). This was similar to the case of Isaac and Jacob who were the heirs of this promise together with Abraham (Hebrews 11:9). A question therefore arises as to how this promise was made good to Abraham.

In answer to this (ignoring for now the typical aspect of the promised land and Abraham's inheritance of the spiritual and heavenly blessings signified by it), observe the following.

---

[5] Genesis 12:6-7
[6] Genesis 12:17; Psalm 105:13-15.

1. That as to those words "to you, and to your seed", the latter may be taken as an interpretation of the former. Then the sense is, "to you, that is, to your seed." The Hebrew particle used here should undoubtedly be taken in this sense in some other places[7] and is to be interpreted not as copulative by "and" but as explicative by "even" or "that is." See 1 Chronicles 21:12 where it is so rendered. The same interpretation must be given of it in 2 Samuel 17:12, "Of him and (rather, that is) of all the men that are with him there will not be left so much as one." Now this rendering removes all appearance of difficulty from the text.

2. A man may have *jus ad rem*[8] who has not *jus in re*.[9] All rights are not presently actionable. A man may have a right to an inheritance by promise without the right of present possession. This he may not enter into until a long time after, or perhaps not himself but his posterity are to possess it by that right which is at present made over to him. Neither does the annexing of such terms render the promise vain or fruitless to him who first receives it. For the assurance that the promised good in its time will certainly accrue to his offspring is a present comfort to him, just as it is an honor for him to be made capable of transmitting such a right to them this way. Therefore it was a pleasing thought to old Jacob when he lay dying that God would surely visit his children and bring them up out of Egypt to inherit the promised land (Genesis 48:5, 20, 21) although he went to his fathers without seeing its accomplishment. Similarly, it was a special favor to Ephraim and Manasseh that by Jacob's blessing each of them obtained a right in Canaan equal with their brothers. Yet they did not enjoy the temporal good of that blessing but their posterity did after them.[10] Indeed, that is properly said to be given to parents which is given to their posterity on the account of that promise which they have received. This makes them the heads of that covenant blessing which descends on their offspring. That the fathers embraced the promise in this sense is put beyond doubt by the express limitation of the time of its accomplishment in Genesis 15:13, 16.

Secondly, the other difficulty arises from the extent of the promise in regard to time. For here God promises to give this land to Abraham and

---

[7] See Ainsw. Annot. [See Ainsworth's *Annotations* previously cited.]

[8] [A right to the matter at hand.]

[9] [A right in a matter (in general).]

[10] *Lege Riveti exercitationem in Locum; ubi dubium hoc proponitur & accurate solvitur.* [Read this passage in Rivet's commentary on Genesis where this ambiguity is set forth and accurately explained.]

to his seed "for ever" and in Genesis 17:8 "for an everlasting possession." Now it is evident they have for many ages been disinherited of it. But the solution to this doubt will be easy to him who consults the use of these terms in other texts, and the necessary restriction of their sense when applied to the state or interests of Abraham's seed in the land of Canaan. For the priesthood of Levi is called an everlasting priesthood (Numbers 25:13) and the gates of the temple, everlasting doors (Psalm 24:5). This is the same sense that Canaan is said to be an everlasting inheritance. No more is intended than the continuance of these for a long time, that is, throughout the Old Testament economy until the days of the Messiah, commonly spoken of by the Jews under the notion of the world to come. In this a new state of things was to be expected when their old covenant right and privilege was to expire, its proper end and design being fully accomplished.

The Promise Renewed and Enlarged

§. 5. In Genesis 15 we have an account of another solemn transaction of God with Abraham in which (besides other things included and intermixed) the promises given to Abraham earlier concerning his carnal seed and their inheritance, are renewed and further explained in various particulars. Abraham was now more stricken in years than when he first received the promise. Yet he still had no son, even though his eternal happiness as well as other blessings depended on the seed that should be given to him. He was now brought to a greater trial of his faith than before. And his present actions were made more illustrious by the difficulties they overcame. So the Holy Spirit is pleased in this place to give an express testimony to it in verse 6, "He believed in the Lord, and he counted it to him for righteousness."[11] This is the first time that either believing or the imputation of righteousness is *in terminis*[12] mentioned in the Scripture. Both of these were true of Abraham before, even from the first giving out of the promise to him (Genesis 12). He then believed in the Lord and he accounted it to him for righteousness. But as his faith was now manifested in a higher degree, so it pleased God from this time to leave on record a more particular encomium[13] of it than formerly. And as a further token of favor, there immediately follows the explanation and

---

[11] Compare Romans 4.

[12] [In express terms or definitely.]

[13] [A formal expression of praise; tribute.]

enlargement of the promise to his natural offspring that was earlier mentioned. I will pass over many things and only note here these few that follow, as directly related to my present purpose.

1. The Lord informs Abraham of the affliction that would befall his posterity, and the seeming death that should be on the promise before they were brought into the inheritance of the land of Canaan. He also particularly limits the time they would be afflicted to four hundred years. This account I suppose must take its rise from the mocking of Isaac, the heir of the promise, by Ishmael the son of Hagar the Egyptian. From this to the deliverance of Israel from their bondage in Egypt is exactly four hundred years.

2. The Lord gives Abraham an assurance that in the appointed time he will redeem them from their servitude by signal judgments on their oppressors and by great favor to them. They would suddenly change their condition from lack and penury to the enjoyment of great riches and substance (Genesis 15:14). And as for Abraham, he would go to his fathers in peace and be buried in a good old age. In the fourth generation the blessing of this promise should certainly come on his posterity (verses 15, 16). The exact accomplishment of all this you may read in the book of Exodus.[14] All the wonders recorded there are the birth of these promises for it was not the goodness of the people but the stability of the promise that all those things are to be ascribed to.

3. A reason is given for referring the accomplishment of the promise to this time: the nations whose land they were to possess were not yet ripe for judgment and the measure of their iniquity had to be filled up before the curse of Canaan was fully executed on them. So we see that although the children of Canaan bore his curse for many generations after him, yet this curse did not descend on them without a full measure of their own sin, as there is no doubt that Canaan's partnership with Ham in his wickedness at first brought the curse of his father on himself.

4. These things are expressly said to have been transacted in a way of covenant with Abraham. Also the bounds of Israel's inheritance are set and those nations marked out by name which were to be dispossessed and destroyed by them.[15]

---

[14] Exodus 2:24; Acts 7:17.
[15] Genesis 15:18-21.

The Seed of Abraham

§. 6. Before we pass on further in the history of God's transactions with Abraham regarding his natural offspring, the following points should be observed.

1. Just as this seed was later raised up to Abraham by virtue of a promise, so the first grant of the land of Canaan to them for an inheritance was also by a gratuitous promise. That promise passed into the form of a covenant with Abraham long before the giving of the law as a condition of their inheritance there, even before the institution of circumcision. Since the origin of their claim was a free promise, the severity of that law which they later came under, was far restrained by it, so that (notwithstanding their manifold breach of covenant with God, and forfeiture of all legal claim of their rights and privileges in the land of Canaan by this) they were never utterly cut off from that good land. Nor did they cease to be a peculiar people to God until the end of their being made such was fully answered. That promise expired with the accomplishment of its design in the introduction of the Israel of God to the full enjoyment of those spiritual blessings which were the substance of what was only darkly shadowed by their temporal enjoyments. This will be of great use in our reflections on the typical state of that people which I will not enlarge on now.

2. Until now it is not expressly signified that Sarah would be the mother of this seed. Therefore in the delay of the promise, Abraham and Sarah (not knowing but it might be fulfilled this way) agreed about Abraham's going in to Hagar, Sarah's hand-maid, that by her they might obtain children (Genesis 16). It will be granted on good grounds that they might have had other apprehensions of the promise before (as it will appear they had by comparing Genesis 15 with Romans 4) and that this proceeded from some vacillation and weakness of faith in them. Yet it was not the kind of thing that directly crossed and called into question the promises given earlier. Nothing appears to the contrary except that Abraham counted Ishmael to be the heir of the promise until the Lord appeared to him again (Genesis 17) and fully completed his covenant with him about his natural offspring.

3. There was not given yet any intimation of a distinction to be made in point of privilege or covenant right between the children that might in one way or another be brought to Abraham. But the claims of these children (supposing, as it later proved, that there might be many) seemed

to be equal until a further statement was given (Genesis 17). Nor was any distinguishing character yet appointed for his seed to be the foundation for their rising up into a church-state such that the solemn institutions of divine service should be appropriate to them and no one counted a member of the visible church but themselves and those who became proselytes to them. However, it is true that all that has been previously mentioned was ordered for this, being in the wise counsel of God directed toward such an end. For known to him are all his works from the beginning. Therefore the former promises are still recollected and taken in, in the later transactions about this people.

4. The promises previously given to Abraham for his natural offspring involve those in remote generations as much as those immediately descended from him. And in some respects they were made good more fully to them than to the others. For it was not until the fourth generation that God was known to them by his name Jehovah (Exodus 6) in the actual accomplishment of his word. The fathers only had his all-sufficiency engaged for the later fulfilling of the promise in its proper season. It was not Abraham's immediate seed, but his mediate, that became as numerous as the dust of the earth and took possession of the land flowing with milk and honey.

The Covenant of Circumcision

§. 7. We will now pass on to Genesis 17. What is more largely recorded there, is briefly pointed at by Stephen in his general view of the history of Israel (Acts 7:8), "and he gave him the covenant of circumcision; and so Abraham became the father of Isaac," etc. By the covenant of circumcision we are to understand that covenant of which circumcision was the sign or token or that covenant in which a restipulation was required by the observation of this rite or ordinance, as in Genesis 17:9-11.

It is noteworthy that in this transaction of God with Abraham we first meet with an express injunction of obedience to a command (and that of positive right) as the condition of covenant interest. It is all ushered in with this prologue (Genesis 17:1), "I am the Almighty God; walk before me and be perfect." First in these words, the all-sufficiency of God is revealed for the ensuring of the promises. Then a strict and entire obedience to his precepts is required in order to inherit the good things that were to be given by this covenant. In this mode of transacting it, the

Lord was pleased to draw the first lines of that form of covenant relationship in which the natural seed of Abraham was fully stated[16] by the law of Moses, which was a covenant of works with its condition or terms, "Do this and live." For although the covenant of grace made with Abraham has in all respects (in point of time and excellency) the precedence to the covenant made with his carnal seed in Isaac's line, yet in the wise counsel of God things were so ordered that the full revelation of the covenant of grace, the actual accomplishment of its great promises, and its being filled up with ordinances proper to it, should succeed the covenant made with Israel after the flesh, and replace it on its dissolution when it waxed old and vanished away. Therefore the covenant interest of the natural seed was to be perfected by the law of Moses before the gospel preached to Abraham was unveiled. Accordingly this chapter leads us a great step toward the Sinai covenant and its terms.

The Promise of the New Covenant Repeated

§. 8. This covenant of circumcision properly and immediately belongs to the natural seed of Abraham and is ordered as a foundation to that economy which they were to be brought under until the times of reformation. Yet by way of preface to it in Genesis 17:4, 5, you have a recapitulation of former transactions and a renewed confirmation of one great promise of the covenant of grace given earlier to Abraham, that is, "A father of many nations have I made you." This is principally to be understood of his believing seed collected indifferently out of all nations as appears from Romans 4:17. That Abraham was constituted the father of the faithful before this covenant of circumcision was made and did not obtain the grant of this privilege by it, has been proven before from Moses' history. It is also argued strongly by the apostle in the first part of Romans 4 previously mentioned. Nevertheless, there are two great reasons for it to be repeated in this place.

1. It makes evident that the covenant of peculiarity with the carnal seed, which took place first, and that wall of separation which was to be raised up between them and other nations (the cornerstone of which was now to be laid in circumcision) should not evacuate or infringe on the covenant of grace, or the right and privilege of the spiritual seed stated[17]

---

[16] [To instate or establish in the covenant.]
[17] [To instate or establish in the covenant.]

in it, or of any part of it. Instead, the former was added and made subservient to the latter's great ends. The springs of new covenant mercy, which God had before opened to all nations, were not to be shut up again by this covenant. Nor were the heathen excluded[18] from inheriting the blessing of Abraham through faith in Jesus Christ by any privilege or right conferred on the Jew. So when the covenant of circumcision was given to the carnal seed to fully separate them from other nations, it pleased God in that to revive the remembrance of that promise of the covenant of grace which should in due time bring salvation to the Gentiles. This was so there might be no color of reason[19] left for interpreting this covenant to their prejudice in the restricting of the grace of the gospel, which was designed by God only to be a handmaid to it.

2. Things were so ordered by God in this covenant, that as their promises would be subordinate to the great promise, so also spiritual blessings should be figuratively[20] implied in them. So Abraham's being the father of believers from many nations was typified in his numerous offspring by Isaac, that is, Israel after the flesh. Therefore, a confirmation and sealing of the one must also include a ratification of the other. And so at the same time to assure Abraham that he would certainly become the father of a multitude,[21] or of many nations, his name is changed to Abraham. Also, circumcision is instituted for the sealing of the promises made to his carnal seed. The mutual relation of these different promises and the order observed in their establishment shows that circumcision itself was so far from subverting the covenant of grace in its promise to the Gentiles, that it became to Abraham a seal of the righteousness of faith (Romans 4:11). It did not become this from its next and peculiar end, or its proper nature with respect to all the carnal seed or others that were to be the subjects of it. But it became this from the disposition[22] of the covenant to which it was annexed, and the present circumstances of Abraham with whom it was made and to whom circumcision was now given for a seal of it. But we must further enlarge on this when speaking to the mutual relation of God's federal transactions with Abraham.

---

[18] Read diligently Galatians 3.

[19] [Appearance or semblance of reason; pretext.]

[20] [The original reads "mystically".]

[21] אַב־הֲמוֹן גּוֹיִם [From Genesis 17:5. Abraham means "a father of a multitude".]

[22] [Ordering, administration, or dispensation.]

At present it will suffice to remind you that there is no way of avoiding confusion and entanglements in our conception of these things except by keeping before our eyes the distinction between Abraham's seed as either spiritual or carnal, and of the respective promises belonging to each. For this whole covenant of circumcision given to the carnal seed, can no more convey spiritual and eternal blessings to them as such, than it can now enright[23] a believer (though a child of Abraham) in their temporal and typical blessings in the land of Canaan. Neither can I see any reason for assigning a covenant interest in all typified spiritual blessings (as well as in the temporal blessings that were the types of them) to the carnal seed, and yet not admit the same covenant to convey temporal blessings to the spiritual seed. I say this since some conceive both are directly included in the same covenant and the promise of both was sealed with the same seal.

But the truth is, despite the relationship this covenant has to the covenant of grace, it yet remains distinct from it. It can give no more than external and typical blessings to a typical seed. The proper end and design of this transaction in Genesis 17 is the stating[24] of their rights and privileges in a subordinate and typical relation to the dispensation of grace to the elect in the new covenant. This will more fully appear in the particular account of the promises given there.

The Distinction of Tribes in Israel

§. 9. The sum of those promises is set before us in Genesis 17:6-8. In the sixth verse the promise of a numerous offspring is repeated in terms that convey, if not enlargement, at least a further explanation of what was earlier promised in Genesis 13:16, "And I will make your seed as the dust of the earth," etc. For here the promise runs, "I will make you exceeding fruitful, and I will make nations of you; and Kings will come out of you."

These words in their first and literal sense had their accomplishment in the natural offspring of Abraham and are particularly intended of his seed by Isaac. For though it is true that other nations besides Israel sprang from Abraham, yet the context will clearly demonstrate it to be that seed with which the covenant of circumcision should be established that is here meant. And that was the seed of Abraham by Isaac only. To

---

[23] [To invest with a right or entitle.]
[24] [To instate or establish in the covenant.]

see, then, the fulfilling of this promise we must look to the twelve tribes of Israel who were like so many distinct peoples and nations with respect to their power and number, though with respect to religion and government were united in one polity, and so were but one people. To this promise Jacob has an eye in his blessing of the sons of Joseph (Genesis 48:19) where he says that Manasseh (the father of one of the tribes of Israel) will be a people and will become great. He means his seed will be numerous and strong, and will make up one people or one of the nations that God had promised should come of Abraham. And yet Ephraim his younger brother must have the preeminence in being the father of another distinct people or tribe that should be stronger and more numerous than Manasseh. This was because his seed would become the fullness of nations (so it is in the Hebrew), that is, a very great nation and people.

That distinction of tribes which was later observed among the Israelites seems to be first pointed at in these words, "I will make nations of you" and the following words "Kings will come out of you." These do not only signify the eminency of Abraham's seed in general, but more particularly relate their forming under a distinct polity and government of their own, or (as Ezekiel speaks in chapter 16) prospering into a kingdom and living under the rule and conduct of judges and princes raised up among themselves. They were like this from Moses' time who was king in Jeshurun, when the heads of the people and the tribes gathered themselves together (Deuteronomy 33:5). By his ministry God settled their state and government by laws peculiar to themselves and in this fulfilled the covenant of their fathers. This branch of the promise contains more than was expressly given to Abraham earlier.

The Meaning of Everlasting in Relation to this Covenant

§. 10. In the words that follow in Genesis 17:7 we have the assurance of this and the ensuing promises. God gives these to Abraham by passing them into a solemn covenant and follows by an interposition[25] of himself and an engagement of all the perfections and properties of his divine nature to be exerted to make them good. Thus you read, "And I will establish my covenant between me and you and your seed after you in

---

[25] [Intervening on another person's behalf; mediation.]

their generations for an everlasting covenant, to be a God to you and to your seed after you."

To this is added the promise of their inheritance in verse 8, "And I will give to you, and to your seed after you, the land in which you are a stranger, all the land of Canaan for an everlasting possession; and I will be their God."

The difficulty arising from those terms in the promise which give the right of the inheritance of Canaan to Abraham in the first place has already been considered and cleared, as well as how the land of Canaan may be said to be an everlasting possession. In the same sense this covenant is said to be everlasting. Israel could not be finally cut off from the promised inheritance until the covenant by which it was given to them expired. As the duration of the inheritance and of Israel's right in it was everlasting, so was the duration of this covenant. This was not absolute but was with such a limitation as the nature of the things spoken of necessarily requires, and as is usual in those Scriptures that speak of things pertaining to the Jewish state. There is, therefore, no more reason to conclude from this term that the covenant of circumcision was directly and properly a covenant of spiritual and eternal blessings, than there is to affirm that the land of Canaan and the good things of it were a spiritual and eternal inheritance.

The Church-State of Israel after the Flesh

§. 11. Nevertheless, from the strict connection of this 7th verse with the 6th, and the assurance given here that God will establish his covenant with the seed of Abraham to be their God, the following is evident.

The number of Abraham's carnal seed and the grandeur of their civil state is not all that is promised in this covenant, nor are these the principal blessings bestowed on them in it. Instead, it is the forming of them into a church-state with the establishment of the ordinances of public worship in which they should walk in a covenant relationship to God as his peculiar people. (Understand this still of the old covenant in which they had their peculiar right and privilege.) No less can be intended in this, "I will be a God to them in their generations." This is also made more evident by the following account of this transaction with respect to Isaac and Ishmael (Genesis 17:18-21).

When the Lord promised Abraham a son by Sarah, whose name should be called Isaac, Abraham prays for Ishmael, "O that Ishmael might live before you!" The Chaldee paraphrases it, "might live and worship before you." No doubt his prayer was that Ishmael might also be an heir of the blessing of this covenant. But that was not granted to him for the Lord would only have his covenant seed called in Isaac. With him God would establish his covenant, having appointed and chosen him alone to be its heir who was to be a child of promise and son of the free-woman. And yet for Ishmael (in special favor to Abraham, whose seed he was) this much is obtained: that he would be fruitful and multiply exceedingly. Twelve princes or heads of great families would spring from him (which imports some analogy to the twelve tribes of Israel after the flesh, whose old covenant-state was typified in Ishmael) and God would make him a great nation. And yet all this lay short of the blessing of Abraham's natural offspring by Isaac from which Ishmael was now excluded. It is plain then, that the privilege of the ecclesiastical, as well as the flourishing of the civil state of Israel, arose to them out of the covenant of circumcision.

The same may be observed later of Esau whom the Lord rejected before he was born, excluding him from the privilege and blessing of this covenant which descended to Jacob only. And yet Esau was also the father of a great nation and of many Kings, and had the inheritance of many outward blessings assigned to him (Genesis 27:39).

So we conclude that the carnal seed of Abraham could not claim a right in the spiritual and eternal blessings of the new covenant, as such, because of their interest in the covenant of circumcision. Yet the privileges and advantages in their church-state, though immediately consisting in things outward and typical, were of far greater value and use than any mere worldly or earthly blessing. This was because they gave them a choice means of the knowledge of God and set them nearer to him than any other nation in the world.

Chapter Six

The Covenant of Circumcision (II)

Two Propositions Laid Down

§. 1. The passages just expounded from Genesis give me an occasion to enlarge on some things deduced from the texts that have been partially considered already. Their further clearing and strengthening will not only confirm what has already been hinted at, but will also contribute greatly to the right understanding of the nature and end of this covenant of circumcision that I am treating. This will remove the grounds of many mistaken deductions from it by those who would from there determine the right subjects of baptism.

What I intend is summed up in these two propositions.

1. The mediate and remote seed of that line to which the promises of the covenant of circumcision belonged were as fully included and interested in them as the immediate seed.
2. From the first establishing of this covenant, some of the immediate seed of Abraham were excluded from interest in it.

The First Proposition Proved

§. 2. I will begin with the first. The truth of it appears sufficiently in the express terms of the promises now given to Abraham which run to him and to his seed after him in their generations. The covenant itself is said to be an everlasting covenant which they are strictly commanded to keep in their generations (Genesis 17:7, 9, 13). These terms are used because it was a covenant in force for the benefit of both more remote and nearer generations. Its promises included and its law equally bound both during the whole state of the Mosaic economy. The right of the remotest generation was as much derived from Abraham and the covenant made with him, as was that of his immediate seed, and did not at all depend on the faithfulness of their immediate parents. Thus, the immediate seed of those Israelites that fell in the wilderness under the displeasure of God were made to inherit the land of Canaan by virtue of this covenant with Abraham. They never could have enjoyed it by virtue of their immediate parent's steadfastness in the covenant.

Its Further Confirmation

§. 3. I suppose it cannot be denied that gross idolatry was a manifest and full breach of this covenant on the part of the idolater. Yet when the Israelites in Ezekiel's time became guilty of the vilest idolatries, the Lord still claims an interest in their children by virtue of this covenant (16:20, 21), "Moreover you have taken your sons and your daughters, whom you have born to me, and these you have sacrificed to them to be devoured. Is this of your whoredoms a small matter that you have slain my children," etc. The children of the apostate Israelite were God's as well as those of his faithful servants. This could not have been if their covenant interest had been suspended on the good behavior of immediate parents.

This agrees with the story we have of Mattathias' proceeding in the reformation of the church in his day. Finding that many had denied their God and forsaken his true worship in that time of persecution, he (according to the law of Moses) executed justice on as many of the apostates as he could lay hands on by slaying them (as Josephus witnesses). But the children that he found to be left uncircumcised in this time of apostasy, he took and circumcised them. The words of the author in 1 Maccabees 2:46 are, "καὶ περιέτεμον τὰ παιδάρια τὰ ἀπερίτμητα ὅσα εὖρον ἐν ὁρίοις Ισραηλ ἐν ἰσχύι."[1] I know this has no further strength than human testimony but it speaks fully of what the sense of those times was concerning the covenant interest of children; that is, that the apostasy of their immediate parents could not prejudice it so as to render them incapable of circumcision. This strongly concludes that their covenant right was derived from Abraham and not suspended on them. Mattathias who did this was not only a man zealous for the law but also one that may be presumed to have understood it better than many others since he was a priest.

Its Support from the Current of Sacred History

§. 4. Not only the passages insisted on before, but the whole current of Scripture where these things are mentioned runs very smoothly this way. It is especially true that the phrase mentioned before, "thy seed in their generations," will admit of no other sense. It is by no means capable of a

---

[1] ["They forcibly circumcised all the uncircumcised boys that they found within the borders of Israel." For this translation see *The Cambridge Annotated Study Apocrypha, New Revised Standard Version* (Cambridge: Cambridge University Press, 1994).]

restraint to the immediate seed. But even as the similar expression in Genesis 9:12 secures Noah's children from drowning by the waters of a universal deluge to the end of the world, so this promise gave a covenant interest to the seed of Abraham until the times of reformation.

The immediate seed, Isaac, is not excluded. But the promise passes on much further and is to be fulfilled in a seed exceedingly multiplied and formed into a kingdom. This did not happen until Isaac and his immediate offspring were laid in the dust.

Furthermore, the inheritance promised in the land of Canaan is given to this seed for an everlasting possession. This was fulfilled in their successive inheriting of it from generation to generation. So the seed intended was such as would be propagated through many generations, the last of which are here as directly spoken of as the first. Circumcision was to be observed by them (on account of the promise and command now given) for an everlasting covenant. The relationship of the carnal seed to God in an external typical covenant, the inheritance of Canaan by its virtue, and the seal of circumcision are all of one date and all expired together.

The Church-State of Israel Built on this Covenant

§ 5. That these things may be the better understood, we must further observe that this covenant of circumcision was the foundation on which the church-state of Israel after the flesh was built.

I do not say that their church-state was exactly and completely formed by this ordinance alone. But I mean that in the covenant of circumcision were contained the first rudiments of the one in the wilderness, and the latter was the filling up and completing of the former. It was made with them in pursuance of it and for the full accomplishment of the promises now made to Abraham. And therefore the privilege of the carnal seed of Abraham by virtue of the covenant of circumcision can rise no higher than the advantage and privilege of a Jew by virtue of the covenant in the wilderness.

Circumcision the Door into Israel's Communion

§. 6. To confirm this I will offer these things. First, circumcision was the entrance into and boundary of communion in the Jewish church. It was made so by the express command of God himself, who strictly enjoined[2] that whoever broke the covenant by the neglect of circumcision should be cut off from his people (Genesis 17:14). As it was to them a gate of privilege, so was it no less a bond of duty. It not only obliged them to obey the will of God so far as it was now made known to Abraham, but also, to the observation of all those laws and ordinances that were delivered later to them by Moses. For the circumcised person was a debtor to keep the whole law (Galatians 5:3). This obligation resulted from its proper use and end in its primitive institution. For we do not read of its appointment to any new end by Moses, nor of any use it was assigned to, *de novo*,[3] which it did not have (at least virtually) from its first appointment. It was from first to last, a visible character on this people as separated to God from other nations, and as such they made their boast of it. Therefore it may be concluded to belong to that covenant from which all their rights and privileges as a people sprang. And where the sign was not varied, there was no essential variation or change in the covenant itself.

How Levi Paid Tithes in Abraham

§. 7. Secondly, all the advantage and privilege of Israel after the flesh is in the New Testament expressly referred to the covenant of circumcision. This is how the Holy Spirit speaks by Paul in Romans 3:1, "What advantage then has the Jew? Or what profit is there of circumcision?" You see these phrases, "the advantage of the Jew" and "the profit of circumcision" are set down as interchangeable. They import the same testamental thing; what belongs to the one, belongs to the other. And wherever circumcision is mentioned in the New Testament, it is spoken of as no less belonging to the Mosaic economy (though the first institution was not of Moses, but of the fathers) than any other part of the law first given by him. Boasting in circumcision is esteemed a boasting in the flesh as much as boasting in any other Old Testament privilege of the Jew (Philippians 3). From all of this we may safely conclude that the covenant of circumcision was of the same kind as the Levitical covenant, which was afterwards annexed to it or rather built on it, for the full accomplishing of its design.

---

[2] [To impose with authority.]
[3] [Afresh or anew.]

I might also insist on the case of Levi's paying tithes in Abraham. This could not have been reckoned to him if he had not been in Abraham, considered as a head in some covenant transaction in which Levi was covenanted for by Abraham. Neither could this have been pleaded by the apostle as it is in Hebrews 7:9, 10 if that covenant in which the Levitical priesthood was founded and to which it belonged, had not been originally made with Abraham. But I pass this.

Israel Brought out of Egypt by Virtue of this Covenant

§. 8. Thirdly, the Scriptures everywhere affirm that the Lord brought up Israel out of Egypt, formed their church-state by establishing the order of his solemn worship among them, and gave them the land of Canaan in possession, in remembrance of his covenant with Abraham and to fulfill its promises. For instance, let these places be well weighed: Exodus 2:24, 25; Deuteronomy 29:10-13; Nehemiah 9:7-9; Psalm 78 with Psalm 105. In these he was known to them by his name Jehovah, this being the actual accomplishment of the promise which their fathers depended on his all-sufficiency for. Compare Exodus 6 with Genesis 17:1. Thus if we follow the clue of Scripture in our inquiries after the origin of the covenant of peculiarity made with Israel after the flesh, it will certainly guide us to that covenant which God made with Abraham for his natural offspring and sealed by circumcision. Yet that covenant of peculiarity is in the New Testament always styled old and carnal. It is a covenant from which the gospel covenant is distinguished and to which it is in many respects opposed (Jeremiah 31:31-34; Hebrews 8:8-13).

Neither can any just exception be made against what has been said from the enlargement of the terms and articles of this covenant in its consummation in the wilderness. For that will not in the least infer any substantial difference of this covenant from the covenant of circumcision. This is no more than God has done by the gospel with respect to the new covenant that was confirmed in Christ to Abraham. What was first summed up in one promise, "In you will all nations be blessed," was abundantly enlarged, cleared, filled up with its own ordinances, and made the entire rule of the church's obedience when the fullness of time came to which that promise was related. And yet the New Testament is not another gospel differing from that preached to Abraham, or another covenant differing from that before confirmed of God in Christ. In the same manner, the filling up of this covenant of circumcision was reserved to the time of God's performing what he now promised to Abraham, without the least change of the nature or design of the covenant itself.

The Second Proposition Proved

§. 9. We now come to the second proposition, that from the first establishment of this covenant some of the immediate seed of Abraham were excluded.

The promises of the covenant belonged to Isaac's line in their generations from age to age. But they did not pertain to the immediate seed of Abraham by Hagar or by Keturah and their extent was restrained by the express caution of God himself, to whom it belonged to set the bounds of this covenant-relation and interest. He did this in the very first making of the covenant of circumcision with Abraham (read diligently Genesis 17:19-21), "In Isaac will your seed be called." It was Isaac's seed and not Ishmael's that the Lord would set apart for himself, give the land of Canaan to, and establish his solemn worship among them to be their God. And yet Abraham was as much a believer and as much in covenant with God as to his personal interest in the covenant of grace when he fathered the one as when he fathered the other.

If it is objected that Ishmael was at first included and interested in the covenant but was afterwards rejected and cast out for his profane mocking at Isaac, it will be answered as follows.

This supposition is against the express words and letter of the text just urged and the limitation which God, the author of the covenant, made of its promises. Before Ishmael was circumcised God declares that he did not give the promises of his covenant to him, but to Isaac with whom it should be established. So Ishmael's being later cast out of Abraham's family in no way infers that until then he was in covenant. It only shows that then it was made more manifest than ever that the covenant did not pertain to him, and that he must be included[4] under the exception that was before laid in against him. And the divine confirmation of what Sarah then required is grounded on that revelation of his will that he now made to Abraham. This will be evident to whoever compares Genesis 17 and 21:12, 13, "Cast out the bond-woman

---

[4] [The original reads "conluded." The *Oxford English Dictionary* has no such word. Presumably this is a printer's error for "conclude," the first given meaning of which is to enclose, comprehend, or include.]

and her son, for in Isaac will your seed be called." Therefore Abraham later voluntarily sent his sons by Keturah far away from Isaac and from the promised land (Genesis 25:1, 6). He did this even though they were not guilty of any such wickedness as Ishmael who mocked at Isaac. From every appearance they might be very holy and good men, the true children of Abraham by faith according to the character of the covenant of grace; though they might not be joint heirs with Isaac according to the character of the covenant of circumcision.

The Example of Esau

§. 10. This also should be observed. Although the covenant seed of Abraham was called in Isaac, and his immediate children were only two sons, Esau and Jacob, yet the right of this covenant blessing did not descend equally on them both. But once more the Lord restrains it by the rejection of Esau and the choosing of Jacob before the children had done either good or evil. This was so the purpose of God according to election might stand and he might set before us an awe-inspiring type of his sovereignty in the later dispensation of the grace of the gospel. Indeed, by the profane selling of his birthright and despising his inheritance, Esau later rendered himself manifestly unworthy of the blessing.[5] But before this God had declared that Jacob and his seed, and not Esau, should inherit the promises of this covenant.

It may be for this reason that Isaac and Jacob are so particularly mentioned in Acts 7:8 because of the special limiting of the promises to them and because they were the seed brought into the world in virtue of the promise given to Abraham.

An Objection Answered

§. 11. These things lie so plainly before us in the scriptural history that they will hardly be called into question if our minds are not prepossessed with some particular notion to which they are not suited. But it is earnestly pleaded by some, "That all the immediate seed of Abraham were interested in this covenant, and that the first right in its promise belonged to them since the seal of the covenant was applied to them all in their circumcision; the

---

[5] Conf. Genesis 25:23 with Malachi 1:2 ff.; Romans 9:10-13. [Compare Genesis 25:23 with Malachi 1:2 and following and Romans 9:10-13.]

doing of which must be absurd and useless if they had not been parties in that covenant to which this seal belonged."[6] To this I answer the following.

1. It is not at all proper for our uncertain conjectures or inferences to be opposed to the express testimony of God himself or that his wisdom should be called into question on their account. Though God laid his command on Abraham to circumcise Ishmael, yet at the same time he tells him that his covenant would be established with Isaac, excluding Ishmael. To him he will not grant a joint interest with Isaac in this covenant even though Abraham interceded for him. God dismisses Ishmael's claim and lays out his portion by himself in another inferior blessing.

2. Abraham was as strictly bound to circumcise all the males in his family (those who were not of his seed bought with his money from the stranger, and the children of those bond-servants that were born in his house) as he was his own children (Genesis 17:12, 13). This obligation remained on the heirs of his covenant in their generations. Yet none of these servants (not even Ishmael) were made parties in the covenant by this, so that the promises of it should be sealed to them by circumcision as their own inheritance.

3. To suppose an interest in the covenant without a right to its promises is to introduce a mere chimera or fancy instead of a real covenant interest. Now the promises of this covenant are that God will give to the seed of Abraham, called in Isaac, the land of Canaan for an everlasting possession, and that he will be a God to them in their generations and they will be a peculiar people to him. Can we suppose that these promises belonged to Ishmael and the bond-servants in Abraham's family? Were they ever made good to them? If they were not, we must conclude they never had their grant or an interest in them. For the performance of these promises was the fulfilling of the covenant on God's part, whose faithfulness is to all generations. And if the promises of the covenant did not belong to them, then they were not parties in covenant; and if not in covenant, then they were not circumcised on the account of their own covenant interest, but in obedience to the particular and positive command of God.

Circumcision, a Seal of the Covenant

§. 12. It appears from what has been already said, that circumcision was a seal of the covenant on all, but not to all, that were circumcised. It was a seal

---

[6] [An unknown reference but probably from Whiston.]

of the covenant to the children of the covenant and gave them admission to all the blessings promised in it. But it did not make their slaves free of the commonwealth of Israel nor was it given for their sakes. They could not claim the outward privilege of an Israelite by it. So it will hardly be granted that only on the account of their being bought by a Jew (though their master himself, perhaps, had no interest in the covenant of grace) they should be made the subjects of a new covenant blessing. This is true whether they knew or were capable of consenting to the terms of that covenant or not. For this might be the case for many of them, since the law involved those who were purchased in their infancy as well as those of riper years. The one as well as the other must be circumcised because of the command given to his master. Perhaps this belonged to the typical holiness of the family of an Israelite. But whether we can fully understand the reason for it or not, it is sufficient that the wise God ordained it to be so.

However, this is certain: that it was the positive command of God and not simply covenant interest that was the rule according to which circumcision was administered, and by which both the subjects and circumstances of it were determined. And so it must be in all things of similar nature, for in matters of positive right we can have no warrant for our practice except from a positive precept. Things of this kind do not fall within the compass of common light or the general principles of natural religion. Instead they have their original from a particular, distinct, and independent will of the lawgiver. And therefore inferences built on general notions may soon lead us into mistakes about them if on such inferences we form a rule to ourselves of larger extent than the express words of the institution warrant.

Some Inferences from the Preceding Discourse

§. 13. With these propositions laid down, explained, and confirmed, I will draw this chapter to a close with an inference or two grounded on the foregoing discourse.

1. He who holds himself obliged by the command and interested in the promises of the covenant of circumcision is equally involved in all of them since together they are that covenant. Therefore,[7] he who applies one promise or branch of this covenant to the carnal seed of a believing parent

---

[7] [Coxe adds parenthetically here, "omitting for now to speak of the yoke of the law belonging to it."]

(esteeming every such parent to have an interest in the covenant coordinate[8] with Abraham's) ought seriously to consider the whole promissory part of the covenant in its true import and extent, and see whether he can make such an undivided application of it without manifest absurdity.

For example, if I may conclude my concern in this covenant is such that by one of its promises I am assured that God has taken my immediate seed into covenant with himself, I must on the same ground conclude also that my seed in remote generations will be no less in covenant with him, since the promise extends to the seed in their generations. I must also conclude that this seed will be separated from other nations as a peculiar people to God and will have the land of Canaan for an everlasting possession since all these things are included in the covenant of circumcision. But because these things cannot be allowed, nor are they pleaded for by anyone that I know of, we must conclude that Abraham was considered in this covenant, not in the capacity or respect of a private believing parent, but of one chosen of God to be the father of and a federal root to a nation that for special ends would be separated to God by a peculiar covenant. When those ends are accomplished, the covenant by which they obtained that right and relation must cease. And no one can plead anything similar without reviving the whole economy built on it.

2. The notion that this covenant interest is the basis of a kind of federal holiness in believer's children under the New Testament that gives them a right to baptism, also labors under the following inconsistencies.

3. They generally narrow the terms of covenant interest (if we consider it as conveyed on Isaac's line) by limiting it to the immediate offspring. Yet in this covenant it was not restrained like this but came just as fully on remote generations. They also exclude the servants and slaves of Christians, with the children born of them, from that privilege which they suppose they enjoyed under the Old Testament in being sealed with the sign or token of the covenant of grace.

4. But then on the other hand, (according to what has already been proved) they make a believer's interest in this covenant of larger extent than Abraham's ever truly was. They have all the immediate seed of believers included in it, while we see only Isaac, of all the sons of Abraham according to the flesh, admitted to the inheritance of the blessing and promises of this covenant.

---

[8] [Equal in importance, rank, or degree.]

Chapter Seven

The Covenant of Circumcision (III)

The True Meaning of the Great Promise

§. 1. It will be expedient in the next place, to more fully search out the true meaning and extent of that great promise in the covenant of circumcision which was only briefly touched on before; that is, "I will establish my covenant to be a God to you, and to your seed after you" (Genesis 17:7). Also, the promise of Canaan to be an everlasting possession for Israel is backed with the same assurance; "and I will be their God" (verse 8). This inquiry is all the more necessary because many conceive that the entire blessing of the new covenant is comprehended in these words since the same promise is given as the summary and assurance of that covenant in Jeremiah 31 and Hebrews 8. On this basis they conclude that it is the covenant of grace God is now making with Abraham which he sealed with circumcision. So then spiritual blessings are by it directly transmitted to him both for himself and his seed. Consequently, it was nothing other than interest in the grace and promise of the new covenant that was sealed to his infant seed by circumcision.

This notion militates against various things that have been pointed at before in the account we have given of this transaction. But on a more thorough disquisition[1] this idea will be found without sufficient strength to shake those principles already laid down and which must yet be built on in the progress of our discourse. So in order to free you from any entanglement by objections raised from it, I will proceed gradually to the solution of the doubt removed.[2]

Several Premises to its Right Understanding

§. 2. That I may not be misunderstood in what is to follow, I will prepare the way by offering these serious thoughts.

1. A considerable time before this transaction recorded in Genesis 17, the covenant of grace was confirmed by God to Abraham in Christ Jesus. Abraham not only acted in the capacity of a private believer but as

---

[1] [Systematic inquiry.]
[2] [The original reads "moved".]

one bearing the relationship of a father to all believers. And this relationship is peculiar to himself; none can claim a partnership with him in it.

2. In the establishment of this covenant there was a seed promised to him that would certainly inherit its spiritual and eternal blessings. The promise was sure to all the seed. But this was a seed of believers collected out of all nations and united to Christ by faith, and not the children of Abraham according to the flesh. This is manifest in almost every page of the New Testament.

3. Furthermore, it has been proved that God chose Abraham to be the root and father of a typical people, a nation whose entire number he would take into a peculiar relation and nearness to himself. On them he would bestow many great favors and privileges until the fullness of time came for the bringing into the world that seed to which the promises of the new covenant especially pertained.

4. One great end of this separation of Abraham and his seed by Isaac from all other families in the earth was to bring into his line the Messiah as the evident accomplishment of the great and first promise. This was a privilege that Abraham had in the flesh, and his seed derived from him, that they were set apart as a special channel through which the promised seed should be derived and brought into the world (Romans 9:4, 5).

5. On this account, their privilege and covenant-state was secured to them. They could never be utterly divested of it in their generations[3] until the great end of it was accomplished by the Messiah's coming in the flesh. Then it was to cease, as the nature of the thing itself sufficiently demonstrates, because it was now brought to the limited time and end appointed to it. And on this all the carnal privileges and ordinances of worship suited to that state necessarily ceased and became useless.

6. During the time in which their covenant retained its full vigor and all their carnal privileges remained good to them to the utmost extent, all their advantage lay short of interest in the covenant of grace. They could never claim this by virtue of a carnal descent from Abraham (Matthew 3:9). For it was not a carnal relationship to Abraham, but walking in the steps of his faith, that alone could interest them in this covenant and its blessings. This the apostle openly discusses in Romans 4 and many other places.

---

[3] See Dr. Owen's *Exercitations on the Hebrews*, Vol. 1. [See John Owen, *Commentary on Hebrews*, Vol. 1, (Edinburgh: Banner of Truth Trust, 1991), 446ff.]

Israel Considered in Two Ways under the Mosaic Economy

§. 3. So then, the carnal and the spiritual seed, like the covenants in which their respective privileges are stated, were distinct from one another in their own nature from the beginning. During the minority of the church, that is, under the Mosaic economy, these different blessings ordinarily met in the same subjects, for in that time the seed of Abraham after the flesh comes under a twofold consideration.

1. The whole body of them is to be considered as a people separated to God for the ends mentioned before and formed into a typical state by the law of Moses. They were vested with carnal privileges and had an earthly inheritance which were both typical of spiritual blessings under the gospel.

2. A great number of them were the true and real members of the spiritual church. They were the assembly of the redeemed of the Lord who by faith inherited and enjoyed these spiritual blessings to which the outward privilege of the carnal Jew was but a shadow. For that nation was so made a typical church that they were also the only true visible church God then had in the world. While the wall of separation stood between them and the Gentiles, the oracles of God were committed to them, his true worship was settled among them, the covenants of promise were given to them, and the way of salvation by a covenant of grace through the promised seed was made known among them though only darkly. The blood of God's special elect generally ran in their veins. The people who were savingly interested in God and truly holy were for the most part found among them while the Gentiles lived without God in the world. This is how it was ordinarily, for even then the grace of God might superabound to a few among the Gentiles. Therefore, that church that was not only typically but really Holiness to the Lord, was found within the compass of their enclosure. Just as Isaac was not only a type of the children of promise in the New Testament, but was also one of those who by faith truly inherited the spiritual blessing of Abraham; and as Jacob was not only a type of the elect seed, but also a real part of it; so the same may be said of all who came later of the circumcision, who were not only of the circumcision, but also walked in the steps of the faith of their father Abraham which he had even though uncircumcised. They were in one respect a type and in another respect true members of the general assembly and church of the firstborn. The first of these they found as pertaining to the flesh, the other they obtained by faith.

The Israel of God in Israel

§. 4. Of this Israel in Israel, two things are to be observed.

1. Despite their interest in the promise by faith, they were not freed from the yoke and discipline of Moses' law until Christ came. They were indeed children, even the children of Abraham on a spiritual account. By the grace of a free promise which the law could not disannul they were relieved from its rigor as to their spiritual and eternal state. But being children under age, the pedagogy they were under differed nothing from that of servants; nor could they be discharged of this school master before Christ came.

2. They were blessed with spiritual blessings and had an interest in eternal life in circumcision and under the law. But none of them obtained this by circumcision or by the law. That whole economy that Israel according to the flesh was under was insufficient and weak in and by itself for the purpose of eternal happiness and the justification of a sinner before God. It could not make those who came to it perfect, nor make the carnal seed heirs of spiritual blessings. But a right to them was always grounded on a spiritual relationship to Abraham and an interest in that promise to which the covenant of circumcision was but a handmaid. And therefore those who rested in their carnal privileges and sought eternal happiness from them perverted their true end and could never obtain what they followed after.

In conclusion, the covenant of circumcision belonged to the body of the carnal seed, even to the Jewish church. The foundation of their state is laid there and their right and privilege is in it expressly stated to be "in their generations." Therefore, as we readily grant the promise now under consideration to belong to the seed of Abraham after the flesh, so we with good reason affirm that it must be taken in such a sense as is verified in that people and nation to whom it belonged and that will in no way contradict or interfere with the general design of the gospel or the plain and indisputable sense of other texts of Scripture.

The Promise Fully Explained

§. 5. These things being premised, we will now come closer to the words themselves and inquire what that good and blessing is which is ensured to this seed of Abraham.

It is evident that this promise, "I will be their God," and the earlier one found in Genesis 17:7 give a general assurance of some good to the people in covenant. But it should not be supposed that they are promises of some particular good or blessing that is of a higher nature than is comprehended in any other promises of the covenant. For the true import of this general promise is "that God has engaged himself and all the properties of his nature for the exact fulfilling of all the promises of the covenant now made with them, according to the true character and conditions of the said covenant."[4] All the divine perfections are laid in as pledges that the promises will not fail on God's part since they will be all exerted, as the need requires, for the good and advantage of this people in fulfilling the promises given to them. But still God's communications to them and acts for them, both in regard to the blessings he will bestow and the terms and conditions on which they will be bestowed, are limited by the covenant he has made with them and the nature and extent of the promises of it.

This will appear more plainly to be the true sense if we properly weigh the terms of the promise, "I will be their God" (that is, a God to them and they will have interest in all the perfections of my nature).

Either God is obliged by this promise to communicate himself in the highest degree possible to all those to whom it is made, and to do the utmost for them that may be done (without implying a contradiction to his being and infinite perfections) and to bring them absolutely to the utmost degree of happiness that omnipotent goodness can raise them to, or else the promised good must fall under some particular limitation. If it falls under any limitation (as it certainly does) those bounds must be set either by the import of the terms in which the promise is made, as considered absolutely and by themselves, or some other way. The first cannot be affirmed, for the terms are general and indeterminate. Therefore, it is to be limited some other way. This must be by the particular promises and conditions of that covenant to which this general promise belongs. And if so, then there is not, nor can there be, any greater good promised than what the nature of that covenant allows and its particular promises give a right in to the involved parties.

These things being so, no one from here can prove a grant of spiritual blessings to or a right in gospel ordinances for the carnal seed of

---

[4] See Mr. Whist. *Prim. Doctr.* p. 124. [Coxe refers his reader to Joseph Whiston, *An Essay to Revive the Primitive Doctrine and Practice of Infant Baptism in the Resolution of Four Questions* (London: Jonathan Robinson, 1676), 124.]

Abraham (or of any believer as such) unless he could produce a particular promise which contained such a grant or give such a right to them.

This Explanation Further Confirmed

§. 6. So what is principally intended and fully expressed in this engagement is no more than the necessary result of any covenant transaction of God with men. For where his truth is once engaged in a promise, all the properties of his nature are engaged respectively for the making good of that promise. Therefore, such a promise in its own nature contains no more than a general assurance of any covenant that God makes with men. It cannot by itself be the distinguishing character of any one covenant in opposition to or contradistinction from another. Neither does it determine the kind of promised blessings or the way in which they will be enjoyed.

And so this promise is equally and indifferently annexed both to the old covenant and the new, the covenant of works and that of grace. The truth of this will be manifest by a diligent comparison of Hebrews 8 with Jeremiah 31 and that with Genesis 17, Exodus 6:7, and Deuteronomy 26:17, 18. There is no reason therefore to conclude because we find this promise in the covenant of grace, that every covenant in which it is found must be of the same nature. For the covenant is not measured by this promise but, *è contra*,[5] its special import is limited by the covenant to which it belongs.

The History of its Accomplishment to Israel

§. 7. So far I have endeavored to set before you the genuine sense and true interpretation of this great promise in the covenant of circumcision, and to give you the reasons by which it is confirmed. It may add some further light to what has been said to briefly represent the history of its accomplishment from the holy Scriptures as follows.

The Lord abundantly blessed Abraham, Isaac, and Jacob and guided them with his eye in all their peregrinations[6] from nation to nation and from one kingdom to another people. When he broke the whole staff of

---

[5] [On the contrary.]
[6] [Journeys.]

bread[7] in the land of Canaan and the adjacent countries, he made provision through a wonderful series of providences to sustain Jacob's family by sending Joseph before them into the land of Egypt. For their sakes he raised him to such a capacity that he not only secured them from lack but also preserved the lives of thousands more. When the house of Jacob was by this means brought into the land of Egypt, the Lord was with them there. And when the time of the promise drew near, he caused them to increase and multiply exceedingly.

The Egyptians sought by all means to oppress and deal slyly with them, yet all their artifice and cruelty could make no earnings of their work, for the more they oppressed them the more they grew. In the midst of their calamitous distress Moses was brought into the world, whom the Lord had designed to be a deliverer and savior to them. For this purpose he was preserved in a miraculous manner from all dangers and temptations from his birth to the time that he was sent about his great work.

When the bondage of Israel grew to its extremity the Lord's eye was still open on them, and he heard their cry, remembered his covenant with their fathers, and sent Moses and Aaron to deliver them. Then his bow was made quite naked (Habakkuk 3:9) in a course of miracles by signs, wonders, and mighty works for which his name is celebrated to all generations. In that very day which he had set in the promise to their fathers he brought them out of the land of Egypt and delivered them from the house of their bondage with a high hand. He even divided the Red Sea before them and led them through the deep as on dry land. But he buried Pharaoh and all his host in the same waters that had been as a wall on the right hand and on the left, while the redeemed of the Lord passed over.

He guided them also in the wilderness and afforded the visible token of his presence with them in a pillar of cloud by day and of fire by night. From his right hand there went out a fiery law for them because he loved them. By it he formed both their civil and ecclesiastical polity by which they were immediately subjected to him and made a kingdom of priests and a holy nation. The Lord's tabernacle was pitched in the midst of them so that there was no nation under heaven that had God so near as the Lord their God was to them in all that they did call on him for. Moreover, he gave his good Spirit to instruct them, who was poured on

---

[7] [Apparently a phrase meaning to bring famine.]

Moses, Aaron, and Miriam with the seventy elders and those prophets which from time to time God raised up among them. He fed them also with manna from heaven and gave them water out of the rock to drink. All the time of their forty years of travel in the wilderness their feet were not swollen neither did their garments grow old.

He also dried up the Jordan, brought them into the land of Canaan, and drove out before them nations more in number and mightier than them. There he blessed them with the blessings of heaven above and of the earth beneath so that nothing failed of any good thing which the Lord had spoken concerning them (Joshua 23:14) but their state was made prosperous and happy because the Lord was their God (Psalm 144:15). Despite all their provocations he had compassion on them when they cried to him in their distresses. He delivered them so that the scepter did not depart from Judah nor a law-giver from between his feet until Shiloh (that is, Christ) came. Much of this you have summed up in Nehemiah 9, Psalm 105, and Psalm 144 with Acts 7.

The Blessings of Israel after the Flesh

§. 8. In all these respects and others of a similar nature asserted before, there was a glory on the ministry of the Old Testament (2 Corinthians 3:7-11). The Jew had a great advantage and there was profit in circumcision. But the chief advantage was this: that to them was committed the oracles of God (Romans 3:1; 9:4). Theirs were the covenants of promise and the solemn worship of God was maintained among them. Salvation was of the Jews (John 4:22). In these things was the promise fulfilled that the Lord would be a God to them in their generations. And yet all this lies short of an actual, personal, and saving interest in the covenant of grace[8] as the apostle Paul argues at large in his epistle to the Romans and particularly in chapters 9, 10, and 11. He could not have affirmed that the committing of the oracles of God to them was the chief profit or greatest benefit of circumcision, if God had ever appointed it to be the seal of their interest in the covenant of grace. For this undoubtedly is much greater than any external benefit or advantage.

---

[8] Many to whom the Lord was a God according to the tenor of the Old covenant, died in their sins, and were eternally lost; but those to whom he is a God, according to the tenor of the New covenant, receive from him, the blessings of a new heart, remission of sins, and eternal salvation.

Furthermore, Jews had the privilege that the son of God was to be made flesh of the seed of Abraham, and to be manifested among them, being made a minister of the circumcision for the fulfilling of the promises made to the fathers (Romans 15:8).

Also, the first offer of the grace and salvation of the gospel rightly belonged to them. The preaching of repentance and remission of sins in Christ's name was to begin at Jerusalem (Luke 24:47). And as this was an argument of God's great favor, so it might be to them a great encouragement to receive the gospel and expect salvation by Christ according to the offer made in it. To this purpose Peter urges, (Acts 2:38, 39) "Repent and be baptized every one of you, in the name of Jesus Christ for the remission of sins, and you will receive the gift of the Holy Spirit. For the promise is to you and to your children..." The promise which he refers to is the one cited earlier of the salvation of all who in the day of the gospel call on the name of the Lord, and the pouring out of his Spirit on all flesh (see verses 17-21).

This promise of the Spirit is also mentioned by Paul as the great blessing of the gospel in Galatians 3:14. The Spirit was then to be poured out on many in the miraculous and extraordinary gifts and on all true believers in a New Testament measure. Accordingly, the apostle exhorts them to the obedience of the gospel that they might obtain the remission of their sins and receive the gift of the Holy Spirit. This he assures them of, on the terms proposed, for he says, "the promise is to you and your children..." You are in no way excluded from the hope of this blessing though you have been betrayers and murderers of Christ himself. But on the contrary, you (as Jews) have a special interest in the promise, for its accomplishment is to begin among you and the first offer of its blessing belongs to you.

They could not have an actual interest in the promise to salvation until they believed and repented. But as was explained earlier, the promise was to them while unbelievers. In a similar sense the apostle Paul says of them that the covenants and the promises (as well as the giving of the law and Levitical service) were theirs (Romans 9:4). Their covenant brought salvation to them. But it was the receiving of it by faith, when so offered, that gave them a particular interest in it. And the interest of their children or posterity in the promises can reach no further than theirs from whom it is supposed to be derived. It is the same thing in effect that Peter urges on the same people to persuade them to obedience to the doctrine of Christ (Acts 3:25, 26). "You are the children of the prophets and of the covenant which God made with our fathers, saying to Abraham, and in your seed will all the kindreds of the earth be blessed. To you first God, having raised up his son Jesus, sent him to bless you in turning every one of you from his iniquities."

Suitable to this we find the apostles in all places, where they came with the glad tidings of the gospel, first applied themselves to the Jews, holding it necessary that the word of God should first be preached to them (Acts 13:46, 47).

The Covenant of Circumcision not the Covenant of Grace

§. 9. From the account which has been given of the covenant of circumcision, and its nature and promises, these corollaries follow.

1. This was a covenant of grace and mercy, originating from the mere goodness and undeserved favor of God toward Israel (Deuteronomy 7:7, 8). In it many excellent privileges were given to them which no other nation under heaven had a right in except themselves. These were conferred on them in pursuit of the great design of God's grace in the covenant of redemption by Christ. Yet it was not that covenant of grace which God made with Abraham for all his spiritual seed, which was earlier confirmed of God in Christ, and through which all nations (that is, true believers in every nation) have been ever since, now are, and will be, blessed with the spiritual and eternal blessing of Abraham.

2. Although it is granted that this covenant ultimately related to spiritual blessings (since it was prepared in the manifold wisdom of God in subordination to the covenant of grace and added to the promise until the fullness of time came) yet it was not immediately and directly a covenant of spiritual blessings. Nor could it ever convey to the carnal seed of Abraham, as such, a right and interest in them.

3. Despite the promises made in this covenant of circumcision, and the separation of Israel to be the peculiar people of God in pursuit of them, their church-state was completed by the covenant in the wilderness. This was when the set time for the fulfilling of those promises in that respect was fully come. Yet for the present this covenant did not confine the solemn worship of God (by sacrifices or otherwise) to Abraham's family. Nor were other holy men living then under any obligation to incorporate themselves into it by circumcision or at all to take on them that sign or seal of this covenant of peculiarity that God

now made with Abraham. Yet without a doubt they should have done this if in its first institution it had been given simply and directly as a seal of the covenant of grace. For then by reason of their interest in that covenant, both in point of duty and privilege, it belonged as much to them as to the seed and family of Abraham.

Other Holy Men then Living Not Bound to be Circumcised

§. 10. From the sacred history it is evident that the command by virtue of which circumcision was administered, extended no further than to Abraham and his family. Therefore we have no ground to conclude that Lot (though closely allied to Abraham) was circumcised. There is nothing in the command of God or the first institution of circumcision that obligated him to it or interested him in it. Yet there is no doubt to be made of his interest in the covenant of grace.

Nor was Lot the only righteous man then living in the world beside those of Abraham's family for the patriarchs Heber, Salah, and Shem were now living. They had their distinct families and interests so there is no question that the pure worship of God was maintained in them and they promoted the interest of true religion to the utmost of their power while they lived.

Melchizedek was alive about this time. Whether he was Shem named earlier or another does not concern us. But this is certain: that it was he who was the priest of the most high God and King of Salem. In both respects he was the most eminent type of Jesus Christ that ever was in the world; a person greater than Abraham, for Abraham paid tithes to him and was blessed by him. Now considering that he was both king and priest, there is no doubt that there was a society of men that were ruled by him and for whom he ministered. For a priest is ordained for men in things pertaining to God.[9] This society was at this time as much a church of God as Abraham's family was and as truly interested in the covenant of grace as any in it. Yet they were not involved as parties in this covenant of circumcision nor to be signed by it. And so it is manifest that circumcision was not at first applied as a seal of the covenant of grace, nor did an interest in it presently render a man the proper subject of it.

Again, to suppose that all good men then living should have been circumcised as Abraham was, and their offspring bound to keep this

---

[9] [Hebrews 5:1.]

covenant in their generations as his were, would necessarily frustrate one great (if not the greatest) end of circumcision and its covenant. This was the separating of one family and people from all others in the world for the bringing out of the Messiah, that promised seed, from them and among them for the establishing of all the promises made to the fathers. Moreover, the promise of this covenant regarding the inheritance of the land of Canaan could never have been made good to them all. And yet certainly the sealing of that promise was one thing intended in circumcision.

From the whole it appears that, on the one hand, there was a positive command which made it necessary to circumcise many that never had interest in the covenant of grace. So, on the other hand, from the first date of circumcision there were many truly interested in the covenant of grace who were under no obligation to be circumcised. This is how far from truth it is that a new covenant interest and right to circumcision may be inferred the one from the other.

Infant Church Membership Considered

§. 11. I would have here closed this chapter except that I judge it convenient in this place to briefly touch on that notion of infant church membership, which is much spoken about with reference to those times, and which history we have already passed through. This is because of the light we may receive from the things already discoursed to guide us to a right understanding of the true state of the question about it. Many affirm such a thing to have been from the beginning and great weight is laid on it in the controversy about the right subjects of baptism. It is judged to afford a sufficient ground for applying the seal of the covenant to the infant seed of believers. For my own part, I do not find in the Scriptures occasion given for any long discourses about it and I will not desire to be wise above what is written. Therefore I will endeavor in a few words to represent some things grounded on the records of matter of fact in the Scripture, which I conceive may be sufficient to determine our thoughts, as to the issue of our present inquiry about it. And they are these that follow.

Five Proposals Considered

§. 12. 1. The term church in the Scriptures is not (that I find) applied to any particular society of men united in one body for the maintaining of the public and solemn worship of God before the children of Israel were completely formed into a church-state by the covenant that God made with them in the wilderness. They are called the church in the wilderness in Acts 7:38. Yet I do no doubt that all good men before that time belonged to that general assembly and church which Christ has redeemed with his blood and made the members of his body. I grant that we may (using the term in a more lax sense) call any family or society of men truly worshiping God, a church of God. Nevertheless, if we consider the circumstances relating to the different state of things in those different times, it will appear that no society before the Jewish church was formed can be called a church in so strict and proper a sense as they might. For no other was so formed into a church-state as they were.

2. Before Abraham's time there was no institution of an outward sign or seal of any covenant to be applied either to infants or adult persons. Therefore there could not be any inauguration of this kind or solemn right of initiation to church privilege in use among them. All that can be said of the children born in those families and societies is that they were under a more special and gracious providence of God than others, being members of a family peculiarly interested in it. They also had the benefit of continual prayers for them and the advantage of early and diligent instruction, being brought up in the nurture and admonition of the Lord. They were preserved from many snares and temptations that others are liable to by the discipline they were under. And being provoked to religion by the pious and holy example of those they conversed with, as soon as they were capable of it (if, when grown up, they did not break through all these fences and revolt to a wicked and irreligious life) they actually joined with that family and society to which they belonged in the solemn worship of God.

3. If we consider church membership in a way agreeable to that time in which circumcision was first instituted, we cannot conclude that a right to circumcision resulted from it. For certainly the patriarchs and other good men then living and their families were as truly church members as Abraham and his family. Yet they were not therefore to be circumcised, but the particular law and positive institution of this ordinance alone determined its subjects.

4. Moreover, it was not membership in Abraham's family singly and simply considered that brought a person under the law of circumcision, without respect to other circumstances of time and sex expressly set down in the institution. For circumcision was to be applied to the males

only, though the right of church-membership belonged as much to the females as to them. And it is no satisfactory answer to say the female is not a subject capable of circumcision. For if it had pleased God to have made church membership the reason and ground of applying this seal of the covenant, he could easily have appointed a sign that all members were capable of.

Besides, how does it appear that the females were utterly incapable of any kind of circumcision, except that God required no such thing? Vitriacus[10] reports that the Jacobites use circumcision of both sexes and so do the Habassines. Therefore the thing in itself is not impossible. That which has been done, may be done. Also, we find the circumcising of the males was limited to the eighth day. It might not be done sooner or delayed longer. The slaves that were bought with money had to be circumcised though they were not church members, nor the children of such. From all this it is manifest that they proceeded not on a notion of church membership, but were strictly governed by divine institution in the matter of circumcising or not circumcising.

5. In conclusion, it is granted that the Jewish infants were born members of that church. This privilege they had in the flesh. But this clearly belongs to the national and typical church-state of that people. This state is dissolved by the gospel and is so inconsistent with its ministry that the placing of the one necessarily infers the abolition of the other. Therefore this right and privilege of the Jew which was in the very foundation of their national church-state, as separated from the Gentiles, cannot be transferred into, because it will not fit with the gospel dispensation.

Besides, it is evident throughout the whole gospel that the right of membership in the Jewish church could never give to any, either infant or adult, the same right of membership in the gospel church. There was never any one received into it, *eo nomine*,[11] because he had such a right according to the state of the old covenant. And there is good reason to conclude, that the carnal seed of believers can derive no higher privilege from the covenant of circumcision than the carnal seed of Abraham obtained by it. It could not bring the latter into the gospel church or give them a right to baptism without an actual compliance by repentance and faith to the terms of the gospel. So, it can by no means do so for the

---

[10] Brecrw. inquir. [This is an unknown reference.]

[11] [On this account.]

former (even if we should suppose them to have a part in the covenant of circumcision, which indeed, they do not).

Therefore it remains true that since circumcision of old was administered according to the positive law and express will of the Lord, so ought baptism to be now and not otherwise. Neither can I see any ground to conclude for paedobaptism until such a divine law can be produced for its warrant, as was given of old for circumcising the male infants of the Jews.

Chapter Eight

The Mutual Reference of the Promises made to Abraham
The General Design of this Chapter

§. 1. In the previous chapters, I have endeavored to distinctly discuss the promises given to Abraham, first those that belong to his spiritual seed and then those that pertain to his carnal seed. These promises, despite their different nature and importance, are frequently found intermixed in the same transaction of God with Abraham, as they are in the sacred history presented to us interwoven with one another. The order of our discourse now leads us to make a more exact inquiry into the mutual relationship between the promises which might give occasion for and make necessary such an intermixture of them.

The Intermixture of the Promises

§. 2. The first thing I will offer to be considered on this point is that this order and disposition of the promises is excellently suited to the dispensation of those times in which they were given and to that state of the Israelite church which was not long after to be built on them. For these things were transacted long before the time appointed for the clear breaking up of gospel light to the world. That was not to be expected until Christ came in the flesh, before whose coming the law was to be given and the economy of the old covenant remain for many generations. So although the gospel was preached to Abraham, it was not delivered to him with the plainness and perspicuity as it is in the New Testament. For the most part it is shadowed and figured by outward things. Thus that which concerns the state of Israel under the Mosaic economy is more expressly and fully declared to Abraham than what concerns his spiritual seed under the gospel. Though the latter is the chief thing intended and aimed at (because it is the perfection of all the rest) in all divine transactions with Abraham, yet it is for the most part spiritually enfolded in and to be inferred from the typical relation of the other to it. This leaves the glory of gospel grace still under that veil which accompanied the Old Testament state of the church. The full opening of those promises that immediately belonged to the covenant of grace was reserved for another state of things in the church. "God having provided some better thing for us, that they without us should not be made perfect" (Hebrews 11:40). A dim light was suited to those times. And it could only be dim as long as the promises lay so much entangled with one another.

The same is to be observed later in the revelation of the mind of God to Israel by the prophets. In the prophetic writings it appears that the temporal deliverances of Israel are considered as typical of the spiritual redemption of the church. So we often meet sudden and seemingly abrupt transitions from the promises of things relating to the present state of Israel after the flesh, to promises and prophecies of those things which are accomplished in the New Testament by the ministry of the Spirit. These are generally delivered in terms suitable to the present dispensation of things. But their typical relationship is woefully perverted to this day by the Jews. They contend they are the only people involved in them, that the promised and prophesied blessings belong to them, and that they are to be fulfilled to them in a way agreeable to their former state and suited to their own carnal lusts and imaginations. By this they harden themselves in their contempt of the grace of God in Christ and the spiritual blessings of the gospel in which the accomplishment of those prophecies according to their true sense is only to be sought. And so Jesus Christ himself became a stone of stumbling and rock of offence to them because the state of his kingdom did not suit their carnal minds nor meet their groundless expectation.

The Mutual Relationship of the Promises

§. 3. It should also be observed that there is a remarkable congruity and fitness in this method of giving out the promises in regard to the time they were made to Abraham and that state of the church which followed the transactions. But there is also in some respects a necessity of it arising from the nature of the things promised and their mutual dependence on one another.

This is because all the promises of a spiritual seed and spiritual blessings to be bestowed on that seed (which belong to the covenant of grace as revealed to Abraham), are "Yes and Amen" in Christ Jesus. This Messiah, in whom the covenant was confirmed, was to be made of the seed of Abraham according to the flesh. The seed of Abraham by Isaac and Jacob was separated to God for a peculiar people and kept distinct from all other families in the world to bring him out according to the promise. In this respect, the blessing of grace and eternal life given to Abraham and his believing seed was suspended on the effect and accomplishment of the promises concerning his natural offspring; and particularly on the promise of Isaac's birth. He was to be begotten by Abraham and brought forth by Sarah at a time when nature in them both was so weakened by age that they were as unable, he to beget and she to conceive a son, as if they had been already dead (Romans 4:19).

It is for this reason that the apostle lays such great weight on Abraham's faith in this particular, even in the business of his justification before God since the object of justifying faith, the Messiah to come, was included in the promise of Isaac's birth. On this account his parents had the greatest cause for rejoicing at the birth of this son who has his name from laughter and rejoicing (Genesis 17:17 and chapter 21). This, in part, may be the reference of the saying of our Savior, "Abraham rejoiced to see my day, and he saw it, and was glad" (John 8:56). He saw it in the birth of Isaac and afterwards in the offering up of him who was a type of Christ and from whom he was to come. His miraculous birth, in virtue of a promise when nature could not have effected it, also afforded some vague foreshadowing of and a *præludium*[1] to the more miraculous birth of Christ who was conceived and brought forth by a pure virgin (the power of the most High overshadowing her). This was the fulfilling of that promise, "The seed of the woman will break the head of the serpent."[2] As Isaac in the type, so Christ more eminently, sprang up as a root out of a dry ground (Isaiah 53).

The Greatness of Abraham's Trial

§. 4. Now from these things we may collect with ease and great clearness the greatness of Abraham's trial and the eminency of his faith in offering up Isaac. To part with an obedient son, a son grown up as Isaac now was, even an only son, was indeed a great trial. But Abraham was not only required to part with him but to sacrifice him. For a father to become the executioner of his son, the son of his old age and the object of his most endeared affections, for him to be appointed the priest that must slay this victim, adds much more to the trial. And in Abraham's addressing himself to such a service (had there been no more in it) without debate,

---

[1] [Prelude; introduction.]
[2] [Genesis 3:15.]

murmuring, or delay we have an unparalleled instance and example of piety and obedience.

But grievously, there is an infinitely greater concern in this case than all that has been yet mentioned. Isaac was the son of the promise. On this account the Holy Spirit places it – "he that had received the promises offered up his only begotten son of whom it was said, in Isaac will your seed be called" (Hebrews 11:17, 18). Abraham had no other son in whom he might expect the fulfilling of the promise when Isaac was lost. And yet on the accomplishment of this promise, in the bringing forth of the Messiah in Isaac's line, the eternal salvation of Abraham and of the whole church depended. Therefore he is called his only begotten, not because Abraham had no other son, but because he was the only heir of the promise. This might have caused the greatest anxiety of mind imaginable in Abraham if he had at all consulted with flesh and blood in the case. But his faith overcame this difficulty and silenced all carnal reasonings about the impossibility of the accomplishment of the promise if this command were obeyed. He was "accounting that God was able to raise him up, even from the dead, from which also he received him in a figure" (Hebrews 11:19).

The result made it abundantly manifest that Abraham's readiness to obey in this case did not put the promise in real hazard, for it brought out means to further confirm his faith by the exhibition of an eminent type of the redemption of the church by the death and resurrection of Christ. To this was added the renewing of God's promises to Abraham, both for his spiritual and carnal seed, and their confirmation by the oath of the great God (Genesis 22:17, 18). But I now return to our present purpose.

From these things we may certainly collect that all the promises made to Abraham were ordered by God to meet in one general issue. For as the promises concerning the carnal seed and their state were subservient to the ends of God's covenant with the spiritual seed, so also the promises peculiarly belonging to the spiritual seed were to have their effect and accomplishment in a seed that must descend from Abraham according to the flesh. And therefore that interchange of the promises which has been observed to you ought not to seem strange in any way.

The Covenant of Peculiarity as a Type

§. 5. The typical relation and analogy of the covenant of peculiarity to the covenant of grace more fully revealed and accomplished in Christ, affords another occasion of and reason for the interweaving of those promises which require a distinct application. Some of them belong directly to the carnal seed and others to the spiritual seed arising from the springs and ordered toward the ministry of two distinct covenants. It is asserted by the Holy Spirit in the Scriptures that there was a ordering of things in the Old Testament in a typical relation to the things of a spiritual nature and concern in the New. This is so full and clear that it is generally acknowledged by those who own their authority. Many things in the transactions of God with Abraham were of this nature. To insist at length on these things is beside my present design, but for the better clearing of the point under consideration, I will briefly touch on something of this kind.

First, let it be observed that the body of the Israelite nation was considered a holy people and the Lord's first-born (Exodus 4:22, 23; Jeremiah 2:3), bearing in their flesh the mark of circumcision which obligated them to perform the righteousness of the law. They were not only a seed separated to God for the bringing forth of the Messiah but were also a spiritual type of Christ. That is, they were of that seed and body of which Christ is the Head and true believers are the members (who in this relationship are considered complete in him). So they eminently pointed at his being made under the law (Galatians 4:4) and by its perfect fulfillment "becoming the end of the law for righteousness to every one that believes" (Romans 10:4).

Much may be fairly gathered from that saying of the prophet in Hosea 11:1,[3] "Out of Egypt have I called my son" by comparing it with Matthew 2:15 where the evangelist applies it to Christ. Probably for this reason Christ is prophesied of by the name of Israel (Isaiah 49:3). Christ was the seed in whom the substance of the righteousness that was foreshadowed in the circumcision of Israel was to be found. From him it is derived on all true believers for their justification before God and their introduction into a state in which they should acceptably walk before God and worship him in newness of spirit. Thus circumcision did not only obligate the keeping of the law (in which respect it was a heavy yoke, Acts 15:10) but also (as subservient to the promise) pointed at the Messiah who was to come under a legal bond to fulfill all righteousness,

---

[3] Vid. Junii *Annotationes in locum, & ejusdem Parallela.* [See Junius' *Annotations* on the passage, and his parallels. "Junius" is Franciscus Junius, 1545-1602, whose comments can presumably be found in his *Testimenti Veteris,* London, 1581 or its English translation of 1643.]

that through faith in his name such a righteousness might be obtained as is witnessed to both by the law and the prophets (Romans 3:21).

It is Christ alone in whom the design of circumcision is fully answered. Under the Old Testament administration no man could enjoy the privileges of the covenant of peculiarity without circumcision since none were admitted to walk before God in that covenant without this sign of a perfect righteousness and purity according to the law. So now none can have entrance into the kingdom of grace or obtain a right in the spiritual blessings and privileges of the new covenant, except by an interest in the righteousness of Christ through faith and by coming under the imputation of his obedience in which the law was fulfilled for us. Seeing that this was the most comforting and chief end of circumcision, since it served the design of the covenant of grace toward the elect, its continuation now in the same relationship which it had in its first institution would be in effect to deny that Christ is come in the flesh.

I do not intend by anything I have said to intimate a denial of the typical relationship of circumcision to the sanctification of believers. Neither is that notion of it in the least weakened, but rather strengthened in its proper place. For as the real holiness of believers springs from their union to Christ, and justification through the faith of his name, so I take circumcision first to look toward that perfect righteousness which we have in Jesus Christ and then to that sincere (though imperfect) holiness that is worked in us by the Spirit of Christ. "For we are the circumcision which worship God in the Spirit; and rejoice in Christ Jesus, and have no confidence in the flesh" (Philippians 3:3).

Colossians 2:11 Explained

§. 6. I conceive if those other texts in the New Testament that look toward the spiritual use of circumcision are weighed well, and the scope of their context is duly considered, they will cast a great light on the notion proposed to you. I cannot stay on all, but for instance, let us repair to Colossians 2:11, "In whom also you are circumcised with the circumcision made without hands, in putting off the body of the sins of the flesh by the circumcision of Christ."

The design of the apostle's discourse in the whole context is to confirm the souls of the believing Colossians in the faith of the gospel, and particularly in that great article of the Christian religion concerning our being justified freely by the grace of God through the redemption that is in Christ Jesus (Romans 3:24). He cautions them not to be led away by the error of the wicked from the simplicity of truth which they had received. But as they had received Christ Jesus the Lord, so they should walk in him, rooted and built up in him and established in the faith (verses 6, 7). Then he says, "Beware lest any man spoil you through philosophy and vain deceit, after the tradition of men, after the rudiments of the world, and not after Christ" (verse 8). The men who the apostle brands in these last words are those that endeavored to subvert the liberty of the Gentile churches by entangling them again in the yoke of legal bondage. To this end these men not only asserted that the Levitical ceremonies continued to be in their own nature acceptable service to God, but also that they were of perpetual use. This was because of the philosophical secrets and mysteries of nature which they pretended were wrapped up in them. They had no ground for this conceit (God having at no time appointed them to such an end) except from the tradition of their elders. This is what the apostle intends by "philosophy and vain deceit after the tradition of men."

To prevent their being ensnared with this corrupt doctrine, he informs them how Christ was the end and substance of all those shadows and that all fullness dwells in him in whom they were complete. For that reason they ought not to turn back to the law or its ceremonies to seek perfection from them since by Christ they were made partakers of the real benefit which was only darkly pointed at and foreshadowed by the ceremonies of the law. So he adds in verse 11, "In whom also you are circumcised..." Notice, they are not said to be circumcised in themselves but in Christ. This is because in him they were completely justified by the imputation of a perfect righteousness which circumcision under the law, as an ordinance of the old covenant, obligated men to and prefigured as subordinate to the promise. Therefore the apostle affirms that believers are the circumcision who place their whole trust in Jesus Christ (Philippians 3:3). They are also described to be those who worship God in the Spirit. This does not restrain the notion of their circumcision to the righteousness of sanctification, but rather describes them by another fruit and property of that grace by which they are justified (compare Romans 8:4).

In the words of this text in Colossians, the circumcision spoken of is said to be "in the putting off the body of the sins of the flesh..." This primarily signifies our justification and includes sanctification as its necessary accompaniment. It is by justification that we are completely delivered from a state of sin and the mass of corruption (as Joshua was from his filthy garments, Zechariah 3:4). This is by an implantation into and union with Christ who died for our sins and rose again for our justification. Therefore this change of their state is said to be by their being "quickened together with Christ" (verse 13). This quickening is that of justification, in which they were raised from that deadly state of guiltiness that they were in while dead in their sins and the uncircumcision of their flesh, to a state of life, righteousness, and acceptance with God who forgives them all their trespasses.

Now this putting off the body of the sins of the flesh is by "the circumcision of Christ." I know expositors generally take this circumcision to be the work of the Spirit of Christ in the soul since they apply the whole verse to our sanctification. But I conceive that our justification is primarily intended in the context, so the scope of the apostle's discourse leads us instead to interpret this to be the circumcision with which Christ was circumcised. The sign is put for the thing signified; that is, the circumcision of Christ for his perfect obedience and fulfilling of the law. In circumcision the yoke of the law was first carried and by it the circumcised person was bound to keep the whole law, otherwise his circumcision became uncircumcision (Romans 2:25). So then the circumcision of Christ is a convincing evidence of his being made under the law. By its perfect fulfillment, he brought in that everlasting righteousness which, through its imputation, all that are in him are justified before God. This communion that believers have with Christ in his benefits through the faith of the operation of God, is in a lively manner held out and signified to them in their baptism, in which they are said to be both buried and risen together with him (Colossians 2:12). The immersion of the body into the water bears an analogy to his burial, just as the raising of it again out of the water does to his resurrection. The apostle means that even their baptism on their first receiving and profession of the Christian religion, taught and obligated them to live on Christ alone and to join no other thing with him in the foundation of their hope.

These things being so, circumcision was no longer of use nor were Christians involved in it. Having accomplished its utmost end in Jesus Christ, it expired in time and vanished away with the whole system of the Mosaic economy. And so far is the apostle from intimating that baptism came in the place of circumcision, that he speaks of them as pertaining to two covenants so different from one another, and in their complete ministry opposed to one another, that they could not by any means (in this last respect) consist together.

Abraham's Family a Type of the Future Church

§. 7. Next it is to be noted that there was a typical representation of the future state of the church (in the days of the gospel) in the present transactions of God with Abraham and the state of his family. The explanation of all the details belonging to this would require an enlargement of this discourse beyond its intended bounds. Therefore, for our present purpose, I will only point at the heads of those things which the apostle sets before us in Galatians 4 from verse 21 to the end of the chapter.

After reading the context, you will observe that the allegory insisted on by the apostle is grounded on the historical verity that Abraham had a twofold seed.

1. One proceeded from him according to the ordinary course and by the strength of nature; the other was produced by virtue of a promise. The one was Ishmael by Hagar, a bond-woman; the other was Isaac by Sarah, a free-woman.

2. The bond-woman and her son had the precedence in time of conception and birth to the free-woman and her son.

3. In the process of time the son of the bond-woman who was born after the flesh persecutes the son of the free-woman who was born after the Spirit; that is, in the virtue of the promise. Because of this the bond-woman and her son are cast out of the family and Isaac remains there as the only heir of his father's blessing.

The apostle affirms that these things were ordered by God in a typical relationship to gospel times and applies them as follows.

Hagar was a type of Mount Sinai and the legal covenant established there. Ishmael was a type of the carnal seed of Abraham under that covenant. Sarah was a type of the new Jerusalem, the gospel church founded on the covenant of grace. Isaac was a type of the true members of that church who are born of the Spirit, being converted by the power of the Holy Spirit for the fulfilling of the promise of the Father to Jesus Christ the mediator. And the ejection of Hagar and Ishmael was to prefigure the abrogation of the Sinaitic covenant and the dissolving of the Jewish church-state so that the inheritance of spiritual blessings might be clearly passed down to the children of God by faith in Jesus Christ.

There are many other things worthy to be observed which are not my present work to insist on, for this general view taken of the context is sufficient to prepare our way to the following observations.

Inferences from this Type

§. 8. First, the apostle who in Galatians 3:8, 17 calls the promise recorded in Genesis 12, "the gospel preached to Abraham" and "the covenant confirmed of God in Christ," here expressly calls that covenant transaction to which circumcision belonged and in which the right and privilege of the natural seed of Abraham was stated,[4] the law. He condemns their desire to be under it as proceeding from their folly and ignorance (Galatians 4:21).

2. Despite all the privileges of Israel after the flesh, they remained in a state of bondage under the law. They were parties in the Sinai covenant and in the covenant of circumcision, and children of the earthly Jerusalem (or members of that church whose state was founded on the covenants just mentioned) and so interested in all the worship to be performed there. All this could no more give them interest in and right to the spiritual blessings of Abraham, than Ishmael's carnal descent from him could either enright[5] himself or his seed in the covenant of peculiarity made with Israel and its outward blessings. For although the seed of Abraham by Isaac was under the dispensation of those blessings that were the shadow and type of the good things of the gospel, yet their birthright and proper claim in the interest of their covenant fell as far short of gospel blessings, as Ishmael's did of their privileges. For as Ishmael was in a literal sense born after the flesh and was the son of a bond-woman, so were they spiritually. And as Ishmael persecuted Isaac, so they (being puffed up with a vain confidence in their carnal privilege and prerogative) did not only reject the gospel themselves, but also persecuted the children of the new Jerusalem. Therefore as he was cast out of Abraham's family and excluded from any part in the inheritance of the son of promise, so they must be excluded from the kingdom of God and the inheritance of its blessings.

---

[4] [To instate or establish in the covenant.]
[5] [To invest with a right or entitle.]

Thus in the very beginning of the covenant-state of Israel after the flesh, God, in this type, set before their eyes its imperfection and the sad end they would bring themselves to by a resting in it and overweening of it.

3. Nevertheless, the covenant of peculiarity made with Israel and the dispensation that God brought them under pursuant to its ends, was typical of the gospel covenant and the state of things in it. In Isaac we have a type of the children of God by faith. As he (in his seed) was the heir of Canaan, so they are heirs of heaven. As he was persecuted by Ishmael, so must they expect trouble in the world and look to be maligned by all carnal and Pharisaic spirits who seek to establish their own righteousness and refuse to submit to the righteousness of God. In a word, the people, their worship, and their inheritance were all typical. And yet, as Abraham's spiritual seed may behold the shadow of their own state and privilege in the spiritual relation and typical economy of the Jewish church, so they again might and ought to consider themselves in their outward state to be but typical.[6] While they were figures of the children of promise, both themselves, their state, and their end were figured in the son of the bond-woman and his rejection.

Now from this we may infer the following.

1. The carnal seed of believers can obtain no greater privilege by the covenant of circumcision than the seed of Abraham by Isaac had. Their privilege did not reach to an interest in gospel blessings or in the new covenant unless they obtained that right for themselves by believing. They had no more right in them by their natural descent from Abraham than Ishmael had in the blessings of their covenant of peculiarity. And their interest in typical privileges necessarily ceased and vanished away when the things typified were exhibited.

---

[6] *Pars [enim] quædam terrenæ Civitatis, Imago cælestis Civitatis effecta est, non se significando, sed alteram, & ideo serviens. Non enim propter se ipsam, sed propter aliam significandam est instituta, & præcEdente alia significantione, & ipsa præfigurans, præfigurata est: Namque; Agar ancilla Sarræ, eiusque; Filius, Imago quædam huius imaginis fuit.* August. *De Civita Dei,* Lib. 15. Cap. 2. [A certain part of the earthly city has been used to make an image of the heavenly city, and since it thus symbolizes not itself but the other, it is in servitude. For it was established not for its own sake but to symbolize another city, and since it too was anticipated by another symbol, the foreshadowing image itself was also foreshadowed. Hagar, who was Sarah's slave, represented together with her son an image of this image. For this translation see Augustine, *The City of God Against the Pagans,* IV, Book 15, Chapter 2, (Cambridge, MA: Harvard University Press, 1966), 418-419.]

2. The state of Israel after the flesh was typical. The Israel of God among them were taught to look above and beyond their external privileges to those things that were foreshadowed by them, as set before their faith in the promises of grace by Christ. They were to live on the grace of that covenant which their outward state and covenant of peculiarity were subservient to. All these things had a spiritual and evangelical use to them which was their principal end and intent. So a fair occasion is furnished for the intermixture of the promises of typical blessing with real blessings, which we have now had under consideration, because the covenant of grace and that of circumcision have their mutual reference, as the type to its antitype.

A Key to Many Promises in the Old Testament

§. 9. These things are not only necessary to the right understanding of those divine transactions with Abraham which we have been treating, but they also are of use for the opening and right application of many prophecies and promises of the Old Testament. They help us avoid those stumbling blocks (and others like them) into which the blind Jews have fallen and do fall on to this day.

The phraseology of the Old Testament will hardly be understood in various places without due regard to many of those things that we have been treating, such as the following.

1. During the time of the law the true church was impaled[7] within the bounds of the commonwealth of Israel which in its entire body was a typical church.

2. The children of God after the Spirit (though as underage children they were subject to the pedagogy of the law, yet) as to their spiritual and eternal state, walked before God and found acceptance with him on terms of the covenant of grace.

3. The whole economy these people were under in its typical respect, promoted the ends of the covenant of grace to the elect, who were the true and spiritual worshipers of God. And the greatest and only visible number of them was to be preserved among that people until the gospel church-state should take place.

4. Yet this spiritual relationship to God according to the terms of the new covenant which the truly godly then had, was not as clearly held out

---

[7] [Surrounded as with a palisade; fenced in.]

under the Old Testament as it is in the times of the New and by the dispensation of the gospel. But the things relating to it were very much wrapped up in dark shadows and figures.

Therefore, many times the typified things and people are spoken of in the prophetic Scriptures under the names of those things and that people which were the types of them. The promises of the choicest gospel blessings and most glorious spiritual state of the New Testament church are given out to Israel of old in those terms that suited their present state of things. They are peculiarly directed to them and their seed. But these promises, given to them because of their relationship to God as his only visible church and covenant people, are not to be applied to Israel after the flesh, as such. Rather, they had their accomplishment in the church when Israel was rejected and the Gentiles were called to inherit the blessing of Abraham. Although they were directly given out to Israel and Jacob, as the only true church then in existence and a people in whom the church was typified, it was only fitting and necessary that the terms used in those prophecies and promises should be accommodated to the economy which the church was then under. (This is especially true considering that the spiritual glory of the gospel and the calling of the Gentiles was a mystery not to be unfolded in those times, but was kept under a veil.) Yet they must be interpreted in a sense agreeable to those times and that dispensation in which they were to have their full accomplishment. Therefore, seeing the church was then continued in a line of natural descent from Abraham, being propagated by generation as long as that old covenant-state remained unshaken, the promises made to the church concerning her future glory, peace, and blessedness in the days of the Messiah, are given to the seed and offspring of the church then in being. This is so even though they really belonged to and were intended for, not a carnal offspring, but those who God would continue to own as his covenant people and church; even those who would walk in the steps of Abraham's faith, Gentiles as well as Jews.

Romans 4:11 Explained

§. 10. All that remains to be done before I draw this discourse to an end is to consider how far the mutual relationship of the promises made to Abraham may guide us toward a right understanding of how circumcision became a seal of the righteousness of faith to Abraham. The apostle affirms this in Romans 4:11. In opening that text, the grand objection against that notion of the covenant of circumcision which I have insisted on, will be effectively disposed of. To this end, I will first set down the text and give you a brief exposition of it. Then I will show you in what way it was verified and offer something for the strengthening and proving of the sense given.

The words of the text are, "And he received the sign of circumcision, a seal of the righteousness of faith which he had being yet uncircumcised; that he might be the father of all them that believe, though they be not circumcised, that righteousness may be imputed to them also."

In these verses the apostle is discoursing concerning the time when Abraham's faith was imputed to him for righteousness. He proves from there the equal right of the uncircumcised Gentile (if a believer) with the circumcised Jew in the blessings of the gospel. This was by means of a spiritual relationship to Abraham, because his faith was reckoned to him for righteousness, not in circumcision, but in uncircumcision.

"And he received the sign of circumcision," that is, circumcision which was a sign. It is *genitivus speciei*,[8] as when we read the "city of Jerusalem" for "the city, Jerusalem" and the like. Some Greek copies read περιτομήν[9] here. This belongs to the general use, nature, and end of circumcision. It was a sign. But more than this, to Abraham it was also the following.

"A seal of the righteousness of the faith which he had being yet uncircumcised..." A seal is for confirmation and assurance. In this notion of a seal there may be some reference to that visible mark and character which remained in the flesh of the one who was circumcised. For we do not read that any other ordinance (not even baptism) is called this in Scripture. But in the New Testament the sealing of believers is attributed to the Holy Spirit.

"Of the righteousness of the faith which he had, being yet uncircumcised," that is, of his being righteous before God through believing. This faith was his and this righteousness was imputed to him (the relative[10] may agree with either antecedent) while he was

---

[8] [An old technical term in Latin and Greek grammar which is today called the genitive of explanation.]

[9] [The accusative case of the word "circumcision".]

[10] [A relative pronoun referring to or qualifying an antecedent or preceding word. Here the pronoun is "which" in the phrase, "the righteousness of the faith which he had" and the antecedents are "righteousness" and "faith".]

uncircumcised. There are some words supplied by the translators to fill up the sense in our English phrase, which the learned Dr. Lightfoot in his *Horae Hebraica* on 1 Corinthians 7:19[11] fills up by another supply that gives a somewhat different sense of the text. While I refer the reader to it as not unworthy of his consideration, I will here rest satisfied with that sense which our translation affords us.

"That he might be the father of all that believe" in uncircumcision. The sense is that he might be manifested to be[12] the father of all believing Gentiles, though they are not circumcised since they are also a part of that spiritual seed promised to him in uncircumcision.

"That righteousness might be imputed to them also." This should be taken as before to mean that it might be made manifest and confirmed that righteousness is and will be imputed to them also (see verses 23 and 24).

Circumcision a Seal to Abraham's Faith

§. 11. Having given this brief explanation of the terms used in the text, the next thing to be asked is where are its contents verified. That is to say, how or in what respect was circumcision a seal of the righteousness of the faith which Abraham had being yet uncircumcised?

For the answer to this inquiry, observe the following.

1. In the prologue to this covenant of circumcision (Genesis 17) God expressly renewed and confirmed to Abraham the great promise of the covenant of grace concerning the justifying of the Gentiles by faith in Christ. This blessing they would receive in the relationship of children to Abraham, and so he would become the father of many nations. The covenant of circumcision was added to the former transactions in which God had confirmed his covenant in Christ with Abraham. So the use of circumcision to Abraham was not limited to that covenant of peculiarity to which it immediately belonged, but necessarily reached further and

---

[11] [This is a reference to John Lightfoot's commentaries on the New Testament. Lightfoot, 1602-1675, was a member of the Westminster Assembly, later Bishop of Durham, and the preeminent scholar of his day in the biblical languages. His commentaries, written in Latin and published between 1658 and 1674, sought to shed light on the text from Hebrew sources. For an English translation see John Lightfoot, *A Commentary on the New Testament from the Talmud and Hebraica*, Vol. 4, (Grand Rapids: Baker Book House, 1979), 212-215.]

[12] [Coxe parenthetically adds here: "things are in Scripture oftentimes said 'to be' when they are by any solemn act declared or confirmed."]

included a confirmation of all the preceding transactions and the promises given in them. This is especially true of what was repeated immediately before its institution. The promises of God to Abraham, though of a different nature, did not interfere with each other, but the latter still implied a confirmation and ratification of the former. This covenant therefore, did not supplant but rather confirmed the truth of the gospel preached earlier to Abraham. It was not added to disannul the promise but to serve its ends. Therefore circumcision did not only seal to Abraham the promises of typical blessings now given, but it also was a seal of the righteousness of the faith which he had being yet uncircumcised, that he might be the father of all that believe in uncircumcision.

2. This is also true, though more indirectly, for the following reason.

Abraham's faith, as we have seen before, was much involved in the promise of Isaac's birth and the separation of his seed from other nations to bring the Messiah into being. He knew well that the covenant of circumcision was made with him in pursuance of the great promises given earlier. So the seal of this covenant became to him a seal of the righteousness of the faith which he had before and confirmed him in his paternal relationship to believers in all nations, which was an honor conferred on him earlier. It is the discovery of the subservience of circumcision, as received by Abraham, to the great end and design of the covenant of grace (which was confirmed to Abraham before he was circumcised) that the apostle particularly aims to explain in this place. And he proves that the covenant of circumcision is so far from excluding the Gentiles from inheriting the blessing of Abraham by faith, that it was to him an assurance and seal of the promise of so great a privilege to them as well as of his own justification through faith while uncircumcised.

In addition, the covenant of circumcision was not complete enough in itself to bring the church to the perfection intended in the eternal counsels of God's sovereign grace. It was not capable of making anything perfect by itself and had to be established as typical and subservient to the covenant of grace in a temporary dispensation that would usher in and then give place to the gospel in the fullness of time. Regarding this arrangement of the covenant now made, the sign by which it was confirmed became ultimately and in its typical respect, a seal of the righteousness of the faith which Abraham had earlier.

The Conclusion of the Treatise

§. 12. It is not difficult to conceive that circumcision might have a different reference according to the differing circumstances and capacity of its subjects. Indeed, that it had this in another instance has already been proved. It was a seal of the inheritance of Canaan to the children of Israel and ensured that promise to them and their seed. But it gave their bond-servants no such right or claim. Even so, it was to Abraham a seal of the righteousness of the faith which he had. But this arose from the peculiar and extraordinary circumstances and capacity that he was in. For it is not possible to conceive that circumcision should be a seal of the righteousness of the faith which he had while uncircumcised (that he might be the father of all that believe in uncircumcision) to one that never had faith, either before or after his circumcision, nor ever had or should have the relationship of a father to all believers as Abraham had.

Now that the apostle speaks here of circumcision with respect to the peculiar circumstances and capacity of Abraham who received it, is evident from the scope of his discourse in the context. The argument he makes there proves that circumcision could not give to anyone an interest in the grace that justifies a sinner before God. Nor could the lack of it hinder anyone from obtaining that interest in the way and on the terms of the gospel. For even Abraham himself did not obtain it by his carnal prerogative but was justified before he was circumcised. The whole stress of his argument lies on the supposition of Abraham's being a believer and justified by his faith before he received circumcision. Remove this and his discourse proves nothing that he intends. And so he infers that Abraham received circumcision so that it was to him a seal not simply of the righteousness of faith or of the new covenant, but of the righteousness of the faith which he had being yet uncircumcised.

It was also a seal of his paternal relationship to all believers though they were not circumcised; for it follows, "that he might be the father of all them that believe." It is equally absurd to say that circumcision was a seal to all its subjects of the righteousness of faith which they had while uncircumcised, as it is to affirm that it was the seal of a paternal relationship to all believers to every one that received it. Both of these must necessarily be resolved into the peculiar circumstances of Abraham, the particular relationship he had in the covenants made with him, and the order of their disposition and not into the nature of circumcision considered simply and in itself.

Moreover, it is notable that immediately after, in continuing his discourse in Romans 4, the apostle refers circumcision to the law in contradistinction from the gospel. For when he has told us that the circumcised Jew could not obtain the blessing of a spiritual relationship to Abraham by virtue of his circumcision, unless he walked in the steps of Abraham's faith which he had while uncircumcised, verse 12, he assigns this as the reason of it in the 13th verse. For the promise that he should be the heir of the world was not to Abraham or to his seed through the law, but through the righteousness of faith. And I cannot see how the conclusion which the apostle makes concerning the inefficacy of circumcision is enforced by this reason, if circumcision immediately and in its own nature had not belonged to the law but to the righteousness of faith or covenant of grace, as an ordinary seal of it.

The interpretation made of this text is further strengthened by comparing other places in the New Testament where we find that circumcision is styled an unsupportable yoke (Acts 5:10) and is said to lay men under an obligation to keep the whole law (Galatians 5:3). The complete dispensation of grace in the gospel according to the new covenant is constantly insisted on as that which renders it utterly useless to the gospel church and manifests the inconsistency of retaining its practice with the liberty of their present state.

For instance, see the epistle to the Galatians 5:13. There the apostle tells them if he still preached circumcision, then the offence of the cross was ceased and he might have lived free from the persecutions he now suffered from the unbelieving Jews. It was the apostles preaching Christ, in which they asserted the shaking and removing of that old covenant to which circumcision belonged and by which the Jews held the right of their peculiar privileges[13] that was the ground of the controversy between them and of their unreasonable opposition to him. For if the controversy had been about the mode of administering the same covenant, and the change only of an external rite by bringing baptism into the place of circumcision to serve for the same use and end now as that had done before, the heat of their contests might soon have been allayed. This is especially the case when we consider that the latter is far less painful and dangerous than the former. But he will certainly find himself engaged in a very difficult task who will seriously endeavor to reconcile the apostles' discourses of circumcision with such a notion of it.

---

[13] [Coxe parenthetically adds here: "though now in truth, the continuance of those could no longer have been a real privilege to them."]

Circumcision was an ordinance of the old covenant and pertained to the law and therefore directly bound its subjects to a legal obedience. But baptism is an ordinance of the gospel and (besides other excellent and most comfortable uses) directly obliges its subjects to gospel obedience. Therefore it is in this respect opposed to, rather than substituted in the place of, circumcision.

Certainly it is safer to interpret one text according to the general current of Scripture and in full harmony with it, than to force such a sense on many texts (which they will in no way admit) to bring them into compliance to a notion with which our minds are prepossessed. It is plain that the notion I have insisted on fully agrees with other places where circumcision is discussed according to its immediate and direct use in the old covenant. For there can be no contradiction in ascribing a different and seemingly opposite use and end to the same thing, if it be done in a different respect. What circumcision was directly and in its immediate use is one thing; what it was as subordinate to a better covenant and promise that had precedence to it, is another. It is easy to conceive that it might be that to the father of the faithful in its extraordinary institution, what it could not be to the children of the flesh or carnal seed in its ordinary use.

To conclude: if circumcision and baptism have the same use and are seals of the same covenant, I can hardly imagine how the application of both to the same subjects should at any time be proper. Yet we find those that were circumcised in their infancy were also baptized on the profession of faith and repentance even before circumcision was abrogated. Yes, according to the opinion that has been argued against, the Jews that believed before Christ suffered were at the same time under a command both of circumcising and baptizing their infant seed. But if the principles that this discourse is built upon are well proved by Scripture, as I take them to be, there must be allowed a vast disparity between circumcision and baptism. The old covenant is not the new; nor that which is abolished, the same with that which remains. Until these become one, baptism and circumcision will never be found so far one that the law for applying the latter should be a sufficient warrant for the administration of the former to infants.

We have now passed through the covenant transactions of God with Abraham. After these we find no significant alteration in the state of the church by any new transactions until the law was given on Mount Sinai. Therefore, I will here put an end to my present discourse because it was intended to address only the covenants that God made with men before the law.

PART II

John Owen

A Brief Life of John Owen

Derived from Samuel Palmer's
The Nonconformist's Memorial[1]

John Owen was a descendant of Welsh royalty through his father, Henry Owen, a strict puritan and minister at Stadham, Oxfordshire. It was there that John, Henry's second son, was born in 1616.

As a young man, he was so proficient at learning that he was admitted to Oxford University at about twelve years of age. He then pursued his studies with such diligence that for several years he allowed himself only four hours of sleep each night. His whole aim and ambition was, as he afterwards confessed with shame and sorrow, to rise to some eminence in church or state.

At this time Archbishop William Laud imposed several superstitious rites on the University. But Owen had received so much light that his conscience could not submit to them for God had made such an impression on his heart that he was inspired with warm zeal for the purity of his worship and reformation in the church. This change of judgment now revealed itself so that his friends renounced him as being infected with Puritanism, and he became so obnoxious to the Laudian party that he was forced to leave the college. About this time he struggled with many perplexing thoughts about his spiritual state. These combined with his outward troubles to throw him into a period of spiritual darkness lasting three months, and it was nearly five years before he attained a settled peace.

When the English Civil War began, he took up Parliament's cause. But his Royalist uncle who had supported him at college, so vehemently resented this decision that he immediately turned against him and pledged his estate to another heir. He then lived as a private chaplain in the home of a gentleman, who though a Royalist, treated him with great civility. Nevertheless, when this gentleman entered the service of the

---

[1]Samuel Palmer, *The Nonconformist's Memorial; Being An Account of the Lives, Sufferings, and Printed Works of the Two Thousand Ministers Ejected from the Church of England, chiefly by the Act of Uniformity, Aug. 24, 1666. Originally Written by Edmund Calamy, D.D.* (London: J. Cundee, 1802), 1:198-208; supplemented by some material from David Bogue and James Bennett, *History of the Dissenters from the Revolution in 1688, to the Year 1808* (London:1809), 2:225-238.

King's army, Owen was forced to seek another means of support. Coming to London as a complete stranger and burdened with profound spiritual struggles, he entered the Aldermanbury Church one Lord's Day in order to hear Edmund Calamy preach. When the expected preacher did not appear, an unknown country minister (whose identity Owen was never able to find) ascended the pulpit and preached on Matthew 8:26, "Why are ye fearful, o ye of little faith?" This sermon removed his doubts and laid the foundation of that spiritual peace and comfort which he enjoyed as long as he lived. His bodily health now fully restored, he wrote his book called *A Display of Arminianism* that brought notice to this previously unknown young theologian.

Parliament's *Committee for Ejecting Scandalous Ministers* (a group charged with the removal of ministers who did not fulfill their responsibilities) was so impressed with this book that they offered him the pastoral position in Fordham, Essex. He filled this role for eighteen months with much blessing and appreciation in both the parish and the surrounding countryside. When the report of his predecessor's death reached the patron who held the living (a man with little regard for Owen), another man was appointed and Owen was thrust from his place. When the people of Coggeshall, Essex, about five miles away heard this, they invited him to their village and the Earl of Warwick, their patron, readily presented him with the living. Here he preached to a more thoughtful and larger (seldom less than 2000) congregation with great success. While at Coggeshall, his study in the Scripture convinced him to abandon Presbyterian principles and adopt those of the Congregational/Independents, and as a result he formed a church on the congregational plan that flourished for many years after his death.

His talents could not be hidden and he was called to preach before Parliament on April 29, 1646, taking Acts 16:2 as his text. On several other special occasions, particularly the day after the death of Charles I, Owen was called to be the preacher. His text on that day was Jeremiah 15:19-20, and his sermon deserves to be recorded as a perpetual monument to his integrity, modesty and wisdom. Soon after, Oliver Cromwell approached him saying, "Sir, you are the person I must be acquainted with," beginning an intimate friendship that lasted until his death. He informed Owen of his intended expedition to Ireland and insisted that he preside over the college at Dublin. With great reluctance and after much deliberation, he complied and stayed about a year and a half, preaching and overseeing the affairs of the college. He then returned to Coggeshall but was soon called to preach at Whitehall.

In September, 1650, Cromwell required him to go with him into Scotland, and since Owen was reluctant to go, he procured an order of Parliament. He stayed in Edinburgh about six months and once more returned to his people at Coggeshall with whom he hoped to spend the remainder of his days. But the House of Commons soon called him to the deanery of Christ Church, Oxford, which he accepted with the consent of his church. In the following year (when he was also made D. D.) he was chosen Vice-chancellor of the university, an office he held about five years. He managed this honor with singular prudence. He took care to restrain the malicious, to encourage the pious, and to advance men of learning and diligence. Under his administration the whole university was put into good order and furnished with a number of excellent scholars and persons of distinguished piety. He demonstrated great moderation toward both Presbyterians and Episcopalians; to the former he gave several vacant livings at his disposal, and the latter he was willing to accommodate. A large congregation of them met regularly near his residence to observe worship according to the suppressed liturgy of the Church of England, and he never gave them the least disturbance even though he was often urged to do so. He was hospitable in his house, generous in his favors, and charitable to the poor, especially to poor scholars. Some of these he took into his own family and maintained at his own charge, giving them an academic education. He still redeemed time for his studies, preaching every other Lord's Day at St. Mary's, and often at Stadham and other adjacent places, and writing some excellent books including his work on the perseverance of the saints. In 1657, Dr. Conant was elected Vice-chancellor of the University and Owen said farewell to them and returned to private life at Stadham, where he possessed a good estate and lived peacefully.

He remained there until after the Restoration of Charles II. But when persecution grew hot he was obliged to move from place to place and at length came to London where he preached as he had opportunity and continued writing. His *Animadversions* on a popish book called *Fiat Lux* recommended him to the esteem of Lord Chancellor Hyde, who assured him that "he had deserved the best of any English Protestant of late years, and that the church was bound to own and advance him." At the same time he offered him preferment if he would accept it, but expressed his surprise that so learned a man should embrace the novel opinion of

Independency. The Doctor offered to prove that it was practiced for several hundred years after Christ against any bishop his lordship should appoint to argue in response. Yet despite all the good service the Doctor had done to the Church of England, he was persecuted from place to place and once very narrowly escaped being seized by some troopers at Oxford. They came in pursuit of him to the house where he was but rode off on being told by the mistress that he was gone early that morning, which she really thought had been the case. For several years he thought of going to New England, where he was invited in 1663 to govern Harvard College and pastor the First Church of Boston, but he was stopped by particular orders from the king. He was afterwards invited to be professor of divinity in the United Provinces (The Netherlands), but he felt such a love for his own country that he could not leave it as long as there was any opportunity of being useful in it.

When Charles II provided an indulgence to tolerate the dissenters, Owen was tireless in preaching and set up a lecture attended by eminent persons. The writings which he still continued to produce drew upon him the admiration and respect of several persons of high rank and honor. When he was at Tunbridge, the Duke of York sent for him and several times discoursed with him concerning the dissenters. After his return to London he was sent for by King Charles himself, who spoke with him for two hours, assuring him of his favor and respect, telling him that he might have access to him whenever he would like. At the same time he assured the Doctor that he was for liberty of conscience and was sensible of the wrong that had been done to the dissenters. As a testimony of this he gave him 1000 guineas to distribute among those who had suffered the most.

His great worth earned him the esteem of many strangers who came to him from foreign places, and many foreign theologians, having read his Latin works, learned English for the benefit of the rest. His correspondence with scholars abroad was great and several traveled into England to see and converse with him. His many labors brought upon him frequent infirmities by which he was greatly taken away from his public service, though not rendered useless, for he was continually writing whenever he was able to sit up. At length he retired to Kensington. On one occasion when he was coming from there to London, two informers seized his carriage but he was discharged by the intervention of Sir Edmund Godfrey, a justice of the peace, who happened to come by at that moment. The Doctor afterwards moved to a house of his own at Ealing, where he spent his last days on earth. There he was taken up with thoughts of the other world as one who was drawing near it, and this produced his *Meditations on the Glory of Christ*, in which he breathed out the devotion of a soul continually growing in a heavenly frame of mind.

He wrote, "I am going to him whom my soul has loved, or rather who has loved me with an everlasting love, which is the whole ground of all my consolation. The passage is very irksome and wearisome, through strong pains of various sorts, which are all issues in an intermitting fever. All things were provided to carry me to London today, according to the advice of my physicians; but we are all disappointed by my utter disability to undertake the journey. I am leaving the ship of the church in a storm, but whilst the great Pilot is in it, the loss of a poor under rower will be inconsiderable. Live and pray, and hope, and wait patiently, and do not despond: the promise stands invincible, that he will never leave us nor forsake us." He died on St. Bartholomew's Day, August 24, 1683, aged 67.

His character may be briefly summed up as follows: as to his person, his stature was tall; his countenance grave, majestic, and handsome; his deportment, genteel; his mental abilities, incomparable; his temper, pleasant and courteous; his common discourse, moderately amusing. He was a great master of his passions, especially of anger, and possessed great serenity of mind, neither elated with honor or wealth, nor depressed with difficulties. He exercised great moderation in his judgment and was of a charitable spirit, willing to think the best of all men as far as he could, not confining Christianity to a party. He was a friend of peace and a diligent promoter of it among Christians. In regard to learning, he was one of the brightest ornaments of the University of Oxford. Even Anthony Wood, no friend of Puritans, wrote that "he was a person well skilled in the languages, Rabbinical learning, and Jewish rites; that he had a great command of his English pen, and was one of the fairest and most refined writers that appeared against the Church of England." His Christian temper in managing controversy was indeed admirable. He was well acquainted with men and things, and would shrewdly guess a man's temper and designs at a first meeting. His labors as a minister of the gospel were incredible. He was an excellent preacher, having good elocution, graceful and affectionate. He could, on all occasions, without any premeditation, express himself pertinently on any subject. Yet his sermons were well studied and digested, though he generally used no notes in the pulpit. His piety and devotion were eminent, and his experimental knowledge of spiritual things very great. In all relations he behaved himself like a great Christian.

His knowledge of ecclesiastical history and polemical theology was vast and profound, so that when the ancient heresies were revived under the modern names of Arminianism and Socinianism, he readily overcame them. The acumen with which he detected the most specious error, and the force with which he crushed the most formidable teachers of it, were only surpassed by the accuracy with which he stated the most profound truths of the Scriptures, and the sanctity with which he directed every truth to the purification of the heart and the regulation of the life. In his exposition of Psalm 130 he developed the wise and benevolent purpose of God in the mental conflicts he had endured, and proved himself qualified to guide the steps of the returning sinner to the God of pardon. His treatises on the mortification of sin in believers, on spiritual mindedness, and on the glory of Christ, prove him equally fitted to guide the Christian in his more advanced stages, and to show him how to finish his course with joy in order to obtain an abundant entrance into Christ's everlasting kingdom. But his grand work is his exposition of the epistle to the Hebrews. To this the studies of his life were more or less directed. And though this epistle may be safely pronounced the most difficult of all the didactic books of Scripture, no part of the sacred writings has received so perfect an exposition in the English or perhaps in any other language.

It ought to be mentioned to Owen's honor, that he seems to have been one of the first to entertain the idea of the right of private judgment and toleration. He was honest and zealous enough to maintain these in his writings when the times were the least encouraging. He not only published two *Pleas* for indulgence and toleration in 1677 when the Dissenters were suffering persecution under Charles II, but took the same side much earlier, pleading against intolerance in an Essay about the beginning of 1647 when the Parliament had arrived at its full power.

Dr. Owen was buried at Bunhill Fields in London with uncommon respect. His tombstone is in Latin, but translated into English reads:

John Owen, D. D.

Born in the county of Oxford: the son of an eminent divine, but more eminent himself, and justly to be ranked among the most illustrious of the age. Furnished with the aids of polite and solid learning, in a very uncommon degree, he led them all, in a well-ordered train, to the service of his great study, Christian divinity, controversial, practical, and casuistical. In each of these, he excelled others, and was ever equal to himself. In the one branch of this most sacred science, he, with powers more than Herculean, seized and vanquished the envenomed monsters, of Arminian, Socinian, and Popish errors. In the other, first experiencing in his own breast, according to the unerring rule of Scripture, the sacred energy of the Holy Spirit, he taught the whole economy of that divine influence. Rejecting lower objects, he constantly cherished and largely experienced that blissful communion with God which he so admirably described. Though a pilgrim on earth, he was next to a spirit in heaven. In Experimental Divinity, all who could have the blessings of his counsels found him as an oracle. He was a scribe every way accomplished for the kingdom of heaven. To many in private dwellings, from the pulpit to more, and from the press to all, who were aiming at the heavenly prize, he shone a pure lamp of gospel doctrine. Thus brightly shining he was gradually consumed, not unobserved by himself and his afflicted friends, till his holy soul, longing for the fuller fruition of its God, quitted the ruins of a body depressed by constant infirmities, emaciated by frequent diseases, but chiefly worn out by severe labors, and so no further suitable for the service of God: a fabric, till thus reduced, most comely and majestic. He left the world on a day, rendered dreadful to the church by the powers of the world, but blissful to himself by the plaudit of his God, the 24th of August 1683, aged 67.

An Exposition
Of
Hebrews 8:6-13

Wherein,
The nature and differences between the Old and New
Covenants is discovered.

By John Owen

Editor's Introduction

The same observations by the Editor of Coxe's piece apply here. Although Owen's piece had the singular advantage of being a copy of the edition by William H. Goold (published by Johnstone & Hunter in 1854-1855 and reprinted by Banner of Truth in 1991), the English language has changed since 1855. Owen's style is particularly difficult for the novice, and even those who have been privileged of reading Owen at length would agree that he is not an easy author to follow. Therefore, we have revised Owen's material using the following grammatical and stylistic guidelines.

1. We have updated spelling and word usage. Archaic words are modernized according to definitions from the Oxford English Dictionary. Some technical theological terms are retained.
2. Grammar and style has been slightly modernized.
3. Only the Latin has been italicized. Owen usually translates the Hebrew, Greek, and Latin used in his exposition. Therefore we have kept these ancient languages in the body of the Commentary, only moving the larger Greek and Latin quotes of the text to a footnote. Amy E. Chifici, M.A. Latin, translated the longer Latin quotes. A few Latin and Greek words and phrases are translated in footnotes.
4. The original footnotes that appear in the Banner of Truth edition are all included. The editor's footnotes are placed in square brackets ([…]).
5. An effort has been made to retain word and paragraph divisions. Most of Owen's numbered outline has been retained; this will help in comparing this edition with the Banner edition. However, words in a sentence are sometimes rearranged for better clarity.
6. Titles and headings have been provided. There are no headings or subheadings in the Banner edition. It is hoped that these artificial divisions will be helpful. The divisions have somewhat altered the original section numbering.
7. The intent has been to make Owen easier to read, however those with the desire and those who are not novices in reading the Puritans will certainly profit much by reading the Banner edition which is readily available.

Francisco Orozco
Iglesia Bautista Betel
Cd. Cuauhtémoc Chihuahua México

Chapter One

Exposition of Verse 6

The Difference Between the Two Covenants

But now he has obtained a more excellent ministry, by how much also he is the mediator of a better covenant, which was established on better promises.[1]

There is no material difference in any translators, ancient or modern, in the rendering of these words; their significance in particular will be given in the exposition.

In this verse begins the second part of the chapter, concerning the difference between the two covenants, the old and the new, with the pre-eminence of the latter above the former, and of the ministry of Christ above the high priests on that account. The whole church-state of the Jews, with all the ordinances and worship of it, and the privileges annexed to it, depended wholly on the covenant that God made with them at Sinai. But the introduction of this new priesthood of which the apostle is discoursing, did necessarily abolish that covenant, and put an end to all sacred ministrations that belonged to it. And this could not well be offered to them without the supply of another covenant, which should excel the former in privileges and advantages. For it was granted among them that it was the design of God to carry on the church to a perfect state, as has been declared on chap. 7; to that end he would not lead it backward, nor deprive it of any thing it had enjoyed, without provision of what was better in its room. This, therefore, the apostle here undertakes to declare. And he does it after his usual manner, from such principles and testimonies as were admitted among them.

Two things to this purpose he proves by express testimonies out of the prophet Jeremiah:

---

[1] Νυνὶ δὲ διαφορωτέρας τέτευχε λειτουργίας, ὅσῳ καὶ κρείττονός ἐστι διαθήκης μεσίτης, ἥτις ἐπὶ κρείττοσιν ἐπαγγελίαις νενομοθέτηται.

Exposition.- Turner remarks that νυνὶ, *now*, is not here so much a mark of time, as a formula to introduce with earnestness something which has close, and may have even logical, connection with what precedes. See also for this use of the term, ch. xi.16, 1 Cor. xv.20, xii.18, 20; in which passages it does not refer to time, but implies strong conviction grounded upon preceding arguments.- Ed. [Banner of Truth Edition.]

1. That besides the covenant made with their fathers in Sinai, God had promised to make another covenant with the church, in his appointed time and season.

2. That this other promised covenant should be of another nature than the former, and much more excellent, as to spiritual advantages, to them who were taken into it.

From both these, fully proved, the apostle infers the necessity of the abrogation of that first covenant in which they trusted and to which they adhered, when the appointed time was come. And on this he takes occasion to declare the nature of the two covenants in various instances, and in which the differences between them did consist. This is the substance of the remainder of this chapter.

This verse is a transition from one subject to another; namely, from the excellence of the priesthood of Christ above that of the law, to the excellence of the new covenant above the old. And in this also the apostle skillfully comprises and confirms his last argument, of the pre-eminency of Christ, his priesthood and ministry, above those of the law. And this he does from the nature and excellence of that covenant of which he was the mediator in the discharge of his office.

There are two parts of the words: First, An assertion of the excellence of the ministry of Christ. And this he expresses by way of comparison; "He has obtained a more excellent ministry:" and after he declares the degree of that comparison; "By how much also." Secondly, He annexes the proof of this assertion; in that he is "the mediator of a better covenant, established on better" or "more excellent promises".

An Assertion of the Excellence of the Ministry of Christ

In the first of these there occur these five things: 1. The note of its introduction; "But now": 2. What is ascribed in the assertion to the Lord Christ; and that is a "ministry": 3. How he came by that ministry; "He has obtained it": 4. The quality of this ministry; it is "better" or "more excellent" than the other: 5. The measure and degree of this excellence; "By how much also." All which must be spoken to, for the opening of the words.

The Introduction of the Assertion

The introduction of the assertion is by the particles νυνὶ δέ, "but now." Νῦν, "now," is a note of time, of the present time. But there are instances where these adverbial particles, thus conjoined, do not seem to denote any time or season, but are merely adversative, Rom. 7:17; 1 Cor. 5:11; 7:14. But even in those places there seems a respect to time also; and therefore I know not why it should be here excluded. As, therefore, there is an opposition intended to the old covenant, and the Levitical priesthood; so the season is intimated of the introduction of the new covenant, and the better ministry by which it was accompanied; '"now," at this time, which is the season that God has appointed for the introduction of the new covenant and ministry.' To the same purpose the apostle expresses himself, treating of the same subject, Rom. 3:26: "To declare ἐν τῷ νῦν καιρῷ, "at this instant season," now the gospel is preached, "his righteousness".

First Practical Observation

God, in his infinite wisdom, gives proper times and seasons to all his dispensations to and towards the church. So the accomplishment of these things was in "the fullness of times," Eph. 1:10; that is, when all things rendered it seasonable and suitable to the condition of the church, and for the manifestation of his own glory. He hastens all his works of grace in their own appointed time, Isa. 60:22. And our duty it is to leave the ordering of all the concerns of the church, in the accomplishment of promises, to God in his own time, Acts 1:7.

What is Ascribed to Christ in the Assertion

That which is ascribed to the Lord Christ is λειτουργία, a "ministry." The priests of old had a ministry; they ministered at the altar, as in the foregoing verse. And the Lord Christ was "a minister" also; so the apostle had said before, he was λειτουργὸς τῶν ἁγίων, verse 2, "a minister of the holy things." To that end he had a "liturgy," a "ministry," a service, committed to him. And two things are included in this:

(1.) That it was an office of ministry that the Lord Christ undertook. He is not called a minister with respect to one particular act of ministration; so are we said to "minister to the necessity of the saints," which yet denotes no office in them that do so. But he had a standing office committed to him, as the word imports. In that sense also he is called διάκονος, a "minister" in office, Rom. 15:8.

(2.) Subordination to God is included in this. With respect to the church his office is supreme, accompanied with sovereign power and authority; he is "Lord over his own house." But he holds his office in subordination to God, being "faithful to him that appointed him." So the angels are said to minister to God, Dan. 7:10; that is, to do all things according to his will, and at his command. So the Lord Christ had a ministry.

Second Practical Observation

And we may observe that the whole office of Christ was designed to the accomplishment of the will and dispensation of the grace of God. For these ends was his ministry committed to him. We can never sufficiently admire the love and grace of our Lord Jesus Christ, in undertaking this office for us. The greatness and glory of the duties which he performed in the discharge of it, with the benefits we receive by that means, are unspeakable, being the immediate cause of all grace and glory. Yet we are not absolutely to rest in them, but to ascend by faith to the eternal spring of them. This is the grace, the love, the mercy of God, all acted in a way of sovereign power. These are everywhere in the Scripture represented as the original spring of all grace, and the ultimate object of our faith, with respect to the benefits which we receive by the mediation of Christ. His office was committed to him of God, even the Father; and his will did he do in the discharge of it.

Third Practical Observation

Yet also, the condescension of the Son of God to undertake the office of the ministry on our behalf is unspeakable, and for ever to be admired. Especially will it appear so to be, when we consider who it was who undertook it, what it cost him, what he did and underwent in the pursuance and discharge of it, as it is all expressed, Phil. 2:6-8. Not only what he continues to do in heaven at the right hand of God belongs to this ministry, but all that he suffered also on the earth. His ministry, in the undertaking of it, was not a dignity, a promotion, a revenue, Matt. 20:28. It is true, it is issued in glory, but not until he had undergone all the evils that human nature is capable of undergoing. And we ought to undergo any thing cheerfully for him who underwent this ministry for us.

Fourth Practical Observation

The Lord Christ, by undertaking this office of the ministry, has consecrated and made honorable that office to all that are rightly called to it, and do rightly discharge it. It is true, his ministry and ours are not of the same kind and nature; but they agree in this, that they are both a ministry to God in the holy things of his worship. And considering that Christ himself was God's minister, we have far greater reason to tremble in ourselves on an apprehension of our own insufficiency for such an office than to be discouraged with all the hardships and contests we meet in the world on the account of it.

How Christ Came into this Ministry

The general way in accordance with which our Lord Christ came to this ministry is expressed: Τέτευχε, "He obtained it." Τυγχάνω is either "*sorte contingo*," "to have a lot or portion;" or to have any thing happen to a man, as it were by accident; or "*assequor*," "*obtineo*," to "attain" or "obtain" any thing which before we had not. But the apostle intends not to express in this word the especial call of Christ, or the particular way in accordance with which he came to his ministry, but only in general that he had it, and was possessed of it, in the appointed season, which before he had not. The way in accordance with which he entered on the whole office and work of his mediation he expresses by κεκληρονόμηκε, Heb. 1:4, he had it by "inheritance;" that is, by free grant and perpetual donation, made to him as the Son. See the exposition on that place.[2]

There were two things that concurred to his obtaining this ministry: (1.) The eternal purpose and counsel of God designing him to that; an act of the divine will accompanied with infinite wisdom, love, and power. (2.) The actual call of God, to which many things did concur, especially his unction with the Spirit above measure for the holy discharge of his whole office. Thus did he obtain this ministry, and not by any legal constitution, succession, or carnal rite, as did the priests of old.

Fifth Practical Observation

And we may see that the exaltation of the human nature of Christ into the office of this glorious ministry depended solely on the sovereign wisdom, grace and love of God. When the human nature of Christ was united to the divine, it

---

[2] [Owen's complete Exposition of Hebrews, as well as his Miscellaneous Works, is available from Banner of Truth. The reader is often directed to his previous writings.]

became, in the person of the Son of God, fit and capable to make satisfaction for the sins of the church, and to procure righteousness and life eternal for all that believe. But it did not merit that union, nor could do so. For as it was utterly impossible that any created nature, by any act of its own, should merit the hypostatical union[3], so it was granted to the human nature of Christ antecedently to any act of its own in way of obedience to God; for it was united to the person of the Son by virtue of that union. To that end, antecedently to it, it could merit nothing. Therefore its whole exaltation and the ministry that was discharged in that respect depended solely on the sovereign wisdom and pleasure of God. And in this election and designation of the human nature of Christ to grace and glory, we may see the pattern and example of our own. For if it was not on the consideration or foresight of the obedience of the human nature of Christ that it was predestinated and chosen to the grace of the hypostatical union, with the ministry and glory which depended for that reason, but of the mere sovereign grace of God; how much less could a foresight of any thing in us be the cause why God should choose us in him before the foundation of the world to grace and glory!

The Quality of this Ministry

The quality of this ministry, thus obtained, as to a comparative excellence, is also expressed: Διαφορωτέρας, "More excellent." The word is used only in this epistle in this sense, chap. 1:4, and in this place. The original word denotes only a difference from other things; but in the comparative degree, as here, it signifies a difference with a preference, or a comparative excellence. The ministry of the Levitical priests, was good and useful in its time and season; this of our Lord Jesus Christ so differed from it as to be better than it, and more excellent; πολλῷ ἄμεινον.[4]

The Preeminence of this Ministry

And, there is added to this the degree of this pre-eminence, so far as it is intended in this place and the present argument, in the word ὅσῳ, "by how much." "So much

---

[3] ["...the union of the two natures in the person of Christ. ...the assumption of a human nature by the preexistent eternal person of the Son of God in such a way as to draw the human nature into the oneness of the divine person without division or separation of natures..., but also without change or confusion of natures...; yet also in such a way that the attributes of both natures belong to the divine-human person and contribute conjointly to the work of salvation" (Muller, *Dictionary*, 316).]

[4] [Greatly the best.]

more excellent, by how much." The excellence of his ministry above that of the Levitical priests, bears proportion with the excellence of the covenant of which he was the mediator above the old covenant in which they administered; of which afterwards.

So we have explained the apostle's assertion, concerning the excellence of the ministry of Christ. And by this means he closes his discourse which he had so long engaged in, about the pre-eminence of Christ in his office above the high priests of old. And indeed, this being the very hinge on what his whole controversy with the Jews did depend, he could not give it too much evidence, or too full a confirmation.

Sixth Practical Observation

And as to what concerns ourselves at present, we are taught by that means, that it is our duty and our safety to consent universally and absolutely in the ministry of Jesus Christ. That which he was so designed to, in the infinite wisdom and grace of God; that which he was so furnished for the discharge of by the communication of the Spirit to him in all fullness; that which all other priesthoods were removed to make way for, must needs be sufficient and effectual for all the ends to which it is designed. It may be said, "This is that which all men, all who are called Christians do fully consent in the ministry of Jesus Christ." But if it be so, why do we hear the bleating of another sort of cattle? What mean those other priests, and reiterated sacrifices, which make up the worship of the church of Rome? If they rest in the ministry of Christ, why do they appoint one of their own to do the same things that he has done, namely, to offer sacrifice to God?

The Proof of the Assertion

Secondly, the proof of this assertion lies in the latter part of these words; "By how much he is the mediator of a better covenant, established on better promises." The words are so disposed, that some think the apostle intends now to prove the excellence of the covenant from the excellence of his ministry in that respect. But the other sense is more suited to the compass of the place, and the nature of the argument with which the apostle presses the Hebrews. For on supposition that there was indeed another, and that a "better covenant," to be introduced and established, than that which the Levitical priests served in, which they could not deny, it plainly follows, that he on whose ministry the dispensation of that covenant did depend must of necessity be "more excellent" in that ministry than they who appertained to that covenant which was to be abolished. However, it may be granted that these things do mutually testify to and illustrate one another. Such as the priest is, such is the covenant; such as the covenant is in dignity, such is the priest also.

In the words there are three things observable: 1. What is in general ascribed to Christ, declaring the nature of his ministry; he was a "mediator": 2. The determination of his mediatory office to the new covenant; "of a better covenant": 3. The proof or demonstration of the nature of this covenant as to its excellence, it was "established on better promises".

The Office of Mediator

His office is that of a mediator, μεσίτης, one that interposed between God and man, for the doing of all those things in accordance with which a covenant might be established between them, and made effectual. Schlichtingius[5] on the place gives this description of a mediator: "Being a mediator is nothing other than being the negotiator of God and the go-between in settling (his) covenant with men; through whom, in other words, both, God might disclose his (own) will to men, and they, in turn, might agree with God, and having been reconciled with him, they might experience peace for the future.."[6] And Grotius speaks much to the same purpose.

But this description of a mediator is wholly applicable to Moses, and suited to his office in giving of the law. See Exod. 20:19; Deut. 5:27, 28. What is said by them does indeed immediately belong to the mediatory office of Christ, but it is not confined to that; yea, it is exclusive of the principal parts of his mediation. And although there is nothing in it but what belongs to the prophetical office of Christ, which the apostle here does not principally intend, it is most improperly applied as a description of such a mediator as he does intend. And therefore, when he comes

---

[5] [Jonas Schlichtingius, a Socinian author. His works form one volume in the "Bibliotheca Fratrum Polonorum".]

[6] *Mediatorem foederis esse nihil aliud est, quam Dei esse interpretem, et internuntium in foedere cum hominibus pangendo; per quem scilicet et Deus voluntatem suam hominibus declaret, et illi vicissim divinae voluntatis notitiâ instructi ad Deum accedant, cumque eo reconciliati, pacem in posterum colant.*

afterwards to declare in particular what belonged to such a mediator of the covenant as he designed, he expressly places it in his "death for the redemption of transgressions," chap. 9:15; affirming that "for that cause he was a mediator." But of this there is nothing at all in the description they give us of this office. But this the apostle does in his writings elsewhere, 1 Tim. 2:5, 6, "There is one God, and one mediator between God and men, the man Christ Jesus; who gave himself a ransom for all." The principal part of his mediation consisted in the "giving himself a ransom," or a price of redemption for the whole church. On that ground this description of a mediator of the new testament is pretended only, to exclude his satisfaction, or his offering himself to God in his death and blood-shedding, with the atonement made by that means.

The Lord Christ, then, in his ministry, is called μεσίτης, the "mediator" of the covenant, in the same sense as he is called ἔγγυος, the "surety;" of which see the exposition on chap. 7:22. He is, in the new covenant, the mediator, the surety, the priest, the sacrifice, all in his own person. The ignorance and lack of a due consideration of this are the great evidence of the degeneracy of Christian religion.

Although this is the first general notion of the office of Christ, that which comprises the whole ministry committed to him, and contains in itself the especial offices of king, priest, and prophet, in accordance with which he discharges his mediation, some things must be mentioned that are declarative of its nature and use. And we may to this purpose observe,

(1.) That to the office of a mediator it is required that there be different persons concerned in the covenant, and that, by their own wills; as it must be in every compact,[7] of whatsoever sort. So says our apostle, "A mediator is not of one, but God is one," Gal. 3:20; that is, if there were none but God concerned in this matter, as it is in an absolute promise or sovereign precept, there would be no need of, no place for a mediator, such a mediator as Christ is. To that end our consent in and to the covenant is required in the very notion of a mediator.

(2.) That the persons entering into covenant be in such a state and condition as that it is no way convenient or morally possible that they should treat immediately with each other as to the ends of the covenant; for if they are so, a mediator to go between is altogether needless. So was it in the original covenant with Adam, which had no mediator. But in the

---

[7] [Covenant.]

giving of the law, which was to be a covenant between God and the people, they found themselves utterly insufficient for an immediate treaty with God, and therefore desired that they might have an internuncio to go between God and them, to bring his proposals, and carry back their consent, Deut. 5:23-27. And this is the voice of all men really convinced of the holiness of God, and of their own condition. Such is the state between God and sinners. The law and the curse of it did so interpose between them, that they could not enter into any immediate treaty with God, Ps. 5:3-5. This made a mediator necessary, that the new covenant might be established; of which we will speak afterwards.

(3.) That he who is this mediator be accepted, trusted, and rested in on either sides of the parties mutually entering into covenant. An absolute trust must be reposed in him, so that each party may be everlastingly obliged in what he undertakes on their behalf; and such as admit not of his terms, can have no benefit by, no interest in the covenant. So was it with the Lord Christ in this matter. On the part of God, he reposed the whole trust of all the concernments of the covenant in him, and absolutely rested in that respect. "Behold," says he of him, "my servant, whom I uphold; mine elect, in whom my soul delights," or is "well pleased," ἐν ᾧ εὐδόκησα, Isa. 42:1; Matt. 3:17. When he undertook this office, and said, "Lo, I come to do your will, O God," the soul of God rested in him, Exod. 23:21; John 5:20-22. And to him he gives an account at last of his discharge of this thing, John 17:4. And on our part, unless we resign ourselves absolutely to a universal trust in him and reliance on him, and unless we accept of all the terms of the covenant as by him proposed, and engage to stand to all that he has undertaken on our behalf, we can have neither share nor interest in this matter.

(4.) A mediator must be a middle person between both parties entering into covenant; and if they be of different natures, a perfect, complete mediator ought to partake of each of their natures in the same person. The necessity of this, and the glorious wisdom of God in this, I have elsewhere at large demonstrated, and will not therefore here again insist on it.

(5.) A mediator must be one who voluntarily and of his own accord undertakes the work of mediation. This is required of every one who will effectually mediate between any persons at variance, to bring them to an agreement on equal terms. So it was required that the will and consent of Christ should concur in his reception of this office; and that they did so, himself expressly testifies, Heb. 10:5-10. It is true, he was designed and appointed by the Father to this office; by reason of this he is called his "servant," and constantly witnesses of himself, that he came to do the will and commandment of him that sent him: but he had that to do in the discharge of this office, which could not, according to any rule of divine righteousness, be imposed on him without his own voluntary consent. And this was the ground of the eternal compact that was between the Father and the Son, with respect to his mediation; which I have elsewhere explained. And the testification[8] of his own will, grace, and love, in the reception of this office, is a principal motive to that faith and trust which the church places in him, as the mediator between God and them. On this his voluntary undertaking does the soul of God rest in him, and he reposes the whole trust in him of accomplishing his will and pleasure, or the design of his love and grace in this covenant, Isa. 53:10-12. And the faith of the church, on what salvation does depend, must have love to his person inseparably accompanying it. Love to Christ is no less necessary to salvation, than faith in him. And as faith is resolved into the sovereign wisdom and grace of God in sending him, and his own ability to save to the uttermost those that come to God by him; so love arises from the consideration of his own love and grace in his voluntary undertaking of this office, and the discharge of it.

(6.) In this voluntary undertaking to be a mediator, two things were required:

[1.] That he should remove and take out of the way whatever kept the covenanters at a distance, or was a cause of enmity between them. For it is supposed that such an enmity there was, or there had been no need of a mediator. Therefore in the covenant made with Adam, there having been no variance between God and man, nor any distance but what necessarily ensued from the distinct natures of the Creator and a creature, there was no mediator. But the design of this covenant was to make reconciliation and peace. On this therefore depended the necessity of satisfaction, redemption, and the making of atonement by sacrifice. For man having sinned and apostatized from the rule of God, making himself by that means subject to his wrath, according to the eternal rule of righteousness, and in particular to the curse of the law, there could be no new peace and agreement made with God unless due satisfaction were made for these things. For although God was willing, in infinite love,

---

[8] [The action or an act of testifying; the testimony borne.]

grace, and mercy, to enter into a new covenant with fallen man, yet would he not do it to the prejudice of his righteousness, the dishonor of his rule, and the contempt of his law. To that end none could undertake to be a mediator of this covenant, but he that was able to satisfy the justice of God, glorify his government, and fulfill the law. And this could be done by none but him, concerning whom it might be said that "God purchased his church with his own blood".

[2.] That he should procure and purchase, in a way suited to the glory of God, the actual communication of all the good things prepared and proposed in this covenant; that is, grace and glory, with all that belong to them, for them and on their behalf whose surety he was. And this is the foundation of the merit of Christ, and of the grant of all good things to us for his sake.

(7.) It is required of this mediator, as such, that he give assurance to and undertake for the parties mutually concerned, as to the accomplishment of the terms of the covenant, undertaking on each hand for them:

[1.] On the part of God towards men, that they will have peace and acceptance with him, in the sure accomplishment of all the promises of the covenant. This he does only declaratively, in the doctrine of the gospel, and in the institution of the ordinances of evangelical worship. For he was not a surety for God, nor did God need any, having confirmed his promise with an oath, swearing by himself, because he had no greater to swear by.

[2.] On our part, he undertakes to God for our acceptance of the terms of the covenant, and our accomplishment of them, by his enabling us to that.

Seventh Practical Observation

These things, among others, were necessary to a full and complete mediator of the new covenant, such as Christ was. And the provision of this mediator between God and man was an outworking of infinite wisdom and grace; yea, it was the greatest and most glorious external accomplishment of them that ever they did produce, or ever will do in this world. The creation of all things at first out of nothing was a glorious work of infinite wisdom and power; but when the glory of that design was eclipsed by the entrance of sin, this provision of a mediator, one in accordance with which all things were restored and retrieved to a condition of bringing more glory to God, and securing for ever the blessed estate of them whose mediator he is, is accompanied with more evidences of the divine excellencies than that was. See Eph. 1:10.

Further Description of His Mediatory Office

Two things are added in the description of this mediator: (1.) That he was a mediator of a covenant; (2.) That this covenant was better than another which respect is had to, of which he was not the mediator:

(1.) He was the mediator of a "covenant." And two things are supposed in this:

[1.] That there was a covenant made or prepared between God and man; that is, it was so far made, as that God who made it had prepared the terms of it in a sovereign act of wisdom and grace. The preparation of the covenant, consisting in the will and purpose of God graciously to bestow on all men the good things which are contained in it, all things belonging to grace and glory, as also to make way for the obedience which he required in this, is supposed to the constitution of this covenant.

[2.] That there was need of a mediator, that this covenant might be effectual to its proper ends, of the glory of God and the obedience of mankind, with their reward. This was not necessary from the nature of a covenant in general; for a covenant may be made and entered into between different parties without any mediator, merely on the equity of the terms of it. Nor was it so from the nature of a covenant between God and man, as man was at first created of God; for the first covenant between them was immediate, without the interposition of a mediator. But it became necessary from the state and condition of them with whom this covenant was made, and the especial nature of this covenant. This the apostle declares, Rom. 8:3, "For what the law could not do, in that it was weak through the flesh, God sending his own Son in the likeness of sinful flesh, and for sin, condemned sin in the flesh." The law was the moral instrument or rule of the covenant that was made immediately between God and man: but it could not continue to be so after the entrance of sin; that is, so as that God might be glorified by that means, in the obedience and reward of men. To that end he "sent his Son in the likeness of sinful flesh;" that is, provided a mediator for a new covenant. The persons with whom this covenant was to be made being all of them sinners, and apostatized from God, it became not the holiness or righteousness of God to treat immediately with them any more. Nor would it have answered his holy ends so to have done. For if when they were in a condition of uprightness and integrity, they kept not the terms of that covenant which was made immediately with them, without a mediator, although they were holy, just, good, and equal; how much less could any such thing be expected from them in their depraved condition of apostasy from God and enmity against him! It therefore became not the wisdom of God to enter anew into covenant with mankind, without security that the terms of the covenant should be accepted, and the grace of it made effectual. This we could not give; yea, we gave all evidences possible to the contrary, in that "GOD saw that every imagination of the thoughts of man's heart was only evil continually," Gen. 6:5. To that end it was necessary there should be a mediator, to be the surety of this covenant. Again, the covenant itself was so prepared, in the counsel, wisdom, and grace of God, as that the principal, yea, indeed, all the benefits of it, were to depend on what was to be done by a mediator, and could not otherwise be accomplished. Such were satisfaction for sin, and the bringing in of everlasting righteousness; which are the foundation of this covenant.

(2.) To proceed with the text; this covenant, of which the Lord Christ is the mediator, is said to be a "better covenant." To that end it is supposed that there was another covenant, of which the Lord Christ was not the mediator. And in the following verses there are two covenants, a first and a latter, an old and a new, compared together. We must therefore consider what was that other covenant, of which this is said to be better; for on the definition of it depends the right understanding of the whole ensuing discourse of the apostle. And because this is a subject wrapped up in much obscurity, and attended with many difficulties, it will be necessary that we use the best of our diligence, both in the investigation of the truth and in the declaration of it, so as that it may be distinctly understood. And I will first explain the text, and then speak of the difficulties which arise from it:

[1.] There was an original covenant made with Adam, and all mankind in him. The rule of obedience and reward that was between God and him was not expressly called a covenant, but it contained the express nature of a covenant; for it was the agreement of God and man concerning obedience and disobedience, rewards and punishments. Where there is a law concerning these things, and an agreement on it by all parties concerned, there is a formal covenant. To that end it may be considered two ways:

1st. As it was a law only; so it proceeded from, and was a consequent of the nature of God and man, with their mutual relation to one another. God being considered as the creator, governor, and benefactor of man; and man as an intellectual creature, capable of moral obedience; this law was necessary, and is eternally indispensable.

2dly. As it was a covenant; and this depended on the will and pleasure of God. I will not dispute whether God might have given a law to men that should have had nothing in it of a covenant, properly so called; as is the law of creation to all other creatures, which has no rewards nor punishments annexed to it. Yet God calls this a covenant also, inasmuch as it is an accomplishment of his purpose, his unalterable will and pleasure, Jer. 33:20-21. But that this law of our obedience should be a formal, complete covenant, there were moreover some things required on the part of God, and some also on the part of man. Two things were required on the part of God to complete this covenant, or he did so complete it by two things:

(1st.) By annexing to it promises and threats of reward and punishment; the first of grace, the other of justice. (2dly.) The expression of these promises and threats in external signs; the first in the tree of life, the latter in that of the knowledge of good and evil. By these God did establish the original law of creation as a covenant, gave it the nature of a covenant. On the part of man, it was required that he accept of this law as the rule of the covenant which God made with him. And this he did in two ways:

[1st.] By the innate principles of light and obedience co-created with his nature. By these he absolutely and universally assented to the law, as proposed with promises and threats, as holy, just, good, what was fit for God to require, what was equal and good to himself.

[2dly.] By his acceptance of the commands concerning the tree of life, and that of the knowledge of good and evil, as the signs and pledges of this covenant. So it was established as a covenant between God and man, without the interposition of any mediator.

This is the covenant of works, absolutely the old, or first covenant that God made with men. But this is not the covenant here intended; for,

1st. The covenant called afterwards "the first," was διαθήκη, a "testament." So it is here called. It was such a covenant as was a testament also. Now there can be no testament, but there must be death for the confirmation of it, Heb. 9:16. But in the making of the covenant with Adam, there was not the death of any thing, from what cause it might be called a testament. But there was the death of beasts in sacrifice in the confirmation of the covenant at Sinai, as we will see afterwards. And it must be observed, that although I use the name of a "covenant," as we have rendered the word διαθήκη, because the true signification of that word will be more properly presented to us in another place, yet I do not understand by that means a covenant properly and strictly so called, but such a one as has the nature of a testament also, in which the good things of him that makes it are bequeathed to them for whom they are designed. Neither the word used constantly by the apostle in this argument, nor the design of his discourse, will admit of any other covenant to be understood in this place. Although, therefore, the first covenant made with Adam was in no sense a testament also, it cannot be here intended.

2dly. That first covenant made with Adam, had, as to any benefit to be expected from it, with respect to acceptance with God, life, and salvation, ceased long before, even at the entrance of sin. It was not abolished or abrogated by any act of God, as a law, but only was made weak and insufficient to its first end, as a covenant. God had provided a way for the salvation of sinners, declared in the first promise. When this is actually embraced, that first covenant ceases towards them, as to its curse, in all its concerns as a covenant, and obligation to sinless obedience as the condition of life; because both of them are answered by the mediator of the new covenant. But as to all those who receive not the grace tendered in the promise, it does remain in full force and efficacy, not as a covenant, but as a law; and that because neither the obedience it requires nor the curse which it threatens is answered. Therefore, if any man believes not, "the wrath of God abides on him." For its commands and curse depending on the necessary relation between God and man, with the righteousness of God as the supreme governor of mankind, they must be answered and fulfilled. To that end it was never abrogated formally. But as all unbelievers are still obliged by it, and to it must stand or fall, so it is perfectly fulfilled in all believers, not in their own persons, but in the person of their surety. "God sending his own Son in the likeness of sinful flesh, and for sin, condemned sin in the flesh, that the righteousness of the law might be fulfilled in us," Rom. 8:3, 4. But as a covenant, obliging to personal, perfect, sinless obedience, as the condition of life, to be performed by them, so it ceased to be, long before the introduction of the new covenant which the apostle speaks of, that was promised "in the latter days." But the other covenant here spoken of was not removed or taken away, until this new covenant was actually established.

3dly. The church of Israel was never absolutely under the power of that covenant as a covenant of life; for from the days of Abraham, the promise was given to them and their seed. And the apostle proves that no law could afterwards be given, or covenant made, that should disannul that promise, Gal. 3:17. But had they been brought under the old covenant of works, it would have disannulled the promise; for that covenant and the promise are diametrically opposite. And moreover, if they were under that covenant, they were all under the curse, and so perished eternally: which is openly false; for it is testified of them that they pleased God by faith, and so were saved. But it is evident that the covenant intended was a covenant in which the church of Israel walked with God, until such time as this better covenant was solemnly introduced. This is plainly declared in the following context, especially in the close of the chapter, where, speaking of this former covenant, he says, it was "become old," and so "ready to disappear." To that end it is not the covenant of works made with Adam that is intended, when this other is said to be a "better covenant".

[2.] There were other federal transactions between God and the church before the giving of the law on Mount Sinai. Two of them there were into which all the rest were resolved:

1st. The first promise given to our first parents immediately after the Fall. This had in it the nature of a covenant, grounded on a promise of grace, and requiring obedience in all that received the promise.

2dly. The promise given and sworn to Abraham, which is expressly called the covenant of God, and had the whole nature of a covenant in it, with a solemn outward seal appointed for its confirmation and establishment. Of this we have treated at large on the sixth chapter.

Neither of these, nor any transaction between God and man that may be reduced to them as explanations, renovations, or confirmations of them, is the "first covenant" here intended. For they are not only consistent with the "new covenant" so as that there was no necessity to remove them out of the way for its introduction, but did indeed contain in them the essence and nature of it, and so were confirmed in that respect. Therefore the Lord Christ himself is said to be "a minister of the circumcision for the truth of God, to confirm the promises made to the fathers," Rom. 15:8. As he was the mediator of the new covenant, he was so far from taking off from, or abolishing those promises, that it belonged to his office to confirm them. To that end,

[3.] The other covenant or testament here supposed, to which that of which the Lord Christ was the mediator is preferred, is none other but that which God made with the people of Israel on Mount Sinai. So it is expressly affirmed, verse 9: "The covenant which I made with your fathers in the day when I took them by the hand to lead them out of the land of Egypt." This was that covenant which had all the institutions of worship annexed to it, Heb. 9:1-3; of which we must treat afterwards more at large. With respect to this it is that the Lord Christ is said to be the "mediator of a better covenant"; that is, of another distinct from it, and more excellent.

It remains to the exposition of the words that we inquire what this covenant was of which our Lord Christ was the mediator, and what is here affirmed of it.

Of What Covenant Was Christ the Mediator?

This can be no other in general but that which we call "the covenant of grace." And it is so called in opposition to that of "works" which was made with us in Adam; for these two, grace and works, do divide the ways of our relation to God, being diametrically opposite, and every way inconsistent, Rom. 11:6. Of this covenant the Lord Christ was the mediator from the foundation of the world, namely, from the giving of the first promise, Revelation 13:8; for it was given on his interposition, and all the benefits of it depended on his future actual mediation.

Difficulties of the Context Answered

But here arises the first difficulty of the context and that in two things; for,

[1.] If this covenant of grace was made from the beginning, and if the Lord Christ was the mediator of it from the first, then where is the privilege of the gospel-state in opposition to the law, by virtue of this covenant, seeing that under the law also the Lord Christ was the mediator of that covenant, which was from the beginning?

[2.] If it be the covenant of grace which is intended, and that be opposed to the covenant of works made with Adam, then the other covenant must be that covenant of works so made with Adam, which we have before disproved.

The answer to this is in the word here used by the apostle concerning this new covenant: νενομοθέτηται, of which meaning we must inquire into. I say, therefore, that the apostle does not here consider the new covenant absolutely, and as it was virtually administered from the foundation of the world, in the way of a promise; for as such it was consistent with that covenant made with the people in Sinai. And the apostle proves expressly, that the renovation of it made to Abraham was no way abrogated by the giving of the law, Gal. 3:17. There was no interruption of its administration made by the introduction of the law. But he treats of such an establishment of the new covenant as by which the old covenant made at Sinai was absolutely inconsistent, and which was therefore to be removed out of the way. To that end he considers it here as it was actually completed, so as to bring along with it all the ordinances of worship which are proper to it, the dispensation of the Spirit in them, and all the spiritual privileges by which they are accompanied. It is now so brought in as to become the entire rule of the church's faith, obedience, and worship, in all things.

This is the meaning of the word νενομοθέτηται: "established", say we; but it is, "reduced into a fixed state of a law or ordinance." All the obedience required in it, all the worship appointed by it, all the privileges exhibited in it, and the grace administered with them, are all given for a statute, law, and ordinance to the church. That which before lay hid in promises, in many things obscure, the principal mysteries of it being a secret hid in God himself, was now brought to light; and that covenant which had invisibly, in the way of a promise, put forth its efficacy under types and shadows, was now solemnly sealed, ratified, and confirmed, in the death and resurrection of Christ. It had before the confirmation of a promise, which is an oath; it had now the confirmation of a covenant, which is blood. That which before had no visible, outward worship, proper and peculiar to it, is now made the only rule and instrument of worship to the whole church, nothing being to be admitted in that respect but what belongs to it, and is appointed by it. The apostle intends this by νενομοθέτηται, the "legal establishment" of the new covenant, with all the ordinances of its worship. On this the other covenant was disannulled and removed; and not only the covenant itself, but all that system of sacred worship in accordance with which it was administered. This was not done by the making of the covenant at first; yea, all this was added into the covenant as given out in a promise, and was consistent with that. When the new covenant was given out only in the way of a promise, it did not introduce worship and privileges expressive of it. To that end it was consistent with a form of worship, rites and ceremonies, and those composed into a yoke of bondage which belonged not to it. And as these, being added after its giving, did not overthrow its nature as a promise, so they were inconsistent with it when it was completed as a covenant; for then all the worship of the church was to proceed from it, and to be conformed to it. Then it was established. Therefore it follows, in answer to the second difficulty, that as a promise, it was opposed to the covenant of works; as a covenant, it was opposed to that of Sinai. This legalizing or authoritative establishment of the new covenant, and the worship to that belonging, accomplished this alteration.

The Proof of the Nature of this Covenant as to its Excellence

In the last place, the apostle tells us on what this establishment was made; and that is ἐπι κρείττοσιν ἐπαγγελίαις, "on better promises." For the better understanding of this we must consider somewhat of the original and use of divine promises in our relation to God. And we may observe,

Every Covenant Established on Promises

That every covenant between God and man must be founded on and resolved into "promises." Therefore essentially a promise and a covenant are all one; and God calls an absolute promise, founded on an absolute decree, his covenant, Gen. 9:11. And his purpose for the continuation of the course of nature to the end of the world, he calls his covenant with day and night, Jer. 33:20. The being and essence of a divine covenant lies in the promise. Therefore they are called "the covenants of promise", Eph. 2:12; such as are founded on and consist in promises. And it is necessary that so it should be. For,

[1.] The nature of God who makes these covenants requires that it should be so. It becomes his greatness and goodness, in all his voluntary transactions with his creatures, to propose that to them in which their advantage, their happiness and blessedness, does consist. We inquire not how God may deal with his creatures as such; what he may absolutely require of them, on the account of his own being, his absolute essential excellencies, with their universal dependence on him. Who can express or limit the sovereignty of God over his creatures? All the disputes about it are fond. We have no measures of what is infinite. May he not do with his own what he pleases? Are we not in his hands, as clay in the hands of the potter? And whether he make or mar a vessel, who will say to him, What are you doing? He gives no account of his matters. But on supposition that he will condescend to enter into covenant with his creatures, and to come to agreement with them according to the terms of it, it becomes his greatness and goodness to give them promises as the foundation of it, in which he proposes to them the things in which their blessedness and reward do consist. For, 1st. In this he proposes himself to them as the eternal spring and fountain of all power and goodness. Had he treated with us merely by a law, he had in that respect only revealed his sovereign authority and holiness; the one in giving of the law, the other in the nature of it. But in promises he reveals himself as the eternal spring of goodness and power; for the matter of all promises is somewhat that is good; and the communication of it depends on sovereign power. That God should so declare himself in his covenant was absolutely necessary to direct and encourage the obedience of the covenanters; and he did so accordingly, Gen. 15:1, 17:1, 2. 2dly. By this means he reserves the glory of the whole to himself. For although the terms of agreement which he proposes between himself and us be in their own nature "holy, just, and good," which sets forth his praise and glory, yet if there were not something on his part which has no antecedent respect to any goodness, obedience, or merit in us, we should have in which to glory in ourselves; which is inconsistent with the glory of God. But the matter of those promises in which the covenant is founded is free, undeserved, and without respect to any thing in us in accordance with which it may in any sense be procured. And so in the first covenant, which was given in a form of law, attended with a penal sanction, yet the foundation of it was in a promise of a free and undeserved reward, even of the eternal enjoyment of God: which no goodness or obedience in the creature could possibly merit the attainment of. So that if a man should by virtue of any covenant be justified by works, though he might have of which to glory before men, yet could he not glory before God, as the apostle declares, Rom. 4:2; and that because the reward proposed in the promise does infinitely exceed the obedience performed.

[2.] It was also necessary on our part that every divine covenant should be founded and established on promises; for there is no state in which we may be taken into covenant with God, but it is supposed we are not yet arrived at that perfection and blessedness of which our nature is capable, and which we cannot but desire. And therefore when we come to heaven, and the full enjoyment of God, there will be no use of any covenant any more, seeing we will be in eternal rest, in the enjoyment of all the blessedness of which our nature is capable, and will immutably adhere to God without any further expectation. But while we are in the way, we have still somewhat, yea principal parts of our blessedness, to desire, expect, and believe. So in the state of innocence, though it had all the perfection which a state of obedience according to a law was capable of, yet the blessedness of eternal rest, for which we were made, did not consist in that respect. Now, while it is thus with us, we cannot but desire and look out after that full and complete happiness, which our nature cannot come to rest without. This, therefore, renders it necessary that there should be a promise of it given as the foundation of the covenant; without which we should lack our principal encouragement to obedience. And much more must it be so in the state of sin and apostasy from God; for we are now not only most remote from our utmost happiness, but involved in a condition of misery, without a deliverance from which we cannot be in any way induced to give ourselves up to covenant obedience. To that end, unless we are prevented in the covenant with promises of deliverance from our present state, and the enjoyment of future blessedness, no covenant could be of use or advantage to us.

[3.] It is necessary from the nature of a covenant. For every covenant that is proposed to men, and accepted by them, requires somewhat to be performed on their part, otherwise it is no covenant; but where any thing is required of them that accept of the covenant, or to whom it is proposed, it does suppose that somewhat be promised on the behalf of them by whom the covenant is proposed, as the foundation of its acceptance, and the reason of the duties required in it.

All this appears most evidently in the covenant of grace, which is here said to be "established on promises"; and that on two accounts. For,

[4.] At the same time that much is required of us in the way of duty and obedience, we are told in the Scripture, and find it by experience, that of ourselves we can do nothing. To that end, unless the precept of the covenant is founded in a promise of giving grace and spiritual strength to us, in accordance with which we may be enabled to perform those duties, the covenant can be of no benefit or advantage to us. And the lack of this one consideration, that every covenant is founded in promises, and that the promises give life to the precepts of it, has perverted the minds of many to suppose ability in ourselves of yielding obedience to those precepts, without grace antecedently received to enable us to that; which overthrows the nature of the new covenant.

[5.] As was observed, we are all actually guilty of sin before this covenant was made with us. To that end unless there be a promise given of the pardon of sin, it is to no purpose to propose any new covenant terms to us. For "the wages of sin is death"; and we having sinned must die, whatever we do afterwards, unless our sins be pardoned. This, therefore, must be proposed to us as the foundation of the covenant, or it will be of no effect. And in this lies the great difference between the promises of the covenant of works and those of the covenant of grace. The first were only concerning things future; eternal life and blessedness on the accomplishment of perfect obedience. Promises of present mercy and pardon it stood in need of none, it was not capable of. Nor had it any promises of giving more grace or supplies of it; but man was wholly left to what he had at first received. Therefore the covenant was broken. But in the covenant of grace all things are founded in promises of present mercy, and continual supplies of grace, as well as of future blessedness. Therefore it comes to be "ordered in all things, and sure".

And this is the first thing that was to be declared, namely, that every divine covenant is established on promises.

The New Covenant is Established on Better Promises

These promises are said to be "better promises." The other covenant had its promises peculiar to it, with respect to which this is said to be "established on better promises." It was, indeed, principally represented under a system of precepts, and those almost innumerable; but it had its promises also, into the nature of which we will immediately inquire. With respect, therefore, to them is the new covenant, of which the Lord Christ is the mediator, said to be "established on better promises." That it should be founded in promises was necessary from its general nature as a covenant, and more necessary from its especial nature as a covenant of grace. That these promises are said to be "better promises" respects those of the old covenant. But this is so said as to include all other degrees of comparison. They are not only better than they, but they are positively good in themselves, and absolutely the best that God ever gave, or will give to the church. And what they are we must consider in our progress. And various things may be observed from these words.

Eighth Practical Observation

There is infinite grace in every divine covenant, inasmuch as it is established on promises. Infinite condescension it is in God that he will enter into covenant with dust and ashes, with poor worms of the earth. And in this lies the spring of all grace, from out of which all the streams of it do flow. And the first expression of it is in laying the foundation of it in some undeserved promises. And this was that which became the goodness and greatness of his nature, the means in accordance with which we are brought to adhere to him in faith, hope, trust, and obedience, until we come to the enjoyment of him; for that is the use of promises, to keep us in adherence to God, as the first original and spring of all goodness, and the ultimate satisfactory reward of our souls, 2 Cor. 7:1.

Ninth Practical Observation

The promises of the covenant of grace are better than those of any other covenant, as for many other reasons, so especially because the grace of them prevents any condition or qualification on our part. I do not say the covenant of grace is absolutely without conditions, if by conditions we intend the duties of obedience which God requires of us in and by virtue of that covenant; but this I say, the principal promises of it are not in the first place remunerative of our obedience in the covenant, but efficaciously assumptive of us into covenant, and establishing or confirming in the covenant. The covenant of works had its promises, but they were all remunerative, respecting an antecedent obedience in us; (so were all those which were peculiar to the covenant of Sinai). They were, indeed, also of grace, in that the reward did infinitely exceed the merit of our obedience; but yet they all supposed it, and the subject of them was formally reward only. In the covenant of grace it is not so; for several of the promises of it are the means of our being taken into covenant, of our entering into covenant with God. The first covenant absolutely was established on promises, in that when men were actually taken into it, they were encouraged to obedience by the promises of a future reward. But those promises, namely, of the pardon of sin and writing of the law in our hearts, on which the apostle expressly insists as the peculiar promises of this covenant, do take place and are effectual antecedently to our covenant obedience. For although faith be required in order of nature antecedently to our actual receiving of the pardon of sin, yet is that faith itself produced in us by the grace of the promise, and so its precedence to pardon respects only the order that God had appointed in the communication of the benefits of the covenant, and intends not that the pardon of sin is the reward of our faith.

A Discourse of Some Things in General

This entrance has the apostle made into his discourse of the two covenants, which he continues to the end of the chapter. But the whole is not without its difficulties. Many things in particular will occur to us in our progress, which may be considered in their proper places. In the meantime there are some things in general which may be here discoursed, by whose determination much light will be communicated to what does follow.

A Dispute Concerning Two Covenants

First, therefore, the apostle does evidently in this place dispute concerning two covenants, or two testaments, comparing the one with the other, and declaring the disannulling of the one by the introduction and establishment of the other. What are these two covenants in general we have declared, namely, that made with the church of Israel at Mount Sinai, and that made with us in the gospel; not as absolutely the covenant of grace, but as actually established in the death of Christ, with all the worship that belongs to it.

Here then arises a difference of no small importance, namely, whether these are indeed two distinct covenants, as to the essence and substance of them, or only different ways of the dispensation and administration of the same covenant. And the reason of the difficulty lies in this: We must grant one of these three things: 1. That either the covenant of grace was in force under the old testament; or, 2. That the church was saved without it, or any benefit by Jesus Christ, who is the mediator of it alone; or, 3. That they all perished everlastingly. And neither of the two latter can be admitted.

Some, indeed, in these latter days, have revived the old Pelagian imagination, that before the law men were saved by the conduct of natural light and reason; and under the law by the directive doctrines, precepts, and sacrifices of it, without any respect to the Lord Christ or his mediation in another covenant. But I will not here contend with them, as having elsewhere sufficiently refuted these imaginations. To that end I will take it here for granted, that no man was ever saved but by virtue of the new covenant, and the mediation of Christ in that respect.

Suppose, then, that this new covenant of grace was extant and effectual under the old testament, so as the church was saved by virtue of it, and the mediation of Christ in that respect, how could it be that there should at the same time be another covenant between God and them, of a different nature from this, accompanied with other promises, and other effects?

On this consideration it is said, that the two covenants mentioned, the new and the old, were not indeed two distinct covenants, as to their essence and substance, but only different administrations of the same covenant, called two covenants from some different outward solemnities and duties of worship attending of them. To clear this it must be observed,

1. That by the old covenant, the original covenant of works, made with Adam and all mankind in him, is not intended; for this is undoubtedly a covenant different in the essence and substance of it from the new.

2. By the new covenant, not the new covenant absolutely and originally, as given in the first promise, is intended; but in its complete gospel administration, when it was actually established by the death of Christ, as administered in and by the ordinances of the new testament. This, with the covenant of Sinai, would be, as most say, but different administrations of the same covenant.

But on the other hand, there is such express mention made, not only in this, but in various other places of the Scripture also, of two distinct covenants, or testaments, and such different natures, properties, and effects, ascribed to them, as seem to constitute two distinct covenants. This, therefore, we must inquire into; and will first declare what is agreed to by those who are sober in this matter, though they differ in their judgments about this question, whether two distinct covenants, or only a twofold administration of the same covenant, be intended. And indeed there is so much agreed on, as that what remains seems rather to be a difference about the expression of the same truth, than any real contradiction about the things themselves. For,

Four Agreements about the Two Administrations

1. It is agreed that the way of reconciliation with God, of justification and salvation, was always one and the same; and that from the giving of the first promise none was ever justified or saved but by the new covenant, and Jesus Christ, the mediator of it. The foolish imagination before mentioned, that men were saved before the giving of the law by following the guidance of the light of nature, and after the giving of the law by obedience to the directions of it, is rejected by all that are sober, as destructive of the Old Testament and the New.

2. That the writings of the Old Testament, namely, the Law, Psalms, and Prophets, do contain and declare the doctrine of justification and salvation by Christ. The church of old believed this, and walked with God in the faith of it. This is undeniably proved, in that the doctrine mentioned is frequently confirmed in the New Testament by testimonies taken out of the Old.

3. That by the covenant of Sinai, as properly so called, separated from its figurative relation to the covenant of grace, none was ever eternally saved.

4. That the use of all the institutions in accordance with which the old covenant was administered, was to represent and direct to Jesus Christ, and his mediation.

These things being granted, the only way of life and salvation by Jesus Christ, under the old testament and the new, is secured; which is the substance of the truth in which we are now concerned. On these grounds we may proceed with our inquiry.

The Judgment of Most Reformed Divines

The judgment of most Reformed divines is, that the church under the old testament had the same promise of Christ, the same interest in him by faith, remission of sins, reconciliation with God, justification and salvation by the same way and means, that believers have under the new. And although the essence and the substance of the covenant consist in these things, they are not to be said to be under another covenant, but only a different administration of it. But this was so different from that which is established in the gospel after the coming of Christ, that it has the appearance and name of another covenant. And the difference between these two administrations may be reduced to the ensuing heads.

Five Differences Between The Two Administrations

1. It consisted in the way and manner of the declaration of the mystery of the love and will of God in Christ; of the work of reconciliation and redemption, with our justification by faith. For in this the gospel, in which "life and immortality are brought to light," does in plainness, clearness, and evidence, much excel the administration and declaration of the same truths under the law. And the greatness of the privilege of the church in this is not easily expressed. For by this means "with open face we behold as in a glass the glory of the Lord," and "are changed into the same image," 2 Cor. 3:18. The man whose eyes the Lord Christ opened, Mark 8:23-25, represents these two states. When he first touched him, his eyes were opened, and he saw, but he saw nothing clearly; by reason of which, when he looked, he said, "I see men as trees, walking," verse 24: but on his second touch, he "saw every man clearly," verse 25. They had their sight under the old testament, and the object was proposed to them, but at a great distance, with such an interposition of mists, clouds, and shadows, as that they "saw men like trees, walking," nothing clearly and perfectly: but now under the gospel, the object, which is Christ, being brought near to us, and all clouds and shadows being departed, we do or may see all things clearly. When a traveler in his way on downs or hills is encompassed with a thick mist and fog, though he be in his way yet he is uncertain, and nothing is presented to him in its proper shape and distance; things near seem to be afar off, and things afar off to be near, and every thing has, though not a false, yet an uncertain appearance. Let the sun break forth and scatter the mists and fogs that are about him, and immediately every thing appears quite in another shape to him, so as indeed he is ready to think he is not where he was. His way is plain, he is certain of it and the entire region about lies evident under his eye; yet is there no alteration made but in the removal of the mists and clouds that interrupted his sight. So was it with them under the law. The types and shadows that they were enclosed in, and which were the only medium they had to view spiritual things in, represented them not to them clearly and in their proper shape. But they being now removed, by the rising of the Sun of righteousness with healing in his wings, in the dispensation of

the gospel, the whole mystery of God in Christ is clearly manifested to them that do believe. And the greatness of this privilege of the gospel above the law is inexpressible; of which, as I suppose, we must speak somewhat afterwards.

2. In the plentiful communication of grace to the community of the church; for now it is that we receive "grace for grace," or a plentiful effusion of it, by Jesus Christ. There was grace given in an eminent manner to many holy persons under the old testament, and all true believers had true, real, saving grace communicated to them; but the measures of grace in the true church under the new testament do exceed those of the community of the church under the old. And therefore, as God winked at some things under the old testament, as polygamy, and the like, which are expressly and severely interdicted under the new, nor are consistent with the present administrations of it; so are various duties, as those of self-denial, readiness to bear the cross, to forsake houses, lands, and habitations, more expressly enjoined to us than to them. And the obedience which God requires in any covenant, or administration of it, is proportional to the strength which the administration of that covenant does exhibit. And if those who profess the gospel do content themselves without any interest in this privilege of it, if they endeavor not for a share in that plentiful effusion of grace which does accompany its present administration, the gospel itself will be of no other use to them, but to increase and aggravate their condemnation.

3. In the manner of our access to God. In this much of all that is called religion does consist; for on this depends all our outward worship of God. And in this the advantages of the gospel-administration of the covenant above that of the law is in all things very eminent. Our access now to God is immediate, by Jesus Christ, with liberty and boldness, as we will afterwards declare. Those under the law were immediately conversant, in their whole worship, about outward, typical things, the tabernacle, the altar, the ark, the mercy-seat, and the like obscure representations of the presence of God. Besides, the manner of the making of the covenant with them at Mount Sinai filled them with fear, and brought them into bondage, so as they had comparatively a servile frame of spirit in all their holy worship.

4. In the way of worship required under each administration. For under that which was legal, it seemed good to God to appoint a great number of outward rites, ceremonies, and observances; and these, as they were dark in their signification, as also in their use and ends, so were

they, by reason of their nature, number, and the severe penalties under which they were enjoined, grievous and burdensome to be observed. But the way of worship under the gospel is spiritual, rational, and plainly subservient to the ends of the covenant itself; so as that the use, ends, benefits and advantages of it are evident to all.

5. In the extent of the dispensation of the grace of God; for this is greatly enlarged under the gospel. For under the old testament it was on the matter confined to the posterity of Abraham according to the flesh; but under the new testament it extends itself to all nations under heaven.

Various other things are usually added by our divines to the same purpose. See Calvin. Institut. lib. 2:cap. xi.; Martyr. Loc. Com. loc. 16, sect. 2; Bucan. loc. 22, etc.

The Lutheran Arguments

The Lutherans, on the other side, insist on two arguments to prove, that not a twofold administration of the same covenant, but that two covenants substantially distinct, are intended in this discourse of the apostle.

1. Because in the Scripture they are often so called, and compared with one another, and sometimes opposed to one another; the first and the last, the new and the old.

2. Because the covenant of grace in Christ is eternal, immutable, always the same, subject to no alteration, no change or abrogation; neither can these things be spoken of it with respect to any administration of it, as they are spoken of the old covenant.

Five Things Concerning This Matter

To state our thoughts aright in this matter, and to give what light we can to the truth, the things ensuing may be observed:

1. When we speak of the "old covenant," we intend not the covenant of works made with Adam, and his whole posterity in him; concerning which there is no difference or difficulty, whether it is a distinct covenant from the new or no.

2. When we speak of the "new covenant," we do not intend the covenant of grace absolutely, as though that were not before in being and efficacy, before the introduction of that which is promised in this place. For it was always the same, as to the substance of it, from the beginning.

It passed through the whole dispensation of times before the law, and under the law, of the same nature and efficacy, unalterable, "everlasting, ordered in all things, and sure." All who contend about these things, only except the Socinians, do grant that the covenant of grace, considered absolutely, that is the promise of grace in and by Jesus Christ, was the only way and means of salvation to the church, from the first entrance of sin. But for two reasons it is not expressly called a covenant, without respect to any other things, nor was it so under the old testament. When God renewed the promise of it to Abraham, he is said to make a covenant with him; and he did so, but it was with respect to other things, especially the proceeding of the promised Seed from his loins. But absolutely under the old testament it consisted only in a promise; and as such only is proposed in the Scripture, Acts 2:39; Heb. 6:14-16. The apostle indeed says, that the covenant was confirmed of God in Christ, before the giving of the law, Gal. 3:17. And so it was, not absolutely in itself, but in the promise and benefits of it. The νομοθεσία, or full legal establishment of it, by reason of which it became formally a covenant to the whole church, was future only, and a promise under the old testament; for it lacked two things to that:

(1.) It lacked its solemn confirmation and establishment, by the blood of the only sacrifice which belonged to it. Before this was done in the death of Christ, it had not the formal nature of a covenant or a testament, as our apostle proves, Heb. 9:15-23. For neither, as he shows in that place, would the law given at Sinai have been a covenant, had it not been confirmed with the blood of sacrifices. To that end the promise was not before a formal and solemn covenant.

(2.) This was lacking, that it was not the spring, rule, and measure of all the worship of the church. This does belong to every covenant, properly so called, that God makes with the church, which it be the entire rule of all the worship that God requires of it; which is that which they are to estipulate in their entrance into covenant with God. But so the covenant of grace was not under the old testament; for God did require of the church many duties of worship that did not belong to that. But now, under the new testament, this covenant, with its own seals and appointments, is the only rule and measure of all acceptable worship. To that end the new covenant promised in the Scripture, and here opposed to the old, is not the promise of grace, mercy, life, and salvation by Christ, absolutely considered, but as it had the formal nature of a covenant given to it, in its establishment by the death of Christ, the procuring cause of all its benefits, and the declaring of it to be the only rule of worship and obedience to the church. So that although by "the covenant of grace," we oftentimes understand no more but the way of life, grace, mercy, and salvation by Christ; yet by "the new covenant," we intend its actual establishment in the death of Christ, with that blessed way of worship which by it is settled in the church.

3. While the church enjoyed all the spiritual benefits of the promise, in which the substance of the covenant of grace was contained, before it was confirmed and made the sole rule of worship to the church, it was not inconsistent with the holiness and wisdom of God to bring it under any other covenant, or prescribe to it what forms of worship he pleased. It was not so, I say, on these three suppositions:

(1.) That this covenant did not disannul or make ineffectual the promise that was given before, but that that does still continue the only means of life and salvation. And that this was so, our apostle proves at large, Gal. 3:17-19.

(2.) That this other covenant, with all the worship contained in it or required by it, did not divert from, but direct and lead to, the future establishment of the promise in the solemnity of a covenant, by the ways mentioned. And that the covenant made in Sinai, with all its ordinances, did so, the apostle proves likewise in the place before mentioned, as also in this whole epistle.

(3.) That it be of present use and advantage to the church in its present condition. This the apostle acknowledges to be a great objection against the use and efficacy of the promise under the old testament, as to life and salvation; namely, "To what end then serves the giving of the law?" to which he answers, by showing the necessity and use of the law to the church in its then present condition, Gal. 3:17-19.

4. These things being observed, we may consider that the Scripture does plainly and expressly make mention of two testaments, or covenants, and distinguish between them in such a way, as what is spoken can hardly be accommodated to a twofold administration of the same covenant. The one is mentioned and described, Exod. 24:3-8, Deut. 5:2-5, namely, the covenant that God made with the people of Israel in Sinai; and which is commonly called "the covenant," where the people under the old testament are said to keep or break God's covenant; which for the most part is spoken with respect to that worship which was peculiar to that. The other is promised, Jer. 31:31-

34, 32:40; which is the new or gospel covenant, as before explained, mentioned Matt. 26:28; Mk. 14:24. And these two covenants, or testaments, are compared one with the other, and opposed one to another, 2 Cor. 3:6-9; Gal. 4:24-26; Heb. 7:22; 9:15-20.

These two we call "the old and the new testament." Only it must be observed, that in this argument, by the "old testament," we do not understand the books of the Old Testament, or the writings of Moses, the Psalms, and the Prophets, or the oracles of God committed then to the church, (I confess they are once so called, 2 Cor. 3:14, "The veil remains untaken away in the reading of the Old Testament," that is, the books of it; unless we should say, that the apostle intends only the reading of the things which concern the old testament in the Scripture;) for this old covenant, or testament, whatever it be, is abrogated and taken away, as the apostle expressly proves, but the word of God in the books of the Old Testament abides for ever. And those writings are called the Old Testament, or the books of the Old Testament, not as though they contained in them nothing but what belongs to the old covenant, for they contain the doctrine of the New Testament also; but they are so termed because they were committed to the church while the old covenant was in force, as the rule and law of its worship and obedience.

5. To that end we must grant two distinct covenants, rather than a twofold administration of the same covenant merely, to be intended. We must, I say, do so, provided always that the way of reconciliation and salvation was the same under both. But it will be said, and with great pretense of reason, for it is that which is the sole foundation they all build on who allow only a twofold administration of the same covenant, "That this being the principal end of a divine covenant, if the way of reconciliation and salvation be the same under both, then indeed are they for the substance of them but one." And I grant that this would inevitably follow, if it were so equally by virtue of them both. If reconciliation and salvation by Christ were to be obtained not only under the old covenant, but by virtue of it, then it must be the same for substance with the new. But this is not so; for no reconciliation with God nor salvation could be obtained by virtue of the old covenant, or the administration of it, as our apostle disputes at large, though all

believers were reconciled, justified, and saved, by virtue of the promise, while they were under the covenant.

Three Things Related to the First Covenant that Prove that It was not an Administration of the Covenant of Grace

As therefore I have showed in what sense the covenant of grace is called "the new covenant," in this distinction and opposition, so I will propose various things which relate to the nature of the first covenant, which manifest it to have been a distinct covenant, and not a mere administration of the covenant of grace.

First, it was not for the Life and Salvation of the Church

This covenant, called "the old covenant," was never intended to be of itself the absolute rule and law of life and salvation to the church, but was made with a particular design, and with respect to particular ends. This the apostle proves undeniably in this epistle, especially in the chapter foregoing, and those two that follow. Therefore it follows that it could abrogate or disannul nothing which God at any time before had given as a general rule to the church. For that which is particular cannot abrogate any thing that was general, and before it; as that which is general does abrogate all antecedent particulars, as the new covenant does abrogate the old. And this we must consider in both the instances belonging to this. For,

(1.) God had before given the covenant of works, or perfect obedience, to all mankind, in the law of creation. But this covenant at Sinai did not abrogate or disannul that covenant, nor in any way fulfill it. And the reason is, because it was never intended to come in the place or room of it, as a covenant, containing an entire rule of all the faith and obedience of the whole church. God did not intend in it to abrogate the covenant of works, and to substitute this in the place of it; yea, in various things it re-enforced, established, and confirmed that covenant. For,

[1.] It revived, declared, and expressed all the commands of that covenant in the Decalogue; for that is nothing but a divine summary of the law written in the heart of man at his creation. And in this the dreadful manner of its delivery or promulgation, with its writing in tables of stone, is also to be considered; for in them the nature of that first covenant, with its inexorableness as to perfect obedience, was represented. And because none could answer its demands, or comply with it in that respect, it was called "the ministration of death," causing fear and bondage, 2 Cor. 3:7.

[2.] It revived the sanction of the first covenant, in the curse or sentence of death which it denounced against all transgressors. Death was the penalty of the transgression of the first covenant: "In the day that you eat of it, you will die the death." And this sentence was revived and represented anew in the curse by which this covenant was ratified, "Cursed be he that confirms not all the words of this law to do them," Deut. 27:26; Gal. 3:10. For the design of God in it was to bind a sense of that curse on the consciences of men, until he came by whom it was taken away, as the apostle declares, Gal. 3:19.

[3.] It revived the promise of that covenant that of eternal life on perfect obedience. So the apostle tells us that Moses thus describes the righteousness of the law, "That the man which does those things will live by them," Rom. 10:5; as he does, Leviticus 18:5.

Now this is no other but the covenant of works revived. Nor had this covenant of Sinai any promise of eternal life annexed to it, as such, but only the promise inseparable from the covenant of works which it revived, saying, "Do this, and live."

Therefore it is, that when our apostle disputes against justification by the law, or by the works of the law, he does not intend the works peculiar to the covenant of Sinai, such as were the rites and ceremonies of the worship then instituted; but he intends also the works of the first covenant, which alone had the promise of life annexed to them.

And therefore it follows also, that it was not a new covenant of works established in the place of the old, for the absolute rule of faith and obedience to the whole church; for then would it have abrogated and taken away that covenant, and all the force of it, which it did not.

(2.) The other instance is in the promise. This also went before it; neither was it abrogated or disannulled by the introduction of this covenant. This promise was given to our first parents immediately after the entrance of sin, and was established as containing the only way and means of the salvation of sinners. Now, this promise could not be abrogated by the introduction of this covenant, and a new way of justification and salvation be by that means established. For the promise being given out in general for the whole church, as containing the way appointed by God for righteousness, life, and salvation, it could not be disannulled or changed, without a change and alteration in the counsels of Him "with whom is no variableness, neither shadow of turning." Much less could this be accomplished by a particular covenant, such as that was, when it was given as a general and eternal rule.

Second, It Did Not Disannul the Promise Made to Abraham

But although there was an especial promise given to Abraham, in the faith of which he became "the father of the faithful," he being their progenitor, it should seem that this covenant did wholly disannul or supersede that promise, and take off the church of his posterity from building on that foundation, and so fix them wholly on this new covenant now made with them. So says Moses, "The LORD made not this covenant with our fathers, but with us, who are all of us here alive this day," Deut. 5:3. God made not this covenant on Mount Sinai with Abraham, Isaac, and Jacob, but with the people then present, and their posterity, as he declares, Deut. 29:14, 15. This, therefore, should seem to take them off wholly from that promise made to Abraham, and so to disannul it. But that this it did not, nor could do, the apostle strictly proves, Gal. 3:17-22; yea, it did in various ways establish that promise, both as first given and as afterwards confirmed with the oath of God to Abraham, in two ways especially:

(1.) It declared the impossibility of obtaining reconciliation and peace with God any other way but by the promise. For representing the commands of the covenant of works, requiring perfect, sinless obedience, under the penalty of the curse, it convinced men that this was no way for sinners to seek for life and salvation by. And by this means it so urged the consciences of men, that they could have no rest or peace in themselves but what the promise would afford them, to which they saw a necessity of committing themselves.

(2.) By representing the ways and means of the accomplishment of the promise, and of that on what all the efficacy of it to the justification and salvation of sinners does depend. This was the death, blood-shedding, oblation, or sacrifice of Christ, the promised seed. This all its offerings and ordinances of worship directed to; as his incarnation, with the inhabitation of God in his human nature, was typed by the tabernacle and temple. To that end it was so far from disannulling the promise, or diverting the minds of the people of God from it, that by all means it established it and led to it.

Third, it had Other Benefits for the Church

But it will be said, as was before observed, "That if it did neither abrogate the first covenant of works, and come in the room of it, nor disannul the promise made to Abraham, then to what end did it serve, or what benefit did the church receive by that means?" I answer,

(1.) There has been, with respect to God's dealing with the church, οἰκονομία τῶν καιρῶν, a "certain dispensation" and disposition of times and seasons, reserved to the sovereign will and pleasure of God. Therefore from the beginning he revealed himself πολυτρόπως[9] and πολυμερῶς,[10] as seemed good to him, Heb. 1:1. And this dispensation of times had a πλήρωμα, a "fullness" assigned to it, in which all things, namely, that belong to the revelation and communication of God to the church, should come to their height, and have as it were the last hand given to them. This was in the sending of Christ, as the apostle declares, Eph. 1:10, "That in the dispensation of the fullness of times he might bring all to a head in Christ." Until this season came, God dealt variously with the church ἐν ποικίλῃ σοφίᾳ, "in manifold" or "various wisdom," according as he saw it needful and useful for it, in that season which it was to pass through, before the fullness of times came. Of this nature was his entrance into the covenant with the church at Sinai; the reasons of which we will immediately inquire into. In the meantime, if we had no other answer to this inquiry but only this, that in the order of the disposal or dispensation of the seasons of the church, before the fullness of times came, God in his manifold wisdom saw it necessary for the then present state of the church in that season, we may well consent in that respect. But,

(2.) The apostle acquaints us in general with the ends of this dispensation of God, Gal. 3:19-24: "To what end then serves the law? It was added because of transgressions, until the seed should come to whom the promise was made; and it was ordained by angels in the hand of a mediator. Now a mediator is not of one, but God is one. Is the law then against the promises of God? God forbid; for if there had been a law given which could have given life, verily righteousness should have been by the law. But the Scripture has concluded all under sin that the promise by faith of Jesus Christ might be given to them that believe. But before

---

[9] [In various times.]

[10] [In various ways.]

faith came, we were kept under the law, shut up to the faith which should afterwards be revealed. To that end the law was our schoolmaster to bring us to Christ, that we might be justified by faith." Much light might be given to the mind of the Holy Spirit in these words, and that in things not commonly discerned by expositors, if we should divert to the opening of them. I will at present only mark from them what is to our present purpose.

A Double Inquiry Concerning the Covenant of Sinai

There is a double inquiry made by the apostle with respect to the law, or the covenant of Sinai: [1.] To what end in general it served. [2.] Whether it was not contrary to the promise of God. To both these the apostle answers from the nature, office, and work of that covenant. For there were, as has been declared, two things in it: [1.] A revival and representation of the covenant of works, with its sanction and curse. [2.] A direction of the church to the accomplishment of the promise. From these two does the apostle frame his answer to the double inquiry laid down.

And to the first inquiry, "to what end it served," he answers, "It was added because of transgressions." The promise being given, there seems to have been no need of it, why then was it added to it at that season? "It was added because of transgressions." The fullness of time was not yet come, in which the promise was to be fulfilled, accomplished and established as the only covenant in which the church was to walk with God; or, "the seed" was not yet come, as the apostle here speaks, to whom the promise was made. In the meantime some order must be taken about sin and transgression that all the order of things appointed of God might not be overflowed by them. And this was done two ways by the law:

[1.] By reviving the commands of the covenant of works, with the sanction of death, it put awe on the minds of men, and set bounds to their lusts, that they should not dare to run forth into that excess which they were naturally inclined to. It was therefore "added because of transgressions;" that, in the declaration of God's severity against them, some bounds might be fixed to them; for "by the law is the knowledge of sin."

[2.] To shut up unbelievers, and such as would not seek for righteousness, life, and salvation by the promise, under the power of the covenant of works, and curse attending it. "It concluded" or "shut up all under sin," says the apostle, Gal. 3:22. This was the end of the law, for this end was it added, as it gave a revival to the covenant of works.

To the second inquiry, which arises out of this supposition, namely, that the law did convince of sin, and condemn for sin, which is, "whether it be not then contrary to the grace of God," the apostle in like manner returns a double answer, taken from the second use of the law, before insisted on, with respect to the promise. And,

[1.] He says, "That although the law does thus rebuke sin, convince of sin, and condemn for sin, so setting bounds to transgressions and transgressors, yet did God never intend it as a means to give life and righteousness, nor was it able so to do." The end of the promise was to give righteousness, justification, and salvation, all by Christ, to whom and concerning whom it was made. But this was not the end for which the law was revived in the covenant of Sinai. For although in itself it requires a perfect righteousness, and gives a promise of life for that reason, ("He that does these things, he will live in them,") yet it could give neither righteousness nor life to any in the state of sin. See Rom. 8:3; 10:4. To that end the promise and the law, having diverse ends, they are not contrary to one another.

[2.] He says, "The law has a great respect to the promise; and was given of God for this very end, that it might lead and direct men to Christ." This is sufficient to answer the question proposed at the beginning of this discourse, about the end of this covenant, and the advantage which the church received by that means.

The Substance of the Whole Truth

What has been spoken may suffice to declare the nature of this covenant in general; and two things do here evidently follow, in which the substance of the whole truth contended for by the apostle does consist:

(1.) That while the covenant of grace was contained and proposed only in the promise, before it was solemnly confirmed in the blood and sacrifice of Christ, and so legalized or established as the only rule of the worship of the church, the introduction of this other covenant on Sinai did not constitute a new way or means of righteousness, life, and salvation; but believers sought for them alone by the covenant of grace as declared in the promise. This follows evidently on what we have discoursed; and it secures absolutely that great fundamental truth, which the apostle in this and all his other epistles so earnestly contends for, namely, that there neither is, nor ever was, either righteousness, justification, life, or salvation, to be attained by any law, or the works of it, (for this covenant at Mount Sinai comprehended every law that God ever gave to the church,) but by Christ alone, and faith in him.

(2.) That although this covenant being introduced in the pleasure of God, there was prescribed with it a form of outward worship suited to that dispensation of times and present state of the church; on the introduction of the new covenant in the fullness of times, to be the rule of all relationship between God and the church, both that covenant and all its worship must be disannulled. This is that which the apostle proves with all sorts of arguments, manifesting the great advantage of the church by that means.

These things, I say, do evidently follow on the preceding discourses, and are the main truths contended for by the apostle.

Six Reasons for the First Covenant

There remains one thing more only to be considered, before we enter on the comparison between the two covenants here directed to by the apostle. And it is how this first covenant came to be an especial covenant to that people: in which we will manifest the reason of its introduction at that season. And to this end various things are to be considered concerning that people and the church of God in them, with whom this covenant was made; which will further evidence the nature, use, and necessity of it:

(1.) This people were the posterity of Abraham, to whom the promise was made that in his seed all the nations of the earth should be blessed. To that end from among them was the promised Seed to be raised up in the fullness of time, or its proper season, from among them was the Son of God to take on him the seed of Abraham. To this end various things were necessary:

[1.] That they should have a certain abiding place or country, which they might freely inhabit, distinct from other nations, and under a rule or scepter of their own. So it is said of them, that "the people should dwell alone, and not be reckoned among the nations," Num. 23:9; and "the scepter was not to depart from them until Shiloh came," Gen. 49:10. For God had regard to his own glory in his faithfulness as to his word and oath given to Abraham, not only that they should be accomplished, but that their accomplishment should be evident and conspicuous. But if this posterity of Abraham, from among whom the promised Seed was to rise, had been, as it is at this day with them, scattered abroad on the face of the earth, mixed with all nations, and under their power, although God might have accomplished his promise really in raising up Christ from among some of his posterity, yet could it not be proved or evidenced that he had so done, by reason of the confusion and mixture of the people with others. To that end God provided a land and country for them which they might inhabit by themselves, and as their own, even the land of Canaan. And this was so suited to all the ends of God towards that people, as might be declared in various instances, that God is said to have "espied this land out for them," Ezek. 20:6. He chose it out, as most fit for his purpose towards that people of all lands under heaven.

[2.] That there should be always kept among them an open confession and visible representation of the end for which they were so separated from all the nations of the world. They were not to dwell in the land of Canaan merely for secular ends, and to make as it were a mute show; but as they were there maintained and preserved to evidence the faithfulness of God in bringing forth the promised Seed in the fullness of time, so there was to be a testimony kept up among them to that end of God to which they were preserved. This was the end of all their ordinances of worship, of the tabernacle, priesthood, sacrifices and ordinances; which were all appointed by Moses, on the command of God, "for a testimony of those things which should be spoken afterwards," Heb. 3:5.

These things were necessary in the first place, with respect to the ends of God towards that people.

(2.) It becomes not the wisdom, holiness, and sovereignty of God, to call any people into an especial relation to himself, to do them good in an eminent and peculiar manner, and then to suffer them to live at their pleasure, without any regard to what he has done for them. To that end, having granted to this people those great privileges of the land of Canaan, and the ordinances of worship relating to the great end mentioned, he moreover prescribed to them laws, rules, and terms of obedience, on what they should hold and enjoy that land, with all the privileges annexed to the possession of it. And these are both expressed and frequently inculcated, in the repetition and promises of the law. But yet in the prescription of these terms, God reserved the sovereignty of dealing with them to himself. For had he left them to stand or fall absolutely by the terms prescribed to them, they might and would have utterly forfeited both the land and all the privileges they enjoyed in that respect. And had it so fallen out, then the great end of God in preserving them a separate people until the Seed should come, and a representation of it among them, had been frustrated. To that end, although he punished them for their transgressions, according to the threats of the law, yet would he not bring חֵרֶם, "curse of the law," on them, and utterly cast them off, until his great end was accomplished, Mal. 4:4-6.

(3.) God would not take this people off from the promise, because his church was among them, and they could neither please God nor be accepted with him but by faith in that respect. But yet they were to be dealt with according as it was proper. For they were generally a stiff-necked people, of a hard heart and lifted up with an opinion of their own righteousness and worth above others. This Moses endeavors, by all manner of reasons and instances to the contrary, to take them off from, in the book of Deuteronomy. Yet it was not performed among the generality of them, nor is to this day; for in the midst of all their wickedness and misery, they still trust to and boast of their own righteousness, and will have it that God has an especial obligation to them on that account. For this cause God saw it necessary, and it pleased him to put a grievous and heavy yoke on them, to subdue the pride of their spirits, and to cause them to breathe after deliverance. This the apostle Peter calls "a yoke that neither they nor their fathers were able to bear," Acts 15:10; that is, with peace, ease, and rest: which therefore the Lord Christ invited them to seek for in himself alone, Matt. 11:29, 30. And this yoke that God put on them consisted in these three things:

[1.] In a multitude of precepts, hard to be understood, and difficult to be observed. The present Jews reckon up six hundred and thirteen of them; about the sense of most of which they dispute endlessly among themselves. But the truth is, since the days of the Pharisees they have increased their own yoke, and made obedience to their law in any tolerable manner altogether impracticable. It would be easy to manifest, for instance, that no man under heaven ever did, or ever can, keep the Sabbath according to the rules they give about it in their Talmud. And they generally scarce observe one of them themselves. But in the law, as given by God himself, it is certain that there are a multitude of arbitrary precepts, and those in themselves not accompanied with any spiritual advantages, as our apostle shows, Heb. 9:9, 10; only they were obliged to perform them by a mere sovereign act of power and authority.

[2.] In the severity by which the observance of all those precepts was enjoined them. And this was the threat of death; for "he that despised Moses' law died without mercy," and "every transgression and disobedience received a just recompense of reward." Therefore was their complaint of old, "Behold, we die, we perish, we all perish. Whosoever comes any thing near to the tabernacle of the LORD will die: will we be consumed with dying?" Num. 17:12, 13. And the curse solemnly denounced against every one that confirmed not all things written in the law was continually before them.

[3.] In a spirit of bondage to fear. This was administered in the giving and dispensation of the law, even as a spirit of liberty and power is administered in and by the gospel. And as this respected their present obedience, and manner of its performance, so in particular it regarded death not yet conquered by Christ. Therefore our apostle affirms, that "through fear of death they were all their lifetime subject to bondage."

This state God brought them into, partly to subdue the pride of their hearts, trusting in their own righteousness, and partly to cause them to look out earnestly after the promised deliverer.

(4.) Into this estate and condition God brought them by a solemn covenant, confirmed by mutual consent between him and them. The tenor, force, and solemn ratification of this covenant, are expressed, Exod. 24:3-8. To the terms and conditions of this covenant was the whole church obliged indispensably, on pain of extermination, until all was accomplished, Mal. 4:4-6. To this covenant belonged the Decalogue, with all precepts of moral obedience from there drawn. So also did the laws of political rule established among them, and the whole system of religious worship given to them. All these laws were brought within the verge of this covenant, and were the matter of it. And it had especial promises and threats annexed to it as such; of which none did exceed the bounds of the land of Canaan. For even many of the laws of it were such as obliged nowhere else. Such was the law of the sabbatical year, and all their sacrifices. There was sin and obedience in them or about them in the land of Canaan, none elsewhere. Therefore,

(5.) This covenant thus made, with these ends and promises, did never save nor condemn any man eternally. All that lived under the administration of it did attain eternal life, or perished for ever, but not by virtue of this covenant as formally such. It did, indeed, revive the commanding power and sanction of the first covenant of works; and in that respect, as the apostle speaks, was "the ministry of condemnation,"

2 Cor. 3:9; for "by the deeds of the law can no flesh be justified." And on the other hand, it directed also to the promise, which was the instrument of life and salvation to all that did believe. But as to what it had of its own, it was confined to things temporal. Believers were saved under it, but not by virtue of it. Sinners perished eternally under it, but by the curse of the original law of works. And,

(6.) On this occasionally fell out the ruin of that people; "their table became a snare to them, and that which should have been for their welfare became a trap," according to the prediction of our Savior, Ps. 69:22. It was this covenant that raised and ruined them. It raised them to glory and honor when given of God; it ruined them when abused by themselves to ends contrary to express declarations of his mind and will. For although the generality of them were wicked and rebellious, always breaking the terms of the covenant which God made with them, so far as it was possible they should, while God determined to reign over them to the appointed season, and repining under the burden of it; yet they would have this covenant to be the only rule and means of righteousness, life, and salvation, as the apostle declares, Rom. 9:31-33; 10:3. For, as we have often said, there were two things in it, both which they abused to other ends than what God designed them:

[1.] There was the renovation of the rule of the covenant of works for righteousness and life. And this they would have to be given to them for those ends, and so sought for righteousness by the works of the law.

[2.] There was ordained in it a typical representation of the way and means in accordance with which the promise was to be made effectual, namely, in the mediation and sacrifice of Jesus Christ; which was the end of all their ordinances of worship. And the outward law of it, with the observance of its institution, they looked on as their only relief when they came short of exact and perfect righteousness.

Against both these pernicious errors the apostle disputes expressly in his epistles to the Romans and the Galatians, to save them, if it were possible, from that ruin they were casting themselves into. On this "the elect obtained," but "the rest were hardened." For by that means they made an absolute renunciation of the promise, in which alone God had enwrapped the way of life and salvation.

This is the nature and substance of that covenant which God made with that people; a particular, temporary covenant it was, and not a mere dispensation of the covenant of grace.

The Difference between the Two Covenants

That which remains for the declaration of the mind of the Holy Spirit in this whole matter, is to declare the differences that are between those two covenants, by reason of which fact the one is said to be "better" than the other, and to be "built on better promises".

The Opinion of the Church of Rome

Those of the Church of Rome do commonly place this difference in three things: 1. In the promises of them: which in the old covenant were temporal only; in the new, spiritual and heavenly. 2. In the precepts of them: which under the old, required only external obedience, designing the righteousness of the outward man; under the new, they are internal, respecting principally the inner man of the heart. 3. In their sacraments: for those under the old testament were only outwardly figurative; but those of the new are operative of grace.

But these things do not express much, if any thing at all, of what the Scripture places this difference in. And besides, as by some of them explained, they are not true, especially the two latter of them. For I cannot but somewhat admire how it came into the heart or mind of any man to think or say, that God ever gave a law or laws, precept or precepts, that should "respect the outward man only, and the regulation of external duties." A thought of it is contrary to all the essential properties of the nature of God, and fit only to ingenerate[11] apprehensions of him unsuited to all his glorious excellencies. The life and foundation of all the laws under the old testament was, "You will love the LORD your God with all your soul;" without which no outward obedience was ever accepted with him. And for the third of the supposed differences, neither were the sacraments of the law so barely "figurative," but that they did exhibit Christ to believers: for

---

[11] [Not generated, self-existent; inborn, innate.]

"they all drank of the spiritual rock; which rock was Christ." Nor are those of the gospel so operative of grace, but that without faith they are useless to them that do receive them.

The Scripture's Doctrine on the Difference
Between the Covenants Expounded on 17 Particulars

The things in which this difference does consist, as expressed in the Scripture, are partly circumstantial, and partly substantial, and may be reduced to the heads ensuing:

1. These two covenants differ in the circumstance of time as to their promulgation, declaration, and establishment. This difference the apostle expresses from the prophet Jeremiah, in the ninth verse of this chapter, where it must be more fully spoken to. In brief, the first covenant was made at the time that God brought the children of Israel out of Egypt, and took its date from the third month after their coming up from there, Exod. 19, 24. From the time of what is reported in the latter place, in which the people give their actual consent to the terms of it, it began its formal obligation as a covenant. And we must afterwards inquire when it was abrogated and ceased to oblige the church. The new covenant was declared and made known "in the latter days," Heb. 1:1, 2; "in the dispensation of the fullness of times," Eph. 1:10. And it took date, as a covenant formally obliging the whole church, from the death, resurrection, ascension of Christ, and sending of the Holy Spirit. I bring them all into the epoch of this covenant, because though principally it was established by the first, yet was it not absolutely obligatory as a covenant until after the last of them.

2. They differ in the circumstance of place as to their promulgation; which the Scripture also takes notice of. The first was declared on Mount Sinai; the manner of which, and the station of the people in receiving the law, I have in my Exercitations to the first part of this Exposition at large declared, and to that place the reader is referred,[12] Exod. 19:18. The other was declared on Mount Zion, and the law of it went forth from Jerusalem, Isa. 2:3. This difference, with many remarkable instances from it, our apostle insists on, Gal. 4:24-26: "These are the two covenants; the one from Mount Sinai, which gives birth to bondage, which is Agar." That is, Agar, the bondwoman whom Abraham took

---

[12] See vol. i, of this Exposition, p. 446. – Ed. [Banner Edition.]

before the heir of promise was born, was a type of the old covenant given on Sinai, before the introduction of the new, or the covenant of promise; for so he adds: "For this Agar is Mount Sinai in Arabia, and answers to Jerusalem which now is, and is in bondage with her children." This Mount Sinai, where the old covenant was given, and which was represented by Agar, is in Arabia, cast quite out of the verge and confines of the church. And it "answers," or "is placed in the same series, rank, and order with Jerusalem," namely, in the opposition of the two covenants. For as the new covenant, the covenant of promise, giving freedom and liberty, was given at Jerusalem, in the death and resurrection of Christ, with the preaching of the gospel which ensued for that reason; so the old covenant, that brought the people into bondage, was given at Mount Sinai in Arabia.

3. They differ in the manner of their promulgation and establishment. There were two things remarkable that accompanied the solemn declaration of the first covenant:

(1.) The dread and terror of the outward appearance on Mount Sinai, which filled all the people, yea, Moses himself, with fear and trembling, Heb. 12:18-21; Exod. 19:16; 20:18, 19. Together by this means was a spirit of fear and bondage administered to all the people, so as that they chose to keep at a distance, and not draw nigh to God, Deut. 5:23-27.

(2.) That it was given by the ministry and "disposition of angels," Acts 7:53; Gal. 3:19. Therefore the people were in a sense "put in subjection to angels," and they had an authoritative ministry in that covenant. The church that then was, was put into some kind of subjection to angels, as the apostle plainly intimates, Heb. 2:5. Therefore the worshipping or adoration of angels began among that people, Col. 2:18; which some, with an addition to their folly and superstition, would introduce into the Christian church, in which they have no such authoritative ministry as they had under the old covenant.

Things are quite otherwise in the promulgation of the new covenant. The Son of God in his own person did declare it. This he "spoke from heaven," as the apostle observes; in opposition to the giving of the law "on the earth," Heb. 12:25. Yet did he speak on the earth also; the mystery of which himself declares, John 3:13. And he did all things that belonged to the establishment of this covenant in a spirit of meekness and condescension, with the highest evidence of love, grace, and compassion, encouraging and inviting the weary, the burdened, the heavy and laden to come to him. And by his Spirit he makes his disciples to carry on the same work until the covenant was fully declared, Heb. 2:3. See John 1:17, 18.

And the whole ministry of angels, in the giving of this covenant, was merely in a way of service and obedience to Christ; and they owned themselves the "fellow-servants" only of them that have "the testimony of Jesus," Rev. 19:10. So that this "world to come," as it was called of old, was not put in subjection to them.

4. They differ in their mediators. The mediator of the first covenant was Moses. "It was ordained by angels in the hand of a mediator," Gal. 3:19. And this was no other but Moses, who was a servant in the house of God, Heb. 3:5. And he was a mediator, as designed of God, so chosen of the people, in that dread and consternation which befell them on the terrible promulgation of the law. For they saw that they could no way bear the immediate presence of God, nor treat with him in their own persons. To that end they desired that there might be a go-between, a mediator between God and them, and that Moses might be the person, Deut. 5:24-27. But the mediator of the new covenant is the Son of God himself. For "there is one God, and one mediator between God and men, the man Christ Jesus; who gave himself a ransom for all," 1 Tim. 2:5. He who is the Son, and the Lord over his own house, graciously undertook in his own person to be the mediator of this covenant; and in this it is unspeakably preferred before the old covenant.

5. They differ in their subject-matter, both as to precepts and promises, the advantage being still on the part of the new covenant. For,

(1.) The old covenant, in the preceptive part of it, renewed the commands of the covenant of works, and that on their original terms. Sin it forbade, that is, all and every sin, in matter and manner, on the pain of death; and gave the promise of life to perfect, sinless obedience only: from what cause the Decalogue itself, which is a transcript of the law of works, is called "the covenant," Exod. 34:28. And besides this, as we observed before, it had other precepts innumerable, accommodated to the present condition of the people, and imposed on them with rigor. But in the new covenant, the very first thing that is proposed is the accomplishment and establishment of the covenant of works, both as to its commands and sanction, in the obedience and suffering of the mediator. On this the commands of it, as to the obedience of the covenanters, are not grievous; the yoke of Christ being easy, and his burden light.

(2.) The old testament, absolutely considered, had, [1.] No promise of grace, to communicate spiritual strength, or to assist us in obedience; nor, [2.] Nor of eternal life, no otherwise but as it was contained in the promise of the covenant of works, "The man that does these things will live in them;" and, [3.] Had promises of temporal things in the land of Canaan inseparable from it. In the new covenant all things are otherwise, as will be declared in the exposition of the ensuing verses.

6. They differ, and that principally, in the manner of their dedication and sanction. This is that which gives any thing the formal nature of a covenant or testament. There may be a promise, there may be an agreement in general, which has not the formal nature of a covenant, or testament, and such was the covenant of grace before the death of Christ, but it is the solemnity and manner of the confirmation, dedication, and sanction of any promise or agreement, that give it the formal nature of a covenant or testament. And this is by a sacrifice, in which there is both blood shedding and death ensuing for that reason. Now this, in the confirmation of the old covenant, was only the sacrifice of beasts, whose blood was sprinkled on all the people, Exod. 24:5-8. But the new testament was solemnly confirmed by the sacrifice and blood of Christ himself, Zech. 9:11; Heb. 10:29; 13:20. And the Lord Christ dying as the mediator and surety of the covenant, he purchased all good things for the church; and as a testator bequeathed them to it. Therefore he says of the sacramental cup, that it is "the new testament in his blood," or the pledge of his bequeathing to the church all the promises and mercies of the covenant; which is the new testament, or the disposition of his goods to his children. But because the apostle expressly handles this difference between these two covenants, chap. 9:18-23, we must to that place refer the full consideration of it.

7. They differ in the priests that were to officiate before God in the behalf of the people. In the old covenant, Aaron and his posterity alone were to discharge that office; in the new, the Son of God himself is the only priest of the church. This difference, with the advantage of the gospel-state for that reason, we have handled at large in the exposition of the previous chapter.

8. They differ in the sacrifices on what the peace and reconciliation with God which is tendered in them depends. And this also must be spoken to in the following chapter, if God permits.

9. They differ in the way and manner of their solemn writing or enrolment. All covenants were of old solemnly written in tables of brass

or stone, where they might be faithfully preserved for the use of the parties concerned. So the old covenant, as to the principal, fundamental part of it, was "engraved in tables of stone," which were kept in the ark, Exod. 31:18; Deut. 9:10; 2 Cor. 3:7. And God did so order it in his providence, that the first draft of them should be broken, to intimate that the covenant contained in them was not everlasting or unalterable. But the new covenant is written in the "fleshy tables of the hearts" of them that do believe 2 Cor. 3:3; Jer. 31:33.

10. They differ in their ends. The principal end of the first covenant was to discover sin, to condemn it, and to set bounds to it. So says the apostle, "It was added because of transgressions." And this it did several ways:

(1.) By conviction: for "by the law is the knowledge of sin"; it convinced sinners, and caused every mouth to be stopped before God.

(2.) By condemning the sinner, in an application of the sanction of the law to his conscience.

(3.) By the judgments and punishments by which on all occasions it was accompanied. In all it manifested and represented the justice and severity of God.

The end of the new covenant is, to declare the love, grace, and mercy of God; and therefore to give repentance, remission of sin, and life eternal.

11. They differed in their effects. For the first covenant being the "ministration of death" and "condemnation," it brought the minds and spirits of them that were under it into servitude and bondage; but spiritual liberty is the immediate effect of the new testament. And there is no one thing in which the Spirit of God does more frequently give us an account of the difference between these two covenants, than in this of the liberty of the one and the bondage of the other. See Rom. 8:15; 2 Cor. 3:17; Gal. 4:1-7, 24, 26, 30, 31; Heb. 2:14, 15. This, therefore, we must explain a little. To that end the bondage which was the effect of the old covenant arose from several causes concurring to the effecting of it:

(1.) The renovation of the terms and sanction of the covenant of works contributed much to that. For the people saw not how the commands of that covenant could be observed, nor how its curse could be avoided. They saw it not, I say, by any thing in the covenant of Sinai; which therefore "gave birth to bondage." The entire prospect they had of deliverance was from the promise.

(2.) It arose from the manner of the delivery of the law, and God's entering for that reason into covenant with them. This was ordered on purpose to fill them with dread and fear. And it could not but do so, whenever they called it to remembrance.

(3.) From the severity of the penalties annexed to the transgression of the law. And God had taken on himself, that where punishment was not exacted according to the law, he himself would "cut them off." This kept them always anxious and solicitous, not knowing when they were safe or secure.

(4.) From the nature of the whole ministry of the law, which was the "ministration of death" and "condemnation," 2 Cor. 3:7, 9; which declared the punishment of every sin to be death, and denounced death to every sinner, administering by itself no relief to the minds and consciences of men. So was it the "letter that killed" them that were under its power.

(5.) From the darkness of their own minds, in the means, ways, and causes of deliverance from all these things. It is true, they had a promise before of life and salvation, which was not abolished by this covenant, even the promise made to Abraham; but this belonged not to this covenant, and the way of its accomplishment, by the incarnation and mediation of the Son of God, was much hidden from them, yea, from the prophets themselves who yet foretold them. This left them under much bondage. For the principal cause and means of the liberty of believers under the gospel arises from the clear light they have into the mystery of the love and grace of God in Christ. This knowledge and faith of his incarnation, humiliation, sufferings, and sacrifice, in accordance with which he made atonement for sin, and brought in everlasting righteousness, is that which gives them liberty and boldness in their obedience, 2 Cor. 3:17, 18. While they of old were in the dark as to these things, they necessarily have been kept under much bondage.

(6.) It was increased by the yoke of a multitude of laws, rites, and ceremonies, imposed on them; which made the whole of their worship a burden to them, and unendurable, Acts 15:10.

In and by all these ways and means there was a spirit of bondage and fear administered to them. And this God did, thus he dealt with them, to the end that they might not rest in that state, but continually look out after deliverance.

On the other hand, the new covenant gives liberty and boldness, the liberty and boldness of children, to all believers. It is the Spirit of the Son in it that makes us free, or gives us universally all that liberty which is any way needful for us or useful to us. For "where the Spirit of the Lord is, there is liberty;" namely, to serve God, "not in the oldness of the letter, but in the newness of the spirit." And it is declared that this was the great end of bringing in the new covenant, in the accomplishment of the promise made to Abraham, namely, "that we being delivered out of the hand of our enemies, might serve God without fear ...... all the days of our life," Luke 1:72-75. And we may briefly consider in which this deliverance and liberty by the new covenant does consist, which it does in the following things:

(1.) In our freedom from the commanding power of the law, as to sinless, perfect obedience, in order to righteousness and justification before God. Its commands we are still subject to, but not in order to life and salvation; for to these ends it is fulfilled in and by the mediator of the new covenant, who is "the end of the law for righteousness to every one that believes," Rom. 10:4.

(2.) In our freedom from the condemning power of the law, and the sanction of it in the curse. This being undergone and answered by him who was "made a curse for us," we are freed from it, Rom. 7:6; Gal. 3:13, 14. And in that respect also we are "delivered from the fear of death," Heb. 2:15, as it was penal and an entrance into judgment or condemnation, John 5:24.

(3.) In our freedom from conscience of sin, Heb. 10:2, that is, conscience disquieting, perplexing, and condemning our persons; the hearts of all that believe being "sprinkled from an evil conscience" by the blood of Christ.

(4.) In our freedom from the whole system of Mosaic worship, in all the rites, and ceremonies, and ordinances of it; which what a burden it was the apostles do declare, Acts 15, and our apostle at large in his epistle to the Galatians.

(5.) From all the laws of men in things pertaining to the worship of God, 1 Cor. 7:23.

And by all these, and the like instances of spiritual liberty, does the gospel free believers from that "spirit of bondage to fear," which was administered under the old covenant.

It remains only that we point out the heads of those ways in accordance with which this liberty is communicated to us under the new covenant. And it is done,

(1.) Principally by the grant and communication of the Spirit of the Son as a Spirit of adoption, giving the freedom, boldness, and liberty of children, John 1:12; Rom. 8:15-17; Gal. 4:6, 7. From this place the apostle lays it down as a certain rule, that "where the Spirit of the Lord is, there is liberty," 2 Cor. 3:17. Let men pretend what they will, let them boast of the freedom of their outward condition in this world, and of the inward liberty or freedom of their wills, there is indeed no true liberty where the Spirit of God is not. The ways in accordance with which he gives freedom, power, a sound mind, spiritual boldness, courage, contempt of the cross, holy confidence before God, a readiness for obedience, and growth of heart in duties, with all other things in which true liberty does consist, or which any way belong to it, I must not here divert to declare. The world judges that there is no bondage but where the Spirit of God is; for that gives that meticulous fear of sin, that awe of God in all our thoughts, actions, and ways, that careful and circumspect walking, that temperance in things lawful, that abstinence from all appearance of evil, in which they judge the greatest bondage on the earth to consist. But those who have received him do know that the whole world does lie in evil, and that all those to whom spiritual liberty is a bondage are the servants and slaves of Satan.

(2.) It is obtained by the evidence of our justification before God, and the causes of it. Men were greatly in the dark to this under the first covenant, although all stable peace with God does depend for that reason; for it is in the gospel that "the righteousness of God is revealed from faith to faith," Rom. 1:17. Indeed "the righteousness of God without the law is witnessed by the law and the prophets," Rom. 3:21; that is, testimony is given to it in legal institutions and the promises recorded in the prophets. But these things were obscure to them, who were to seek for what was intended under the veils and shadows of priests and sacrifices, atonements and expiations. But our justification before God, in all the causes of it, being now fully revealed and made manifest, it has a great influence into spiritual liberty and boldness.

(3.) By the spiritual light that is given to believers into the mystery of God in Christ. This the apostle affirms to have been "hid in God from the beginning of the world," Eph. 3:9. It was contrived and prepared in the counsel and wisdom of God from all eternity. Some intimation was given of it in the first promise, and it was afterwards shadowed out by various legal institutions; but the depth, the glory, the beauty and fullness of it, were "hid in God," in his mind and will, until it was fully revealed in the gospel. The saints under the old testament believed that they should be delivered by the promised Seed, that they should be saved for the Lord's sake, that the Angel of the covenant would save them, yea, that the Lord himself would come to his temple; and they diligently inquired into what was signified before concerning "the sufferings of Christ, and the glory that should follow." But all this while their thoughts and conceptions were exceedingly in the dark as to those glorious things which are made so plain in the new covenant, concerning the incarnation, mediation, sufferings, and sacrifice of the Son of God, concerning the way of God's being in Christ reconciling the world to himself. Now as darkness gives fear, so light gives liberty.

(4.) We obtain this liberty by the opening of the way into the holiest, and the entrance we have by that means with boldness to the throne of grace. On this also the apostle insists peculiarly in various places of his following discourses, as chap. 9:8; 10:19-22: where it must be spoken to, if God permits, at large; for a great part of the liberty of the new testament does consist in this.

(5.) By all the ordinances of gospel-worship. How the ordinances of worship under the old testament did lead the people into bondage has been declared; but those of the new testament, through their plainness in signification, their immediate connection to the Lord Christ, with their use and efficacy to guide believers in their communion with God, do all conduce to our evangelical liberty. And of such importance is our liberty in this instance of it, that when the apostles saw it necessary, for the avoiding of offense and scandal, to continue the observance of one or two legal institutions, in abstinence from some things in themselves indifferent, they did it only for a season, and declared that it was only in case of scandal that they would allow this temporary abridgment of the liberty given us by the gospel.

12. They differ greatly with respect to the dispensation and grant of the Holy Spirit. It is certain that God did grant the gift of the Holy Spirit under the old testament, and his operations during that season, as I have at large elsewhere declared;[13] but it is no less certain, that there was always a promise of his more distinguished effusion on the confirmation and establishment of the new covenant. See in particular that great promise to this purpose, Joel 2:28, 29, as applied and expounded by the apostle Peter, Acts 2:16-18. Yea, so sparing was the communication of

---

[13] See vol. iii. p. 125, of his miscellaneous works. – Ed. [Banner Edition.]

the Holy Spirit under the old testament, compared with his effusion under the new, as that the evangelist affirms that "the Holy Spirit was not yet, because that Jesus was not yet glorified," John 7:39; that is, he was not yet given in that manner as he was to be given on the confirmation of the new covenant. And those of the church of the Hebrews who had received the doctrine of John, yet affirmed that "they had not so much as heard whether there were any Holy Spirit" or no, Acts 19:2; that is, any such gift and communication of him as was then proposed as the chief privilege of the gospel. Neither does this concern only the plentiful effusion of him with respect to those miraculous gifts and operations by which the doctrine and establishment of the new covenant was testified to and confirmed: however, that also gave a distinguished difference between the two covenants; for the first covenant was confirmed by dreadful appearances and operations, accomplished by the ministry of angels, but the new by the immediate operation of the Holy Spirit himself. But this difference principally consists in this, that under the new testament the Holy Spirit has graciously condescended to bear the office of the comforter of the church. That this unspeakable privilege is peculiar to the new testament, is evident from all the promises of his being sent as a comforter made by our Savior, John 14-16; especially by that in which he assures his disciples that "unless he went away" (in which going away he confirmed the new covenant) "the Comforter would not come; but if he so went away, he would send him from the Father," chap. 16:7. And the difference between the two covenants which resulted from this is inexpressible.

13. They differ in the declaration made in them of the kingdom of God. It is the observation of Augustine, that the very name of "the kingdom of heaven" is peculiar to the new testament. It is true, God reigned in and over the church under the old testament; but his rule was such, and had such a relation to secular things, especially with respect to the land of Canaan, and the flourishing condition of the people in that respect, as that it had an appearance of a kingdom of this world. And that it was so, and was so to be, consisting in empire, power, victory, wealth, and peace, was so deeply fixed on the minds of the generality of the people, that the disciples of Christ themselves could not free themselves of that apprehension, until the new testament was fully established. But now in the gospel, the nature of the kingdom of God, where it is, and in which it consists, is plainly and evidently declared, to the unspeakable consolation of believers. For although it is now known and experienced

to be internal, spiritual, and heavenly, they have no less assured interest in it and advantage by it, in all the troubles which they may undergo in this world, than they could have in the fullest possession of all earthly enjoyments.

14. They differ in their substance and end. The old covenant was typical, shadowy, and removable, Heb. 10:1. The new covenant is substantial and permanent, as containing the body, which is Christ. Now, consider the old covenant comparatively with the new, and this part of its nature, that it was typical and shadowy, is a great debasement of it. But consider it absolutely, and the things in which it was so were its greatest glory and excellence; for in these things alone was it a token and pledge of the love and grace of God. For those things in the old covenant which had most of bondage in their use and practice, had most of light and grace in their signification. This was the design of God in all the ordinances of worship belonging to that covenant, namely, to typify, shadow, and represent the heavenly, substantial things of the new covenant, or the Lord Christ and the work of his mediation. The tabernacle, ark, altar, priests, and sacrifices did this; and it was their glory that so they did. However, compared with the substance in the new covenant, they have no glory.

15. They differ in the extent of their administration, according to the will of God. The first was confined to the posterity of Abraham according to the flesh, and to them especially in the land of Canaan, Deut. 5:3, with some few proselytes that were joined to them, excluding all others from the participation of the benefits of it. And therefore it was, that although the personal ministry of our Savior himself, in preaching of the gospel, was to precede the introduction of the new covenant, it was confined to the people of Israel, Matt. 15:24. And he was the "minister of the circumcision," Rom. 15:8. Such narrow bounds and limits had the administration of this covenant affixed to it by the will and pleasure of God, Ps. 147:19, 20. But the administration of the new covenant is extended to all nations under heaven; none being excluded, on the account of tongue, language, family, nation, or place of habitation. All have an equal interest in the rising Sun. The partition wall is broken down, and the gates of the New Jerusalem are set open to all comers on the gospel invitation. This is frequently taken notice of in the Scripture. See Matt. 28:19; Mark 16:15; John 11:51, 52; 12:32; Acts 11:18; 17:30; Gal. 5:6; Eph. 2:11-16; 3:8-10; Col. 3:10, 11; 1 John 2:2; Rev. 5:9. This is the grand charter of the poor wandering Gentiles. Having willfully

fallen off from God, he was pleased, in his holiness and severity, to leave all our ancestors for many generations to serve and worship the devil. And the mystery of our recovery was "hid in God from the beginning of the world," Eph. 3:8-10. And although it was so foretold, so prophesied of, so promised under the old testament, yet, such was the pride, blindness, and obstinacy, of the greatest part of the church of the Jews, that its accomplishment was one great part of that stumbling-block whereat they fell; yea, the greatness and glory of this mystery was such, that the disciples of Christ themselves comprehended it not, until it was testified to them by the pouring out of the Holy Spirit, the great promise of the new covenant, on some of those poor Gentiles, Acts 11:18.

16. They differ in their efficacy; for the old covenant "made nothing perfect," it could accomplish none of the things it did represent, nor introduce that perfect or complete state which God had designed for the church. But this we have at large insisted on in our exposition of the previous chapter. Lastly,

17. They differ in their duration: for the one was to be removed, and the other to abide for ever; which must be declared on the ensuing verses.

It may be other things of like nature may be added to these that we have mentioned, in which the difference between the two covenants does consist; but these instances are sufficient to our purpose. For some, when they hear that the covenant of grace was always one and the same, of the same nature and efficacy under both testaments, that the way of salvation by Christ was always one and the same, are ready to think that there was no such great difference between their state and ours as is pretended. But we see that on this supposition, that covenant which God brought the people into at Sinai, and under the yoke of which they were to abide until the new covenant was established, had all the disadvantages attending it which we have insisted on. And those who understand not how excellent and glorious those privileges are which are added to the covenant of grace, as to the administration of it, by the introduction and establishment of the new covenant, are utterly unacquainted with the nature of spiritual and heavenly things.

A Response to the Socinians

There remains yet one thing more, which the Socinians give us occasion to speak to from these words of the apostle, that the new covenant is "established on better promises." For from this place they do conclude that there were no promises of life under the old testament; which, in the latitude of it, is a senseless and brutish opinion. And,

1. The apostle in this place intends only those promises on what the new testament was legally ratified, and reduced into the form of a covenant; which were, as he declares, the promises of especial pardoning mercy, and of the efficacy of grace in the renovation of our natures. But it is granted that the other covenant was legally established on promises which respected the land of Canaan. To that end it is granted, that as to the promises in accordance with which the covenants were actually established, those of the new covenant were better than the other.

2. The old covenant had express promise of eternal life: "He that does these things will live in them." It was, indeed, with respect to perfect obedience that it gave that promise; however that promise it had, which is all that at present we inquire after.

3. The institutions of worship which belonged to that covenant, the whole ministry of the tabernacle, as representing heavenly things, had the nature of a promise in them; for they all directed the church to seek for life and salvation in and by Jesus Christ alone.

4. The question is not, What promises are given in the law itself, or the old covenant formally considered as such? But, What promises had they who lived under that covenant, and which were not disannulled by it? For we have proved sufficiently, that the addition of this covenant did not abolish or supersede the efficacy of any promise that God had before given to the church. And to say that the first promise, and that given to Abraham, confirmed with the oath of God, were not promises of eternal life, is to overthrow the whole Bible, both Old Testament and New.

Tenth Practical Observation

And we may observe from the previous discourses that although one state of the church has had great advantages and privileges above another, yet no state has had of which to complain, while they observed the terms prescribed to them. We have seen in how many things, and those most of them of the highest importance, the state of the church under the new covenant excels that under the old; yet that was in itself a state of unspeakable grace and privilege. For,

1. It was a state of near relation to God, by virtue of a covenant. And when all mankind had absolutely broken covenant with God by sin, to call any of them into a new covenant relation with himself, was an act of

sovereign grace and mercy. In this were they distinguished from the rest of mankind, whom God permitted to walk in their own ways, and winked at their ignorance, while they all perished in the pursuit of their foolish imaginations. A great part of the Book of Deuteronomy is designed to impress a sense of this on the minds of the people. And it is summarily expressed by the psalmist, Ps. 147:19, 20; and by the prophet, "We are *yours*: you never bore rule over them; they were not called by your name," Isa. 43:19.

2. This covenant of God was in itself holy, just, and equal. For although there was in it an imposition of various things burdensome, they were such as God in his infinite wisdom saw necessary for that people, and such as they could not have been without. Therefore on all occasions God refers it even to themselves to judge whether his ways towards them were not equal, and their own unequal. And it was not only just, but attended with promises of unspeakable advantages above all other people whatever.

3. God dealing with them in the way of a covenant, to which the mutual consent of all parties covenanting is required, it was proposed to them for their acceptance, and they did accordingly willingly receive it, Exod. 24, Deut. 5; so as that they had not of which to complain.

4. In that state of discipline in which God was pleased to order them, they enjoyed the way of life and salvation in the promise; for, as we have showed at large, the promise was not disannulled by the introduction of this covenant. To that end, although God reserved a better and more complete state for the church under the new testament, having "ordained better things for us, that they without us should not be made perfect;" yet was that other state in itself good and holy, and sufficient to bring all believers to the enjoyment of God.

Eleventh Practical Observation

The state of the gospel, or of the church under the new testament, being accompanied with the highest spiritual privileges and advantages that it is capable of in this world, two things follow from there:

1. The great obligation that is on all believers to holiness and fruitfulness in obedience, to the glory of God. We have in this the utmost condescension of divine grace, and the greatest effects of it that God will communicate on this side of glory. That which all these things tend to, that which God requires and expects on them, is the thankful and fruitful

obedience of them that are made partakers of them. And they who are not sensible of this obligation are strangers to the things themselves, and are not able to discern spiritual things, because they are to be spiritually discerned.

2. The heinousness of their sin by whom this covenant is neglected or despised is therefore abundantly manifest. The apostle particularly asserts and insists on this, Heb. 2:2, 3; 10:28, 29.

Chapter Two

Exposition of Verse 7

The Necessity of a New and Better Covenant

For if that first [*covenant*] had been blameless, then should no place
have been sought for the second.[1]

In this verse, and so also in those that follow to the end of this chapter,
the apostle designs a confirmation of what he had before asserted and
undertaken to prove. And this was that there is a necessity of a new and
better covenant, accompanied with better promises and more excellent
ordinances of worship than the former. On this it follows that the first
was to be disannulled and abolished; which was the main thesis he had to
prove. And there are two parts of his argument to this purpose. For first
he proves that on the supposition of another and better covenant to be
introduced, it did unavoidably follow that the first was to be abolished, as
that which was not perfect, complete, or sufficient to its end; which he
does in this verse. Secondly, he proves that such a new, better covenant
was to be introduced, in the verses following.

What he had before confirmed in various particular instances, he
summarily concludes in one general argument in this verse, and that built
on a principle generally acknowledged. And it is this, 'All the privileges,
all the benefits and advantages of the Aaronical priesthood and
sacrifices, do all belong to the covenant to which they were annexed, a
chief part of whose outward administrations consisted in them.' The
Hebrews neither could nor did question this. The whole of what they
pleaded for, the only charter and tenure of all their privileges, was the
covenant that God made with their fathers at Sinai. To that end that
priesthood, those sacrifices, with all the worship belonging to the
tabernacle or temple, would be necessarily commensurate to that
covenant. While that covenant continued, they were to continue; and if
that covenant ceased, they were to cease also. These things were agreed
between the apostle and them.

On this he subsumes, 'But there is mention of another covenant to be
made with the whole church, and to be introduced long after the making

---

[1] Εἰ γὰρ ἡ πρώτη ἐκείνη ἦν ἄμεμπτος, οὐκ ἂν δευτέρας ἐζητεῖτο τόπος.

of that at Sinai.' Neither could this be denied by them. However, to put it out of controversy, the apostle proves it by an express testimony of the prophet Jeremiah. In that testimony it is peculiarly declared, that this new covenant, that was promised to be introduced "in the latter days," should be better and more excellent than the former, as is manifest from the promises on what it is established; yet in this verse the apostle proceeds no further but to the general consideration of God's promising to make another covenant with the church, and what would follow for that reason.

From this supposition the apostle proves that the first covenant is imperfect, blamable, and removable. And the force of his inference depends on a common notion or presumption, that is clear and evident in its own light, And it is this, when once a covenant is made and established, if it will serve to and effect all that he who makes it does design, and exhibit all the good which he intends to communicate, there is no reason why another covenant should be made. The making of a new for no other ends or purposes but what the old was every way sufficient for, argues lightness and mutability in him that made it. To this purpose does he argue, Gal. 3:21, "If there had been a law given which could have given life, verily righteousness should have been by the law." Could the first covenant have perfected and consecrated the church, could it have communicated all the grace and mercy that God intended to indulge to the children of men, the wise and holy author of it would have had no thought about the introduction and establishment of another. It would have been no way agreeable to his infinite wisdom and faithfulness so to do. To that end the promise of this does irrefutably prove, that both the first covenant and all the services of it were imperfect, and therefore to be removed and taken away.

Indeed this promise of a new covenant, diverse from that made at Sinai, or not like to it, as the prophet speaks, is sufficient of itself to overthrow the vain pretences of the Jews in which they are hardened to this day. The absolute perpetuity of the law and its worship, that is, of the covenant at Sinai, is the principal, fundamental article of their present faith, or rather unbelief. But this is framed by them in direct opposition to the promises of God. For let it be demanded of them, whether they believe that God will make another covenant with the church, not according to the covenant which he made with their fathers at Sinai. If they will say they do not believe it, then do they plainly renounce the prophets, and the promises of God given by them. If they do grant it, I desire to know of them with what sacrifices this new covenant will be established; by what priest, with what worship, it will be administered. If they say that they will be done by the sacrifices, priests, and worship of the law, they deny what they granted before, namely, that it is a new and another covenant; for the sacrifices and priests of the law cannot confirm or administer any other covenant, but that which they belong and are confined to. If it be granted that this new covenant must have a new mediator, a new priest, a new sacrifice, as it is undeniable it must, or it cannot be a new covenant, then must the old cease and be removed, that this may come into its place. Nothing but obstinacy and blindness can resist the force of this argument of the apostle.

The general design of the apostle in this verse being cleared, we may consider the words more particularly. And there are two things in them: 1. A positive assertion, included in a supposition, "If the first covenant had been blameless," had not been defective; that is, it was so. 2. The proof of this assertion: "If it had not been so, place would not have been sought for the second;" which that there was, he proves in the following verses.

A Positive Assertion

In the first part of the words there is, (1.) A causal conjunction, rendering a reason: "for"; (2.) The subject spoken of: "That first covenant"; (3.) What is affirmed of it, as the affirmation is included in a negative supposition: It was not blameless, it is not blameless:

(1.) The conjunction, γάρ, "for," shows that the apostle intends the confirmation of what he had before discoursed. But he seems not to refer only to what he had immediately before affirmed concerning the better promises of the new testament, but to the whole argument that he has in hand. For the general reason on which here he insists, proves all that he had before delivered concerning the imperfection of the Levitical priesthood, and the whole worship of the first covenant depending for that reason.

(2.) The subject spoken of is ἡ πρώτη ἐκείνη, "that first;" that is, προτέρα διαθήκη, that "former covenant:" the covenant made with the fathers at Sinai, with all the ordinances of worship to that belonging, whose nature and use we have before declared.

(3.) Of this it is said, εἰ ἄμεμπτος ἦν. Vulg. Lat., "*si culpâ vacasset.*" And so we, "if it had been faultless." I am sure the expression is a little too harsh in our translation, and such as the original word will not bear, at least does not require. For it seems to intimate, that absolutely there was something faulty or blameworthy in the covenant of God. But this must not be admitted. For besides that the author of it, which was God himself, does free it from any such charge or imputation, it is in the Scripture everywhere declared to be "holy, just, and good." There is, indeed, an intimation of a defect in it; but this was not with respect to its own particular end, but with respect to another general end, for which it was not designed. That which is defective with respect to its own particular end to which it is ordained, or which it is designed to accomplish, is really faulty; but that which is or may be so with respect to some other general end, which it was never designed to accomplish, is not so in itself. The apostle discourses concerning this, Gal. 3:19-22. We must therefore state the significance of the word from the subject-matter that he treats about in this place; and this is the perfection and consummation, or the sanctification and salvation of the church. With respect to this alone it is that he asserts the insufficiency and imperfection of the first covenant. And the inquiry between him and the Hebrews was, not whether the first covenant was not in itself holy, just, good, and blameless, every way perfect with respect to its own especial ends; but whether it was perfect and effectual to the general ends mentioned. This it was not, says the apostle; and proves it undeniably, from the promise of the introduction of another general covenant for the effecting of them. Although, therefore, to be not ἄμεμπτος, is either to have some fault or vice accompanying any thing and adhering to it, in accordance with which it is unsuited to or insufficient for its own proper end; or it is that to which somewhat is lacking with respect to another general end which is much to be desired, but such as it was never designed to accomplish; as the art of arithmetic, if it be perfectly taught, is sufficient to instruct a man in the whole science of numeration; if it be not, it is faulty as to its particular end; but it is no way sufficient to the general end of making a man wise in the whole compass of wisdom, a thing far to be preferred before its particular end, be it never so perfect in its own kind; it is in the latter sense only that the apostle affirms that the first covenant was not ἄμεμπτος," or "blameless." If it had been such as to which nothing more was required or needful perfectly to complete and sanctify the church, which was the general end God aimed, it had been absolutely perfect. But this it was not, in that it never was designed for the means of it. To the same purpose he argues, Heb. 7:11, 19. And with respect to this end it is said that "the law was weak," Rom. 8:3; Gal. 3:21; Acts 13:38, 39.

In brief, that which the apostle designs to prove is, that the first covenant was of such constitution, that it could not accomplish the perfect administration of the grace of God to the church, nor was ever designed to that end; as the Jews then falsely, and their posterity still foolishly also imagine it to have done.

The Proof of this Assertion

The ensuing words in this verse include the general proof of his assertion concerning the insufficiency of the first covenant to the ends of God towards the church: Οὐκ ἂν δευτέρας ἐζητεῖτο τόπος.[2] His argument is plainly this: 'The promise of a new covenant does unavoidably prove the insufficiency of the former, at least to the ends for which the new one is promised. For otherwise to what end serves the promise, and covenant promised?' But there is some difficulty in the manner of the expression: "The place of the second had not been sought;" so the words lie in the original. But "the place of the second" is no more but "the second taking place;" the bringing in, the introduction and establishment of it. And this is said to be "sought"; but improperly, and after the manner of men. When men have entered into a covenant which proves insufficient for some end they do intend, they take counsel and seek out after other ways and means, or an agreement and covenant on such other terms as may be effectual to their purpose. To that end this signifies no alteration, no defect in the wisdom and counsel of God, as to what is now to be done, but only the outward change which he would now effect in the introduction of the new covenant. For as such changes among men are the issue of the alteration of their minds, and the effect of new counsels for the seeking out of new means for their end, so is this outward change, in the taking away of the old covenant and introduction of the new, represented in God; being only the second part of his counsel or purpose "which he had purposed in himself before the foundation of the world." And we may therefore observe:

---

[2] [Then no place would have been sought for a second.]

First Practical Observation

That whatever God had done before for the church, yet he ceased not, in his wisdom and grace, until he had made it partaker of the best and most blessed condition of which in this world it is capable. He found out place for this better covenant.

Second Practical Observation

Let those to whom the terms of the new covenant are proposed in the gospel take heed to themselves that they sincerely embrace and improve them; for there is neither promise nor hope of any further or fuller administration of grace.

Chapter Three

Exposition of Verse 8

The New Covenant

For finding fault with them, [*complaining of them,*] he says, Behold, the days come, says the LORD, and I will make [*when I will make*] a new covenant with the house of Israel and the house of Judah.[1]

In this verse the apostle enters on the proof of his argument laid down in that previous one. And this was, that the first covenant was not ἄμεμπτος, "unblamable," or every way sufficient for God's general end; because there was room left for the introduction of another, which was done accordingly.

Of this covenant, so to be introduced, he declares, in the testimony of the prophet afterwards, two things: 1. The qualification of it, or its especial adjunct; it was "new," verse 8. 2. A description of it: (1.) Negative, with respect to the old, verse 9. (2.) Positive, in its nature and effectual properties, verses 10-12. From all which he infers the conclusion which he was contending for, enforced with a new consideration confirming it, verse 13: which is the sum of the last part of this chapter.

There are two general parts of this verse: 1. The introduction of the testimony, to be improved from the occasion of it, as expressed by the apostle. 2. The testimony itself which he insists on.

The Introduction of the Testimony

The FIRST is in these words: "For finding fault with them, he says." In which we have, 1. The note of connection; 2. The ground on what the testimony is built; 3. The true reading of the words to be considered.

---

[1] Μεμφόμενος γὰρ αὐτοῖς λέγει, Ἰδού, ἡμέραι ἔρχονται, λέγει Κύριος, καὶ συντελέσω ἐπὶ τὸν οἶκον Ἰσραὴλ καὶ ἐπὶ τὸν οἶκον Ἰούδα διαθήκην καινήν.

Translation. – Stuart and Conybeare and Howson connect the αὐτοῖς with λέγει: "But finding fault [with the first covenant], he says to them;" *i.e.*, the Jews. Μεμφόμενος, according to the first of these critics, appears to reduplicate upon the ἄμεμπτος of the preceding verse. – Ed. [Banner Edition.]

Its Connection

There is the causal conjunction, γάρ, "for," which gives them connection to the previous verse. That which is designed is the confirmation of the previous argument. This is the proof of the assertion, that place was sought for another covenant, which evinced the insufficiency of the former; "for." And the reason it intimates does not consist in the words by which it is joined, "finding fault with them"; but respects those following, "he says," "For......he says, Behold, the days come" which directly prove what he had affirmed.

Its Ground

There is the ground intimated of what is affirmed in the following testimony. For the new covenant was not to be introduced absolutely, without the consideration of anything foregoing, but because the first was not ἄμεμπτος, or "unblamable." Therefore the apostle shows that God introduced it in a way of blame. He did it "finding fault with them."

Its True Reading

These words may be diversely distinguished and read. For, (1.) Placing the note of distinction thus, Μεμφόμενος γὰρ, αὐτοῖς λέγει, the sense is, "For finding fault," complaining, blaming, "he says to them"; so that expression, μεμφόμενος, "finding fault," respects the covenant itself. Piscator was the first that I know of, who thus distinguished the words; who is followed by Schlichtingius and others. But, (2.) Place the note of distinction at αὐτοῖς, as it is by most interpreters and expositors, and then the sense of the words is rightly expressed in our English translation, "For finding fault with them," (that is, with the people,) "he says." And αὐτοῖς may be regulated either by μεμφόμενος or λέγει.

The reasons for fixing the distinction in the first place are, (1.) Because μεμφόμενος, "finding fault," answers directly to οὐκ ἄμεμπτος, "was not without fault." And this contains the true reason why the new covenant was brought in. And, (2.) It was not God's complaint of the people that was any cause of the introduction of the new covenant, but of the old covenant itself, which was insufficient to sanctify and save the church.

But these seem not of force to change the usual interpretation of the words, for,

(1.) Although the first covenant was not every way perfect with respect to God's general end towards his church, yet it may be it is not so safe to say that God complained of it. When things or persons change the state and condition in which they were made or appointed of God, he may complain of them, and that justly. So when man filled the world with wickedness, it is said that "it repented the LORD that he had made man on the earth." But when they abide unaltered in the state in which they were made by him, he has no reason to complain of them. And so it was with the first covenant. So our apostle disputes about the law, that all the weakness and imperfection of it arose from sin; where there was no reason to complain of the law, which in itself was holy, just, and good.

(2.) God does in this testimony actually complain of the people, namely, that they "broke his covenant;" and expresses his indignation for that reason, "he regarded them not." But there is not in this testimony, nor in the whole context or prophecy from what source it is taken, nor in any other place of Scripture, any word of complaint against the covenant itself, though its imperfection as to the general end of perfecting the church-state is here intimated.

(3.) There is an especial remedy expressed in the testimony against the evil which God complains of, or finds fault with in the people. This was, that "they continued not in his covenant." This is expressly provided against in the promise of this new covenant, verse 10. To that end,

(4.) God gives this promise of a new covenant together with a complaint against the people, that it might be known to be an effect of free and sovereign grace. There was nothing in the people to procure it, or to qualify them for it, unless it were that they had wickedly broken the former. And we may therefore observe,

First Practical Observation

God has often just cause to complain of his people, when yet he will not utterly cast them off. It is on mere mercy and grace that the church at all seasons lives; but in some seasons, when it falls under great provocations, they are warned.

Second Practical Observation

It is the duty of the church to take deep notice of God's complaints of them. This, indeed, is not in the text, but ought not to be passed by on this occasion of the mention of God's complaining, or "finding fault with them." And God does not thus find fault only when he speaks immediately by new revelations, as our Lord Jesus Christ found fault with and rebuked his churches in the revelation made to the apostle John; but he does it continually, by the rule of the word. And it is the especial duty of all churches, and of all believers, to search diligently into what God finds fault with, in his word, and to be deeply impressed with that, so far as they find themselves guilty. Lack of this is that which has laid most churches in the world under a fatal security. Therefore they say, or think, or carry themselves, as though they were "rich and increased in goods, and had need of nothing," when indeed "they are wretched, and miserable, and poor, and blind, and naked." To consider what God blames, and to affect our souls with a sense of guilt is that "trembling at his word" which he so approves of. And every church that intends to walk with God to his glory ought to be diligent in this duty. And to guide them in this, they ought carefully to consider:

1. The times and seasons that are passing over them. God brings his church under a variety of seasons; and in them all requires especial duties from them, as those in which he will be glorified in each of them. If they miss it in this, it is that which God greatly blames and complains of. Faithfulness with God in their generation, that is, in the especial duties of the times and seasons in which they lived, is that which Noah, and Daniel, and other holy men, are commended for. Thus there are seasons of the great abounding of wickedness in the world; seasons of great apostasy from truth and holiness; seasons of judgment and of mercy, of persecution and tranquility. In all these, and the like, God requires especial duties of the church; on what his glory in them does much depend. If they fail here, if they are not faithful as to their especial duty, God in his word finds fault with them, and lays them under blame. And as much wisdom is required to this, so I do not judge that any church can discharge its duty in any competent measure without a due consideration of it. For in a due observation of the times and seasons, and an application of ourselves to the duties of them, consists that testimony which we are to give to God and the gospel in our generation. That church which considers not its especial duty in the days in which we live,

is fast asleep; and it may be doubted whether, when it is awaked, it will find oil in its vessel or no.

2. The temptations which are prevalent, and which unavoidably we are exposed to. Every age and time has its especial temptations; and it is the will of God that the church should be exercised with them and by them. And it would be easy to manifest, that the darkness and ignorance of men, in not discerning the especial temptations of the age in which they have lived, or neglecting of them, have been always the great causes and means of the apostasy of the church. By this means has superstition prevailed in one age, and profaneness in another; as false and noxious opinions in a third. Now, there is nothing that God requires more strictly of us, than that we should be watchful against present prevalent temptations; and he charges us with guilt where we are not so. And those which are not awake with respect to those temptations which are at this day prevalent in the world are far enough from walking well-pleasing before God. And various other things of the like nature might be mentioned to the same purpose.

Third Practical Observation

God often surprises the church with promises of grace and mercy. In this place, where God complains of the people, finds fault with them, charges them for not continuing in his covenant, and declares, that, as to any thing in themselves, he "regarded them not," it might be easily expected that he would proceed to their utter casting off and rejection. But instead of this, God surprises them, as it were, with the most eminent promise of grace and mercy that ever was made, or could be made to them. So he does in like manner, Isa. 7:13, 14; 57:17-19. And this he will do,

1. That he may glorify the riches and freedom of his grace. This is his principal end in all his dispensations towards his church. And how can they be made more conspicuous than in the exercise of them then, when a people are so far from all appearance of any desert of them, as that God declares his judgment that they deserve his utmost displeasure?

2. That none who have the least remainder of sincerity, and desire to fear the name of God, may utterly faint and despond at any time, under the greatest confluence of discouragements. God can come in, and will often, in a way of sovereign grace, for the relief of the most dejected sinners. But we must proceed with our exposition.

The Testimony Itself

The SECOND thing contained in this verse, is the testimony itself insisted on. And there is in the testimony, 1. The author of the promise declared in it, "He says;" as afterwards, "Says the Lord." 2. The note of its introduction, indicating the thing intended, "Behold." 3. The time of the accomplishment of what is here foretold and here promised, "The days come in which." 4. The thing promised is "a covenant:" concerning which is expressed,' (1.) He that makes it, "I," "I will make;" (2.) Those with whom it is made, "the house of Israel, and the house of Judah;" (3.) The manner of its making, συντελέσω;[2] (4.) The property of it, it is "a new covenant".

The Author of the Promise

He who gives this testimony is included in the word λέγει, "he says," "For finding fault with them, he says." He who complains of the people for breaking the old covenant, promises to make the new. So in the next verse it is expressed, "Says the Lord." The ministry of the prophet was made use of in the declaration of these words and things, but they are properly his words from whom they are by immediate inspiration.

Fourth Practical Observation

"He says," that is, נְאֻם יְהֹוָה, "says the LORD ," is the formal object of our faith and obedience. To this are they to be referred, in this do they acquiesce, and in nothing else will they so do. All other foundations of faith, as, 'Thus says the pope,' or 'Thus says the church,' or 'Thus said our ancestors,' are all but, delusions. "Thus says the LORD," gives rest and peace.

The Note of Introduction

There is the note of introduction, calling to attendance, הִנֵּה, Ἰδού, "Behold." It is always found eminent, either in itself or in some of its circumstances that is thus prefaced. For the word calls for a more than ordinary diligence in the consideration of and attention to what is

---

[2] [I will make.]

proposed. And it was needful to indicate this promise; for the people to whom it was given were very difficultly drawn from their adherence to the old covenant, which was inconsistent with that now promised. And there seems to be somewhat more intimated in this word than a call to special attention; and that is, that the thing spoken of is plainly proposed to them concerned, so as that they may look on it, and behold it clearly and speedily. And so is this new covenant here proposed so evidently and plainly, both in the entire nature and properties of it, that unless men willfully turn away their eyes, they cannot but see it.

Fifth Practical Observation

Where God places a note of observation and attention, we should carefully fix our faith and consideration. God sets not any of his marks in vain. And if, on the first view of any place or thing so signalized, the evidence of it does not appear to us, we have a sufficient call to further diligence in our inquiry. And if we are not lacking in our duty, we will discover some especial impression of divine excellence or another on every such thing or place.

Sixth Practical Observation

The things and concernments of the new covenant are all of them objects of the best of our consideration. As such are they here proposed; and what is spoken of the declaration of the nature of this covenant in the next verse is sufficient to confirm this observation.

The Time of the Accomplishment

The time is prefixed for the accomplishment of this promise: יָמִים בָּאִים, ἡμέραι ἔρχονται, "the days come." "Known to God are all his works from the foundation of the world;" and he has determined the times of their accomplishment. As to the particular precise times or seasons of them, while they are future, he has reserved them to himself, unless where he has seen good to make some especial revelation of them. So he did of the time of the sojourning of the children of Israel in Egypt, Gen. 15:13; of the Babylonish captivity, and of the coming of the Messiah after the return of the people, Dan. 9. But from the giving of the first promise, in which the foundation of the church was laid, the accomplishment of it is frequently referred to "the latter days." See our exposition on chap. 1:1, 2. Therefore under the old testament the days of the Messiah were called "the world to come," as we have showed, chap. 2:5. And it was a periphrasis of him, that he was ὁ ἐρχόμενος, Matt. 11:3, "He that was to come." And the faith of the church was principally exercised in the expectation of his coming. And this time is here intended. And the expression in the original is in the present tense, ἡμέραι ἔρχονται, from the Hebrew, יָמִים בָּאִים, "the days coming;" not the days that come, but "the days come." And two things are denoted by that means:

(1.) The near approach of the days intended. The time was now hastening apace, and the church was to be awakened to the expectation of it: and this accompanied with their earnest desires and prayers for it; which were the most acceptable part of the worship of God under the old testament.

(2.) A certainty of the thing itself was by this means fixed in their minds. Long expectation they had of it, and now stood in need of new security, especially considering the trial they were falling into in the Babylonish captivity; for this seemed to threaten a defeat of the promise, in the casting away of the whole nation. The manner of the expression is suited to confirm the faith of them that were real believers among them against such fears. Yet we must observe that from the giving of this promise to the accomplishment of it was near six hundred years. And yet about ninety years after, the prophet Malachi, speaking of the same season, affirms, "That the Lord, whom they sought, should suddenly come to his temple," Mal. 3:1.

Seventh Practical Observation

There is a time limited and fixed for the accomplishment of all the promises of God, and all the purposes of his grace towards the church. See Hab. 2:3, 4. And the consideration of this is very necessary to believers in all ages: (1.) To keep up their hearts from desponding, when difficulties against their accomplishment do arise, and seem to render it impossible. Lack of this has turned aside many from God, and caused them to cast their lot and portion into the world. (2.) To preserve them from putting themselves on any irregular ways for their accomplishment. (3.) To teach them to search diligently into the wisdom of God, who has disposed times and seasons, as to his own glory, so to the trial and real benefit of the church.

The Thing Promised

The subject-matter of the promise given is a "covenant," בְּרִית. The LXX renders it by διαθήκη, "a testament." And that is more proper in this place than "a covenant." For if we take "covenant" in a strict and proper sense, it has indeed no place between God and man. For a covenant, strictly taken, ought to proceed on equal terms, and a proportionate consideration of things on both sides; but the covenant of God is founded on grace, and consists essentially in a free, undeserved promise. And therefore בְּרִית, "a covenant," is never spoken of between God and man, but on the part of God it consists in a free promise, or a testament. And "a testament," which is the proper signification of the word here used by the apostle, is suited to this place, and nothing else. For,

(1.) Such a covenant is intended as is ratified and confirmed by the death of him that makes it. And this is properly a testament: for this covenant was confirmed by the death of Christ, and that both as it was the death of the testator, and as it was accompanied with the blood of a sacrifice; of which we must treat afterwards at large, if God wills.

(2.) It is such a covenant, as in which the covenanter, he that makes it, bequeaths his goods to others in the way of a legacy; for this is done by Christ in this, as we must also declare afterwards. To that end our Savior calls this covenant "the new testament in his blood." This the word used by the apostle does properly signify; and it is evident that he intends not a covenant absolutely and strictly so taken. With respect to this the first covenant is usually called the "old testament." For we intend not by this means the books of Scripture, or oracles of God committed to the church of the Jews, (which yet, as we have observed, are once called "the Old Testament," 2 Cor. 3:14,) but the covenant that God made with the church of Israel at Sinai, of which we have spoken at large.

And this was called a "testament" for three reasons:

[1.] Because it was confirmed by death; that is, the death of the sacrifices that were slain and offered at its solemn establishment. So says our apostle, "The first testament was not dedicated without blood," Heb. 9:18. But there is more required to this; for even a covenant properly and strictly so called may be confirmed with sacrifices. To that end,

[2.] God did in that respect make over and grant to the church of Israel the good things of the land of Canaan, with the privileges of his worship.

[3.] The principal reason of this denomination, "the old testament," is taken from its being typically indicative of the death and legacy of the great testator, as we have showed.

Three Things Concurring in the New Covenant

We have treated somewhat before concerning the nature of the new testament, as considered in distinction from and opposition to the old. I will here only briefly consider what concurs to the constitution of it, as it was then future, when this promise was given, and as it is here promised. And three things do concur to this:

(1.) A recapitulation, collection, and confirmation of all the promises of grace that had been given to the church from the beginning, even all that was spoken by the mouth of the holy prophets that had been since the world began, Lk. 1:70. The first promise contained in it the whole essence and substance of the covenant of grace. All those afterwards given to the church, on various occasions, were but explications and confirmations of it. In the whole of them there was a full declaration of the wisdom and love of God in sending his Son, and of his grace to mankind by that means. And God solemnly confirmed them with his oath, namely, that they should be all accomplished in their appointed season. Although, therefore, the covenant here promised included the sending of Christ for the accomplishment of those promises, they are all gathered into one head in that respect. It is a constellation of all the promises of grace.

(2.) All these promises were to be reduced into an actual covenant or testament in two ways:

[1.] In that, as to the accomplishment of the grace principally intended in them, they received it in the sending of Christ; and as to the confirmation and establishment of them for the communication of grace to the church, they received it in the death of Christ, as a sacrifice of agreement or atonement.

[2.] They are established as the rule and law of reconciliation and peace between God and man. This gives them the nature of a covenant; for a covenant is the solemn expression of the terms of peace between various parties, with the confirmation of them.

(3.) They are reduced to such form of law, as to become the only rule of the ordinances of worship and divine service required of the church. Nothing to these ends is now presented to us, or required of us, but what belongs immediately to the administration of this covenant, and the grace of it. But the reader must consult what has been discoursed at large to this purpose on the 6th verse.

Why Called A Covenant?

And we may see from this place what it is that God here promises and foretells, as that which he would do in the "days that were coming." For although they had the promise before, and so virtually the grace and mercy of the new covenant, it may be inquired: 'What is yet lacking, that should be promised solemnly under the name of a covenant?' For the full resolution of this question, I must, as before, refer the reader to what has been discoursed at large about the two covenants, and the difference between them, on verse 6. Here we may briefly name some few things, sufficient to the exposition of this place; as,

(1.) All those promises which had before been given out to the church from the beginning of the world were now reduced into the form of a covenant, or rather of a testament. The name of "a covenant" is indeed sometimes applied to the promises of grace before or under the old testament; but בְּרִית, the word used in all those places, denotes only "a free, gratuitous promise," Gen. 9:9; 17:4. But they were none of them, nor all of them together, reduced into the form of a testament; which they could not be but by the death of the testator. And what blessed privileges and benefits were included in this has been showed before, and must yet further be insisted on in the exposition of the ninth chapter, if God permits.

(2.) There was another covenant superadded to the promises, which was to be the immediate rule of the obedience and worship of the church. And according to their observance of this superadded covenant, they were esteemed to have kept or broken covenant with God. This was the old covenant on Sinai, as has been declared. To that end the promises could not be in the form of a covenant to the people, inasmuch as they could not be under the power of two covenants at once, and those, as it afterwards appeared, absolutely inconsistent. For this is that which our apostle proves in this place, namely, that when the promises were brought into the form and had the use of a covenant to the church, the former covenant must needs disappear, or be disannulled. Only, they had their place and efficacy to convey the benefits of the grace of God in Christ to them that did believe; but God here foretells that he will give them such an order and efficacy in the administration of his grace, as that all the fruits of it by Jesus Christ will be bequeathed and made over to the church in the way of a solemn covenant.

(3.) Notwithstanding the promises which they had received, yet the whole system of their worship sprang from, and related to the covenant made at Sinai. But now God promises a new state of spiritual worship, relating only to the promises of grace as brought into the form of a covenant.

Eighth Practical Observation

The new covenant, as re-collecting into one all the promises of grace given from the foundation of the world, accomplished in the actual exhibition of Christ, and confirmed in his death, and by the sacrifice of his blood, by that means becoming the sole rule of new spiritual ordinances of worship suited to that, was the great object of the faith of the saints of the old testament, and is the great foundation of all our present mercies.

The Things Contained in the New Covenant

All these things were contained in that new covenant, as such, which God here promises to make. For,

(1.) There was in it a recapitulation of all the promises of grace. God had not made any promise, any intimation of his love or grace to the church in general, or to any particular believer, but he brought it all into this covenant, so as that they should be esteemed, all and every one of them, to be given and spoken to every individual person that has an interest in this covenant. Therefore all the promises made to Abraham, Isaac, and Jacob, and all the other patriarchs, and the oath of God in accordance with which they were confirmed, are all of them made to us, and do belong to us no less than they did to them to whom they were first given, if we are made partakers of this covenant. Of this the apostle gives an instance in the singular promise made to Joshua, which he applies to believers, Heb. 13:5. There was nothing of love or grace in any of them but was gathered up into this covenant.

(2.) The actual exhibition of Christ in the flesh belonged to this promise of making a new covenant; for without it, it could not have been made. This was the desire of all the faithful from the foundation of the world; this they longed after, and fervently prayed for continually. And the prospect of it was the sole ground of their joy and consolation. "Abraham saw his day, and rejoiced." This was the great privilege which God granted to them that walked uprightly before him; such a one, says he, "will dwell on high: his place of defense will be the fortress of rocks: bread will be given him; his waters will be sure. Your eyes will see the King in his beauty: they will behold the land that is very far off," Isa. 33:16, 17. That prospect they had by faith of the King of saints in his beauty and glory, though yet at a great distance, was their relief and their reward in their sincere obedience. And those who understand not the glory of this privilege of the new covenant, in the incarnation of the Son of God, or his exhibition in the flesh, in which the depths of the counsels and wisdom of God, in the way of grace, mercy, and love, opened themselves to the church, are strangers to the things of God.

(3.) It was confirmed and ratified by the death and blood shedding of Christ, and therefore included in it the whole work of his mediation. This is the spring of the life of the church; and until it was opened, great darkness was on the minds of believers themselves. What peace, what assurance, what light, what joy, depend on this, and proceed from it, no tongue can express.

(4.) All ordinances of worship do belong to this. What is the benefit of them, what are the advantages which believers receive by them, we must declare when we come to consider that comparison that the apostle makes between them and the carnal ordinances of the law, chap. 9.

Although, therefore, all these things were contained in the new covenant, as here promised of God, it is evident how great was the concernment of the saints under the old testament to have it introduced; and how great also ours is in it, now that it is established.

The Author of this Covenant

The author or maker of this covenant is expressed in the words, as also those with whom it was made:

(1.) The first is included in the person of the verb, "I will make;" "I will make, says the Lord." It is God himself that makes this covenant, and he takes it on himself so to do. He is the principal party covenanting:

"I will make a covenant." God has made a covenant: "He has made with me an everlasting covenant." And various things we are taught in that respect:

[1.] The freedom of this covenant, without respect to any merit, worth, or condignity[3] in them with whom it is made. What God does, he does freely, "*ex mera gratia et voluntate*."[4] There was no cause outside himself for which he should make this covenant, or which should move him so to do. And this we are eminently taught in this place, where he expresses no other occasion of his making this covenant but the sins of the people in breaking that which he formerly made with them. And it is expressed on purpose to declare the free and sovereign grace, the goodness, love, and mercy, which alone were the absolute springs of this covenant.

[2.] The wisdom of its contrivance. The making of any covenant to be good and useful, depends solely on the wisdom and foresight of them by whom it is made. Therefore men do often make covenants, which they design for their good and advantage, but they are so ordered, for lack of wisdom and foresight, that they turn to their hurt and ruin. But there was infinite wisdom in the constitution of this covenant; by reason of which fact it is, and will be, infinitely effective of all the blessed ends of it. And they, who are not stricken with a holy admiration of divine wisdom in its contrivance, are utterly unacquainted with it. A man might comfortably spend his life in the contemplation of it, and yet be far enough from finding out the Almighty in it to perfection. Therefore is it that it is so divine a mystery in all the parts of it, which the wisdom of the flesh cannot comprehend. Nor, without a due consideration of the infinite wisdom of God in the contrivance of it, can we have any true or real conceptions about it: Ἑκὰς ἑκὰς ἔστε βέζηλοι.[5] Profane, unsanctified minds can have no insight into this effect of divine wisdom.

[3.] It was God alone who could prepare and provide a surety for this covenant. Considering the necessity there was of a surety in this covenant, seeing no covenant between God and man could be firm and stable without one, by reason of our weakness and mutability; and considering of what a nature this surety must be, even God and man in one person; it is evident that God himself must make this covenant. And

---

[3] [In Scholastic Theology that worthiness of eternal life which a man may possess through good works performed while in a state of grace.]

[4] [Out of his grace and will alone.]

[5] ["Let the profane ones depart!" from the *Rite of Pharmakos*, a Greek hymn.]

the provision of this surety does contain in it the glorious manifestation of all the divine excellencies, beyond any act or work of God whatever.

[4.] There is in this covenant a sovereign law of divine worship, in which the church is consummated, or brought into the most perfect estate of which in this world it is capable, and established for ever. This law could be given by God alone.

[5.] There is ascribed to this covenant such an efficacy of grace, as nothing but almighty power can make good and accomplish. The grace here mentioned in the promises of it, directs us immediately to its author. For who else but God can write the divine law in our hearts, and pardon all our sins? The sanctification or renovation of our natures, and the justification of our persons, being promised in this, seeing infinite power and grace are required to them, he alone must make this covenant with whom all power and grace do dwell. "God has spoken once; twice have I heard this; that power belongs to God. Also to you, O Lord, belongs mercy," Ps. 62:11, 12.

[6.] The reward promised in this covenant is God himself: "I am your reward." And who but God can ordain himself to be our reward?

Ninth Practical Observation

All the efficacy and glory of the new covenant do originally arise from, and are resolved into, the author and supreme cause of it, which is God himself. And we might consider, to the encouragement of our faith, and the strengthening of our consolation,

[1.] His infinite condescension, to make and enter into covenant with poor, lost, fallen, sinful man. This no heart can fully conceive, no tongue can express; only we live in hope to have yet a clearer prospect of it, and to have a holy admiration of it to eternity.

[2.] His wisdom, goodness, and grace, in the nature of that covenant which he has condescended to make and enter into. The first covenant he made with us in Adam, which we broke, was in itself good, holy, righteous, and just; it must be so, because it was also made by him. But there was no provision made in it absolutely to preserve us from that woeful disobedience and transgression which would make it void, and frustrate all the holy and blessed ends of it. Nor was God obliged so to preserve us, having furnished us with a sufficiency of ability for our own preservation, so as we could in no way fall but by a willful apostasy from him. But this covenant is of that nature, as that the grace administered in it will effectually preserve all the covenanters to the end, and secure to them all the benefits of it. For,

[3.] His power and faithfulness are engaged to the accomplishment of all the promises of it. And these promises do contain every thing that is spiritually and eternally good or desirable to us. "O LORD, our Lord, how excellent is your name in all the earth!" How glorious are you in the ways of your grace towards poor sinful creatures, who had destroyed themselves! And,

[4.] He has made no created good, but himself only to be our reward.

The Persons with Whom this Covenant is Made

The persons with whom this covenant is made are also expressed: "The house of Israel, and the house of Judah." Long before the giving of this promise, that people were divided into two parts. The one of them, in way of distinction from the other, retained the name of Israel. These were the ten tribes, which fell off from the house of David, under the conduct of Ephraim; by reason of which fact they are often also in the Prophets called by that name. The other, consisting of the tribe properly so called, with that of Benjamin and the greatest part of Levi, took the name of Judah; and with them both the promise and the church remained in a peculiar manner. But although they all originally sprang from Abraham, who received the promise and sign of circumcision for them all, and because they were all equally in their forefather brought into the bond of the old covenant, they are here mentioned distinctly, that none of the seed of Abraham might be excluded from the tender of this covenant. To the whole seed of Abraham according to the flesh it was that the terms and grace of this covenant were first to be offered. So Peter tells them, in his first sermon, that "the promise was to them and their children" who were then present, that is, the house of Judah; and "to all that were afar off," that is, the house of Israel in their dispersions, Acts 2:39. So again he expresses the order of the dispensation of this covenant with respect to the promise made to Abraham, Acts 3:25, 26, "You are the children of the prophets, and of the covenant which God made with our fathers, saying to Abraham, And in your seed will all the kindreds of the earth be blessed. To you first, God having raised his Son Jesus, sent him to bless you;" namely, in the preaching of the gospel. So our apostle, in his sermon to them, affirmed that "it was necessary that the word should be first spoken to them," Acts 13:46. And this was all the privilege that was now left to them; for the partition-wall was now broken down, and all obstacles against the Gentiles taken out of the way. To that end this house of Israel and house of Judah may be considered in two ways: [1.] As that people who were the whole entire posterity of Abraham. [2.] As they were typical, and spiritually symbolic of the whole church of God. Because of this fact alone it is that the promises of grace under the old testament are given to the church under these names, because they were types of them who should really and effectually be made partakers of them.

[1.] In the first sense, God made this covenant with them, and this on various accounts:

1st. Because he in and through whom alone it was to be established and made effectual was to be brought forth among them of the seed of Abraham, as the apostle Peter plainly declares, Acts 3:25.

2dly. Because all things that belonged to the ratification of it were to be transacted among them.

3dly. Because, in the outward dispensation of it, the terms and grace of it were first in the counsel of God to be tendered to them.

4thly. Because by them, by the ministry of men of their posterity, the dispensation of it was to be carried to all nations, as they were to be blessed in the seed of Abraham; which was done by the apostles and other disciples of our Lord Jesus Christ. So the law of the Redeemer went forth from Zion. By this means "the covenant was confirmed with many" of them "for one week," before the calling of the Gentiles, Dan. 9:27. And because these things belonged equally to them all, mention is made distinctly of "the house of Israel, and the house of Judah." For the house of Judah was, at the time of the giving of this promise, in the sole possession of all the privileges of the old covenant; Israel having cut off themselves, by their revolt from the house of David; being cast out also, for their sins, among the heathen. But God, to declare that the covenant he designed had no respect to those carnal privileges which were then in the possession of Judah alone, but only to the promise made to Abraham he equals all his seed with respect to the mercy of this covenant.

[2.] In the second sense the whole church of elect believers is intended under these denominations, being typified by them. These are they alone, being one made of two, namely, Jews and Gentiles, with whom the covenant is really made and established, and to whom the grace of it is actually communicated. For all those with whom this covenant is made will as really have the law of God written in their hearts, and their sins pardoned, according to the promise of it, as the people of old were brought into the land of Canaan by virtue of the covenant made with Abraham. These are the true Israel and Judah, prevailing with God, and confessing to his name.

Tenth Practical Observation

The covenant of grace in Christ is made only with the Israel of God, the church of the elect. For by the making of this covenant with any, the effectual communication of the grace of it to them is principally intended. Nor can that covenant be said to be made absolutely with any but those whose sins are pardoned by virtue of it, and in whose hearts the law of God is written; which are the express promises of it. And it was with respect to those of this sort among that people that the covenant was promised to be made with them. See Rom. 9:27-33; 11:7. But in respect of the outward dispensation of the covenant, it is extended beyond the effectual communication of the grace of it. And in respect to that did the privilege of the carnal seed of Abraham lie.

Eleventh Practical Observation

Those who are first and most advanced as to outward privileges, are oftentimes last and least advantaged by the grace and mercy of them. Thus was it with these two houses of Israel and Judah. They had the privilege and pre-eminence, above all nations of the world, as to the first tender, and all the benefits of the outward dispensation of the covenant; yet, "though the number of them was as the sand of the sea, a remnant only was saved." They came behind the nations of the world as to the grace of it; and this by reason of their unbelief, and the abuse of the privileges granted to them. Let not those, therefore, who now enjoy the greatest privileges be high-minded, but fear.

The Manner of Making the New Covenant

The manner of making this covenant is expressed by συντελέσω *"perficiam,"* *"consummabo,"* "I will perfect" or "consummate." In the Hebrew it is only אֶכְרֹת, *"pangam,"* *"feriam,"* "I will make;" but the apostle renders it by this word, to denote that this covenant was at once perfected and consummated, to the exclusion of all additions and alterations. Perfection and unalterable establishment are the properties of this covenant: "An everlasting covenant, ordered in all things, and sure."

Its Distinguishing Character

As to its distinguishing character, it is called "a new covenant." So it is with respect to the old covenant made at Sinai. To that end by this covenant, as here considered, is not understood the promise of grace given to Adam absolutely; nor that to Abraham, which contained the substance and matter of it, the grace exhibited in it, but not the complete form of it as a covenant. For if it were only the promise, it could not be called "a new covenant," with respect to that made at Sinai; for so it was before it absolutely two thousand five hundred years, and in the person of Abraham four hundred years at the least. But it must be considered as before described, in the establishment of it, and its law of spiritual worship. And so it was called "new" in time after that on Sinai eight hundred years. Although it may be called "a new covenant" in other respects also. As, first, because of its eminency; so it is said of an eminent work of God, "Behold, I work a new thing in the earth" and its duration and continuance, as that which will never wax old, is denoted by that means.

Chapter Four

Exposition of Verse 9

The Newness of the New Covenant

> Not according to that covenant which I made with their fathers, in the
> day when I took them by the hand to lead them out of the land of
> Egypt; because they continued not in my covenant, and I regarded them
> not, says the Lord.[1]

כָּרַתִּי the apostle in this place renders by ἐποίησα, and in this place only;
the reason of which we will see afterwards. אֲשֶׁר־הֵמָּה הֵפֵרוּ אֶת־בְּרִיתִי
"which my covenant they broke," "rescinded," "dissipated;" the apostle
renders αὐτοὶ οὐκ ἐνέμειναν ἐν διαθήκῃ μου, "and they continued
not in my covenant:" for not to abide faithful in covenant is to break it.
וְאָנֹכִי בָּעַלְתִּי בָם "and I was an husband to them," or rather, "a lord over
them;" in the apostle, κἀγὼ ἠμέλησα αὐτῶν, "and I regarded them
not." On what reason and grounds the seeming alteration is made, we
will inquire in the exposition.

Οὐ κατὰ τὴν διαθήκην, "non secundum testamentum;" "secundum
illud testamentum;" and so the Syriac, לָא אֵיךְ הָי דִּיתִיקָא, "not according
to that testament;" others, "foedus," and "illud foedus." Of the different
translation of this word by a "testament" and a "covenant," we have
spoken before.

Ἣν ἐποίησα. Syr., דִּיהָבֵת, "which I gave;" "quod feci," "which I
made." Τοῖς πατράσιν, for σὺν τοῖς πατράσιν, "with the fathers;" for
that is required to be joined to the verb ἐποίησα. And therefore the
Syriac, omitting the preposition, turns the verb into "gave," "gave to the
fathers;" which is properly אֶת־אֲבוֹתָם, "cum patribus eorum."

Οὐκ ἐνέμειναν. Vulg., "non permanserunt;" others, "perstiterunt."
So the Syriac, לָא קָיּוּ, "they stood not," "they continued not." "Maneo"
is used to express stability in promises and covenants: "At tu dictis,
Albane, maneres," Virg. Æn. viii. 643; and, "Tu modo promissis
maneas," Æn. ii. 160. So is "permaneo in officio, in armis, in amicitia,"

---

[1] Οὐ κατὰ τὴν διαθήκης ἣν ἐποίησα τοῖς πατράσιν αὐτῶν, ἐν ἡμέρᾳ
ἐπιλαζομένου μου τῆς χειρὸς αὐτῶν, ἐξαγαγεῖν αὐτοὺς ἐκ γῆς Αἰγύπτου· ὅτι
αὐτοὶ οὐκ ἐνέμειναν ἐν τῇ διαθήκῃ μου, κἀγὼ ἠμέλησα αὐτῶν, λέγει Κύριος.

to continue steadfast to the end. To that end it is as well so rendered as by *"persisto."* Ἐμμένω is so used by Thucydides: Ἐμμένειν ταῖς διαθήκαις, "to abide firm and constant in covenants." And ἐμμενής is he who is "firm," "stable," "constant" in promises and engagements.

Κἀγὼ ἡμέλησα, *"ego neglexi,"* *"despexi,"* *"neglectui habui."* Syr., בְּסִית, "I despised," "I neglected," "I rejected them." Ἀμελέω, is *"curæ non habeo,"* *"negligo,"* *"contemno;"* a word denoting a casting out of care with contempt.[2]

The Reasons for a Different Covenant

The greatest and utmost mercies that God ever intended to communicate to the church, and to bless it with, were enclosed in the new covenant. Nor does the efficacy of the mediation of Christ extend itself beyond the verge and compass of it; for he is only the mediator and surety of this covenant. But now God had before made a covenant with his people. A good and holy covenant it was; such as was meet for God to prescribe, and for them thankfully to accept of. Yet notwithstanding all the privileges and advantages of it, it proved not so effectual, but that multitudes of them with whom God made that covenant were so far from obtaining the blessedness of grace and glory by that means, as that they came short, and were deprived of the temporal benefits that were included in that respect. To that end, as God, on this promises to make a "new covenant" with them, seeing they had forfeited and lost the advantage of the former, yet if it should be of the same kind with that, it might also in like manner prove ineffectual. So must God give, and the church receive, one covenant after another, and yet the ends of them never be obtained.

To obviate this objection, and the fear that from it might arise, God, who provides not only for the safety of his church, but also for their comfort and assurance, declares beforehand to them that it will not be of the same kind with the former, nor liable to be so frustrated, as to the ends of it, as that was.

---

[2] Exposition.- Κἀγὼ ἡμέλησα. This is the Septuagint rendering. The Hebrew, according to A.V., is, "though I was an husband to them." Some explain the discrepancy by conjecturing that the Greek translators had the guttural *cheth* instead of *ayin* in their copies. As the Arabic cognate word signifies to *despise* or *reject*, Kimchi and Pococke adopt this translation of the Hebrew word in this passage. Hengstenberg in his Christology denies that the word can bear this sense.- Ed. [Banner Edition.]

And there are some things remarkable in this:

1. That the preface to the promise of this new covenant is a blame charged on the people, "finding fault with them," blaming them, charging them with sin against the covenant that he had made with them.

2. That yet this was not the whole ground and reason of making this new covenant. It was not so, I say, that the people were not steadfast in it and to the terms of it. For had it been so, there would have no more been needful to reinstate them in a good condition, but only that God should pardon their former sins, and renew the same covenant to them again, and give them another venture or trial for that reason. But inasmuch as he would do so no more, but would make another covenant of another nature with them, it is evident that there was some defect in the covenant itself, it was not able to communicate those good things with which God designed to bless the church.

3. These two things being the only reason that God gives why he will make this new covenant, namely, the sins of the people, and the insufficiency of the first covenant to bring the church into that blessed estate which he designed them; it is manifest that all his dealings with them for their spiritual and eternal good are of mere sovereign grace, and such as he has no motive to but in and from himself alone. There are various things contained in these words.

A Former Covenant

First, An intimation that God had made a former covenant with his people: Τὴν διαθήκην ἥν ἐποίησα. There is in these verses a repetition three times of making covenant; and in every place in the Hebrew the same words are used, כָּרַתִּי בְּרִית. But the apostle changes the verb in every place. First, he expresses it by συντελέσω, verse 8; and in the last place by διαθήσομαι, which is most proper, verse 10, (ζεῖναι and διατιθέναι διαθήκην are usual in other authors.) Here he uses ἐποίησα, in reference to that covenant which the people broke and God disannulled. And it may be he did so, to distinguish their alterable covenant from that which was to be unalterable, and was confirmed with greater solemnity. God made this covenant as others of his outward works, which he resolved to alter, change, or abolish, at the appointed season. It was a work whose effects might be shaken, and itself afterwards be removed; so he speaks, Heb. 12:27. The change of the things that are shaken is ὡς πεποιημένων, "as of things that are made,"

made for a season; so made as to abide and endure for an appointed time only: such were all the things of this covenant, and such was the covenant itself. It had no "*criteria æternitatis*" on it, no evidences of an eternal duration. Nothing has so but what is founded in the blood of Christ. He is אֲבִי־עַד, "the everlasting Father," or the immediate author and cause of every thing that is or will be everlasting in the church. Let men labor and contend about other things while they please; they are all shaken, and must be removed.

First Practical Observation

The grace and glory of the new covenant are much set off and manifested by the comparing of it with the old. This is done here by God, on purpose for the illustration of it. And it is greatly made use of in this epistle; partly to prevail with us to accept of the terms of it, and to abide faithful in that respect; and partly to declare how great is their sin, and how sore will be the destruction of them by whom it is neglected or despised. As these things are insisted on in other places, so are they the subject of the apostle's discourse, chap. 12 from verse 15 to the end.

Second Practical Observation

All God's works are equally good and holy in themselves; but as to the use and advantage of the church, he is pleased to make some of them means of communicating more grace than others. Even this covenant, which the new was not to be like to, was in itself good and holy; which those with whom it was made had no reason to complain of. Although God had ordained that by another covenant he would communicate the fullness of his grace and love to the church. And if every thing that God does be improved in its season, and for its proper ends, we will have benefit and advantage by it, though he has yet other ways of doing us more good, whose seasons he has reserved to himself. But this is an act of mere sovereign goodness and grace, that although any have neglected or abused mercies and kindnesses that they have received, instead of casting them off on that account, God takes this other course of giving them such mercies as will not be so abused. This he did by the introduction of the new covenant in the room of the old; and this he does every day. So Isa. 57:16-18. We live in days in which men variously endeavor to obscure the grace of God and to render it inglorious in the eyes of men; but he will for ever be "admired in them that believe."

Third Practical Observation

Though God makes an alteration in any of his works, ordinances of worship, or institutions, yet he never changes his intention, or the purpose of his will. In all outward changes there is with him "neither variableness nor shadow of turning." "Known to him are all his works from the foundation of the world;" and whatever change there seems to be in them, it is all accomplished in pursuance of the unchangeable purpose of his will concerning them all. It argued not the least change or shadow of turning in God that he appointed the old covenant for a season, and for some certain ends, and then took it away, by making of another that should excel it both in grace and efficacy.

The Recipients of the Former Covenant

Secondly, it is declared with whom this former covenant was made: πατράσιν αὐτῶν, "with their fathers." Some Latin copies read, "*cure patribus vestris,*" "with your fathers;" but having spoken before of "the house of Israel and of the house of Judah" in the third person, he continues to speak still in the same. So likewise is it in the prophet, אֲבוֹתָם, "their fathers".

"Their fathers," their progenitors, were those that this people always boasted of. For the most part, I confess, they rose higher in their claim from them than those here principally intended, namely, to Abraham, Isaac, Jacob, and the twelve patriarchs. But in general their fathers it was of which they made their boast; and they desired no more but only what might descend to them in the right of these fathers. And to these God here sends them and that for two ends:

(1.) To let them know that he had more grace and mercy to communicate to the church than ever those fathers of theirs were made partakers of. So he would take them off from boasting of them, or trusting in them.

(2.) To give warning by them to take heed how they behaved themselves under the tender of this new and greater mercy. For the fathers here intended were those with whom God made the covenant at Sinai; but it is known, and the apostle has declared at large in the third chapter of this epistle, how they broke and rejected this covenant of God, through their unbelief and disobedience, so perishing in the wilderness. These were those fathers of the people with whom the first covenant was made; and so they perished in their unbelief. A great warning this was to those that should live when God would enter into the new covenant with his church, lest they should perish after the same example. But yet was it not effectual towards them; for the greatest part of them rejected this new covenant, as their fathers did the old, and perished in the indignation of God.

Fourth Practical Observation

The disposal of mercies and privileges, as to times, persons, seasons, is wholly in the hand and power of God. Some he granted to the fathers, some to their posterity, and not the same to both. Our wisdom it is to improve what we enjoy, not to repine at what God has done for others, or will do for them that will come after us. Our present mercies are sufficient for us, if we know how to use them. He that lacks not a believing heart will lack nothing else.

Who Were Those "Fathers"?

Who those fathers were with whom God made this covenant, is further evident from the time, season, and circumstances of the making of it:

(1.) For the time of it, it was done ἐν ἡμέρα, that is, ἐκείνῃ, "in that day." That a "day" is taken in the Scripture for an especial time and season in which any work or duty is to be performed, is obvious to all. The reader may see what we have discoursed concerning such a day on the third chapter. And the time here intended is often called the day of it: Ezek. 20:6, "In the day I lifted up mine hand to them to bring them forth of the land of Egypt;" at that time or season. A certain, determinate, limited time, suited with means to any work, occasion, or duty, is so called a "day." And it answers to the description of the time of making the new covenant given in the verse foregoing, "Behold, the days are coming," the time or season approaches. It is also used in a way of eminency; a day, or a signal eminent season: Mal. 3:2, "Who may abide the day of his coming?" the illustrious glory and power that will appear and be exerted at his coming. "In the day," is, at that great, eminent season, so famous throughout all their generations.

(2.) This day or season is described from the work of it: ἐπιλαζομένου μου τῆς χειρὸς αὐτῶν, הֶחֱזִיקִי, "that I firmly laid hold." And ἐπιλαμζάνω, is "to take hold of" with a design of helping or delivering; and various things are intimated as well as the way and manner of the deliverance of that people at that time:

[1.] The woeful, helpless condition that they were in then in Egypt. So far were they from being able to deliver themselves out of their captivity and bondage, that, like children, they were not able to stand or go, unless God took them and led them by the hand. So he speaks, Hos. 11:3, "I taught them to go, taking them by their arms." And certainly never were weakly, stubborn children, so awkward to stand and go of themselves, as that people were to comply with God in the work of their deliverance. Sometimes they refused to stand, or to make a trial of it; sometimes they cast themselves down after they were set on their feet; and sometimes with all their strength went backwards as to what God directed them to. He that can read the story of their deliverance with any understanding will easily discern what pains God was at with that people to teach them to go when he thus took them by the hand. It is therefore no new thing that the church of God should be in a condition of itself able neither to stand nor go. But yet if God will take them by the hand for their help, deliverance will ensue.

[2.] It expresses the infinite condescension of God towards this people in that condition that he would bow down to take them by the hand. In most other places the work which he then accomplished is ascribed to the lifting up or stretching out of his hand, Ezek. 20:6. See the description of it, Deut. 4:34; 26:8. It was towards their enemies a work of mighty power, of the lifting up of his hand; but towards them it was a work of infinite condescension and patience, a bowing down to take them by the hand. And this was the greatest work of God. For such were the perverseness and unbelief, so multiplied were the provocations and temptations of that people, that if God had not held them fast by the hand, with infinite grace, patience, forbearance, and condescension, they had inevitably ruined themselves. And we know in how many instances they endeavored perversely and obstinately to wrest themselves out of the hand of God, and to cast themselves into utter destruction. To that end this word, "When I took them by the hand," for the end mentioned, comprises all the grace, mercy, and patience, which God exercised towards that people, while he worked out their deliverance by lifting up his hand among and against their adversaries.

And indeed no heart can conceive or tongue can express that infinite condescension and patience which God exercises towards every one of us, while he holds us by the hand to lead us to rest with him. Our own hearts, in some measure, know with what contrariness and perverseness, with what wanderings from him and withdrawing from his holy conduct, we exercise and are ready to weary his patience continually; yet do not mercy and grace let go that hold which they have taken on us. O that our souls might live in a constant admiration of that divine grace and patience on which they live; that the remembrance of the times and seasons in which, if God had not strengthened his hand on us, we had utterly destroyed ourselves, might increase that admiration daily, and enliven it with thankful obedience!

[3.] The power of this work intended is also included in this; not directly, but by consequence. For, as was said, when God took them by the hand by his grace and patience, he lifted up the hand of his power, by the mighty works which he did among their adversaries. What he did in Egypt, at the Red Sea, in the wilderness, is all included in this. These things made the day mentioned eminent and glorious. It was a great day, in which God so magnified his name and power in the sight of the entire world.

[4.] All these things had respect to and issued in that actual deliverance which God then accomplished for that people. And this was the greatest mercy which that people ever were or ever could be made partakers of, in that condition in which they were under the old testament. As to the outward part of it, consider what they were delivered from, and what they were led into, and it will evidently appear to be as great an outward mercy as human nature is capable of. But besides, it was gloriously typical, and representative of their own and the whole church's spiritual deliverance from sin and hell, from our bondage to Satan, and glorious translation into the liberty of the sons of God. And therefore did God engrave the memorial of it on the tables of stone, "I am the LORD your God, which brought you out of the land of Egypt, out of the house of bondage." For what was typified and signified by that means is the principal motive to obedience throughout all generations. Not is any moral obedience acceptable to God that does not proceed from a sense of spiritual deliverance.

And these things are here called over in this promise of giving a new covenant, partly to remind the people of the mercies which they had sinned against, and partly to remind them that no concurrence of outward mercies and privileges can secure our covenant-relation to God, without the special mercy which is administered in the new covenant, of which Jesus Christ is the mediator and surety.

Thus great on all accounts the day was, and the glory of it, in which God made the old covenant with the people of Israel; yet had it no glory in comparison of that which does excel. The light of the sun of glory was on this day "seven-fold, as the light of seven days," Isa. 30:26. A perfection of light and glory was to accompany that day, and all the glory of God's work and his rest in that respect, the light of seven days, was to issue in it.

From the things we have observed, it is fully evident both what was the "covenant" that God made, and who were "the fathers" with whom it was made. The covenant intended is none other but that made at Sinai, in the third month after the coming of the people out of Egypt, Exod. 19:1; which covenant, in the nature, use, and end of it, we have before described. And the fathers were those of that generation, those who came out of Egypt, and solemnly in their own persons, they and their children, entered into the covenant, and took on them to do all that was required in that respect; on what they were sprinkled with the blood of it, Exod. 24:3-8, Deut. 5:27. It is true, all the posterity of the people to whom the promise was now given were bound and obliged by that covenant, no less than those who first received it; but those only are intended in this place that actually in their own persons entered into covenant with God. Which consideration will give light to what is affirmed, that "they broke his covenant," or "continued not in it".

A comparison being intended between the two covenants, this is the first general part of the foundation of it with respect to the old.

The Breaking of the Former Covenant

The second part of it is in the event of making this covenant; and this is expressed both on the part of man and God, and in what the people did towards God, and how he carried it towards them for that reason.

First, the event on the part of the people is in these words, "Because they continued not in my covenant," Ὅτι αὐτοὶ οὐκ ἐνέμειναν ἐν τῇ διαθήκῃ μου.

אֲשֶׁר, "which," in the original, is expressed by ὅτι, which we render "because;" ὅτι, as it is sometimes a relative, sometimes a correlative, "which," or "because." If we follow our translation, "because," it seems to give a reason why God made a covenant with them not like the former; namely, because they continued not in the former, or broke it. But this indeed was not the reason of it. The reason, I say, why God made this new covenant not according to the former, was not because they abode not in the first. This could be no reason of it, nor any motive to it. It is therefore mentioned only to illustrate the grace of God, that he would make this new covenant notwithstanding the sin of those who broke the former; as also the excellence of the covenant itself, in accordance with which those who are taken into it will be preserved from breaking it, by the grace which it does administer. To that end I had rather render ὅτι here by "which," as we render אֲשֶׁר in the prophet, "which my covenant;" or "for," "for they abode not." And if we render it "because," it respects not God's making a new covenant, but his rejecting them for breaking the old.

That which is charged on them is, that they "continued not," they "abode not" in the covenant made with them. This God calls his covenant, "They continued not in my covenant;" because he was the author of it, the sole contriver and proposer of its terms and promises, הֵפֵרוּ, they "broke," they rescinded, removed it, made it void. The Hebrew word expresses the matter of fact, what they did; they "broke" or made void the covenant: the word used by the apostle expresses the manner how they did it; namely, by not continuing faithful in it, not abiding by the terms of it. The use of the word μένω, and ἐμμένω, to this purpose, has been before declared. And what is intended by this means we must inquire:

1. God made this covenant with the people on Sinai, in the authoritative proposition of it to them; and for that reason the people solemnly accepted of it, and took it on themselves to observe, do, and fulfill the terms and conditions of it, Exod. 19:8, especially chap. 24:3, 7, "The people answered with one voice, and said, All the words which the LORD has said, will we do." And, "All that the LORD has said, will we do, and be obedient." So Deut. 5:27. On this the covenant was ratified and confirmed between God and them, and for that reason the blood of the covenant was sprinkled on them, Exod. 24:8. This gave that covenant its solemn ratification.

2. Having thus accepted of God's covenant, and the terms of it, Moses ascending again into the Mount, the people made the golden calf. And this fell out so suddenly after the making of the covenant, that the apostle expresses it by, "They continued not in it," 'they made haste to

break it.' He expresses the sense of the words of God on this, Exod. 32:7, 8, "Go, get down; for your people, which you brought out of the land of Egypt, have corrupted themselves: they have turned aside quickly out of the way which I commanded them: they have made them a molten calf, and have worshipped it, and have sacrificed to that, and said, These be your gods, O Israel, which have brought you up out of the land of Egypt." For there they broke the covenant in which God had in a peculiar manner assumed the glory of that deliverance to himself.

3. To that end the breaking of the covenant, or their not continuing in it, was firstly and principally the making of the molten calf. After this, indeed, that generation added many other sins and provocations, before all things proceeded so far that "God swore in his wrath that they should not enter into his rest." This fell out on their professed unbelief and murmuring on the return of the spies, Num. 14, of which we have treated at large on chap. 3. To that end this expression is not to be extended to the sins of the following generations, neither in the kingdom of Israel nor in that of Judah, although they variously transgressed against the covenant, disannulling it so far as lay in them. But it is their sin that personally first entered into covenant with God that is reflected on. That generation with whom God made that first covenant immediately broke it, continued not in it. And therefore let that generation look well to themselves to whom this new covenant will be first proposed. And it so fell out, that the unbelief of that first generation that lived in the first days of the promulgation of the new covenant, has proved an occasion of the ruin of their posterity to this day. And we may observe,

Fifth Practical Observation

That, sins have their aggravations from mercies received. This was that which rendered this first sin of that people of such a shameful nature in itself, and so provoking to God, namely, that they who contracted personally the guilt of it had newly received the honor, mercy and privilege, of being taken into covenant with God. Therefore is that threat of God with respect to this, "Nevertheless in the day when I visit, I will visit their sin on them," Exod. 32:34. He would have a remembrance of this provoking sin in all their following visitations. Let us therefore take heed how we sin against received mercies, especially spiritual privileges, such as we enjoy by the gospel.

Sixth Practical Observation

Nothing but effectual grace will secure our covenant obedience one moment. Greater motives to obedience, or stronger outward obligation to that, no people under heaven could have than this people had newly received; and they had publicly and solemnly engaged themselves to that. But they "quickly turned out of the way." And therefore in the new covenant is this grace promised in a peculiar manner, as we will see on the next verse.

The Annulling of the Former Covenant

Secondly, the acting of God towards them on this is also expressed: "And I regarded them not." There seems to be a great difference between the translation of the words of the prophet and these of the apostle taken from them. In the former place we read, "Although I was a husband to them;" in this, "I regarded them not." And by this means the utmost difference that can be objected to the rendering of these words by the apostle is represented. But there was no need of rendering the words in the prophet, וְאָנֹכִי בָּעַלְתִּי בָם, "Although I was a husband to them," as we will see. Although many learned men have exceedingly perplexed themselves and others in attempting reconciliation between these passages or expressions, because they seem to be of a direct contrary sense and importance. I will therefore premise some things which abate and take off from the weight of this difficulty, and then give the true solution of it. And to the first end we may observe,

1. That nothing of the main controversy, nothing of the substance of the truth which the apostle proves and confirms by this testimony, does any way depend on the precise signification of these words. They are but occasional, as to the principal design of the whole promise; and therefore the sense of it does not depend on their significance. And in such cases liberty in the variety of expositions may be safely used.

2. Take the two different senses which the words, as commonly translated, do present, and there is nothing of contradiction, or indeed the least disagreement between them. For the words, as we have translated them in the prophet, express an aggravation of the sin of the people: "They broke my covenant, although I was" (that is, in that respect) "a husband to them," exercising singular kindness and care towards them. And as they are rendered by the apostle, they express the effect of that

sin so aggravated, He "regarded them not;" that is, with the same tenderness as formerly: for he denied to go with them as before, and exercised severity towards them in the wilderness until they were consumed. Each way, the design is to show that the covenant was broken by them, and that they were dealt with accordingly.

But expositors do find or make great difficulties in this. It is generally supposed that the apostle followed the translation of the LXX in the present copy of which the words are so expressed. But how they came to render בָּעַלְתִּי by ἠμέλησα, they are not agreed. Some say the original copies might differ in some letters from those we now enjoy. Therefore it is thought they might read, as some think, בְּהֶלְתִּי, "*neglexi*," or גָּעַלְתִּי, "*fastidivi*," "I neglected" or "loathed them." And those who speak most modestly, suppose that the copy which the LXX made use of had one of these words instead of בָּעַלְתִּי, which yet is the truer reading; but because this did not belong to the substance of the argument which he had in hand, the apostle would not depart from that translation which was then in use among the Hellenistic Jews.

But the best of these conjectures is uncertain, and some of them by no means to be admitted. Uncertain it is that the apostle made any of his quotations out of the translation of the LXX; yea, the contrary is certain enough, and easy to be demonstrated. Neither did he write this epistle to the Hellenistic Jews, or those who lived in or belonged to their dispersions, in which they made use of the Greek tongue; but to the inhabitants of Jerusalem and Judea principally and in the first place, who made no use of that translation. He expressed the mind of the Scripture as he was directed by the Holy Spirit, in words of his own. And the coincidence of them with those in the present copies of the LXX has been accounted for in our Exercitations.

Dangerous it is, as well as untrue, to allow of alterations in the original text, and then on our conjectures to supply other words into it than what are contained in it. This is not to explain, but to corrupt the Scripture. To that end one learned man (Pococke[3] in Miscellan.) has endeavored to prove that בְּהֶלְתִּי, by all rules of interpretation, in this place must signify to "despise and neglect," and ought to have been so translated. And this he confirms from the use of it in the Arabic language. The reader may find it in the place referred to, with great satisfaction.

---

[3] [Edward Pococke (1604-1691).]

My apprehensions are grounded on what I have before observed and proved. The apostle neither in this nor in any other place does bind up himself precisely to the translation of the words, but infallibly gives us the sense and meaning; and so he has done in this place. For although בַּעַל signifies a "husband," or to be a husband or a lord, בְּ being added to it in construction, as it is here, בָם בָּעַלְתִּי, it is as much as "*jure usus sum maritali*," 'I exercised the right, power, and authority of a husband towards them; I dealt with them as a husband with a wife that breaks covenant:' that is, says the apostle, '"I regarded them not" with the love, tenderness, and affection of a husband.' So he dealt indeed with that generation which so suddenly broke covenant with him. He provided no more for them as to the enjoyment of the inheritance, he took them not home to him in his habitation, his resting-place in the land of promise; but he allowed them all to wander, and bear their adulteries in the wilderness, until they were consumed. So God did exercise the right, and power, and authority of a husband towards a wife that had broken covenant. And in this, as in many other things in that dispensation, did God give a representation of the nature of the covenant of works, and the issue of it.

The Truth of These Things

Thirdly, there is a confirmation of the truth of these things in that expression, "Says the Lord." This assertion is not to be extended to the whole matter, or the promise of the introduction of the new covenant; for that is secured with the same expression, verse 8, Λέγει Κύριος, "Says the Lord." But it has a peculiar πάθος[4] in it, being added in the close of the words, נְאֻם־יְהוָה, and respects only the sin of the people, and God's dealing with them for that reason. And this manifests the meaning of the preceding words to be God's severity towards them: 'I used the authority of a husband, I regarded them not as a wife any more, says the Lord.'

Now, God thus uttered his severity towards them that they might consider how he will deal with all those who despise, break, or neglect his covenant. 'So,' says he, 'I dealt with them; and so will I deal with others who offend in like manner.'

This was the issue of things with them with whom the first covenant was made. They received it, entered solemnly into the bonds of it, took

---

[4] [Strong emotion.]

on themselves expressly the performance of its terms and conditions, were sprinkled with the blood of it; but they "continued not in it," and were dealt with accordingly. God used the right and authority of a husband with whom a wife breaks covenant; he "neglected them," shut them out of his house, deprived them of their dowry or inheritance, and slew them in the wilderness.

The Promise of Another Covenant

On this declaration, God promises to make another covenant with them, in which all these evils should be prevented. This is the covenant which the apostle designs to prove better and more excellent than the former. And this he does principally from the mediator and surety of it, compared with the Aaronical priests, whose office and service belonged wholly to the administration of that first covenant. And he confirms it also from the nature of this covenant itself, especially with respect to its efficacy and duration. And to this the testimony is express, evidencing how this covenant is everlastingly, by the grace administered in it, preventive of that evil success which the former had by the sin of the people.

Therefore he says of it, Οὐ κατὰ τήν, "Not according to it;" a covenant agreeing with the former neither in promises, efficacy, nor duration. For what is principally promised here, namely, the giving of a new heart, Moses expressly affirms that it was not done in the administration of the first covenant. It is neither a renovation of that covenant nor a reformation of it, but utterly of another nature, by whose introduction and establishment that other was to be abolished, abrogated, and taken away, with all the divine worship and service which was peculiar to that. And this was that which the apostle principally designed to prove and convince the Hebrews of. And from the whole we may observe various things.

Seventh Practical Observation

No covenant between God and man ever was, or ever could be stable and effectual, as to the ends of it, that was not made and confirmed in Christ. God first made a covenant with us in Adam. There was nothing in that respect but the mere defectibility[5] of our natures as we were creatures that could render it ineffectual. And from there did it proceed. In him we all sinned, by breach of covenant. The Son of God had not then interposed himself, nor undertaken on our behalf. The apostle tells us that "in him all things consist;" without him they have no consistency, no stability, no duration. So this first covenant was immediately broken. It was not confirmed by the blood of Christ. And those who suppose that the efficacy and stability of the present covenant do depend solely on our own will and diligence, had need not only to assert our nature free from that depravation which it was under when this covenant was broken, but also from that defectibility that was in it before we fell in Adam. And such as, neglecting the interposition of Christ, do commit themselves to imaginations of this kind, surely know little of themselves, and less of God.

Eighth Practical Observation

No external administration of a covenant of God's own making, no obligation of mercy on the minds of men, can enable them to steadfastness in covenant obedience, without an effectual influence of grace from and by Jesus Christ. For we will see in the next verses that this is the only provision which is made in the wisdom of God to render us steadfast in obedience and his covenant effectual to us.

Ninth Practical Observation

God, in making a covenant with any, in proposing the terms of it, retains his right and authority to deal with persons according to their behavior in and towards that covenant: "They broke my covenant, and I regarded them not."

Tenth Practical Observation

God's casting men out of his especial care, on the breach of his covenant, is the highest judgment that in this world can fall on any persons.

And we are concerned in all these things. For although the covenant of grace be stable and effectual to all who are really partakers of it, yet as

---

[5] [Liability to become defective.]

to its external administration, and our entering into it by a visible
profession, it may be broken, to the temporal and eternal ruin of persons
and whole churches. Take heed of the golden calf.

Chapter Five

Exposition of Verses 10-12

The Promises of the New Covenant

For this is the covenant that I will make with the house of Israel after those days, says the Lord; I will give my laws into their mind, and write them on their hearts: and I will be to them a God, and they will be to me a people. And they will not teach every man his neighbor, and every man his brother, saying, Know the Lord: for all will know me, from the least to the greatest. For I will be merciful to their unrighteousness, and their sins and their iniquities will I remember no more.[1]

The design of the apostle, or what is the general argument which he is in pursuit of, must still be borne in mind throughout the consideration of the testimonies he produces in the confirmation of it. And this is, to prove that the Lord Christ is the mediator and surety of a better covenant than that in which the service of God was managed by the high priests according to the law. For therefore it follows that his priesthood is greater and far more excellent than theirs. To this end he does not only prove that God promised to make such a covenant, but also declares the nature and properties of it, in the words of the prophet. And so, by comparing it with the former covenant, he manifests its excellence above it. In particular, in this testimony the imperfection of that covenant is demonstrated from its result. For it did not effectually continue peace and mutual love between God and the people; but being broken by them, they were for that reason rejected of God. This rendered all the other benefits and advantages of it useless. To that end the apostle insists from the

---

[1] Ὅτι αὕτη ἡ διαθήκη ἣν διαθήσομαι τῷ οἴκῳ Ἰσραὴλ μετὰ τας ἡμέρας ἐκείνας, λέγει Κύριος, διδοὺς νόμους μου εἰς τὴν διάνοιαν αὐτῶν, καὶ ἐπι καρδίας αὐτῶν ἐπιγράψω αὐτούς· καὶ ἔσομαι αὐτοῖς εἰς Θεὸν, καὶ αὐτοὶ ἔσονταί μοι εἰς λαόν· καὶ οὐ μὴ διδάξωσιν ἕκαστος τὸν πλησίον αὐτοῦ, καὶ ἕκαστος τὸν ἀδελφον αὐτοῦ, λέγων, Γνῶθι τὸν Κύριον· ὅτι πάντες εἰδήσουσί με, ἀπὸ μικροῦ αὐτῶν ἕως μεγάλου αὐτῶν· ὅτι ἵλεως ἔσομαι ταῖς ἀδικίαις αὐτῶν, καὶ τῶν ἁμαρτιῶν καὶ τῶν ἀνομιῶν αὐτῶν οὐ μὴ μνησθῶ ἔτι.

Various Readings.- Τὸν πλησίον has been rejected, and τὸν πολίτην substituted as the proper reading, by Griesbach, Scholz, Lachmann, and Tischendorf. All the uncial MSS., with most of the versions, vindicate the propriety of the change.- Ed. [Banner Edition.]

prophet on those properties of this other covenant which infallibly prevent the like result, securing the people's obedience for ever, and so the love and relation of God to them as their God.

To that end these three verses give us a description of that covenant of which the Lord Christ is the mediator and surety, not absolutely and entirely, but as to those properties and effects of it in which it differs from the former, so as infallibly to secure the covenant relation between God and the people. That covenant was broken, but this will never be so, because provision is made in the covenant itself against any such event.

And we may consider in the words, 1. The particle of introduction, ὅτι, answering the Hebrew כִּי. 2. The subject spoken of, which is διαθήκη; with the way of making it, ἥν διαθήσομαι, "which I will make." 3. The author of it, the Lord Jehovah; "I will... says the Lord." 4. Those with whom it was to be made, "the house of Israel." 5. The time of making it, "after those days." 6. The properties, privileges, and benefits of this covenant, which are of two sorts: (1.) Of sanctifying, inherent grace; described by a double consequent: [1.] Of God's relation to them, and theirs to him; "I will be to them a God, and they will be to me a people," verse 10. [2.] Of their advantage by that means, without the use of such other aids as formerly they stood in need of, verse 11. (2.) Of relative grace, in the pardon of their sins, verse 12. And various things of great weight will fall into consideration under these several heads.

Exposition of Verse 10

> "For this is the covenant that I will make with the house of Israel after those days, says the Lord; I will give my laws into their mind, and write them on their hearts: and I will be to them a God, and they will be to me a people."

Introduction of the Declaration of the New Covenant

The introduction of the declaration of the new covenant is by the particle ὅτι. The Hebrew כִּי, which is rendered by it, is variously used, and is sometimes redundant. In the prophet, some translate it by an exceptive, "*sed*;" some by an illative, "*quoniam*." And in this place ὅτι, is rendered by some "*quamborem*," "to that end;" and by others "*nam*," or "*enim*," as we do it by "for." And it does intimate a reason of what was spoken before, namely, that the covenant which God would now make should not be according to that, like to it, which was before made and broken.

The Subject Spoken Of: The Making of a Covenant

The thing promised is a "covenant:" in the prophet בְּרִית, here διαθήκη. And the way of making it, in the prophet אֶכְרֹת; which is the usual word in accordance with which the making of a covenant is expressed. For signifying to "cut," to "strike," to "divide," respect is had in it to the sacrifices by which covenants were confirmed. From there also were *"foedus percutere,"* and *"foedus ferire."*[2] See Gen. 15:9, 10, 18. אֵת, or עִם, that is, *"cum,"* which is joined in construction with it, Gen. 15:18; Deut. 5:2. The apostle renders it by διαθήσομαι, and that with a dative case without a preposition, τῷ οἴκῳ, "I will make" or "confirm to." He had used before συντελέσω to the same purpose.

We render the words בְּרִית and διαθήκη in this place by a "covenant," though afterward the same word is translated by a "testament." A covenant properly is a compact or agreement on certain terms mutually stipulated by two or more parties. As promises are the foundation and rise of it, as it is between God and man, so it comprises also precepts, or laws of obedience, which are prescribed to man on his part to be observed. But in the description of the covenant here annexed, there is no mention of any condition on the part of man, of any terms of obedience prescribed to him, but the whole consists in free, gratuitous promises, as we will see in the explication of it. Some therefore conclude that it is only one part of the covenant that is here described. Others observe from this place that the whole covenant of grace as a covenant is absolute, without any conditions on our part; which sense Estius[3] on this place contends for. But these things must be further inquired into:

(1.) The word בְּרִית, used by the prophet, does not only signify a "covenant" or compact properly so called, but a free, gratuitous promise also. Yea, sometimes it is used for such a free purpose of God with respect to other things, which in their own nature are incapable of being obliged by any moral condition. Such is God's covenant with day and night, Jer. 33:20, 25. And so he says that he "made his covenant," not to destroy the world by water any more, "with every living creature," Gen.

---

[2] [Strike a compact.]
[3] [Williem Hessels van Estius (1542-1613).]

9:10, 11. Nothing, therefore, can be argued for the necessity of conditions to belong to this covenant from the name or term in accordance with which it is expressed in the prophet. A covenant properly is συνθήκη, but there is no word in the whole Hebrew language of that precise signification.

(2.) The making of this covenant is declared by כָּרַתִּי. But yet neither does this require a mutual stipulation, on terms and conditions prescribed, to an entrance into covenant. For it refers to the sacrifices by which covenants were confirmed; and it is applied to a mere gratuitous promise, Gen. 15:18, "In that day did the LORD make a covenant with Abram, saying, To your seed will I give this land."

As to the word διαθήκη, it signifies a "covenant" improperly; properly it is a "testamentary disposition." And this may be without any conditions on the part of them to whom any thing is bequeathed.

(3.) The whole of the covenant intended is expressed in the ensuing description of it. For if it were otherwise, it could not be proved from there that this covenant was more excellent than the former, especially as to security that the covenant relation between God and the people should not be broken or disannulled. For this is the principal thing which the apostle designs to prove in this place; and the lack of an observation of that has led many out of the way in their exposition of it. If, therefore, this be not an entire description of the covenant, there might yet be something reserved essentially belonging to that which might frustrate this end. For some such conditions might yet be required in it as we are not able to observe, or could have no security that we should abide in the observation of them: and for that reason this covenant might be frustrated of its end, as well as the former; which is directly contrary to God's declaration of his design in it.

(4.) It is evident that there can be no condition previously required, to our entering into or participation of the benefits of this covenant, antecedent to the making of it with us. For none think there are any such with respect to its original constitution; nor can there be so in respect of its making with us, or our entering into it. For,

[1.] This would render the covenant inferior in a way of grace to that which God made with the people at Horeb. For he declares that there was not any thing in them that moved him either to make that covenant, or to take them into it with himself. Everywhere he asserts this to be an act of his mere grace and favor. Yea, he frequently declares, that he took them into covenant, not only without respect to any thing of good in them, but although they were evil and stubborn. See Deut. 7:7, 8; 9:4, 5.

[2.] It is contrary to the nature, ends, and express properties of this covenant. For there is nothing that can be thought or supposed to be such a condition, but it is comprehended in the promise of the covenant itself; for all that God requires in us is proposed as that which himself will effect by virtue of this covenant.

(5.) It is certain, that in the outward dispensation of the covenant, in which the grace, mercy, and terms of it are proposed to us, many things are required of us in order to a participation of the benefits of it; for God has ordained, that all the mercy and grace that is prepared in it will be communicated to us ordinarily in the use of outward means, by which a compliance is required of us in a way of duty. To this end he has appointed all the ordinances of the gospel, the word and sacraments, with all those duties, public and private, which are needful to render them effectual to us. For he will take us ordinarily into this covenant in and by the rational faculties of our natures, that he may be glorified in them and by them. To that end these things are required of us in order to the participation of the benefits of this covenant. And if, therefore, any one will call our attendance to such duties of the condition of the covenant, it is not to be contended about, though properly it is not so. For,

[1.] God does work the grace of the covenant, and communicate the mercy of it, antecedently to all ability for the performance of any such duty; as it is with elect infants.

[2.] Among those who are equally diligent in the performance of the duties intended he makes a discrimination, preferring one before another. "Many are called, but few are chosen;" and what has any one that he has not received?

[3.] He actually takes some into the grace of the covenant while they are engaged in an opposition to the outward dispensation of it. An example of this grace he gave in Paul.

(6.) It is evident that the first grace of the covenant, or God's putting his law in our hearts, can depend on no condition on our part. For whatever is antecedent to that, being only a work or act of corrupted nature, can be no condition on what the dispensation of spiritual grace is superadded. And this is the great ground of them who absolutely deny the covenant of grace to be conditional; namely, that the first grace is absolutely promised, on what and its exercise the whole of it does depend.

(7.) To a full and complete interest in all the promises of the covenant, faith on our part, from which evangelical repentance is inseparable, is required. But although these also are produced in us by virtue of that promise and grace of the covenant which are absolute, it is a mere strife about words to contend whether they may be called conditions or no. Let it be granted on the one hand, that we cannot have an actual participation of the relative grace of this covenant in adoption and justification, without faith or believing; and on the other, that this faith is produced in us, given to us, bestowed on us, by that grace of the covenant which depends on no condition in us as to its discriminating administration, and I will not concern myself what men will call it.

(8.) Though there are no conditions properly so called of the whole grace of the covenant, yet there are conditions in the covenant, taking that term, in a large sense, for that which by the order of divine constitution precedes some other things, and has an influence into their existence; for God requires many things of them whom he actually takes into covenant, and makes partakers of the promises and benefits of it. Of this nature is that whole obedience which is prescribed to us in the gospel, in our walking before God in uprightness; and there being an order in the things that belong to this, some acts, duties, and parts of our gracious obedience, being appointed to be means of the further additional supplies of the grace and mercies of the covenant, they may be called conditions required of us in the covenant, as well as duties prescribed to us.

(9.) The benefits of the covenant are of two sorts: [1.] The grace and mercy which it does collate. [2] The future reward of glory which it does promise. Those of the former sort are all of them means appointed of God, which we are to use and improve to the obtaining of the latter, and so may be called conditions required on our part. They are only collated on us, but conditions as used and improved by us.

(10.) Although διαθήκη, the word here used, may signify and be rightly rendered a "covenant," in the same manner as בְּרִית does, yet that which is intended is properly a "testament," or a "testamentary disposition" of good things. It is the will of God in and by Jesus Christ, his death and blood shedding, to give freely to us the whole inheritance of grace and glory. And under this notion the covenant has no condition, nor are any such either expressed or intimated in this place.

First Practical Observation

The covenant of grace, as reduced into the form of a testament, confirmed by the blood of Christ, does not depend on any condition or qualification in our persons, but on a free grant and donation of God; and so do all the good things prepared in it.

Second Practical Observation

The precepts of the old covenant are turned all of them into promises under the new. Their preceptive, commanding power is not taken away, but grace is promised for the performance of them. So the apostle having declared that the people broke the old covenant, adds that grace will be supplied in the new for all the duties of obedience that are required of us.

Third Practical Observation

All things in the new covenant being proposed to us by the way of promise; it is faith alone in accordance with which we may attain a participation of them. For faith only is the grace we ought to exercise, the duty we ought to perform, to render the promises of God effectual to us, Heb. 4:1, 2.

Fourth Practical Observation

Sense of the loss of an interest in and participation of the benefits of the old covenant, is the best preparation for receiving the mercies of the new.

The Author of this Covenant

The author of this covenant is God himself: "I will make it, says the Lord." This is the third time that this expression, "Says the Lord," is repeated in this testimony. The work expressed, in both the parts of it, the disannulling of the old covenant and the establishment of the new, is such as calls for this solemn interposition of the authority, veracity, and grace of God. "I will do it, says the Lord." And the mention of this is thus frequently inculcated, to beget a reverence in us of the work which he so emphatically assumes to himself. And it teaches us that,

Fifth Practical Observation

God himself, in and by his own sovereign wisdom, grace, goodness, all-sufficiency, and power, is to be considered as the only cause and author of the new covenant; or, the abolishing of the old covenant, with the introduction and establishment of the new, is an act of the mere sovereign wisdom, grace, and authority of God. It is his gracious disposal of us, and of his own grace; that of which we had no contrivance, nor indeed the least desire.

With Whom the New Covenant is Made

It is declared with whom this new covenant is made: "With the house of Israel." Verse 8, they are called distinctly "the house of Israel, and the house of Judah." The distribution of the posterity of Abraham into Israel and Judah ensued on the division that fell out among the people in the days of Rehoboam. Before, they were called Israel only. And as in verse 8 they were mentioned distinctly, to testify that none of the seed of Abraham should be absolutely excluded from the grace of the covenant, however they were divided among themselves; so here they are all jointly expressed by their ancient name of Israel, to manifest that all distinctions on the account of precedent privileges should be now taken away, that "all Israel might be saved." But we have showed before, that the whole Israel of God, or the church of the elect, is principally intended by this means.

The Time of Making the Covenant

The time of the accomplishment of this promise, or making of this covenant, is expressed, "After those days." There are various conjectures about the sense of these words, or the determination of the time limited in them.

Some suppose respect is had to the time of giving the law on Mount Sinai. Then was the old covenant made with the fathers; but after those days another should be made. But although that time, "those days," were so long past before this prophecy was given out by Jeremiah, namely, about eight hundred years, it was impossible but that the new covenant, which was not yet given, must be "after those days;" to that end it was to no purpose so to express it that it should be after those days, seeing it was impossible that otherwise it should be.

Some think that respect is had to the captivity of Babylon and the return of the people from there; for God then showed them great kindness, to win them to obedience. But neither can this time be intended; for God then made no new covenant with the people, but strictly obliged them to the terms of the old, Mal. 4:4-6. But when this new covenant was to be made, the old was to be abolished and removed, as the apostle expressly affirms, verse 13. The promise is not of new obligation, or new assistance to the observance of the old covenant, but of making a new one quite of another nature, which then was not done.

Some judge that these words, "after those days," refer to what went immediately before, "And I regarded them not:" which words include the total rejection of the Jews. 'After those days in which both the house of Judah and the house of Israel will be rejected, I will make a new covenant with the whole Israel of God.' But neither will this hold the trial; for,

(1.) Supposing that expression, "And I regarded them not," to intend the rejection of the Jews, yet it is manifest that their excision and cutting off absolutely was not in nor for their non-continuance in the old covenant, or not being faithful in that respect, but for the rejection of the new when proposed to them. Then they fell by unbelief, as the apostle fully manifests, chap. 3 of this epistle, and Rom. 11. To that end the making of the new covenant cannot be said to be after their rejection, seeing they were rejected for their refusal and contempt of it.

(2.) By this interpretation the whole house of Israel, or all the natural posterity of Abraham, would be utterly excluded from any interest in this promise. But this cannot be allowed: for it was not so *"de facto,"*[4] a remnant being taken into covenant; which though but a remnant in comparison of the whole, yet in themselves so great a multitude, as that in them the promises made to the fathers were confirmed. Nor on this supposition would this prediction of a new covenant have been any promise to them, or any of them, but rather a severe denunciation of judgment. But it is said expressly, that God would make this covenant with them, as he did the former with their fathers; which is a promise of grace and mercy.

---

[4] [In fact.]

To that end "after those days," is as much as in those days, an indeterminate season for a certain. So, "in that day," is frequently used in the prophets, Isa. 24:21, 22; Zech. 12:11. A time, therefore, certainly future, but not determined, is all that is intended in this expression, "after those days." And by this means most expositors are satisfied. Yet there is, as I judge, more in the words.

"Those days," seem to me to comprise the whole time allotted to the economy of the old testament, or dispensation of the old covenant. Such a time there was appointed to it in the counsel of God. During this season things fell out as described, verse 9. The certain period fixed to these days is called by our apostle "the time of reformation," Heb. 9:10. "After those days," that is, in or at their expiration, when they were coming to their end, in accordance with which the first covenant waxed old and decayed, God would make this covenant with them. And although much was done towards it before those days came absolutely to an end and did actually expire, yet is the making of it said to be "after those days," because being made in the wane and declension of them, it did by its making put a full and final end to them.

The Precise Time of the Accomplishment of this Promise

This in general was the time here designed for the making and establishing of the new covenant. But we must yet further inquire into the precise time of the accomplishment of this promise. And I say, the whole of it cannot be limited to any one season absolutely, as though all that was intended in God's making of this covenant did consist in any one individual act. The making of the old covenant with the fathers is said to be "in the day in which God took them by the hand, to bring them out of the land of Egypt." During the season intended there were many things that were preparatory to the making of that covenant, or to the solemn establishment of it. So was it also in the making of the new covenant. It was gradually made and established, and that by various acts preparatory for it or confirmatory of it. And there are six degrees observable in it,

(1.) The first peculiar entrance into it was made by the ministry of John the Baptist. God had raised him to send under the name and in the spirit and power of Elijah, to prepare the way of the Lord, Mal. 4. Therefore is his ministry called "the beginning of the gospel," Mark 1:1, 2. Until his coming, the people were bound absolutely and universally to the covenant in Horeb, without alteration or addition in any ordinance of worship. But his ministry was designed to prepare them, and to cause them to look out after the accomplishment of this promise of making the new covenant, Mal. 4:4-6. And these by whom his ministry was despised, did "reject the counsel of God against themselves," that is, to their ruin; and made themselves liable to that utter excision with the threat of which the writings of the Old Testament are closed, Mal. 4:6. He therefore called the people off from resting in or trusting to the privileges of the first covenant, Matt. 3:8-10; preached to them a doctrine of repentance; and instituted a new ordinance of worship, in accordance with which they might be initiated into a new state or condition, a new relation to God. And in his whole ministry he pointed at, and directed and gave testimony to Him who was then to come to establish this new covenant. This was the beginning of the accomplishment of this promise.

(2.) The coming in the flesh and personal ministry of our Lord Jesus Christ himself, was an eminent advance and degree in that respect. The dispensation of the old covenant did yet continue; for he himself, as "made of a woman," was "made under the law," yielding obedience to it, observing all its precepts and institutions. But his coming in the flesh laid an axe to the root of that whole dispensation; for in that respect the main end that God designed by that means towards that people was accomplished. The interposition of the law was now to be taken away, and the promise to become all to the church. Therefore on his nativity this covenant was proclaimed from heaven, as that which was immediately to take place, Lk. 2:13, 14. But it was more fully and evidently carried on in and by his personal ministry. The whole doctrine of it was preparatory to the immediate introduction of this covenant. But especially there was in that respect and by that means, by the truth which he taught, by the manner of his teaching, by the miracles which he did, in conjunction with an open accomplishment of the prophecies concerning him, evidence given that he was the Messiah, the mediator of the new covenant. In this was a declaration made of the person in and by whom it was to be established: and therefore he told them, that unless they believed it was he who was so promised, they should die in their sins.

(3.) The way for the introduction of this covenant being thus prepared, it was solemnly enacted and confirmed in and by his death; for in this he offered that sacrifice to God in accordance with which it was established. And by this means the promise properly became διαθήκη, a "testament," as our apostle proves at large, Heb. 9:14-16. And he declares in the same place, that it answered those sacrifices whose blood was sprinkled on the people and the book of the law, in the confirmation of the first covenant; which things must be treated of afterwards. This was the center in which all the promises of grace did meet, and from which source they derived their efficacy. From this point on the old covenant, and all its administrations, having received their full accomplishment, did abide only in the patience of God, to be taken down and removed out of the way in his own time and manner; for really and in themselves their force and authority did then cease, and was taken away. See Eph. 2:14-16; Col. 2:14, 15. But our obligation to obedience and the observance of commands, though formally and ultimately it be resolved into the will of God, yet immediately it respects the revelation of it, by which we are directly obliged. To that end, although the causes of the removal of the old covenant had already been applied to that, yet the law and its institutions were still continued not only lawful but useful to the worshippers, until the will of God concerning their abrogation was fully declared.

(4.) This new covenant had the complement of its making and establishment in the resurrection of Christ. For in order to this the old was to have its perfect end. God did not make the first covenant, and in that respect revive, represent, and confirm the covenant of works, with the promise annexed to it, merely that it should continue for such a season, and then die of itself, and be arbitrarily removed; but that whole dispensation had an end which was to be accomplished, and without which it was not consistent with the wisdom or righteousness of God to remove it or take it away. Yea, nothing of it could be removed, until all was fulfilled. It was easier to remove heaven and earth than to remove the law, as to its right and title to rule the souls and consciences of men, before all was fulfilled. And this end had two parts:

[1.] The perfect fulfilling of the righteousness which it required. This was done in the obedience of Christ, the surety of the new covenant, in the stead of them with whom the covenant was made.

[2.] That the curse of it should be undergone. Until this was done, the law could not quit its claim to power over sinners. And as this curse was undergone in the suffering, so it was absolutely discharged in the resurrection of Christ. For the pains of death being loosed and he delivered from the state of the dead, the sanction of the law was declared to be void, and its curse answered. By this means did the old covenant so expire, as that the worship which belonged to it was only for a while continued, in the patience and forbearance of God towards that people.

(5.) The first solemn promulgation of this new covenant, so made, ratified, and established, was on the day of Pentecost, seven weeks after the resurrection of Christ. And it answered the promulgation of the law on Mount Sinai, the same space of time after the delivery of the people out of Egypt. From this day forward the ordinances of worship, and all the institutions of the new covenant, became obligatory to all believers. Then was the whole church absolved from any duty with respect to the old covenant, and the worship of it, though it was not manifest as yet in their consciences.

(6.) The question being stated about the continuance of the obligatory force of the old covenant, the contrary was solemnly proclaimed by the apostles, under the infallible conduct of the Holy Spirit, Acts 15.

These were the articles, or the degrees of the time intended in that expression, "after those days;" all of them answering the several degrees in accordance with which the old vanished and disappeared.

The Nature of the Promises of the New Covenant

The circumstances of the making of this covenant being thus cleared, the nature of it in its promises is next proposed to us. And in the exposition of the words we must do these two things: 1. Inquire into the general nature of these promises. 2. Particularly and distinctly explain them.

The General Nature of These Promises

FIRST, the general nature both of the covenant and of the promises in accordance with which it is here expressed must briefly be inquired into, because there are various apprehensions about them. For some suppose that there is an especial efficacy towards the things mentioned intended in these promises, and no more; some judge that the things themselves, the event and end, are so promised.

In the first way Schlichtingius expresses himself on this place: "Not, 'For a good while I will see to it that my laws are written on stone tablets only, but I will make such a covenant with them that my laws might be engraved upon their very minds and hearts.' It is evident that these words must be understood within the limits of (their) power and efficacy, certainly not necessarily extending to the result itself of the inscribing, which always has been placed in the free power of man; which very fact the following words of God also teach, verse 12. By which (words) God himself reveals the reason or the manner and matter of this fact which is held together by his vast grace and by holding out mercy to the people. By this (mercy) he describes the future so that the people might be devoted to him with so much ardor and might keep his laws. Therefore the meaning is 'I will make a covenant of such a kind that will produce the greatest and most sufficient resources for keeping my people in allegience.'"[5]

And another: "I will, instead of these external, carnal ordinances and observations, give them spiritual commands for the regulating of their affections, precepts most agreeable to all men, [made] by the exceeding greatness of that grace and mercy. In this and many other particulars I will incline their affections willingly to receive my law."

The sense of both is, that all which is here promised consists in the nature of the means, and their efficacy from it, to incline, dispose, and engage men to the things here spoken of, but not to produce them certainly and infallibly in them to whom the promise is given. And it is supposed that the efficacy granted arises from the nature of the precepts of the gospel, which are rational, and suited to the principles of our intellectual natures. For these precepts, enlivened by the promises made to the observance of them, with the other mercies by which they are accompanied in God's dealing with us, are meet to prevail on our minds and wills to obedience; but yet, when all is done, the whole issue depends on our own wills, and their determination of themselves one way or other.

---

[5] *Non 'ut olim curabo leges meas in lapidëis tantum tabulis inscribi, sed tale foedus cum illis feriam ut meæ leges ipsis eorum mentibus et cordibus insculpantur:' apparet hæc verba intra vim et efficaciam accipienda esse, non vero ad ipsum inscriptionis effectum necessariò porrigenda, qui semper in libera hominis potestate positus est; quod ipsum docent et sequentia Dei verba, ver. 12. Quibus ipse Deus causam seu modum ac rationem hujus rei aperit, quæ ingenti illius gratia ac misericordia populo exhibenda continetur. Hac futurum dicit ut populus tanto ardore sibi serviat, suásque leges observet. Sensus ergo est, 'tale percutiam foedus quod maximas et sufficientissimas vires habebit populum meum in officio continendi.*

Rebuttal of the Socinian Interpretation
And Demonstration of the True Interpretation
In Six Particulars

But these things are not only liable to many just exceptions, but do indeed overthrow the whole nature of the new covenant, and the text is not expounded but corrupted by them; to that end they must be removed out of the way. And,

1. The exposition given can no way be accommodated to the words, so as to grant a truth in their plain literal sense. For although God says, "He will put his laws in their mind, and write them in their heart, and they will all know him," which declares what he will effectually do; the sense of their exposition is, that indeed he will not do so, only he will do that which will move them and persuade them to do that themselves which he has promised to do himself, and that whether they ever do so or no! But if any one concerning whom God says that he will write his law in his heart, have it not so written, be it on what account it will, suppose it be that the man will not have it so written, how can the promise be true, that God will write his law in his heart? It is a sorry apology, to say that God in making that promise did not foresee the obstruction that would arise, or could not remove it when it did so.

2. It is the event, or the effect itself, that is directly promised, and not any such efficacy of means as might be frustrated. For the weakness and imperfection of the first covenant was evidenced by this means, that those with whom it was made continued not in it. On this God neglected them, and the covenant became unprofitable, or at least unsuccessful as to the general end of continuing the relation between God and them, of his being their God, and they being his people. To redress this evil, and prevent the like for the future, that is, effectually to provide that God and his people may always abide in that blessed covenant relation, he promises the things themselves in accordance with which it might be secured. That which the first covenant could not effect, God promised to work in and by the new.

3. It is nowhere said nor intimated in the Scripture, that the efficacy of the new covenant, and the accomplishment of the promises of it, should depend on and arise from the suitableness of its precepts to our reason, or natural principles; but it is universally and constantly ascribed to the efficacy of the Spirit and grace of God, not only enabling us to

obedience, but enduing us with a spiritual, supernatural, vital principle, from which it may proceed.

4. It is true, that our own wills, or the free actions of them, are required in our faith and obedience; by reason of which it is promised that we will be "willing in the day of his power." But that our wills are left absolutely in this to our own liberty and power, without being inclined and determined by the grace of God, is that Pelagianism which has long attacked the church, but which will never absolutely prevail.

5. The putting the laws of God in our minds, and the writing of them in our hearts, that we may know him, and fear him always, is promised in the same way and manner as is the forgiveness of sin, verse 12; and it is hard to affix such a sense to that promise, as that God will use such and such means that our sins may be pardoned, which yet may all of them fail.

6. As this exposition is no way suited to the words of the text, nor of the context, or scope of the place, so indeed it overthrows the nature of the new covenant, and the grace of our Lord Jesus Christ, which comes by that means. For,

(1.) If the effect itself, or the things mentioned are not promised, but only the use of means, left to the liberty of men's wills whether they will comply with them or no, then the very being of the covenant, whether it ever will have any existence or no, depends absolutely on the wills of men, and so may not be. For it is not the proposal of the terms of the covenant, and the means in accordance with which we may enter into it, that is called the making of this covenant with us; but our real participation of the grace and mercy promised in it. This alone gives a real existence to the covenant itself, without which it is not a covenant; nor without it is it properly made with any.

(2.) The Lord Christ would be made by this means the mediator of an uncertain covenant. For if it depends absolutely on the wills of men whether they will accept of the terms of it and comply with it or no, it is uncertain what will be the event, and whether ever any one will do so or no; for the will being not determined by grace, what its actions will be is altogether uncertain.

(3.) The covenant can, on this, in no sense be a testament; which our apostle afterwards proves that it is, and that irrevocably ratified by the death of the testator. For there can, on this supposition, be no certain heir to whom Christ did bequeath his goods, and the inheritance of mercy, grace, and glory. This would make this testament inferior to that of a wise man, who determines in particular to whom his goods will come.

(4.) It takes away that difference between this and the former covenant which it is the main scope of the apostle to prove; at least it leaves the difference to consist only in the gradual efficacy of outward means; which is most remote from his purpose. For there were by the old covenant means supplied to induce the people to constant obedience, and those in their kind powerful. This is pleaded by Moses, in almost the whole book of Deuteronomy. For the scope of all his exhortations to obedience is to show that God had so instructed them in the knowledge of his will by giving of the law, and had accompanied his teachings with so many signal mercies, such effects of his mighty power, goodness, and grace; that the covenant was accompanied with such promises and threats, that in that respect life and death temporal and eternal were set before them; all which made their obedience so reasonable and necessary, that nothing but profligacy in wickedness could turn them from it. To this purpose are discourses multiplied in that book. And yet notwithstanding all this, it is added, "that God had not circumcised their hearts to fear him and obey him always," as it is here promised. The communication of grace effectual, producing infallibly the good things proposed and promised in the minds and hearts of men, belonged not to that covenant. If, therefore, there be no more in the making of the new covenant but only the adding of more forcible outward means and motives, more suitable to our reasons, and meet to work on our affections, it differs only in some unnoticeable degrees from the former. But this is directly contrary to the promise in the prophet, that it will not be according to it, or of the same kind; no more than Christ, the high priest of it, should be a priest after the order of Aaron.

(5.) It would on this supposition follow, that God might fulfill his promise of "putting his laws in the minds of men, and writing them in their hearts," and yet none have the laws put into their minds, nor written in their hearts; which things are not reconcilable by any distinction to the ordinary reason of mankind.

To that end we must grant that it is the effect, the event in the communication of the things promised, that is ascribed to this covenant, and not only the use and application of means to their production. And this will yet further appear in the particular exposition of the several parts of it. But yet, before we enter for that reason, two objections must be removed, which may in general be laid against our interpretation.

Two Objections Removed

First, "This covenant is promised as that which is future, to be brought in at a certain time, 'after those days,' as has been declared. But it is certain that the things here mentioned, the grace and mercy expressed, were really communicated to many both before and after the giving of the law, long before this covenant was made; for all who truly believed and feared God had these things accomplished in them by grace: to that end their effectual communication cannot be esteemed a property of this covenant which was to be made afterwards."

Answer: This objection was sufficiently prevented in what we have already discoursed concerning the efficacy of the grace of this covenant before itself was solemnly consummated. For all things of this nature that belong to it do arise and spring from the mediation of Christ, or his interposition on the behalf of sinners. To that end this took place from the giving of the first promise; the administration of the grace of this covenant did in that respect and then take its date. Although the Lord Christ had not yet done that in accordance with which it was solemnly to be confirmed, and that on what all the virtue of it did depend. To that end this covenant is promised now to be made, not in opposition to what grace and mercy was derived from it both before and under the law, nor as to the first administration of grace from the mediator of it; but in opposition to the covenant of Sinai, and with respect to its outward solemn confirmation.

Secondly, "If the things themselves are promised in the covenant, then all those with whom this covenant is made must be really and effectually made partakers of them. But this is not so; they are not all actually sanctified, pardoned, and saved, which are the things here promised."

Answer: The making of this covenant may be considered two ways: 1. As to the preparation and proposition of its terms and conditions. 2. As to the internal stipulation between God and the souls of men. In this sense alone God is properly said to make this covenant with any. The preparation and proposition of laws are not the making of the covenant. And therefore all with whom this covenant is made are effectually sanctified, justified, and saved.

The Blessed Properties and Effects of the New Covenant

SECONDLY, These things being premised, as it was necessary they should be, to the right understanding of the mind of the Holy Spirit, I will proceed to the particular parts of the covenant as here expressed, namely, in the blessed properties and effects of it, in accordance with which it is distinguished from the former.

First General Blessing–
Restoration of the Image of God in Us

The first two expressions are of the same nature and tendency, "I will put my laws in their mind, and write them in their hearts." In general it is the reparation of our nature by the restoration of the image of God in us, that is, our sanctification, which is promised in these words. And there are two things in the words both doubly expressed: 1. The subject acted on; which is the "mind" and the "heart." 2. The manner of producing the effect mentioned in them; and that is by "putting" and "writing." And, 3. The things by these means so communicated; which are the "laws" of God.

The Subject Acted On

The subject spoken of is the mind and heart. When the apostle treats of the depravation and corruption of our nature, he places them ἐν τῇ διανοίᾳ and ἐν τῇ καρδίᾳ, Eph. 4:18; that is, "the mind and the heart." These are, in the Scripture, the seat of natural corruption, the residence of the principle of alienation from the life of God which is in us. To that end the renovation of our natures consists in the rectifying and curing of them, in the furnishing them with contrary principles of faith, love, and adherence to God. And we may observe, that,

Sixth Practical Observation

The grace of our Lord Jesus Christ in the new covenant, in its being and existence, in its healing, repairing efficacy, is as large and extensive as sin is in its residence and power to deprave our natures. This is the difference about the extent of the new covenant, and the grace of it: Some would have it to extend to all persons, in its tender and conditional proposition; but not to all things, as to its efficacy in the reparation of our natures. Others assert it to extend to all the effects of sin, in the removal of them, and the cure of our natures by that means; but as to persons, it is really extended to none but those in whom these effects are produced, whatever be its outward administration, which was also always limited: to whom I do subscribe.

On Their Minds

The first thing mentioned is the "mind." קֶרֶב, the apostle renders by διάνοια, "the inward part." The mind is the most secret, inward part or power of the soul. And the prophet expresses it by the "inward part," because it is the only safe and useful repository of the laws of God. When they are there laid up, we will not lose them; neither men nor devils can take them from us. And he also declares in which the excellence of covenant obedience does consist. It is not in the conformity of our outward actions to the law, although that be required in that respect also; but it principally lies in the inward parts, where God searches for and regards truth in sincerity, Ps. 51:6. To that end διάνοια is the "mind and understanding," whose natural depravation is the spring and principle of all disobedience; the cure of which is here promised in the first place. In the outward administration of the means of grace, the affections, or, if I may so speak, the more outward part of the soul, are usually first impressed and acted on: but the first real effect of the internal promised grace of the covenant is on the mind, the most spiritual and inward part of the soul. This in the New Testament is expressed by the renovation of the mind, Rom. 12:2, Eph. 4:23; and the opening of the eyes of our understandings, Eph. 1:17, 18; God shining into our hearts, to give us the knowledge of his glory in the face of Jesus Christ, 2 Cor. 4:6. By this means the enmity against God, the vanity, darkness, and alienation from the life of God, with which the mind naturally is possessed and filled, are taken away and removed, of the nature of which work I have treated at large elsewhere;[6] for the law of God in the mind, is the saving knowledge of the mind and will of God, of which the law is the revelation, communicated to it and implanted in it.

---

[6] See his treatise on the Holy Spirit, vol. iii. of his miscellaneous works.- Ed. [Banner Edition.]

The Manner of Producing the Effect

The way in accordance with which God in the covenant of grace
thus works on the mind is expressed by διδούς: so the apostle
renders נָתַתִּי, "I will give." Διδούς, "giving," may by a substitution
be put for δώσω, "I will give." So is it expressed in the next clause,
ἐπιγράψω, in the future tense, "I will write." The word in the
prophet is, "I will give;" we render it, "I will put." But there are two
things intimated in the word: (1.) The freedom of the grace
promised; it is a mere grant, gift, or donation of grace. (2.) The
efficacy of it. That which is given of God to any is received by
them, otherwise it is no gift. And this latter is well expressed by the
word used by us, "I will put;" which expresses an actual
communication, and not a fruitless tender. This the apostle renders
emphatically, διδούς; that is, εἰμί, 'This is that which I do, am
doing in this covenant; namely, freely giving that grace in
accordance with which my laws will be implanted on the minds of
men.'

The Things Communicated: My Laws

To show in general, before we proceed to the nature of this work, so
far as is necessary to the exposition of the words, we may here
consider what was observed in the third place, namely, what it is
that is thus promised to be communicated, and so carry it on with us
to the other clause of this promise.

That which is to be put into this spiritual receptacle is, in these
words, τοὺς νόμους μου, "My laws;" in the plural number.
Expositors inquire what laws are here intended, whether the moral
law only, or others also. But there is no need of such inquiry. There
is a metonymy of the subject and effect in the words. It is that
knowledge of the mind and will of God which is revealed in the law,
and taught by it, which is promised. The "laws of God," therefore,
are here taken largely, for the whole revelation of the mind and will
of God. So does תּוֹרָה originally signify "doctrine" or "instruction."
By whatsoever way or revelation God makes known himself and his
will to us, requiring our obedience in that respect, it is all comprised
in that expression of "his laws".

The Nature of the Grace in the First Promise

From these things we may easily discern the nature of that grace which is contained in this first branch of the first promise of the covenant. And this is, the effectual operation of his Spirit in the renovation and saving illumination of our minds, in accordance with which they are habitually made conformable to the whole law of God, that is, the rule and the law of our obedience in the new covenant, and enabled to all acts and duties that are required of us. And this is the first grace promised and communicated to us by virtue of this covenant, as it was necessary that so it should be. For, 1. The mind is the principal seat of all spiritual obedience. 2. The proper and peculiar actions of the mind, in discerning, knowing, judging, must go before the actions of the will and affections, much more all outward practices. 3. The depravation of the mind is such, by blindness, darkness, vanity, and enmity, that nothing can inflame our souls, or make an entrance towards the reparation of our natures, but an internal, spiritual, saving operation of grace on the mind. 4. Faith itself is principally ingenerated by an infusion of saving light into the mind, 2 Cor. 4:4, 6. So,

Seventh Practical Observation

All the beginnings and entrances into the saving knowledge of God, and for that reason of obedience to him, are effects of the grace of the covenant.

On Their Hearts

The second part of this first promise of the covenant is expressed in these words, "And will write them on their hearts;" which is that which renders the former part actually effectual.

Expositors generally observe, that respect is had in this to the giving of the law on Mount Sinai, that is, in the first covenant; for then the law (that is, "the ten words") was written in tables of stone. And although the original tables were broken by Moses, when the people had broken the covenant, yet would not God alter that dispensation, nor write his laws any other way, but commanded new tables of stone to be made, and wrote them in that place. And this was done, not so much to secure the outward letter of them, as to represent the hardness of the hearts of the people to whom they were given. God did not, God would not by virtue of that covenant otherwise dispose of his law. And the event that followed this was that they broke these laws, and abode not in obedience. This event God promises to anticipate and prevent under the new covenant, and that by writing these laws now in our hearts, which he wrote before only in tables of stone; that is, he will effectually work that obedience in us which the law does require, for he "works in us both to will and to do of his own good pleasure." The heart, as distinguished from the mind, comprises the will and the affections; and they are compared to the tables in which the letter of the law was engraved. For as by that writing and engraving, the tables received the impression of the letters and words in which the law was contained, which they did firmly retain and represent, so as that although they were stones still in their nature, yet were they nothing but the law in their use; so by the grace of the new covenant there is a durable impression of the law of God on the wills and affections of men, in accordance with which they fulfill it, represent it, comply with it, and have a living principle of it abiding in them. To that end, as this work must necessarily consist of two parts, namely, the removal out of the heart of whatever is contrary to the law of God, and the implanting of principles of obedience in that respect; so it comes under a double description or denomination in the Scripture. For sometimes it is called a "taking away of the heart of stone," or "circumcising of the heart;" and sometimes the "giving of an heart of flesh," the "writing of the law in our hearts;" which is the renovation of our natures into the image of God in righteousness and the holiness of truth. To that end in this promise the whole of our sanctification, in its beginning and progress, in its work on our whole souls and all their faculties, is comprised. And we may observe,

Eighth Practical Observation

The work of grace in the new covenant happens on the whole soul, in all its faculties, powers, and affections, to their change and renovation. The whole was corrupted, and the whole must be renewed. The image of God was originally in and on the whole, and on the loss of it the whole was depraved. See 1 Thes. 5:23.

Ninth Practical Observation

To take away the necessity and efficacy of renewing, changing, sanctifying grace, consisting in an internal, efficacious operation of the principles, habits, and acts of internal grace and obedience, is plainly to overthrow and reject the new covenant.

Tenth Practical Observation

We bring nothing to the new covenant but our hearts, as tables to be written in, with the sense of the insufficiency of the precepts and promises of the law, with respect to our own ability to comply with them.

"I will be to them a God, and they will be to me a people."

The last thing in the words is the relation that follows on this between God and his people: "I will be to them a God, and they will be to me a people." This is indeed a distinct promise by itself, summarily comprising all the blessings and privileges of the covenant. And it is placed in the center of the account given of the whole, as that from which source all the grace of it does spring, in which all the blessings of it do consist, and in accordance with which they are secured. Although in this place it is peculiarly mentioned, as that which has its foundation in the foregoing promise. For this relation, which implies mutual acquiescence in each other, could not be, nor ever had been, if the minds and hearts of them who are to be taken into it were not changed and renewed. For neither could God approve of and rest in his love towards them, while they were enemies to him in the depravation of their natures; nor could they find rest or satisfaction in God, whom they neither knew, nor liked, nor loved.

This is the general expression of any covenant relation between God and men, "He will be to them a God, and they will be to him a people." And it is frequently made use of with respect to the first covenant, which yet was disannulled. God owned the people in that respect for his peculiar portion, and they avouched him to be their God alone.

Nor can this be spoken of God and any people, but on the ground of an especial covenant. It is true, God is the God of all the world and all people are his; yea, he is a God to them all. For as he made them, so he sustains, rules, and governs them in all things, by his power and providence. But with respect to this God does not freely promise that he will be a God to any, nor can so do; for his power over all, and his rule of all things, is essential and natural to him, so as it cannot otherwise be. To that end, as thus declared, it is a peculiar expression of an especial covenant relation. And the nature of it is to be expounded by the nature and properties of that covenant which it does respect.

The Nature of this Relation

Two things we must therefore consider, to discover the nature of this relation: 1. The foundation of it. 2. The mutual actions in it by virtue of this relation.

The Foundation

To the manifestation of the foundation of it, some things must be premised:

(1.) On the entrance of sin there continued no such covenant relation between God and man, as that by virtue of it he should be their God, and they should be his people. God continued still in the full enjoyment of his sovereignty over men; which no sin, or rebellion, or apostasy of man could in the least impeach. And man continued under an obligation to dependence on God and subjection to his will in all things. For these cannot be separated from his nature and being until final judgment be executed; after which God rules over them only by power, without any respect to their wills or obedience. But that especial relation of mutual interest by virtue of the first covenant ceased between them.

(2.) God would not enter into any other covenant with sinful, fallen man, to be "a God to them," and to take them to be a "peculiar people" to him, immediately in their own persons. Nor was it consistent with his wisdom and goodness so to do; for if man was not steadfast in God's covenant, but broke and disannulled it when he was sinless and upright, only created with a possibility of defection, what expectations could there be that now he was fallen, and his nature wholly depraved, any new covenant should be of use to the glory of God or advantage of man? To enter into a new covenant that must necessarily be broken, to the aggravation of the misery of man, became not the wisdom and goodness of God. If it be said, 'God might have so made a new covenant immediately with men as to secure their future obedience, and to have made it firm and stable,' I answer, it would not have become the divine wisdom and goodness to have dealt better with men after their rebellion and apostasy than before, namely, on their own account. He did in our first creation communicate to our nature all that grace and all those privileges with which in his wisdom he thought meet to endow it, and all that was necessary to make them who were partakers of it everlastingly blessed. To suppose that he, on his own account alone, would immediately collate more grace on it, is to suppose him singularly well pleased with our sin and rebellion. This, then, God would not do. To that end,

(3.) God provided in the first place that there should be a mediator, a sponsor, an undertaker, with whom alone he would treat about a new covenant, and so establish it. For in the contrivance of his grace and wisdom concerning it, there were many things necessary to it that could no otherwise be enacted and accomplished. Nay, there was not any one thing in all the good which he designed to mankind in this covenant, in a way of love, grace, and mercy, that could be communicated to them, so as that his honor and glory might be advanced by that means, without the consideration of this mediator, and what he undertook to do. Nor could mankind have yielded any of that obedience to God which he would require of them, without the interposition of this mediator on their behalf. It was therefore with him that God firstly made this covenant.

The Mediator Must Be Christ

How it was needful that this mediator should be God and man in one person; how he became so to undertake for us, and in our stead; what was the especial covenant between God and him as to the work which he undertook personally to perform; have, according to our poor weak measure and dark apprehension of these heavenly things, been declared at large in our Exercitations on this epistle, and yet more fully in our discourse of the mystery and glory of the person of Christ.[7] To that end, as to this new covenant, it was firstly made with Jesus Christ, the surety of it and undertaker in it. For,

(1.) God neither would nor, "*salvâ justitiâ, sapientiâ, et honore*,"[8] could, treat immediately with sinful, rebellious men on terms of grace for

---

[7] See Exerc. xxv.-xxxiv.; and vol. i. of the author's miscellaneous works. [Banner Edition.]

[8] [Saving justice, wisdom and honor.]

the future, until satisfaction was undertaken to be made for sins past, or such as should afterwards fall out. This was done by Christ alone; who was therefore the πρῶτον δεκτικόν[9] of this covenant and all the grace of it. See 2 Cor. 5:19, 20; Gal. 3:13, 14; Rom. 3:25.

(2.) No restipulation[10] of obedience to God could be made by man, which might be a ground of entering into a covenant intended to be firm and stable. For seeing we had broken our first covenant engagement with God in our best condition, we were not likely of ourselves to make good a new engagement of a higher nature than the former. Who will take the word or the security of a bankrupt for thousands, who is known not to be worth one farthing; especially if he had wasted a former estate in luxury and riot, continuing an open slave to the same lusts? To that end it was absolutely necessary that in this covenant there should be a surety, to undertake for our answering and firm standing to the terms of it. Without this, the event of this new covenant, which God would make as a singular effect of his wisdom and grace, would neither have been glory to him nor advantage to us.

(3.) That grace which was to be the spring of all the blessings of this covenant, to the glory of God and salvation of the church, was to be deposited in some safe hand, for the accomplishment of these ends. In the first covenant, God at once committed to man that whole stock of grace which was necessary to enable him to the obedience of it. And the grace of reward which he was to receive on the performance of it, God reserved absolutely in his own hand; yea, so as that perhaps man did not fully understand what it was. But all was lost at once that was committed to our keeping, so as that nothing at all was left to give us the least relief as to any new endeavors. To that end God will now secure all the good things of this covenant, both as to grace and glory, in a third hand, in the hand of a mediator. On this the promises are made to him, and the fullness of grace is laid up in him, John 1:14; Col. 1:19; 2:3; Eph. 3:8; 2 Cor. 1:20.

(4.) As he was the mediator of this covenant, God became his God, and he became the servant of God in a peculiar manner. For he stood before God in this covenant as a public representative of all the elect. See our comment on chap. 1:5, 8, 9; 2:13. God is a God to him in all the

---

[9] [First recipient.]

[10] [To stipulate again – to agree again. See also footnote 4 in Chapter One of Coxe's treatment.]

promises he received on the behalf of his spiritual body; and he was his servant in the accomplishment of them, as the pleasure of the Lord was to prosper in his hand.

(5.) God being in this covenant a God and Father to Christ, he came by virtue of it to be our God and Father, John 20:17; Heb. 2:12, 13. And we became "heirs of God, joint-heirs with Christ;" and his people, to yield him all sincere obedience.

And these things may suffice briefly to declare the foundation of that covenant relation which is here expressed.

Eleventh Practical Observation

To that end, the Lord Christ, God and man, undertaking to be the mediator between God and man, and a surety on our behalf, is the spring and head of the new covenant, which is made and established with us in him.

The Mutual Actions

The nature of this covenant relation is expressed on the one side and the other: "I will be to them a God, and they will be to me a people:"

The Relation of God to Man

On the part of God it is, "I will be to them a God" or, as it is elsewhere expressed, "I will be their God." And we must make a little inquiry into this unspeakable privilege, which eternity only will fully unfold:

[1.] The person speaking is included in the verb, καὶ ἔσομαι, "I will be;" 'I, Jehovah, who make this promise.' And in this God proposes to our faith all the glorious properties of his nature: 'I, who am that I am, Jehovah, goodness and being itself, and the cause of all being and goodness to others; infinitely wise, powerful, righteous, etc. I, that am all this, and in all that I am will be so.' Here lies the eternal spring of the infinite treasures of the supplies of the church, here and for ever. Whatever God is in himself, whatever these properties of his nature extend to, in it all God has promised to be our God: Gen. 17:1, "I am God Almighty; walk before me." Therefore, to give establishment and security to our faith, he has in his word revealed himself by so many names, titles, properties, and that so frequently; it is that we may know him who is our God, what he is, and what he will be to us. And the knowledge of him, as so revealing himself, is that which secures our confidence, faith, hope, fear, and trust. "The LORD will be a refuge for the oppressed, a refuge in times of trouble; and they that know your name will put their trust in you," Ps. 9:9, 10.

[2.] What he promises is, that "he will be a God to us." Now, although this comprises absolutely every thing that is good, yet may the notion of being a God to any be referred to two general heads: 1st. An all-sufficient preserver; and, 2dly. An all-sufficient rewarder: so himself declares the meaning of this expression, Gen. 17:1; 15:1. 'I will be all this to them that I am a God to in the way of preservation and recompense,' Heb. 11:6.

[3.] The declared rule and measure of God's actions towards us as our God, are the promises of the covenant, both of mercy, grace, pardon, holiness, perseverance, protection, success, and spiritual victory in this world, and of eternal glory in the world to come. In and by all these things will he, in all that he is in himself, be a God to those whom he takes into this covenant.

[4.] It is included in this part of the promise that they that take him to be their God, will say, "You are my God," Hos. 2:23; and carry it towards him according to what infinite goodness, grace, mercy, power, and faithfulness, do require.

Twelfth Practical Observation

And we may observe, as nothing less than God becoming our God could relieve, help, and save us, so nothing more can be required to that.

Thirteenth Practical Observation

The efficacy, security, and glory of this covenant, depend originally on the nature of God, immediately and actually on the mediation of Christ. It is the covenant that God makes with us in him as the surety of it.

Fourteenth Practical Observation

It is from the engagement of the properties of the divine nature that this covenant is "ordered in all things and sure." Infinite wisdom has provided it, and infinite power will make it effectual.

Fifteenth Practical Observation

As the grace of this covenant is inexpressible, so are the obligations it puts on us to obedience.

The Relation of Man to God

The relation of man to God is expressed in these words, "And they will be to me a people;" or, "They will be my people." And two things are contained in this:

[1.] God's owning of them to be his in a peculiar manner, according to the tenor and promise of this covenant, and dealing with them accordingly. Λαὸς περιούσιος, Tit. 2:14, "A peculiar people." Let others take heed how they meddle with them, lest they entrench on God's propriety, Jer. 2:3.

[2.] There is included in it that which is essentially required to their being his people, namely, the profession of all subjection or obedience to him, and all dependence on him. To that end this also belongs to it, namely, their avouching this God to be their God, and their free engagement to all that obedience which in the covenant he requires. For although this expression, "And they will be to me a people," seems only to denote an act of God's grace, assuming of them into that relation to himself, yet it includes their avouching him to be their God, and their voluntary engagement of obedience to him as their God. When he says, "You are my people;" they also say, "You are my God," Hos. 2:23.

Sixteenth Practical Observation

Yet is it to be observed, that God does as well undertake for our being his people as he does for his being our God. And the promises contained in this verse do principally aim at that end, namely, the making of us to be a people to him.

Seventeenth Practical Observation

Those, with whom God makes a covenant, are his in a peculiar manner. And the profession of this is that which the world principally maligns in them, and ever did so from the beginning.

Exposition of Verse 11

"And they will not teach every man his neighbor, and every man his brother, saying, Know the Lord: for all will know me, from the least to the greatest."

The second general promise, declaring the nature of the new covenant, is expressed in this verse. And the matter of it is set down, 1. Negatively, in opposition to what was in use and necessary under the first covenant. 2. Positively, in what should take place in the room of it, and be enjoyed under this new covenant, and by virtue of it.

The Negative Part of the Promise

First, in the former part we may observe,

1. The vehemence of the negation, in the redoubling of the negative particle, οὐ μή: 'They will by no means do so; that will not be the way and manner with them with whom God makes this covenant.' And this is designed to fix our minds on the consideration of the privilege which is enjoyed under the new covenant, and the greatness of it.

2. The thing thus denied is teaching, not absolutely, but as to a certain way and manner of it. The negation is not universal as to teaching, but restrained to a certain kind of it, which was in use and necessary under the old covenant. And this necessity was either from God's institution, or from practice taken up among themselves, which must be inquired into.

3. The subject-matter of this teaching, or the matter to be taught, was the knowledge of God, "Know the Lord." The whole knowledge of God prescribed in the law is here intended. And this may be reduced to two heads: (1.) The knowing of him, and the taking him for that reason to be God, to be God alone; which is the first command. (2.) Of his mind and will, as to the obedience which the law required in all the institutions and precepts of it; all the things which God revealed for their good: Deut.

29:29, "Revealed things belong to us and to our children for ever, that we may do all the words of this law."

4. The manner of the teaching, whose continuation is denied, is exemplified in a distribution into teachers and them that are taught: "Every man his neighbor and every man his brother." And in this, (1.) The universality of the duty, "every one," is expressed; and therefore it was reciprocal. Every one was to teach, and every one was to be taught; in which yet respect was to be had to their several capacities. (2.) The opportunity for the discharging of the duty is also declared, from the mutual relation of the teachers and them that are taught: "Every one his neighbor and his brother."

The Positive Part of the Promise

Secondly, the positive part of the promise consists of two parts:

1. The thing promised, which is the knowledge of God: "They will all know me." And this is placed in opposition to what is denied: "They will not teach one another, saying, Know the Lord." But this opposition is not as to the act or duty of teaching, but as to the effect, or saving knowledge itself. The principal efficient cause of our learning the knowledge of God under the new covenant is included in this part of the promise. This is expressed in another prophet and promise, "They will be all taught of God." And the observation of this will be of use to us in the exposition of this text.

2. There is added the universality of the promise with respect to them with whom this covenant is made: "All of them, from the least to the greatest;" a proverbial speech, signifying the generality intended without exception: Jer. 8:10, "Every one, from the least even to the greatest, is given to covetousness."

Rebuttal of a Misinterpretation of this Text

This text has been looked on as attended with great difficulty and much obscurity; which expositors generally rather conceal than remove. For from the vehement denial of the use of that sort or kind of teaching which was in use under the old testament, some have apprehended and contended that all outward stated ways of instruction under the new testament are useless and forbidden. On this by some all the ordinances of the church, the whole ministry and guidance of it, has been rejected;

which is, in sum, that there is no such thing as a professing church in the world. But yet those who are thus minded are no way able to advance their opinion, but by a direct contradiction to this promise in their own sense of it. For they endeavor in what they do to teach others their opinion, and that not in the way of a public ordinance, but every one his neighbor; which, if any thing, is here denied in an especial manner. And the truth is, that if all outward teaching be absolutely and universally forbidden, as it would quickly fill the world with darkness and brutish ignorance, so, if any one should come to the knowledge of the sense of this or any other text of Scripture, it would be absolutely unlawful for him to communicate it to others; for to say, 'Know the Lord, or the mind of God in this text,' either to neighbor or brother, would be forbidden. And of all kinds of teaching, that by a public ministry, in the administration of the ordinances of the church, which alone is contended against from these words, seems least to be intended; for it is private, neighborly, brotherly instruction only, that is expressed. To that end, if, on a supposition of the prohibition of such outward instruction, any one will go about to teach another that the public ordinances of the church are not to be allowed as a means of teaching under the new testament, he directly falls under the prohibition here given in his own sense, and is guilty of the violation of it. To that end these words must necessarily have another sense, as we will see they have in the exposition of them, and that plain and obvious.

Be that as it may, some learned men have been so moved with this objection, as to affirm that the accomplishment of this promise of the covenant belongs to heaven and the state of glory; for in that respect alone, they say, we will have no more need of teaching in any kind. But as this exposition is directly contrary to the design of the apostle, as respecting the teaching of the new covenant and the testator of it; when he intends only that of the old, and exalts the new above it; so there is no such difficulty in the words as to force us to carry the interpretation of them into another world.

Correct Interpretation of the Text

To the right understanding of them various things are to be observed:

1. That various things seem in the Scripture oftentimes to be denied absolutely as to their nature and being, when indeed they are so only comparatively with respect to somewhat else which is preferred before

them. Many instances might be given of this. I will direct only to one that is liable to no exception: Jer. 7:22, 23, "I spoke not to your fathers, nor commanded them in the day that I brought them out of the land of Egypt, concerning burnt-offerings or sacrifices: but this thing commanded I them, saying, Obey my voice, and I will be your God, and you will be my people: and walk in all the ways that I have commanded you, that it may be well to you." The Jews of that time preferred the ceremonial worship by burnt-offerings and sacrifices above all moral obedience, above the great duties of faith, love, righteousness, and holiness. And not only so, but in a pretended diligent observation of it, they countenanced themselves in an open neglect and contempt of moral obedience, placing all their confidence for acceptance with God in these other duties. To take them off from this vain, ruining presumption, as God by various other prophets declared the utter insufficiency of these sacrifices and burnt-offerings by themselves to render them acceptable to him, and then prefers moral obedience above them; so here he affirms that he commanded them not. And the instance is given in that time in which it is known that all the ordinances of worship by burnt-offerings and sacrifices were solemnly instituted. But a comparison is made between ceremonial worship and spiritual obedience; in respect of which God says he commanded not the former, namely, so as to stand in competition with the latter, or to be trusted to in the neglect of it, in which the evils and failures reproved did consist. So our blessed Savior expounds this and the like passages in the prophets, in a comparison between the lowest instances of the ceremonial law, such as tithing of mint and cumin, and the great duties of love and righteousness. "These things," says he, speaking of the latter, "you ought to have done;" that is, principally and in the first place have attended to, as those which the law chiefly designed. But what then will become of the former? Why, says he, "Them also you ought not to leave undone;" in their proper place obedience was to be yielded to God in them also. So is it in this present case. There was an outward teaching of "every man his neighbor, and every man his brother," enjoined under the old testament. The people trusted to and rested in this, without any regard to God's teaching by the inward circumcision of the heart. But in the new covenant, there being an express promise of an internal, effectual teaching by the Spirit of God, by writing his law in our hearts, without which all outward teaching is useless and ineffectual, it is here denied to be of any use; that is, it is not so absolutely, but in comparison of and in competition with this other effectual way of teaching and instruction. Even at this day we have not a few who set these teachings in opposition to one another, although in God's institution they are subordinate. And on this, rejecting the internal, efficacious teaching of the Spirit of God, they commit themselves only to their own endeavors in the outward means of teaching; in which for the most part there are none more negligent than themselves. But so it is, that the ways of God's grace are not suited, but always lie contrary to the corrupt reasoning of men. Therefore some reject all the outward means of teaching by the ordinances of the gospel, under a pretense that the inward teaching of the Spirit of God is all that is needful or useful in this kind. Others, on the other hand, adhere only to the outward means of instruction, despising what is affirmed concerning the inward teaching of the Spirit of God, as a mere imagination. And both sorts run into these pernicious mistakes, by opposing those things which God has made subordinate.

2. The teaching intended, whose continuance is here denied, is that which was then in use in the church; or rather, was to be so when the new covenant state was solemnly to be introduced. And this was twofold: (1.) That which was instituted by God himself; and, (2.) That which the people had superadded in the way of practice:

(1.) The first of these is, as in other places, so particularly expressed, Deut. 6:6-9, "And these words which I command you this day, will be in your heart; and you will teach them diligently to your children, and will talk of them when you sit in your house, and when you walk by the way, and when you lie down, and when you rise up. And you will bind them for a sign on your hand, and they will be as frontlets between your eyes. And you will write them on the posts of your house, and on your gate." Add to this the institution of fringes for a memorial of the commandments; which was one way of saying, "Know the Lord," Num. 15:38, 39.

Two things may be considered in these institutions: [1.] What is natural and moral, included in the common mutual duties of men one towards another; for of this nature is that of seeking the good of others by instructing them in the knowledge of God, in which their chief happiness does consist. [2.] That which is ceremonial, as to the manner of this duty, is described in various instances, as those of frontlets and fringes, writing on posts and doors. The first of these is to abide for ever. No promise of the gospel does evacuate any precept of the law of nature; such as that is of seeking the good of others, and that their chief good, by means and ways proper to that. But as to the latter, which the Jews did principally attend to and rely on, it is by this promise, or the new covenant, quite taken away.

(2.) As to the practice of the church of the Jews in these institutions, it is not to be expressed what extremities they ran into. It is probable that about the time spoken of in this promise, which is that of the Babylonian captivity, they began that intricate, perplexed way of teaching which afterwards they were wholly addicted to. For all of them who pretended to be serious, gave up themselves to the teaching and learning of the law. But with this they mixed so many vain curiosities and traditions of their own, that the whole of their endeavor was disapproved of God. Therefore, in the very entrance of their practice of this way of teaching, he threatens to destroy all them that attended to it: Mal. 2:12, "The LORD will cut off the master and the scholar out of the tabernacles of Jacob." It is true, we have not any monuments or records of their teaching all that time, neither what they taught, nor how; but we may reasonably suppose it was of the same kind with what flourished afterwards in their famous schools derived from these first inventors. And of such reputation were those schools among them, that none was esteemed a wise man, or to have any understanding of the law, who was not brought up in them. The first record we have of the manner of their teaching, or what course they took in that respect, is in the Mishna. This is their interpretation of the law, or their saying one to another, "Know the LORD." And he that will seriously consider but one section or chapter in that whole book, will quickly discern of what kind and nature their teaching was; for such an tedious, laborious, curious, fruitless work, there is not another instance to be given of in the whole world. There is not any one head, doctrine, or precept of the law, suppose it be of the Sabbath, of sacrifices, or offerings, but they have filled it with so many needless, foolish, curious, superstitious questions and determinations, as that it is almost impossible that any man in the whole course of his life should understand them, or guide his course according to them. These were the burdens that the Pharisees bound on the shoulders of their disciples, until they were utterly weary and fainted under them. And this kind of teaching had possessed the whole church then, when the new covenant was solemnly to be introduced, no other being in use. And this is absolutely intended in this promise, as that which was utterly to cease. For God would take away the law, which in itself was "a burden," as the apostle speaks, "which neither their fathers nor they were able to bear." And the weight of that burden was unspeakably increased by the expositions and additions of which this teaching consisted. To that end the removal of it is here proposed in the way of a promise, evidencing it to be a matter of grace and kindness to the church. But the removal of teaching in general is always mentioned as a threat and punishment.

What Was The Removal of Teaching?

To that end the denial of the continuation of this teaching may be considered two ways:

(1.) As it was external, in opposition to and comparison of the effectual internal teaching by the grace of the new covenant; so it is laid aside, not absolutely, but comparatively, and as it was solitary.

(2.) It may be considered in the manner of it, with especial respect to the ceremonial law, as it consisted in the observance of various rites and ceremonies. And in this sense it was utterly to cease; above all, with respect to the additions which men had made to the ceremonial institutions in which it did consist. Such was their teaching by writing parts of the law on their fringes, frontlets, and doors of their houses; especially as these things were enlarged, and precepts concerning them multiplied in the practice of the Jewish church. It is promised concerning these things, that they will be absolutely removed, as useless, burdensome, and inconsistent with the spiritual teaching of the new covenant. But as to that kind of instruction, whether by public, stated preaching of the word, or that which is more private and occasional, which is subservient to the promised teaching of the Spirit of God, and which he will and does make use of in and for the communication of the knowledge itself here promised, there is nothing intimated that is derogatory to its use, continuance, or necessity. A supposition of it would overthrow the whole ministry of Jesus Christ himself and of his apostles, as well as the ordinary ministry of the church.

What Was No Longer To Be Taught?

And these things are spoken in exposition of this place, taken from the meaning and intention of the word teaching, or the duty itself, whose continuance and further use is denied. But yet, it may be, more clear light into the mind of the Holy Spirit may be attained, from a due consideration of what it is that is so to be taught. And this is, "Know the Lord." Concerning which two things may be observed:

1. That there was a knowledge of God under the old testament, so revealed as that it was hidden under types, wrapped up in veils, expressed only in parables and dark sayings. For it was the mind of God, that as to the clear perception and revelation of it, it should lie hid until the Son came from his bosom to declare him, to make his name known, and to "bring life and immortality to light;" yea, some things belonging to this, though virtually revealed, yet were so compassed with darkness in the manner of their revelation, as that the angels themselves could not clearly and distinctly look into them. But that there were some such great and excellent things concerning God and his will laid up in the revelation of Moses and the prophets, with their institutions of worship, they did understand. But the best and wisest of them knew also, that notwithstanding their best and utmost inquiry, they could not comprehend the time, nature, and state of the things so revealed; for it was revealed to them, that not to themselves, but to us, they did minister in their revelation of those things, 1 Peter 1:12. And as our apostle informs us, Moses in his ministry and institutions gave "testimony to the things which were to be spoken" (that is, clearly) "afterwards," Heb. 3:5. This secret, hidden knowledge of God principally concerned the incarnation of Christ, his mediation and suffering for sin, with the call of the Gentiles for that reason. These, and such like mysteries of the gospel, they could never attain the comprehension of. But yet they stirred up each other diligently to inquire into them, as to what they were capable of attaining, saying one to another "Know the Lord." But it was little that they could attain to, "God having provided some better things for us, that they without us should not be made perfect." And when that church ceased to make this the principal part of their religion, namely, a diligent inquiry into the hidden knowledge of God, in and by the promised seed, with a believing desire and expectation of its full manifestation, contenting themselves with the letter of the word, looking on types and shadows as things present and substances, they not only lost the glory of their profession, but were hardened into an unbelief of the things signified to them in their real exhibition. Now this kind of teaching, by mutual encouragement to look into the veiled things of the mystery of God in Christ, is now to cease, at the solemn introduction of the new covenant, as being rendered useless by the full, clear revelation and manifestation of them made in the gospel. They will no more, that is,

they will need no more, to teach, so to teach this knowledge of God; for it will be made plain to the understanding of all believers. And this is that which I judge to be principally intended by the Holy Spirit in this part of the promise, as that which the positive part of it does so directly answer to.

2. The knowledge of the LORD may be here taken, not objectively and doctrinally, but subjectively, for the renovation of the mind in the saving knowledge of God. And this neither is nor can be communicated to any by external teaching alone, in respect to which it may be said comparatively to be laid aside, as was intimated before.

Several Observations on Particular Expressions

We have, I hope, sufficiently freed the words from the difficulties that seem to attend them, so as that we will not need to refer the accomplishment of this promise to heaven, with many ancient and modern expositors; nor yet, with others, to restrain it to the first converts to Christianity, who were miraculously illuminated; much less so to interpret them as to exclude the ministry of the church in teaching, or any other effectual way of it. Something may be observed of the particular expressions used in them:

1. There is in the original promise the word עוֹד, ἔτι, "*amplius*," "no more." This is omitted by the apostle, yet so as that it is plainly included in what he expresses. For the word denotes the time and season which was limited to that kind of teaching which was to cease. This season being to expire at the publication of the gospel, the apostle affirms absolutely then, "They will not teach," what the prophet before declared with the limited season now expired, "They will do so no more."

2. The prophet expresses the subject spoken of indefinitely, אִישׁ אֶת־אָחִיו אֶת, "A man his neighbor, a man his brother;" that is, any man: the apostle by the universal ἕκαστος, "every man;" which is also reducible to any one, every one that is or may be called to this work, or has occasion or opportunity for it. For of this teaching, the rule is ability and opportunity: he that can do it, and has an opportunity for it.

3. That which they taught or intended in that expression, "Know the Lord," is the same with what is promised in the latter part of the verse, where it must be spoken to.

Some things, according to our method and design, may be observed from the exposition of these words.

Eighteenth Practical Observation

The instructive ministry of the old testament, as it was such only, and with respect to the carnal rites of it, was a ministry of the letter, and not of the Spirit, which did not really effect in the hearts of men the things which it taught. The spiritual benefit which was obtained under it proceeded from the promise, and not from the efficacy of the law, or the covenant made at Sinai. For as such, as it was legal and carnal and had respect only to outward things, it is here laid aside.

Nineteenth Practical Observation

There is a duty incumbent on every man to instruct others, according to his ability and opportunity, in the knowledge of God; the law of which, being natural and eternal, is always obligatory on all sorts of persons. This is not here either prohibited or superseded; but only it is foretold, that as to a certain manner of the performance of it, it should cease. That it generally ceases now in the world, is no effect of the promise of God, but a cursed fruit of the unbelief and wickedness of men. The highest degree in religion which men now aim at is but to attend to and learn by the public teaching of the ministry. And, alas, how few are there who do it conscientiously, to the glory of God and the spiritual benefit of their own souls! The whole business of teaching and learning the knowledge of God is generally turned into a formal spending, if not squander of so much time. But as for the teaching of others according to ability and opportunity, to endeavor for abilities, or to seek for opportunities of it, it is not only for the most part neglected, but despised. How few are there who take any care to instruct their own children and servants! But to carry this duty farther, according to opportunities of instructing others, is a thing that would be looked on almost as madness, in the days in which we live. We have far more that mutually teach one another sin, folly, yea, villainy of all sorts, than the knowledge of God and the duty we owe to him. This is not what God here promises in a way of grace, but what he has given up careless, unbelieving professors of the gospel to, in a way of vengeance.

Twentieth Practical Observation

It is the Spirit of grace alone, as promised in the new covenant, which frees the church from a laborious but ineffectual way of teaching. Such was that in use among the Jews of old; and it is well, if somewhat not much unlike, it do not prevail among many at this day. Whoever he be who, in all his teaching, does not take his encouragement from the internal, effectual teaching of God under the covenant of grace, and bends not all his endeavors to be subservient to that, has but an old testament ministry, which ceases as to any divine approbation.

Twenty-First Practical Observation

There was a hidden treasure of divine wisdom, of the knowledge of God, laid up in the spiritual revelations and institutions of the old testament, which the people were not then able to look into, nor to comprehend. The confirmation and explanation of this truth is the principal design of the apostle in this whole epistle. This knowledge, those among them that feared God and believed the promises stirred up themselves and one another to look after and to inquire into, saying to one another, "Know the Lord;" although their attainments were but small, in comparison of what is contained in the following promise.

Twenty-Second Practical Observation

The whole knowledge of God in Christ is both plainly revealed and savingly communicated, by virtue of the new covenant, to them who do believe, as the next words declare.

The Positive Part of the Promise (Continued)

The positive part of the promise remains to consideration. And two things must be inquired into: 1. To whom it is made. 2. What is the subject-matter of it.

To Whom it is Made

Those to whom it is made are so expressed in the prophet, כֻּלָּם, "all of them," לְמִקְטַנָּם וְעַד־גְּדוֹלָם, "from the least of them to the greatest of them." The expression of them absolutely, and then by a distribution, is emphatic. The former the apostle renders in the plural number, as the words are in the original, πάντες αὐτῶν, "all of them," but the terms of the distribution he renders in the singular number, which increases the emphasis, ἀπὸ μικροῦ αὐτῶν ἕως μεγάλου αὐτῶν, "from the least of them to the greatest of them."

The proposition is universal, as to the modification of the subject, πάντες, "all;" but in the word αὐτῶν, "of them," it is restrained to those alone with whom this covenant is made.

The distribution of them is made in a proverbial speech, "From the least to the greatest," used in a peculiar manner by this prophet, Jer. 6:13; 8:10; 31:34; 42:1; 44:12. It is only once more used in the Old Testament, and not elsewhere, Jon. 3:5. And it may denote either the universality or the generality of them that are spoken of, so as none be particularly excluded or excepted, though all absolutely be not intended. Besides, several sorts and degrees of persons are intended. So there ever were and ever will be, naturally, politically, and spiritually, in the church of God. None of them, on the account of their difference from others on the one hand or the other, be they the least or the greatest, are excepted or excluded from the grace of this promise. And this may be the sense of the words, if only the external administration of the grace of the new covenant be intended: None are excluded from the tender of it, or from the outward means of the communication of it, in the full, plain revelation of the knowledge of God.

But although it is the internal, effectual grace of the covenant, and not only the means, but the infallible event for that reason, not only that they will be all taught to know, but that they will all actually know the Lord, all individuals are intended; that is, that whole church all whose children are to be taught of God, and so to learn as to come to him by saving faith in Christ. So does this part of the promise hold proportion with the other, of writing the law in the hearts of the covenanters. As to all these, it is promised absolutely that they will know the Lord.

But yet among them there are many distinctions and degrees of persons, as they are variously differenced by internal and external circumstances. There are some that are greatest, and some that are least, and various intermediate degrees between them. So it has been, and so it ever must be, while the natural, acquired, and spiritual abilities of men have great variety of degrees among them; and while men's outward advantages and opportunities do also differ. Although, therefore, it is promised that they will all of them know the Lord, it is not implied that they will all do so equally, or have the same degree of spiritual wisdom and understanding. There is a measure of saving knowledge due to, and provided for all in the covenant of grace, such as is necessary to the participation of all other blessings and privileges of it; but in the degrees of this some may and do very much excel others. And we may observe,

Twenty-Third Practical Observation

There are, and ever were, different degrees of persons in the church, as to the saving knowledge of God. Therefore is that distribution of them into fathers, young men, and children, 1 John 2:13, 14. All have not one measure, all arrive not to the same stature: but yet as to the ends of the covenant, and the duties required of them in their walk before God, they that have most have nothing over, nothing to spare; and they that have least will have no lack. Every one's duty it is to be content with what he receives, and to improve it to the uttermost.

Twenty-Fourth Practical Observation

Where there is not some degree of saving knowledge, there no interest in the new covenant can be pretended.

What is its Subject-Matter

The thing promised, is the knowledge of God: "They will all know me." No duty is more frequently commanded than this is, nor any grace more frequently promised. See Deut. 29:6; Jer. 24:7; Ezek. 11:10; 36:23, 26, 27. For it is the foundation of all other duties of obedience, and of all communion with God in them. All graces as to their exercise, as faith, love, and hope, are founded in that respect. And the woeful lack of it which is visible in the world is evidence how little there is of true evangelical obedience among the generality of them that are called Christians. And two things may be considered in this promise: (1.) The object, or what is to be known. (2.) The knowledge itself, of what kind and nature it is:

(1.) The first is God himself: "They will all know me, says the LORD." And it is so not absolutely, but as to some especial revelation of himself. For there is a knowledge of God, as God, by the light of nature. This is not here intended, nor is it the subject of any gracious promise, but is common to all men. There was, moreover, a knowledge of God by revelation under the old covenant, but attended with great obscurity in various things of the highest importance. To that end there is something further intended, as is evident from the antithesis between the two states in this declared. In brief, it is the knowledge of him as revealed in Jesus Christ under the new testament. To show what is contained in this doctrinally would be to go over the principal articles of our faith, as declared in the gospel. The sum is, To "know the Lord," is to know God as he is in Christ personally, as he will be to us in Christ graciously, and what he requires of us and accepts in us through the Beloved. In all these things, notwithstanding all their teaching and diligence in that respect, the church was greatly in the dark under the old testament; but they are all of them more clearly revealed in the gospel.

(2.) The knowledge of these things is that which is promised. For notwithstanding the clear revelation of them, we abide in ourselves unable to discern them and receive them. For such a spiritual knowledge is intended as in accordance with which the mind is renewed, being accompanied with faith and love in the heart. This is that knowledge which is promised in the new covenant, and which will be brought about in all them who are interested in that respect. And we may observe,

Twenty-Fifth Practical Observation

The full and clear declaration of God, as he is to be known of us in this life, is a privilege reserved for and belonging to the days of the new testament. Before, it was not made; and more than is now made is not to be expected in this world. And the reason of this is, because it was made by Christ. See the exposition on chap. 1:1, 2.

Twenty-Sixth Practical Observation

To know God as he is revealed in Christ, is the highest privilege of which in this life we can be made partakers; for this is life eternal, that we may know the Father, the only true God, and Jesus Christ whom he has sent, John 17:3.

Twenty-Seventh Practical Observation

Persons destitute of this saving knowledge are utter strangers to the covenant of grace; for this is a principal promise and effect of it, wherever it does take place.

Exposition of Verse 12

> "For I will be merciful to their unrighteousness, and their sins and their iniquities will I remember no more."

This is the great fundamental promise and grace of the new covenant; for though it be last expressed, yet in order of nature it precedes the other mercies and privileges mentioned, and is the foundation of the collation or communication of them to us. This the causal ὅτι, "for," in accordance with which the apostle renders כִּי, "for" in the prophet, does demonstrate. 'What I have spoken, says the Lord, will be accomplished, "for I will be merciful,"' etc.; without which there could be no participation of the other things mentioned. To that end, not only an addition of new grace and mercy is expressed in these words, but a reason also is rendered why, or on what grounds he would bestow on them those other mercies.

The house of Israel and the house of Judah, with whom this covenant was made in the first place, and who are spoken of as representatives of all others who are taken into it, and who for that reason become the Israel of God, were such as had broken and disannulled God's former covenant by their disobedience; "Which my covenant they broke." Nor is there any mention of any other qualification in accordance with which they should be prepared for or disposed to an entrance into this new covenant. To that end the first thing in order of nature that is to be done to this end; is the free pardon of sin. Without a supposition of this, no other mercy can they be made partakers of; for while they continue under the guilt of sin, they are also under the curse. To that end a reason is here rendered, and that the only reason, why God will give to them the other blessings mentioned: "For I will be merciful."

Twenty-Eighth Practical Observation

Free and sovereign, undeserved grace in the pardon of sin is the original spring and foundation of all covenant mercies and blessings. By this means, and by this means alone, are the glory of God and the safety of the church provided for. And those who like not God's covenant on these terms (as none do by nature) will eternally fall short of the grace of it. By this means all glorying and all boasting in ourselves is excluded; which was that which God aimed at in the contrivance and establishment of this covenant, Rom. 3:27; 1 Cor. 1:29-31. For this could not be if the fundamental grace of it did depend on any condition or qualification in ourselves. If we let go the free pardon of sin, without respect to any thing in those that receive it, we renounce the gospel. Pardon of sin is not merited by antecedent duties, but is the strongest obligation to future duties. He that will not receive pardon unless he can one way or other deserve it, or make himself meet for it; or pretends to have received it, and finds not himself obliged to universal obedience by it, neither is nor will be partaker of it.

The Promise Considered

In the promise itself we may consider, 1. To whom it is made. And, 2. What it is that is promised.

To Whom it is Made

The first is expressed in the pronoun αὐτῶν, "their," three times repeated. All those absolutely, and only those with whom God makes this covenant, are intended. Those whose sins are not pardoned do in no sense partake of this covenant; it is not made with them. For this is the covenant that God makes with them, that he will be merciful to their sins; that is, to them in the pardon of them. Some speak of a universal conditional covenant, made with all mankind. If there be any such thing, it is not that here intended; for they are all actually pardoned with whom this covenant is made. And the indefinite declaration of the nature and terms of the covenant is not the making of a covenant with any. And what should be the condition of this grace here promised of the pardon of sin? "It is," say they, "that men repent, and believe, and turn to God, and yield obedience to the gospel." If so, then men must do all these things before they receive the remission of sins? "Yes." Then must they do them while they are under the law, and the curse of it, for so are all men whose sins are not pardoned. This is to make obedience to the law, and that to be performed by men while under the curse of it, to be the condition of gospel-mercy; which is to overthrow both the law and the gospel.

Objection and Answer

"But then, on the other hand it will follow," they say, "that men are pardoned before they do believe; which is expressly contrary to the Scripture." Answer: (1.) The communication and donation of faith to us is an effect of the same grace in accordance with which our sins are pardoned; and they are both bestowed on us by virtue of the same covenant. (2.) The application of pardoning mercy to our souls is in order of nature consequent to believing, but in time they go together. (3.) Faith is not required to the procuring of the pardon of our sins, but to the receiving of it: "Whosoever believes in him will receive remission of sins," Acts 10:43. But that which we will observe from this place is, that,

Twenty-Ninth Practical Observation

The new covenant is made with them alone who effectually and eventually are made partakers of the grace of it. "This is the covenant that I will make with them... I will be merciful to their unrighteousness," etc. Those with whom the old covenant was made were all of them actual partakers of the benefits of it; and if they are not so with whom the new is made, it comes short of the old in efficacy, and may be utterly frustrated. Neither does the indefinite proposal of the terms of the covenant prove that the covenant is made with them, or any of them, who enjoy not the benefits of it. Indeed this is the excellence of this covenant, and so it is here declared, that it does effectually communicate all the grace and mercy contained in it to all and every one with whom it is made; with whomsoever it is made, his sins are pardoned.

What it is that is Promised

The subject-matter of this promise is the pardon of sin. And that which we have to consider for the exposition of the words, is. (1.) What is meant by sins. (2.) What by the pardon of them. (3.) What is the reason of the peculiar expression in this place.

What is Meant by Sins

Sin is spoken of with respect to its guilt especially; so is it the object of mercy and grace. Guilt is the desert of punishment, or the obligation of the sinner to punishment, by and according to the sentence of the law. Pardon is the dissolution of that obligation.

Sin is here expressed by three terms, ἀδικία, ἁμαρτία, ἀνομία, "unrighteousness," "sin," and "lawlessness," as we render the words. In the prophet there is only חַטָּאת and עָוֹן; פֶּשַׁע, is lacking. But they are elsewhere all three used, where mention is made of the pardon of sin, or the causes of it; as, [1.] In the declaration of the name of God with respect to that, Exod. 34:7, וּפֶשַׁע וְחַטָּאָה נֹשֵׂא עָוֹן, "pardoning iniquity, transgression, and sin." [2.] In the confession of sin, for the removal of it by the expiatory sacrifice, Lev. 16:21: "Aaron will confess over him עֲוֹנֹת־אֶת־כָּל לְכָל־חַטֹּאתָם לְכָל־פִּשְׁעֵיהֶם וְאֶת־כָּל־," "all their iniquities, all their transgressions, in all their sins." [3.] In the expression of the forgiveness of sin in justification, Ps. 32:1, 2. To that end the apostle might justly make up the expression and general enumeration of sins, here defective in the prophet, seeing it is elsewhere so constantly used to the same purpose, and on the like occasion.

Nor are those terms needlessly multiplied, but various things we are taught by that means; as, [1.] That those whom God graciously takes into covenant are many of them antecedently subject to all sorts of sins. [2.] That in the grace of the covenant there is mercy provided for the pardon of them all, even of them "from which they could not be justified by the law of Moses," Acts 13:39. And that, [3.] Therefore none should be discouraged from resting on the faithfulness of God in this covenant, who are invited to a compliance with this.

But there is yet more intended in the use of these words. For they do distinctly express all those respects of sin in general by which the conscience of a sinner is stricken, burdened, and terrified; as also on what the equity of the curse and punishment for sin does depend.

The first is ἀδικία, "unrighteousness." This is usually taken for sins against the second table, or the transgression of that rule of righteousness among men which is given by the moral law. But here, as in many other places, it expresses a general disposition of sin against God. A thing unequal and unrighteous it is, that man should sin against God, his sovereign ruler and benefactor. As God is the supreme lord and governor of all, as he is our only benefactor and rewarder, as all his laws and ways towards us are just and equal, the first notion of righteousness in us is the rendering to God what is due to him; that is, universal obedience to all his commands. Righteousness towards man is but a branch springing from this root; and where this is not, there is no righteousness among men, whatever is pretended. If we give not to God the things that are God's, it will not avail us to give to Caesar the things that are Caesar's, nor to other men what is their own. And this is the first consideration of sin that renders the sinner subject to punishment, and manifests the equity of the sanction of the law; it is an unrighteous thing. By this means the conscience of the sinner is stricken, if he be convinced of sin in a due manner. The original perfection of his nature consisted in this righteousness towards God, by rendering his due to him in a way of obedience. This is overthrown by sin; which is therefore both shameful and ruinous: which distresses the conscience, when awakened by conviction.

The second is ἁμαντία, "sin." This is properly a missing of, an erring from that end and scope which it is our duty to aim at. There is a certain end for which we were made, and a certain rule proper to us in accordance with which we may attain it. And this end being our only blessedness, it is our interest, as it was in the principles of our natures, to be always in a tendency towards it. This is the glory of God, and our eternal salvation in the enjoyment of him. To that the law of God is a perfect guide. To sin, therefore, is to forsake that rule, and to forego in that respect our aim at that end. It is to place self and the world as our end, in the place of God and his glory, and to take the imaginations of our hearts for our rule. To that end the perverse folly that is in sin, in wandering away from the chief good as our end, and the best guide as our rule, embracing the greatest evils in their stead, is ἁμαρτία, rendering punishment righteous, and filling the sinner with shame and fear.

There is, thirdly, ἀνομία, "lawlessness." We have no one word in our language properly to express the sense of this; nor is there so in the

Latin. We render it "transgression of the law." Ἄνομος is a lawless person; whom the Hebrews call "a son of Belial," one who owns no yoke nor rule; and ἀνομία is a voluntary unconformity to the law. In this the formal nature of sin consists, as the apostle tells us, 1 John 3:4. And this is that which in the first place happens on the conscience of a sinner.

To that end, as all sorts of particular sins are included in these multiplied names of sin; so the general nature of sin, in all its causes and respects, terrifying the sinner, and manifesting the righteousness of the curse of the law, is declared and represented by them. And we may learn,

Thirtieth Practical Observation

That the aggravations of sin are great and many which the consciences of convinced sinners ought to have regard to.

Thirty-First Practical Observation

There are grace and mercy in the new covenant provided for all sorts of sins, and all aggravations of them, if they be received in a due manner.

Thirty-Second Practical Observation

Aggravations of sin do glorify grace in pardon. Therefore God does here so express them, that he may declare the glory of his grace in their remission.

Thirty-Third Practical Observation

We cannot understand aright the glory and excellence of pardoning mercy, unless we are convinced of the greatness and vileness of our sins in all their aggravations.

What is Meant by the Pardon of Sins

That which is promised with respect to these sins is two ways expressed: First, ἵλεως ἔσομαι, "I will be merciful." Secondly, οὐ μὴ μνησθῶ ἔτι "I will remember no more." It is pardon of sin that is intended in both these expressions; the one respecting the cause of it, the other its perfection and assurance. And two things are considerable in the pardon of sin:

[1.] A respect to the mediator of the covenant, and the propitiation for sin made by him. Without this there can be no remission, nor is any promised.

[2.] The dissolution of the obligation of the law binding over the guilty sinner to punishment. These are the essential parts of evangelical pardon, and respect is had in these words to them both:

1st. ἵλεως, which we translate "merciful," is "propitious," "gracious" through a propitiation. But the Lord Christ is the only ἱλαστήριον or "propitiation" under the new testament, Rom. 3:25; 1 John 2:2. And he died εἰς τὸ ἱλάσκεσθαι, to "propitiate" God for sin; to render him propitious to sinners, Heb. 2:17. In him alone God is ἵλεως, "merciful" to our sins.

2dly. The law, with the sanction of it, was the means appointed of God to bring sin to a judicial remembrance and trial. To that end the dissolution of the obligation of the law to punishment, which is an act of God, the supreme rector and judge of all, belongs to the pardon of sin. This is variously expressed in the Scripture; here by "remembering sin no more." The assertion of which is fortified by a double negative. Sin will never be called legally to remembrance. But the whole doctrine of the pardon of sin I have so largely handled, in the exposition of Ps. 130, that I must not here again resume the same argument.[11]

---

[11] See vol. vi. of the author's miscellaneous works.- Ed. [Banner Edition.]

Chapter Six

Exposition of Verse 13

The Necessity and Certainty of the Abolition

Of the First Covenant

> In that he says, A new [*covenant*], he has made the first old. Now that
> which decays and waxes old is ready to vanish away.[1]

Having in the previous verses proved in general the insufficiency of the
old covenant, the necessity of the new, the difference between the one
and the other, with the preference of the latter above the former, in all
confirming the excellence of the priesthood of Christ above that of
Aaron, in this last verse of the chapter he makes an especial inference
from one word in the prophetical testimony, in which the main truth
which he endeavored to confirm with respect to the Hebrews was
asserted. It was their persuasion, that of whatsoever sort this promised
covenant should be, yet the former was still to continue in force, obliging
the church to all the institutions of worship to that appertaining. On this
depended the main controversy that the apostle had with them; for he
knew that this persuasion was destructive to the faith of the gospel, and
would, if pertinaciously adhered to, prove ruinous to their own souls. To
that end the contrary to this, or the total cessation of the first covenant, he
presses on them with all sorts of arguments; as from the nature, use, and
end of it; from its insufficiency to consecrate or make perfect the state of
the church; from the various prefigurations and certain predictions of the
introduction of another covenant, priesthood, and ordinances of worship,
which were better than those that belonged to it, and inconsistent with
them; with many other cogent evidences to the same purpose. Here he
fixes on a new argument in particular, to prove the necessity and
certainty of its abolition; and by this means, according to his usual
manner, he makes a transition to his following discourse, in which he
proves the same truth from the distinct consideration of the use and end
of the institutions, ordinances, and sacrifices belonging to that covenant.
This he pursues to the 19th verse of the 10th chapter; and so returns to

---

[1] Ἐν τῷ λέγειν, Καινήν, πεπαλαίωκε τὴν πρώτην· τὸ δὲ παλαιούμενον καὶ
γηράσκον ἐγγὺς ἀφανισμοῦ.

the parenetical[2] part of the epistle, making due applications of what he had now fully showed.

A double argument the apostle here makes use of: 1. From a special word or testimony. 2. From a general maxim of truth in all kinds.

The Special Word or Testimony

1. In the former we may consider, (1.) The testimony he makes use of; (2.) The inference to his own purpose which he makes from it:

(1.) The first consists in the adjunct of this other promised covenant. It is called by God himself new: Ἐν τῷ λέγειν, Καινήν, "In that," or "Although it is said, A new;" or, "In that he calls it, names it, A new." So it is expressly in the prophet, "Behold, I will make a new covenant." Thus every word of the Holy Spirit, though but occasional to the principal subject spoken of, is sufficient evidence of what may be deduced from it. And by this kind of arguing we are taught, that the word of God is full of holy mysteries, if with humility, and under the conduct of his Holy Spirit, we do, as we ought, diligently inquire into them. This, therefore, he lays down as the foundation of his present argument, that God himself does not call this promised covenant another covenant, or a second, nor only declare the excellence of it; but signally calls it "a new covenant".

(2.) That which he infers from this place is, that πεπαλαίωκε τὴν πρώτην, "he has made the first old." The force of the argument does not lie in this, that he calls the second new; but that he would not have done so had not he made the first old. For πεπαλαίωκε is of an active signification, and denotes an authoritative act of God on the old covenant, of which the calling the other new was a sign and evidence. He would not have done so, but that he made the other old; for with respect to that this is called new. But yet it was the designation of the new covenant that was the foundation of making the other old.

The word respecting the time past, we must inquire what time it does refer to. And this must be either the time of the prediction and promise of the new covenant, or the time of its introduction and establishment. And it is the first season that is intended. For the introduction of the new covenant did actually take away and abolish the old, making it to disappear; but the act of God here intended, is only his making it old in

---

[2] [Hortatory; encouraging; persuasive.]

order to that. And he did this on and by the giving of this promise, and afterwards by various acts, and in various degrees.

[1.] He did it by calling the faith of the church from resting in it, through the expectation of the bringing in of a better in the room of it. This brought it under decay in their minds, and gave it an undervaluation to what it had before. They were now assured that something much better would in due time be introduced. Therefore, although they abode in the observation of the duties and worship it required, it being the will of God that so they should do, yet this expectation of and longing after the better covenant now promised, made it decay in their minds and affections. So God did make it old.

[2.] He did it by a plain declaration of its infirmity, weakness, and insufficiency for the great ends of a perfect covenant between God and the church. Many things to this purpose might have been collected out of the nature of its institutions and promises, from the first giving of it, as is done by our apostle in his present discourses. But these things were not clearly understood by any in those days; and as to the most, the veil was on them, so that they could not see at all to the end of the things that were to be done away. But now, when God himself comes positively to declare by that prophet that it was weak and insufficient, and therefore he would make another, a better, with them; this made it old, or declared it to be in a tendency to dissolution.

[3.] From the giving of this promise, God did variously by his providence break in on and weaken its administration; which by its decaying age was more and more manifested. For,

1st. Immediately after the giving of this promise, the Babylonian captivity gave a total intermission and interruption to the whole administration of it for seventy years. This, having never before fallen out from the making of it on Mount Sinai, was an evident token of its approaching period, and that God would have the church to live without it.

2dly. On the return of the people from their captivity, neither the temple, nor the worship of it, nor any of the administrations of the covenant, nor the priesthood, were ever restored to their pristine beauty and glory. And although the people in general were much distressed at the apprehension of its decay, God comforts them, not with any intimation that things under that covenant should ever be brought into a better condition, but only with an expectation of His coming among them who would put an utter end to all the administrations of it, Hag. 2:6-9.

And from that time forward it would be easy to trace the whole process of it, and to manifest how it continually declined towards its end.

Thus did God make it old, by variously disposing of it to its end; and to give an evidence of it, called the other covenant which he would make, a new one. And it did not decay of itself. For no institution of God will ever wax old of itself; will ever decay, grow infirm, or perish, unless it be disannulled by God himself. Length of time will not consume divine institutions; nor can the sins of men abate their force. He only that sets them up can take them down.

And this is the first argument of the apostle, taken from this testimony, to prove that the first covenant was to be abolished.

A General Maxim of Truth

But although it may be questioned whether it directly follows or no, that it must be taken away because it is made old, he confirms the truth of his inference from a general maxim, which has the nature of a new argument also. "Now," says he, "that which decays and waxes old, is ready to vanish away."

"Old" is indicative of that which is to have an end, and which draws towards its end. Every thing that can wax old has an end; and that which does so, draws towards that end. So the psalmist affirming that the heavens themselves will perish, adds, as a proof of it, "They will wax old as a garment;" and then none can doubt but they must have an end, as to their substance or their use.

There are in the words,

(1.) The notation of the subject, τὸ δέ, "but that," or "that, whatever it be." The general rule gives evidence to the former inference, "Whatever it be that waxes old."

(2.) The description of it in a double expression, παλαιούμενον and γηράσκον. The words are generally supposed to be synonymous, and to be used for emphasis only. We express the first by decay, "that which decays," to avoid the repetition of the same word, we having no other to express "waxing old," or "made old," by. But παλαιούμενον is not properly "that which decays;" it is that which has the effect passively of πεπαλαίωκε, "that which is made old;" and it properly respects things. Things are so said to be made old, not persons. But the other word, γηράσκον, respects persons, not things. Men, and not inanimate things, are said γηράσκειν. To that end although the apostle might have used a pleonasm to give emphasis to his assertion, and to aver the certainty of the end of the old covenant, yet nothing hinders but that we may think that he had respect to the things and persons that belonged to its administration.

That which is affirmed of this subject of the proposition, is, that it is ἐγγὺς ἀφανισμοῦ, "near to a disappearance;" that is, an abolition and taking out of the way. The proposition is universal, and holds absolutely in all things, as is evident in the light of nature. Whatever brings things to a decay and age will bring them to an end; for decay and age are the expressions of a tendency to an end. Let an angel live never so long, he waxes not old, because he cannot die. Waxing old is absolutely opposed to an eternal duration, Ps. 102:26, 27.

It being the removal of the old covenant and all its administrations that is respected, it may be inquired why the apostle expresses it by ἀφανισμός, "a disappearance," or "vanishing out of sight." And respect may be had in this, (1.) To the glorious outward appearance of its administrations. This was that which greatly captivated the minds and affections of those Hebrews to it. They were carnal themselves, and these things, the fabric of the temple, the ornaments of the priests, the order of their worship, had a glory in them which they could behold with their carnal eyes, and cleave to with their carnal affections. The ministration of the letter was glorious. 'All this glory,' says the apostle, 'will shortly disappear, will vanish out of your sight,' according to the prediction of our Lord Jesus Christ, Matt. 24. (2.) To the gradual removal of it. It departs as a thing by its removal out of our sight. We by little and little lose the prospect of it, until it utterly disappears. How it was made so to disappear, at what time, in what degrees, by what acts of divine authority, must be spoken to distinctly elsewhere. All the glorious institutions of the law were at best but as stars in the firmament of the church, and therefore were all to disappear at the rising of the Sun of Righteousness.

Τῷ Θεῷ δόξα.[3]

---

[3] [To God be the glory.]

Appendix One

Outline of Coxe

A Discourse of the Covenants That God made with men before the Law, Nehemiah Coxe

Chapter One: Covenant Relationships to God in General
- A General Introduction
- God's Covenant Proposed to Men and their Response
- The General Notion of a Covenant and its Inferences
- God has Always Dealt with Men by Way of Covenant
- God's Covenant Always Transacted with a Representative Head
- General Directions to Rightly Understand Covenant Transactions

Chapter Two: God's Transactions with Adam
- The Importance of the Study
- Man's Original State and the Law
- The Promise of a Reward Proved
- The Reward and Punishment of the Law
- Adam a Public Person
- God's Transaction with Adam a Covenant
- The General Nature of the Covenant with Adam
- The Sin of our First Parents
- The State and Condition of Fallen Man
- God's Mercy to Fallen Man
- A Promise of Redemption in a Treaty
- The State and Condition of Adam's Posterity

Chapter Three: God's Covenant with Noah
- A New Relationship Established
- God's Revealed Word is Men's Rule of Faith
- Enoch
- The General Propagation of the Church
- The Ark as a Type
- God Establishes his Covenant with Noah
- The Noahic Covenant Developed

- Blessing and Curse to Noah's Sons
- Babel and the Confusion of Tongues
- The Evils in the Confusion of Language

Chapter Four: The Covenant of Grace Revealed to Abraham
- God Specially Honors Abraham by this Covenant
- Abraham's History and Apparent Incapacity
- Abraham's Double Role in the Covenant
- The Covenant of Grace Revealed to Abraham
- The Timing of the Covenant and its Inferences
- All Spiritual Blessings Included in the Covenant
- This Covenant Confirmed in Christ
- Abraham a Root of Covenant Blessings and Parent of Believers
- The Way of Salvation by Faith in Christ in this Covenant
- The Promise Given before Circumcision

Chapter Five: The Covenant of Circumcision (I)
- The Promises to Abraham for his Natural Offspring
- Abraham Called out of Ur
- Abraham's Journeys and Renewed Promises
- How the Promise of Canaan was Made Good to Abraham
- The Promise Renewed and Enlarged
- The Seed of Abraham
- The Covenant of Circumcision
- The Promise of the New Covenant Repeated
- The Distinction of Tribes in Israel
- The Meaning of Everlasting in Relation to this Covenant
- The Church-State of Israel after the Flesh

Chapter Six: The Covenant of Circumcision (II)
- Two Propositions Laid Down
- The First Proposition Proved
- Its Further Confirmation
- Its Support from the Current of Sacred History
- The Church-State of Israel Built on this Covenant
- Circumcision the Door into Israel's Communion
- How Levi Paid Tithes in Abraham

Appendix Two

JOHN OWEN AND NEW COVENANT THEOLOGY:
Owen on the Old and New Covenants and the Functions of the Decalogue in Redemptive History in Historical and Contemporary Perspective[1]

Richard C. Barcellos

John Owen was a giant in the theological world of seventeenth century England. He is known today as quite possibly the greatest English theologian ever. His learning was deep and his writings thorough and profound. He has left the Christian Church with a legacy few have equaled in volume, fewer yet in content. In saying this of Owen, however, it must also be recognized that some things he said are difficult to understand. Some statements may even appear to contradict other statements if he is not followed carefully and understood in light of his comprehensive thought and the Reformation and Post-Reformation Protestant Scholastic world in which he wrote.

If one reads some of the difficult sections of Owen's writings, either without understanding his comprehensive thought and in light of the theological world in which he wrote, or in a superficial manner, some statements can easily be taken to mean things they do not. When this is done, the result is that authors are misunderstood and sometimes, subsequent theological movements are aligned with major historical figures without substantial and objective warrant. Two such instances of this involve John Owen and New Covenant Theology (NCT).

John G. Reisinger claims that Owen viewed the Old Covenant[2] as "a legal/works covenant."[3] He goes on and says:

> This covenant was conditional because it was a legal/works covenant that promised life and threatened death. Israel failed to earn the blessings promised in the covenant. But under the New Covenant, the Church becomes the Israel of God and all her members are kings and

---

[1] Used by permission from *Reformed Baptist Theological Review*.

[2] The phrase 'Old Covenant' will be used throughout as a synonym for 'Mosaic or Sinai Covenant.'

[3] John G. Reisinger, *Tablets of Stone* (Southbridge, MA: Crown Publications, Inc., 1989), 36.

priests (a kingdom of priests). Christ, as our Surety (Heb. 7:22), has kept the Old Covenant for us and earned every blessing it promised.[4]

The reader of Owen's treatise on the Old and New Covenants in his Hebrews commentary, however, will quickly realize that Reisinger's comments above do not give the full picture of Owen's position. For Owen did not view the Old Covenant as a covenant of works *in itself.* He viewed it as containing a renewal of the original covenant of works imposed upon Adam in the Garden of Eden,[5] something emphatically denied by Reisinger.[6] Neither did Owen teach that Christ "kept the Old Covenant for us and earned every blessing it promised."[7] On the

---

[4] Reisinger, *Tablets of Stone*, 37.

[5] John Owen, *The Works of John Owen* (Edinburgh: The Banner of Truth Trust, 1991), XXII:78, 80, 81, 89, 142. Owen viewed the Old Covenant as containing a works-inheritance principle of the broken covenant of works. The reintroduction of this element of the covenant of works, however, functioned on a typological level under the Old Covenant and applied to temporal promises and threats alone. See Mark W. Karlberg, *Covenant Theology in Reformed Perspective* (Eugene, OR: Wipf and Stock Publishers, 2000), 167, 184, 217, 218, 248, 273, 346, and 366 for a similar understanding of the works principle of the Old Covenant as it relates to the covenant of works on the typological level of kingdom administration.

[6] The following is taken from John G. Reisinger *Abraham's Four Seeds* (Frederick, MD: New Covenant Media, 1998), 129. In it he denies both the covenant of works and the covenant of grace as traditionally understood. "Some time ago I discussed the basic theme of this book with a group of Reformed ministers that was about equally divided on the subject of Covenant Theology, Dispensationalism, and the view that I hold. Several of those who held strongly to Covenant Theology insisted on using the term covenant of grace as if it had the authority of a verse of Scripture. They made no attempt to prove their assertions from Scripture texts. They kept speaking in terms of logic and theology. I finally said, 'We agree that the Bible is structured around two covenants. However, the two covenants that you keep talking about, namely, a covenant of works with Adam in the garden of Eden and a covenant of grace made with Adam immediately after the fall, have no textual basis in the Word of God. They are both theological covenants and not biblical covenants. They are the children of one's theological system. Their mother is Covenant Theology and their father is logic applied to that system. Neither of these two covenants had their origin in Scripture texts and biblical exegesis. Both of them were invented by theology as the necessary consequences of a theological system.'" Though Reisinger denies the Edenic covenant of works, he does not deny the theology of the covenant of works entirely. He simply does not go back far enough in redemptive history for its basis (cf. Hosea 6:7 and Romans 5:12ff). Because of holding to a modified covenant of works position (i.e., the Mosaic Covenant is *the* covenant of works), Reisinger's writings uphold the law/gospel distinction which is crucial in maintaining the gospel of justification by faith alone. For this he is to be commended.

[7] Reisinger, *Tablets of Stone*, 37.

contrary, Owen taught that obedience or disobedience to the Old Covenant in itself neither *eternally* saved nor *eternally* condemned anyone and that its promises were temporal and only for Israel while under it.[8] According to Owen, what Christ kept for us was the original Adamic covenant of works, not the Old Covenant as an end in itself. Owen says:

> But in the new covenant, the very first thing that is proposed, is the accomplishment and establishment of the covenant of works, both as to its commands and sanction, in the obedience and suffering of the mediator.[9]

Reisinger appears to make the Old Covenant the first covenant of works, a sort of new covenant of works in Owen's thought, something he clearly denies.[10] Reisinger also appears to make the Old Covenant contain in itself the promise of *eternal* life and the threat of *eternal* condemnation, thus necessitating Christ's obedience to it.[11] Owen denies both of these. He says:

> This covenant [Sinai] thus made, with these ends and promises, did never save nor condemn any man eternally. All that lived under the administration of it did attain eternal life, or perished for ever, but not by virtue of this covenant as formally such. It did, indeed, revive the commanding power and sanction of the first covenant of works; and therein, as the apostle speaks, was "the ministry of condemnation," 2 Cor. iii. 9; for "by the deeds of the law can no flesh be justified." And on the other hand, it directed also unto the promise, which was the instrument of life and salvation unto all that did believe. But as unto what it had of its own, it was confined unto things temporal. Believers were saved under it, but not by virtue of it. Sinners perished eternally under it, but by the curse of the original law of works.[12]

---

[8] Owen, *Works*, XXII:85, 90, 92.

[9] Ibid., 89-90.

[10] Ibid., 78.

[11] See Richard C. Barcellos, *In Defense of the Decalogue: A Critique of New Covenant Theology* (Enumclaw, WA: WinePress Publishing, 2001), 57-59, for more statements by Reisinger which substantiate this along with my comments. In his book *Tablets of Stone*, he argues that the Old Covenant was for Israel alone and also, contradicting himself, that Christ fulfilled its terms for New Covenant Christians. Owen teaches that Christ fulfilled the terms of the Adamic covenant of works for Christians and not the Old Covenant as a covenant of works in itself.

[12] Owen, *Works*, XXII:85-86.

Using Owen as Reisinger did could lead some to think that Owen and Reisinger are one on the nature of the Old Covenant. But this is far from the truth of the matter.

It must be granted, however, that Owen and Reisinger agree in some aspects of the Old Covenant, though even this acknowledgement must be carefully qualified. Both teach that the Old Covenant was made with Israel and was a temporary covenant and abrogated by the New Covenant, though Reisinger has some inconsistencies in his position (see above). Both teach that the Old Covenant was not an administration of the covenant of grace and deny the 'one covenant two administration' motif of other covenant theologians.[13] Both view the Decalogue as a unit as abrogated under the New Covenant; however, Owen in a relative and highly qualified manner (see below) and Reisinger in an absolute manner and with the inconsistencies mentioned above.[14]

Another NCT advocate, Tom Wells, claims that John G. Reisinger "has adopted John Owen's view of the Mosaic and New covenants, without adding Owen's 'creation ordinance' view of the Sabbath."[15] Wells also claims that Owen held a mediating position on the relationship between the Mosaic and New Covenants and that Owen's position is substantially that of Reisinger and hence, NCT.[16]

Wells defines what he means by mediating position, when he says:

> The mediating position is as follows: a law of any kind may be the property of more than one covenant, but no covenant is still in force in any way after it has reached its end. Applied to the present discussion that means this: many (indeed all) of the moral commands of the Mosaic Covenant reappear in the Law of Christ. But they do not do so because they are part of the Ten Commandments or the Mosaic Covenant. That covenant, with every one of its laws and with every demand it lays on anyone whatsoever, has passed away forever. That

---

[13] See Ibid., 76, 86 and Reisinger, *Abraham's*, 129ff.

[14] In Reisinger's *Tablets of Stone*, he asserts several times and in various ways that the Tablets of Stone were given to ancient Israel, and ancient Israel alone, as a legal covenant. But, as noted above, he also claims that Christ died under the curse of and to secure the blessings of that very covenant for the New Covenant Israel of God, His church.

[15] Tom Wells, *Is John G. Reisinger and Antinomian?* (Frederick, MD: New Covenant Media, 2001), 6.

[16] Wells, *Reisinger*, 6. I added 'hence, NCT' because Wells admits that Reisinger is part of the movement called NCT on page 5.

was John Owen's position, and that is the position of John Reisinger. It has also been the position of many others.[17]

In Sinclair B. Ferguson's *John Owen on the Christian Life*, cited by Wells in the Reisinger pamphlet, Ferguson also calls Owen's position on the Old Covenant a mediating position.[18] But Ferguson's explanation of Owen's mediating position does not have to do with the relationship between the law of the Old Covenant and the Law of Christ (as per Wells above). In fact, Ferguson does not even discuss this matter in this section of his book. Instead, Ferguson's understanding of Owen's mediating position has to do with the nature and function of the Old Covenant and its relation to the Adamic covenant of works, the covenant of grace, and the New Covenant. Unlike others, Owen did not believe that the Old Covenant was a covenant of works in itself or simply an administration of the covenant of grace. In the words of Ferguson:

> Sinai should not then be thought of as the covenant of works; but Sinai does involve a renewal of the principles which partly constituted the covenant of works.
>   On the other hand, the Sinai covenant cannot be thought of as the covenant of grace.[19]

> His [Owen's] conclusion then is that the Sinaitic covenant revived the commands, sanctions and promises of the covenant of works, and that when the apostle Paul disputes about works or law-righteousness it is the renovation of the Edenic covenant in the Sinaitic covenant he has in mind. Sinai therefore is a 'particular, temporary covenant ... and not a mere dispensation of the covenant of grace.'[20]

It now appears that what Wells meant by Owen's mediating position and what Ferguson meant is not identical.[21] Ferguson's meaning

---

[17] Wells, *Reisinger*, 8.
[18] Sinclair B. Ferguson, *John Owen on the Christian Life* (Edinburgh: The Banner of Truth Trust, 1987), 28. In an email discussion concerning his view of Owen's mediating position, Ferguson affirmed that my understanding of him (and Owen) is correct.
[19] Ferguson, *John Owen*, 29.
[20] Ibid., 30.
[21] In an email discussion and subsequent telephone conversation with Tom Wells, he affirmed that he probably intended to use the phrase with Ferguson's meaning. After examining Wells and Ferguson, however, I have come to believe that they, in fact, cannot mean the same thing and that Wells probably misunderstood both Ferguson and Owen.

concentrates on Owen being in the middle of those who taught that the Old Covenant was the covenant of works and those who taught it was the covenant of grace. Owen taught neither. Wells' meaning concentrates on the introduction of moral law from the Old Covenant into the New Covenant and how that's done with the Old Covenant abolished.

Using the phrase as Wells did (i.e., putting a different meaning on it) could easily cause confusion. Wells' pamphlet cited above is an attempt to clear Reisinger of accusations of doctrinal antinomianism. He uses Owen's mediating position (as he defines it), in part, attempting to clear Reisinger of this charge. By referencing Ferguson in the pamphlet, and even Ferguson's use of the phrase mediating position,[22] however, Wells allows his readers to assume he and Ferguson mean the same thing by mediating position. But this, in fact, is not the case.

It must be granted, however, that Owen held a mediating position on the Old Covenant. There were differences of opinion on this issue within Puritanism, as Ferguson acknowledges.[23] Owen did not view the Old Covenant merely as an administration of the covenant of grace. He did not avow the 'one covenant two administrations' motif of many of his comrades.[24] He viewed it as a distinct, subservient covenant with a very limited and temporal purpose.[25] He saw within it a revival of the Edenic covenant of works,[26] superadded to the promises of grace.[27] He also viewed it as abolished by the New Covenant.[28] Hence, Owen's mediating position put him between those who held that the Old Covenant was the covenant of works and those who held that it was the covenant of

---

[22] Wells, *Reisinger*, 10.

[23] Ferguson, *John Owen*, 28.

[24] Owen, *Works*, XXII:76, 86.

[25] Ibid., 76, 77, 85, 90.

[26] Owen, *Works*, XXII:78, 80, 81, 89, 142. Geerhardus Vos acknowledges that other Reformed theologians have used similar language as Owen concerning the relationship between the covenant of works and the Sinai covenant. He says, "...we can also explain why the older theologians did not always clearly distinguish between the covenant of works and the Sinaitic covenant. At Sinai it was not the 'bare' law that was given, but a reflection of the covenant of works *revived* [emphasis added], as it were, in the interests of the covenant of grace continued at Sinai." See Geerhardus Vos, *Redemptive History and Biblical Interpretation* (Phillipsburg, NJ: P&R Publishing, 1980), 255. See also Karlberg, *Covenant Theology*, 76, 184, 248, and 273.

[27] Ibid., 113, 142.

[28] Ibid., 100.

grace.[29] But it cannot be granted that his mediating position be considered as a forerunner to John G. Reisinger and NCT, unless highly qualified on several fronts.[30]

In claiming that Reisinger "has adopted John Owen's view of the Mosaic and New covenants, without adding Owen's 'creation ordinance' view of the Sabbath,"[31] Wells leads his readers to believe that the only difference between Owen and Reisinger and NCT on these issues is Owen's creation-based Sabbath position. This has already been proven to be untrue. As shown above, Owen and Reisinger (and NCT) do not agree on many issues related to the nature and functions of the Old Covenant.

There is another reason, however, why this is not the case. It has to do with the function of the Decalogue in Owen's thought. While explaining what he means by Reisinger's mediating position, Wells claims that Owen and Reisinger both hold that once a covenant, and the laws attached to it, has run its course, then "[t]hat covenant, with every one of its laws and with every demand it lays on anyone whatsoever, has passed away forever."[32] For Reisinger and NCT, this means that the Decalogue as a unit, including its Sabbath, has passed away forever and that if any of its laws are binding on New Covenant Christians, then they must reappear in the law of Christ.[33] This appears to be the standard NCT position. But is this what Owen teaches? If it is true that Reisinger "has adopted John Owen's view of the Mosaic and New covenants, without adding Owen's 'creation ordinance' view of the Sabbath,"[34] and Reisinger teaches that the Decalogue as a unit, along with its Sabbath, has been abrogated in all senses by the New Covenant, then we should find this teaching in Owen as well. In fact, if Wells' claim is true, then the only way Owen can have the Sabbath functioning under the New Covenant is either to base it solely upon its status as creation ordinance

---

[29] Ferguson, *John Owen*, 28. Cf. also Samuel Bolton, *The True Bounds of Christian Freedom* (Edinburgh: The Banner of Truth Trust, 1978), 88-109 (cf. also 173-174), for a discussion on the various views of the nature and function of the Old Covenant among seventeenth-century divines. Bolton holds, substantially, the same position as Owen. The Old Covenant is not a covenant of works in itself, nor a 'legal' administration of the covenant of grace. It is a subservient covenant to the covenant of grace. Fisher and Boston held similar views.

[30] Neither Reisinger nor Wells have provided these necessary qualifications for us. I will suggest some qualifications at the end of this appendix.

[31] Wells, *Reisinger*, 6.

[32] Wells, *Reisinger*, 8.

[33] Ibid., 8-9.

[34] Ibid., 6.

or to contradict himself. But, as we shall see, Owen does neither. He does not base the perpetuity of the Sabbath on its status as creation ordinance alone, nor does he contradict himself by smuggling the Decalogue into the New Covenant against his principles.

Simply put, Tom Wells, as Reisinger above, has overstated his case. In doing so, he reveals that he (1) misunderstands Owen on more than one front, (2) attributes a position to him that he did not, in fact, hold, (3) claims that Reisinger "has adopted Owen's view of the Mosaic and New covenants, without adding Owen's "creation ordinance" view of the Sabbath"[35] without objective warrant, and (4) forces Owen to either base the Sabbath on creation alone or contradict himself by introducing it into the New Covenant on other grounds, something which, in fact, Owen does repeatedly (see below).

The Purpose of this Appendix

The remainder of this appendix attempts to show the following:
  (1) The abrogation of Old Covenant law as defined by Owen. This will demonstrate that he can be easily misunderstood if not followed very carefully and allowed to define his own terms.
  (2) That Owen, very late in his writing career, taught the perpetuity of the Decalogue as a unit under the New Covenant, including its Sabbath, while adhering to the view of abrogation mentioned above. This contradicts Wells' theory that Reisinger "has adopted John Owen's view of the Mosaic and New covenants, without adding Owen's 'creation ordinance' view of the Sabbath."[36] This is so because Owen's view of the New Covenant includes a Sabbath on grounds other than its status as creation ordinance alone.
  (3) That Owen's interpretation and application of Matt. 5:17 preclude the elimination of the Decalogue as a unit from the New Covenant. This also contradicts Wells' theory as per above.
  (4) That Owen held to the multifunctional utility of the Decalogue expressed in his Confession, the *Savoy Declaration of Faith* (Savoy), as well as in the *Westminster Confession of Faith* (WCF), the *Second London Confession of Faith* (2nd LCF), and the writings of the Reformers and Post-Reformation Reformed

---

[35] Wells, *Reisinger*, 6.
[36] Ibid.

Scholastics. In other words, Owen taught the transcovenantal utility of the Decalogue, as others before and after him.

After this, some relevant conclusions will be drawn.

In displaying these things, it will become evident that Owen's latter writings fully comport with his earlier writings, proving that Owen did not change his views or contradict himself. It will also become evident that all of this fits Owen's confessional theology and the theology of Reformation and Post-Reformation Reformed Scholasticism, on the main. And finally, it will become evident that Wells and Reisinger misunderstood Owen on some very crucial points.

The Concept of Abrogation in Owen and others

1. John Owen and Abrogation

Owen teaches that the whole law of Moses (even the moral element as will be seen below) has been abrogated. This is the NCT position and is probably why Wells says in *Reisinger* that Reisinger holds Owen's view.

In this section, we will look at some of the Owen statements which led Wells to conclude what he did. The next three Owen quotes were cited by Wells in *Reisinger*. Commenting on Heb. 7:18-19, Owen says:

> I have proved before that "the commandment" in this verse [Heb. 7:18] is of equal extent and signification with "the law" in the next. And "the law" there doth evidently intend the whole law, in both the parts of it, moral and ceremonial, **as it was given by Moses unto the church of Israel** [emphasis added].[37]

Commenting on Heb. 7:12, Owen says:

> It was the whole "law of commandments contained in ordinances," or the whole law of Moses, **so far as it was the rule of worship and obedience unto the church** [emphasis added]; for that law it is that followeth the fates of the priesthood.[38]

> Wherefore the whole law of Moses, **as given unto the Jews** [emphasis added], whether as used or abused by them, was repugnant unto and inconsistent with the gospel, and the mediation of Christ, especially his

---

[37] Owen, *Works*, XXI:464. Cited by Wells in *Reisinger*, 7.
[38] Ibid., 428. Cited by Wells in *Reisinger*, 7.

priestly office, therein declared; neither did God either design, appoint, or direct that they should be co-existent.[39]

Owen goes on to say that this whole law has been abrogated.

While Owen does teach this, however, he also carefully qualifies what he means by the whole law and its abrogation. What does he mean? Commenting on Heb. 7:18-19, the same text he is commenting on above which Wells cited, Owen says:

> Nor is it the whole ceremonial law only that is intended by "the command" in this place, but the moral law also, **so far as it was compacted with the other into one body of precepts for the same end** [emphasis added]; for with respect unto the efficacy of the whole law of Moses, as unto our drawing nigh unto God, it is here considered.[40]

Again, speaking of the abrogation of the whole law of the Old Covenant (moral and ceremonial), Owen says:

> By all these ways was the church of the Hebrews forewarned that the time would come when the whole Mosaical law, **as to its legal or covenant efficacy** [emphasis added], should be disannulled, unto the unspeakable advantage of the church.[41]

This comes in his section which seeks to explain what he means by the whole law being abrogated. In it, he is showing how "the whole law may be considered ...absolutely in itself" or "with respect ...unto the end for which it was given ..." or "... unto the persons unto whom it was given ..."[42] He calls the law "the whole system of Mosaical ordinances, as it was the covenant which God made with the people of Horeb. For the apostle takes 'the commandment,' and 'the law' for the same in this chapter; and 'the covenant,' in the next, for the same in them both."[43] Owen appears to be concentrating on the whole Mosaic law, as it related to the ancient covenant people and was, in fact, their covenant. It is the law in its totality as it related to that people that has been abrogated. Part

---

[39] Ibid., 429. Cited by Wells in *Reisinger*, 7.
[40] Ibid., 458.
[41] Ibid., 469.
[42] Owen, *Works,* XXI:466.
[43] Ibid., 471.

of Owen's burden in his Hebrews commentary was to show that the apostle was dealing with Hebrew Christians and their relation to the Old Covenant; they thought they could still have one, but the author [Paul according to Owen] is showing otherwise. So the abrogation of the whole law in Owen refers to the whole law as it functioned with Old Covenant Israel. This abrogation is used as an argument for the superiority of the New Covenant in the face of the Hebrew audience Paul was writing to. That law, as such (moral/decalogue and ceremonial), is abrogated.[44]

We will now examine other Reformed theologians to show that Owen stands clearly within Reformed orthodoxy concerning his views of abrogation.

2. John Calvin and Abrogation

This understanding of abrogation is found in Calvin also. According to Calvin, the abrogation of the law under the New Covenant in no way abrogates the Decalogue in every sense of the word. Commenting on Rom. 7:2, Calvin says:

> ...but we must remember, that Paul refers here only to **that office of the law which was peculiar to Moses** [emphasis added]; for as far as God has in the ten commandments taught what is just and right, and given directions for guiding our life, no abrogation of the law is to be dreamt of; for the will of God must stand the same forever. We ought carefully to remember that **this is not a release from the righteousness which is taught in the law, but from its rigid requirements, and from the curse which thence follows** [emphasis added]. The law, then, as a rule of life, is not abrogated; but what

---

[44] I defended this view of abrogation in chapter 3 of my book *In Defense of the Decalogue: A Critique of New Covenant Theology* (*IDOTD*). "Hearty agreement must be given when New Covenant theologians argue for the abolition of the Old Covenant. This is clearly the teaching of the Old and New Testaments (see Jeremiah 31:31-32; Second Corinthians 3; Galatians 3, 4; Ephesians 2:14-15; Hebrews 8-10). The whole law of Moses, *as it functioned under the Old Covenant*, has been abolished, including the Ten Commandments. Not one jot or tittle of the law of Moses functions *as Old Covenant law* anymore and to act as if it does constitutes redemptive-historical retreat and neo-Judaizing. However, to acknowledge that the law of Moses no longer functions *as Old Covenant law* is not to accept that it no longer functions; it simply no longer functions *as Old Covenant law*. This can be seen by the fact that the New Testament teaches *both* the abrogation of the law of the Old Covenant *and* its abiding moral validity under the New Covenant." See Barcellos, *IDOTD*, 61.

belongs to it as opposed to the liberty obtained through Christ, that is, as it requires absolute perfection...[45]

It is important to note that "[t]he term "law" for Calvin may mean (1) the whole religion of Moses...; (2) the special revelation of the moral law to the chosen people, i.e., chiefly the Decalogue and Jesus' summary...; or (3) various bodies of civil, judicial, and ceremonial statutes ..."[46] Calvin says, "I understand by the word "law" not only the Ten Commandments, which set forth a godly and righteous rule of living, but the form of religion handed down by God through Moses."[47] Calvin views the law in various ways. So when he speaks of abrogation, he does not intend absolute abrogation, but relative abrogation in terms of the law considered not in itself, but in its redemptive-historically conditioned use. Commenting on the concept of abrogation in Calvin, one Calvin scholar said, "...the Law was not in itself abrogated by the Christ, but only the slavery and malediction attaching to it under the ancient Covenant."[48] According to Calvin, therefore, the Moral Law has not been abrogated, as such. What has been abrogated or fulfilled in Christ for believers is its function as a curse. "The law itself is not abolished for the believer, but only the *maledictio legis*... [F]or Calvin the law is related above all to believers for whom, however, the *maledictio* is removed."[49] Notice that Hesselink uses the same language that Owen does (i.e., 'the law itself').

3. Zacharias Ursinus and Abrogation

In *The Commentary of Dr. Zacharias Ursinus on the Heidelberg Catechism*, while discussing the question of the extent that Christ has abrogated the law and to what extent it is still in force, Ursinus says:

---

[45] John Calvin, *Calvin's Commentaries, Volume XIX* (Grand Rapids: Baker Book House, re. 1984), 246.

[46] John Calvin, *Institutes of the Christian Religion* (Philadelphia: The Westminster Press, 1960), II.vii, n. 1.

[47] Calvin, *Institutes,* II.vii.1. The same phenomena of viewing the law from different theological vantage points can be found in Owen also. I will provide evidence for this below.

[48] I. John Hesselink, *Calvin's Concept of the Law* (Allison Park, PA: Pickwick Publications, 1992), 203.

[49] Hesselink, *Calvin's Concept,* 256.

The ordinary and correct answer to this question is, that the ceremonial and judicial law, as given by Moses, has been abrogated in as far as it relates to obedience; and that the moral law has also been abrogated **as it respects the curse** [emphasis added], but not as it respects obedience.[50]

The moral law has, **as it respects one part** [emphasis added], been abrogated by Christ; and **as it respects another** [emphasis added], it has not.[51]

But the moral law, or Decalogue, has not been abrogated **in as far as obedience to it is concerned** [emphasis added]. God continually, no less now than formerly, requires both the regenerate and the unregenerate to render obedience to his law.[52]

These statements by Ursinus are similar to both Owen and Calvin. These theologians carefully and repeatedly qualify what they mean by abrogation.

4. Francis Turretin and Abrogation

A similar understanding of abrogation can be found in Turretin. In his *Institutes of Elenctic Theology, II,* the table of contents entitles chapter XXIII as follows:

THE ABROGATION OF THE MORAL LAW
XXIII. Whether the moral law is abrogated entirely under the New Testament. Or whether in a certain respect it still pertains to Christians. The former we deny; the latter we affirm against the Antinomians.[53]

Notice Turretin's careful qualifications (i.e., "...entirely..." and "...in a certain respect..."). While discussing the abrogation of the moral law, he says, "In order to apprehend properly the state of the question, we must ascertain in what sense the law may be said to have been abrogated and

---

[50] Zacharias Ursinus, *The Commentary of Dr. Zacharias Ursinus on the Heidelberg Catechism* (Edmonton, AB, Canada: Still Waters Revival Books, re. n.d.), 492.

[51] Ibid., 495.

[52] Ibid., 496.

[53] Francis Turretin, *Institutes of Elenctic Theology* (Phillipsburg, PA: P&R Publishing, 1994), II:ix.

in what sense not."[54] He then lists three senses in which the law has been abrogated. Then he says, "But the question only concerns its directive use—whether we are now freed from the direction and observance of the law. This the adversaries maintain; we deny."[55]

Turretin does what we have seen in others. He has a view of abrogation which both includes the Decalogue and does not include the Decalogue. This is due to the fact that the law can be viewed from different theological and redemptive-historical vantage points.

5. Protestant Scholasticism[56] and Abrogation

Finally, concerning the *lex Mosaica* [law of Moses], which he defines as the moral law as given to Israel by God in a special revelation to Moses on Mount Sinai, Richard Muller says, "As a norm of obedience belonging to the [covenant of grace], the law remains in force under the economy of the New Testament."[57] Hence, Muller recognizes the fact that Protestant Scholastics considered the law in different ways. So when they spoke of abrogation, the fact that they considered the law in different ways must be taken into consideration. If we do not, we may take their statements on the abrogation of the law in an absolute manner and make them mean something they did not.

6. Conclusion

It has been shown that Owen's view of abrogation was similar to Calvin, Ursinus, Turretin, and Protestant Scholasticism. His view of abrogation neither necessarily demands the elimination of the Decalogue as a unit in all senses under the New Covenant, nor is it contradicted by the inclusion of the Decalogue as a unit under the New Covenant. Though with his own nuances and emphases, Owen's view is substantially that of others in his day. It was Calvin's, Ursinus', Turretin's, Protestant Scholasticism's, as well as that of the WCF, the Savoy, and the 2nd LCF.[58]

---

[54] Turretin, *Institutes*, II:141.

[55] Ibid., 141-142.

[56] The sections dealing with Protestant Scholasticism reflect the general teaching of that school of thought. Other sections may and do deal with specific representatives of that school.

[57] Richard A. Muller, *Dictionary of Latin and Greek Theological Terms* (Grand Rapids: Baker Book House, 1985), 174.

[58] See chapters 4 and 19 of these Confessions.

It appears that Wells takes the concept of abrogation absolutely. Hence, he cannot allow the Decalogue to function in more ways than Old Covenant law, unless its individual commands reappear in the law of Christ (New Testament). This, of course, leads to its elimination from the New Covenant, the position of NCT. From what has been shown above, however, Wells' understanding of Owen on abrogation is not necessary. Others held similar views and yet did not eliminate the Decalogue from the New Covenant.

From the evidence presented, Owen must be understood to view abrogation as both including and not including the Decalogue, depending on how it is viewed (more on this later). If this is the case, then his understanding of abrogation, though with its own nuances and emphases, has clear and ample precedent in Calvin, Ursinus, Turretin, and Protestant Scholasticism.

The Perpetuity of the Decalogue under the New Covenant in Owen and others

1. John Owen and the perpetuity of the Decalogue under the New Covenant

Owen teaches that Jer. 31:33 and 2 Co. 3:3 refer to the Decalogue being written on the heart of New Covenant saints in his Hebrews commentary. Commenting on Heb. 9:5, he says:

> This law, as unto the substance of it, was the only law of creation, the rule of the first covenant of works; for it contained the sum and substance of that obedience which is due unto God from all rational creatures made in his image, and nothing else. It was the whole of what God designed in our creation unto his own glory and our everlasting blessedness. What was in the tables of stone was nothing but a transcript of what was written in the heart of man originally; and which is returned thither again by the grace of the new covenant, Jeremiah 31:33; 2 Corinthians 3:3.[59]

Consider these observations, relevant to our discussion. *First*, the law, in the context of Owen's discussion, refers to the law contained on the tables of stone (i.e., the Decalogue). *Second*, Owen is considering the Decalogue "as unto the substance of it" and not necessarily the form

---

[59] Owen, *Works*, XXII:215.

and/or function of it under the Old Covenant.[60] *Third,* he claims that the Decalogue "was the only law of creation, the rule of the first covenant of works." *Fourth,* he claims that the Decalogue, as to the substance of it, "contained the sum and substance of that obedience which is due unto God from all rational creatures made in his image." *Fifth,* he claims that "what was in the tables of stone was nothing but a transcript of what was written in the heart of man originally." *Sixth,* he claims that "what was in the tables of stone [and written on the heart of man at creation]" is that "which is returned thither again by the grace of the new covenant." And *finally,* he does this referencing Jer. 31:33 and 2 Co. 3:3. This clearly has direct reference to the perpetuity of the entire Decalogue under the New Covenant.

Owen continues:

> Although this law as a covenant was broken and disannulled by the entrance of sin, and became insufficient as unto its first ends, of the justification and salvation of the church thereby, Rom viii. 3; yet as a law and rule of obedience it was never disannulled, nor would God suffer it to be. Yea, one principal design of God in Christ was, that it might be fulfilled and established, Matt. v. 17, 18; Rom iii. 31. For to reject this law, or to abrogate it, had been for God to have laid aside that glory of his holiness and righteousness which in his infinite wisdom he designed therein. Hence, after it was again broken by the people as a covenant, he wrote it a second time himself in tables of stone, and caused it to be safely kept in the ark, as his perpetual testimony. That, therefore, which he taught the church by and in all this, in the first place, was, that this law was to be fulfilled and accomplished, or they could have no advantage of or benefit by the covenant.[61]

---

[60] Protestant Scholasticism taught that the Decalogue summarily contains the moral law and is the inscripturated form of the natural law, as to its *substance*. A distinction was made between *substance* and *form*. *Substance* is one; *form* may vary. Hence, when the Westminster Larger Catechism Q. 98 says, "The moral law is summarily comprehended in the ten commandments," it refers to the fact that the *substance* (i.e., the underlying essence) of the Moral Law is assumed and articulated in the propositions of the Decalogue as contained in Exo. 20 and Deut. 5. The *form* fits the redemptive-historical circumstances in which it was given. The *substance* or underlying principles are always relevant and applicable to man. The application may shift based on redemptive-historical changes, such as the inauguration of the New Covenant, but its *substance* and utility never changes.

[61] Owen, *Works,* XXII:215-216.

The following observations are also relevant to our discussion. *First*, Owen makes a distinction between how the Decalogue functioned in the covenant of works and how it functions "as a law and rule of obedience." *Second*, he connects this law with God's holiness and righteousness. We see from these two observations that Owen views the Decalogue as a perpetual "law and rule of obedience" because it is related to God's holiness and righteousness (i.e., His unchanging nature).

Continuing the discussion and concentrating on how Christ is the true ark [the antitype of the Old Covenant's Ark of the Covenant], he says:

> In his *obedience unto God* according unto the law he is the true *ark*, wherein the law was kept inviolate; that is, was fulfilled, answered, and accomplished, Matt. v. 17; Rom. viii. 3, x. 4. Hence by God's gracious dealing with sinners, pardoning and justifying them freely, the law [i.e., Decalogue in context] is not disannulled, but established, Rom. iii. 31. That this was to be done, that without it no covenant between God and man could be firm and stable, was the principal design of God to declare in all this service; without the consideration thereof it was wholly insignificant. This was the original mystery of all these institutions, that in and by the obedience of the promised seed, the everlasting, unalterable law should be fulfilled.[62]

Several observations are worthy of note. *First*, in the context of Owen's discussion, the law refers to that which was placed in the ark (i.e., the Decalogue as written by God on stone tablets). *Second*, he says that it was this law that was fulfilled, answered, and accomplished by Christ. *Third*, he says that the obedience of Christ to this law effects our justification. *Fourth*, he says that the law is not disannulled but established. *Fifth*, he teaches that all of this was typified in the Ark of the Covenant. And *finally*, he says that the law is *everlasting* and *unalterable*, probably due to its reflection of God's holiness and righteousness.[63]

Owen's use of Jer. 31:33 and 2 Co. 3:3 was not novel as will be seen below. Others who held to his basic understanding of abrogation argued

---

[62] Ibid., 217-218.
[63] Owen, *Works*, XXII:215.

the perpetuity of the Decalogue under the New Covenant upon the same exegetical grounds (see below).[64]

2. Herman Witsius and the perpetuity of the Decalogue under the New Covenant

In his *The Economy of the Covenants Between God and Man*, while discussing the reason that God "engraved them [the Ten Commandments] with his own finger,"[65] Witsius says:

> Both because they contained the declaration or testimony of the divine will, and because the preservation of them by the Israelites, was a testimony of the law given to, and received by them at Sinai. This writing also signified the purpose of God, to write the law on the hearts of his elect, according to the promise of the covenant of grace, Jer. xxxi. 33.
> XVII. Nor is it for nothing that God himself would be the author of this writing, without making use of any man or angel. For this is the meaning of the Holy Spirit, when he says, that the tablets were written with the finger of God, Exod. xxxi. 18. and that the writing was the writing of God, Exod. xxxii. 16. The reasons were, 1st. To set forth the pre-eminence of this law, which he permitted to be written by Moses. 2dly. To intimate, that it is the work of God alone, to write the law on the heart, which is what neither man himself, nor the ministers of God can do, but the Spirit of God alone. And thus believers are "the epistle of Christ, written not with ink, but with the Spirit of the living God," 2 Cor. iii. 3.[66]

He goes on to discuss the effects of God's grace and says, "But the grace of God will cancel that writing of sin, and in the room of it, will the graver of his most Holy Spirit, engrave on the same table of our heart the characters of his law."[67]

---

[64] In *IDOTD*, I provided exegetical evidence that Jer. 31:33 and 2 Co. 3:3 speak directly to the issue of the perpetuity of the Decalogue under the New Covenant. I provided references to Old Testament and New Testament scholars to this end. The scholars I referenced are not all Reformed confessionalists. I did this on purpose to show that one's confessional commitments do not necessarily cloud one's exegetical lenses. See Barcellos, *IDOTD*, 16-24 and 34-38.

[65] Herman Witsius, *The Economy of the Covenants Between God and Man* (Escondido, CA: The den Dulk Christian Foundation, re. 1990), II:170.

[66] Ibid., II:170-171.

[67] Ibid., II:171.

The context is very clear. Witsius sees Jer. 31:33 and 2 Co. 3:3 as testimonies to the perpetuity of the Decalogue under the New Covenant. As shown above, Owen used these texts in a very similar context and with the same practical result.

3. Francis Turretin and the perpetuity of the Decalogue under the New Covenant

In the same section quoted above concerning abrogation, Turretin references both Jer. 31:33 and 2 Cor. 3:3. His use of these texts corresponds with Owen's and Witsius', at least to a degree. He is discussing how abrogation as it related to the Moral Law (Decalogue in context) is not to be considered absolutely, but relatively and that the law must be viewed in the same light–not absolutely, but relatively. Here are a few examples of Turretin making this distinction.

> It is one thing to be under the law as a covenant to acquire life by it (as Adam was) or as a schoolmaster and a prison to guard men until the advent of Christ; another to be under the law as a rule of life to regulate our morals piously and holily. [68]

> The law is compared by Paul to "a dead husband" (Rom. 7:2, 3), not simply, but relatively with regard to the sway and rigorous dominion it obtained over us and the curse to which it subjected sinners; but not with regard to liberation from the duty to be performed to it. Thus the law threatening, compelling, condemning, is not "made for a righteous man" (1 Tim. 1:9) because he is impelled of his own accord to duty and is no longer influenced by the spirit of bondage and the fear of punishment (Rom. 8:15; Ps. 110:3), but the law directive and regulative of morals is always laid down for him and he ought to be under it. [69]

> What was given to the Jews as Jews can be for the use of the Jews alone; but what is given to the Jews as covenanted (or as the people of God simply) does not refer to them alone, but to all those who hold the same relation of people of God. [70]

Turretin makes many more statements similar to this. Suffice to say that he, as with others, makes distinctions in the way the law is viewed. This

---

[68] Turretin, *Institutes*, II:143.
[69] Ibid.
[70] Ibid., 145.

is done to protect the Moral Law from an absolutist view of abrogation and to promote its perpetual utility. It is within this discussion and context that Turretin says, "'If ye be led of the Spirit, ye are not under the law' (Gal. 5:18, viz., compelling and cursing), but under it directing, inasmuch as the Spirit works that law upon our hearts (2 Cor. 3:2; Jer. 31:33)."[71] In this context, the law which directs is the Moral Law (Decalogue). Hence, it is the Decalogue, which "the Spirit works upon our hearts", and He does this according to 2 Corinthians 3 and Jeremiah 31 in the thinking of Francis Turretin.

4. Thomas Boston and the perpetuity of the Decalogue under the New Covenant

Thomas Boston's notes to *The Marrow of Modern Divinity* reveal to us that at least one 18th century Reformed theologian held that Jer. 31:33 referred to the writing of the Decalogue on the heart under the New Covenant. Boston says:

> One will not think it strange to hear, that the ten commandments were, as it were, razed out of man's heart by the fall, if one considers the spirituality and vast extent of them, and that they were, in their perfection engraven on the heart of man, in his creation, and doth withal take notice of the ruin brought on man by the fall. Hereby he indeed lost the very knowledge of the law of nature, if the ten commandments are to be reckoned, as certainly they are, the substance and matter of that law; although he lost it not totally, but some remains thereof were left with him. Concerning these the apostle speaks, Rom. i. 19, 20; and ii. 14, 15. And our author teaches expressly, that the law is partly known by nature, that is, in its corrupt state, See page 181. And here he says, not simply, that the ten commandments were razed, though in another case (page 44), he speaks after that manner, where yet it is evident he means not a razing quite; but he says, "They were, as it were, razed." But what are these remains of them in comparison with that body of natural laws, fairly written, and deeply engraven, on the heart of innocent Adam? If they were not, as it were, razed, what need is there of writing a new copy of them in the hearts of the elect, according to the promise of the new covenant? "I will put my laws into their hearts, and in their minds I will write them," Heb. x. 16, and viii. 10; Jer. xxxi. 33.[72]

---

[71] Ibid., 143-144.

[72] Edward Fisher, *The Marrow of Modern Divinity* (Edmonton, AB, Canada: Still Waters Revival Books, re. 1991), 177.

Like Witsius and Turretin before him, Boston proves that there were some in the 17th and 18th centuries who argued for the perpetuity of the Decalogue from Jer. 31:33 (and 2 Co. 3:3) on the same exegetical ground as Owen.

5. Conclusion

Though Owen's statements concerning Jer. 31:33 are not all equally clear, those provided above are clear enough to conclude that he used it and 2 Co. 3:3 in a context which argues for the perpetuity of the Decalogue under the New Covenant. He does this in similar fashion as Witsius, Turretin, and Boston.

We have seen that abrogation in Owen and others is not absolute. We have also seen that he did, in fact, reference Jer. 31:33 and 2 Co. 3:3 in a context arguing for the perpetuity of the Decalogue under the New Covenant. He did both of these things in a manner done by others before and after him.

The statements of Owen examined thus far came toward the end of his life. Tom Wells rightly claims that the Hebrews commentary reflects Owen's "mature thoughts on the covenants."[73] But Owen's mature thoughts on the covenants include the perpetuity of the entire Decalogue, including the Sabbath commandment, under the New Covenant. Wells claims that Reisinger "has adopted John Owen's view of the Mosaic and New covenants, without adding Owen's 'creation ordinance' view of the Sabbath."[74] But from our study thus far, we have seen that Owen taught the perpetuity of the Decalogue as a unit under the New Covenant. Hence, Owen did not base the Sabbath under the New Covenant solely upon its status as creation ordinance. Wells' claim, therefore, needs modification and qualification in light of a proper understanding of Owen on the Mosaic and New Covenants.

Matthew 5:17 as it Relates to the Perpetuity of the Decalogue under the New Covenant in Owen and others

1. John Owen and Matthew 5:17 as it relates to the perpetuity of the Decalogue under the New Covenant

Owen argues for the perpetuity of the Decalogue under the New Covenant from Matt. 5:17 in his Hebrews commentary.

---

[73] Wells, *Reisinger*, 17.
[74] Ibid., 6.

While discussing the foundations of the Sabbath, Owen says:

From these particular instances we may return to the consideration of the law of the decalogue in general, and the perpetual power of exacting obedience wherewith it is accompanied. That in the Old Testament it is frequently declared to be universally obligatory, and has the same efficacy ascribed unto it, without putting in any exceptions to any of its commands or limitations of its number, I suppose will be granted. The authority of it is no less fully asserted in the New Testament, and that also absolutely without distinction, or the least intimation of excepting the fourth command from what is affirmed concerning the whole. It is of the law of the decalogue that our Savior treats, Matt. v. 17-19. This he affirms that he came not to dissolve, as he did the ceremonial law, but to fulfill it; and then affirms that not one jot or tittle of it shall pass away. And making thereon a distribution of the whole into its several commands, he declares his disapprobation of them who shall break, or teach men to break, any one of them. And men make bold with him, when they so confidently assert that they may break one of them, and teach others so to do, without offense. That this reaches not to the confirmation of the seventh day precisely, we shall after-wards abundantly demonstrate.[75]

Commenting on Heb. 9:3-5, Owen says:

Although this law as a covenant was broken and disannulled *by the entrance of sin,* and became insufficient as unto its first ends, of the justification and salvation of the church thereby, Rom. viii. 3; yet as a *law and rule of obedience* it was never disannulled, nor would God suffer it to be. Yea, one principal design of God in Christ was, that it might be fulfilled and established, Matt. v. 17, 18; Rom. iii. 31. For to reject this law, or to abrogate it, had been for God to have laid aside that glory of his holiness and righteousness which in his infinite wisdom he designed therein. Hence, after it was again broken by the people as a covenant, he wrote it a second time himself in tables of stone, and caused it to be safely kept in the ark, as his perpetual testimony. That, therefore, which he taught the church by and in all this, in the first place, was, that this law was to be fulfilled and accomplished, or they could have no advantage of or benefit by the covenant.[76]

---

[75] Owen, *Works*, XVIII:372.
[76] Owen, *Works*, XXII:215-216.

These two quotes show that both early in the Hebrews commentary and late, Owen held that Matt. 5:17 did not eliminate the Decalogue from the New Covenant. It is of interest for our purposes to note that this latter use of Matt. 5:17 both agrees with the former and comes after the statements Tom Wells used to conclude that Owen's view was John G. Reisinger's and that of NCT. This also proves that Owen based the Sabbath on its presence in the Decalogue as well as its status as creation ordinance.

This consistent understanding of Matt. 5:17, which includes the perpetuity of the Decalogue under the New Covenant, does not necessarily contradict Owen on the abrogation of the whole law–Decalogue included. We have seen that abrogation for Owen, and many others, is not absolute, especially when it comes to the Decalogue. Owen used Jer. 31:33 and 2 Co. 3:3 as proof for the perpetuity of the Decalogue. His use of Matt. 5:17 is to the same end.[77]

2. Zacharias Ursinus and Matthew 5:17 as it relates to the perpetuity of the Decalogue under the New Covenant

While discussing how abrogation affects the Moral Law, Ursinus makes the point that "the moral law, or Decalogue, has not been abrogated in as far as obedience to it is concerned."[78] He then argues, "God continually, no less now than formerly, requires both the regenerate and the unregenerate to render obedience to his law."[79] He seeks to prove this by three reasons. The third reason is:

From the testimony of Scripture: "Think not that I am come to destroy the law, or the prophets; I am not come to destroy, but to fulfill." (Matt.

---

[77] In *IDOTD*, I argued that Mt. 5:17 can be understood in such a way as not to eliminate the Decalogue from the New Covenant. As a matter of fact, I argued that it could be understood in such a way as not to eliminate the Old Testament from the New Covenant. For instance, after providing exegetical observations and conclusions and then testing my interpretation with the rest of the New Testament, I said: "The law of God, even the whole Old Testament, has its place under Christ, finding its realization in Him and its modified application in His kingdom. If the whole of the Old Testament is still binding, then certainly all its parts are as well." See Barcellos, *IDOTD*, 65. I realize my explanation has nuances Owen's may not. The point is that Owen is not the only one in history to so understand Mt. 5:17 as not to eliminate the Decalogue from the New Covenant, as will be further illustrated below.

[78] Ursinus, *Heidelberg Catechism*, 496.

[79] Ibid.

5:17.) This is spoken, indeed, of the whole law, but with a special reference to the moral law, which Christ has fulfilled in four respects [80] ...

Ursinus understands Matt. 5:17 in such a way as to demand the perpetuity of the Decalogue under the New Covenant. This shows that someone who held similar views with Owen on abrogation also upheld the perpetuity of the Decalogue under the New Covenant from Matt. 5:17.

3.   Francis Turretin and Matthew 5:17 as it relates to the perpetuity of the Decalogue under the New Covenant

While offering "Proof that the law is not abrogated as to direction"[81], Turretin says, "...Christ 'did not come to destroy but to fulfill the law' (Mt. 5:17). Therefore as it was not abolished but fulfilled by Christ, neither is its use among us to be abolished."[82] Once again, one who held similar views with Owen concerning abrogation and the use of Jer. 31:33 and 2 Co. 3:3 uses Matt. 5:17 to support the perpetuity of the Decalogue under the New Covenant.

4.   Conclusion

It has now become clear that Owen's view of Matt. 5:17 does not require the elimination of the Decalogue under the New Covenant. This was Owen's position in the Hebrews commentary itself. His view on Matt. 5:17 was the view of Ursinus and Turretin. These men also held similar views on abrogation and the perpetuity of the Decalogue based on various grounds. Taking all that we have seen thus far in Owen and others who held similar views, it is becoming more and more unlikely that his mediating position can be claimed as that of John G. Reisinger or NCT. They may and do hold to his view in part, but certainly not in whole, and the difference is not as simple as Owen's addition of the Sabbath as a creation ordinance.

---

[80] Ibid.

[81] Turretin, *Institutes*, II:142.

[82] Ibid.

The Multi-functional Utility of the Decalogue in Owen and others

1. John Owen and the multi-functional utility of the Decalogue

Owen viewed the Decalogue as having more than one function. Unlike Reisinger and NCT, he did not view it as Old Covenant law alone. His understanding of the multi-functional utility of the Decalogue can be seen very clearly in several places of his Hebrews commentary. For instance, commenting on Heb. 9:5, referenced above, he says, "The law [Decalogue in context], as unto the substance of it, was the only law of creation, the rule of the first covenant of works."[83] Later he claims that "[w]hat was in the tables of stone was nothing but a transcript of what was written in the heart of man originally; and which is returned thither again by the grace of the new covenant."[84] Notice that he views the Decalogue as functioning several ways; first, "as unto the substance of it, ...the only law of creation;" second, "the rule of the first covenant of works;" third, that which "was in the tables of stone;" fourth, "a transcript of what was written in the heart of man originally;" and fifth, that "which is returned [to the heart of man] again by the grace of the new covenant."

Commenting on Heb. 7:18-19, also referenced previously, he says:

> Nor is it the whole *ceremonial law* only that is intended by "the command" in this place, but the *moral law* also, **so far as it was compacted with the other into one body of precepts for the same end** [emphasis added]; for with respect unto the efficacy of the whole law of Moses, as unto our drawing nigh unto God, it is here considered.[85]

Here he views the Decalogue as a unit "so far as it was compacted with the other [ceremonial law] into one body of precepts for the same end." In other words, he is considering the Decalogue not absolutely or in itself (see below), but relatively or as it was "compacted" with the ceremonial law under the Old Covenant.

While discussing the causes of the Sabbath and arguing for the morality and immutability of the essence of the fourth commandment, he

---

[83] Owen, *Works*, XXII:215.
[84] Ibid.
[85] Owen, *Works*, XXI:458.

makes this statement concerning the nature and function of the Decalogue under the Old Covenant:

> The nature of the decalogue, and the distinction of its precepts from all commands, ceremonial or political, comes now under consideration. The whole decalogue, I acknowledge, as given on mount Sinai to the Israelites, had a political use, as being made the principal instrument or rule of the polity and government of their nation, as peculiarly under the rule of God. It had a place also in that economy or dispensation of the covenant which that church was then brought under; wherein, by God's dealing with them and instructing of them, they were taught to look out after a further and greater good in the promise than they were yet come to the enjoyment of. Hence the Decalogue itself, in that dispensation of it, was a schoolmaster unto Christ.[86]

First, Owen views the Decalogue as the core of the law of the Old Covenant. He says, "The whole decalogue, ...as given on mount Sinai to the Israelites, had a political use, as being made the principal instrument or rule of the polity and government of their nation." Second, he makes the point that the Decalogue was "made the principal instrument or rule of the polity and government" of Israel under the Old Covenant. This is something it was not until that time. He viewed it as already in existence, though in a different form and revealed in a different manner, but now being "made" something it was not. It was now "made" to fit the redemptive-historical conditions of the Old Covenant. This seems even more likely, since he goes on to say, "Some, indeed, of the precepts of it, as the first, fourth, and fifth, have either prefaces, enlargements, or additions, which belonged peculiarly to the then present and future state of that church in the land of Canaan."[87] Third, he also viewed it as "a schoolmaster unto Christ."

Next, he is going to consider the Decalogue "in itself, and materially."[88] He says:

> But in itself, and materially considered, it was wholly, and in all the preceptive parts of it, absolutely moral. Some, indeed, of the precepts of it, as the first, fourth, and fifth, have either prefaces, enlargements, or additions, which belonged peculiarly to the then present and future

---

[86] Owen, *Works*, XVIII:365-366.
[87] Ibid., 366.
[88] Ibid.

state of that church in the land of Canaan; but these especial applications of it unto them change not the nature of its commands or precepts, which are all moral, and, as far as they are esteemed to belong to the Decalogue, are unquestionably acknowledged so to be.[89]

Notice that he has transitioned from viewing the Decalogue in its Old Covenant functions to the Decalogue in itself. We might say that he was considering it relatively speaking, as it functioned under the Old Covenant, and now he is considering it absolutely or in itself, as it functions transcovenantally. *First*, he makes a distinction between the Decalogue "as being made the principal instrument or rule of the polity and government of their [Old Covenant Israel's] nation" and "in itself." Hence, "in itself" and "in all the preceptive parts of it" the Decalogue is "absolutely moral." *Second*, he says that the Decalogue under the Old Covenant had redemptive-historical "prefaces, enlargements, or additions" peculiar to the conditions in which they [the church in the land of Canaan] lived. These are positive, covenantal appendages, added to the Decalogue and applicable to Old Covenant Israel in the land of Canaan.

From these statements, the following observations are relevant to our purposes. *First*, Owen viewed the Decalogue both relatively and absolutely, depending on its function in redemptive history. *Second*, he viewed the Decalogue (i.e., that which "was in tables of stone... as unto the substance of it") functioning various ways and in all of the epochs of redemptive history. First of all, he saw it functioning in the Garden of Eden. He viewed it as being the law of creation, the rule of the Adamic covenant of works, and that which was written on Adam's heart. He then saw it functioning in a special manner under the Old Covenant. He also saw it functioning under the New Covenant. He taught that it was this same law, as unto its substance, "which is returned thither [to the heart of man] again by the grace of the new covenant."[90] He also viewed it as the rule of life for all men,[91] because "in all the preceptive parts of it" it is "absolutely moral." And as stated earlier, he viewed it as related to the

---

[89] Ibid.
[90] Owen, *Works*, XXII:215.
[91] Ibid.

active and passive obedience of Christ and hence, connected and essential to the doctrine of justification.[92]

Hence, Owen adheres to the multi-functional utility of the Decalogue. It functioned in the garden as the law of creation written on Adam's heart, as the rule of the covenant of works, as that which is required of all image bearers, as the principal instrument or rule of the Old Covenant, and as the basic rule of life under the New Covenant. Hence, its broken commands were the cause of Christ's suffering and its precepts the rule of His obedience.[93]

2. John Calvin and the multi-functional utility of the Decalogue[94]

Calvin very clearly and in many places identified the Decalogue as a special form of the Natural Law. For instance, Calvin said, "Now that inward law, which we have above described as written, even engraved, upon the hearts of all, in a sense asserts the very same things that are to be learned from the two Tables."[95] Calvin "saw the revealed law as given in the ten commandments as a specially accommodated restatement of

---

[92] Ibid., 89-90. "But in the new covenant, the very first thing that is proposed, is the accomplishment and establishment of the covenant of works, both as to its commands and sanction, in the obedience and suffering of the mediator."

[93] In *IDOTD*, I argued for a multi-functional utility of the Decalogue. For instance, I said: "In light of the exposition above [Jer. 31:33; 2 Cor. 3:3; Eph. 6:2-3; and 1 Tm. 1:8-11], we may assert that the Decalogue functions three ways in Scripture: *first* as the basic, fundamental law of the Old Covenant; *second*, as the basic, fundamental law of the New Covenant; and *third*, as the basic, fundamental law common to all men, the Moral Law." See Barcellos, *IDOTD*, 59. Elsewhere, I use the language "transcovenantal utility" to refer to the same concept. In other words, the Decalogue has more than one function. It is transcovenantal and applies to all men at all times, though not always in the same way. In my article published by *Tabletalk*, "The Death of the Decalogue," I added these observations which comport with Owen. "The essence of righteousness in man is the same from Creation to consummation. The righteousness demanded of Adam is essentially the same demanded of us. The righteousness procured by Christ's life (His active obedience) and imputed to believers is the same for all the elect. NCT unwittingly tampers with what constitutes essential righteousness in man. This is so because NCT sees the moral law as a dynamic concept in Scripture and therefore in process, both changing and advancing as revelation unfolds. This impinges upon the active obedience of Christ, the imputation of righteousness, and the ground of justification. The Bible teaches one justification based on one righteousness, not various levels of righteousness depending on what moral law one is under." See Richard C. Barcellos, "The Death of the Decalogue," *Tabletalk* (Orlando, FL: Ligonier Ministries, September 2002), 55.

[94] Some of the following material comes from Barcellos, *IDOTD*, 92-93, and is used with permission from Founders Press.

[95] Calvin, *Institutes*, II.viii.1.

the law of nature for the Jews."[96] He clearly held that by nature Gentiles without special revelation possessed the general knowledge of the Decalogue, though obscured by sin.[97] Hesselink says, "There is no denying that for Calvin the content of the moral law is essentially the same as that inscribed on the hearts of humans 'by nature'."[98] Francois Wendel says, "One can even say that, for Calvin, the Decalogue is only a special application of the natural law which God came to attest and confirm."[99]

Calvin's view of the multi-functional utility of the Decalogue is no secret. It is also evidenced by the fact that he clearly upheld the perpetuity of both Tables of the law for New Covenant believers.[100] For instance, he says:

> The whole law is contained under two heads. Yet our God, to remove all possibility of excuse, willed to set forth more fully and clearly by the Ten Commandments everything connected with the honor, fear, and love of him, and everything pertaining to the love toward men, which he for his own sake enjoins upon us.[101]

Calvin clearly held that the Decalogue, all Ten Commandments, functioned as the basic, fundamental law of the Bible and as a universal ethical canon for all men based on creation. He also believed in the basic centrality of the entire Decalogue under the New Covenant.

Similar to Owen, Calvin holds to the multi-functional utility of the Decalogue.

3. Zacharias Ursinus and the multi-functional utility of the Decalogue

As stated above, in his *Commentary on the Heidelberg Catechism*, while discussing the question: To What Extent Has Christ Abrogated The Law, And To What Extent Is It Still In Force, Ursinus says: "The moral law has, as it respects one part, been abrogated by Christ; and as it respects

---

[96] Hesselink, *Calvin's Concept*, 51.

[97] Calvin, *Institutes*, II.viii.1.

[98] Hesselink, *Calvin's Concept*, 10.

[99] Francois Wendel, *Calvin, Origins and Developments of His Religious Thought* (Grand Rapids: Baker Book House, re. 1997), 206.

[100] Calvin, *Institutes*, II.vii.13.

[101] Ibid., II.viii.12.

another, it has not."[102]   He continues and says, "...But the moral law, or Decalogue, has not been abrogated in as far as obedience to it is concerned."[103]

It is clear that Ursinus, like Owen and Calvin, holds to a multi-functional utility of the Decalogue.

4. Francis Turretin and the multi-functional utility of the Decalogue

While discussing the use of the Moral Law, Turretin says:

> A twofold use of the law may be laid down—absolute and relative. The former regards the law in itself; the latter regards the law in relation to the various states of man. The absolute (which obtains in every state of man) is that it may be a unique, full and certain rule of things to be done and avoided by each of us as well towards God as his neighbor. Thus there is no work truly and properly good and acceptable to God which does not agree with the law and is not prescribed by it; and whatsoever is not commanded nor forbidden by it is to be considered in its own nature indifferent and left to the freedom of man, unless this freedom has been restricted by some positive law.[104]

In Turretin, the Moral Law or Decalogue is the inscripturated form of the Natural Law.[105] Notice above that Turretin views the Moral Law absolutely and relatively. Viewing it absolutely, it is applicable "in every state of man." How does he view the Moral Law relatively? He continues:

> The relative use is manifold according to the different states of man. (1) In the instituted state of innocence, it was a contract of a covenant of works entered into with man and the means of obtaining life and happiness according to the promise added to the law...
>
> (2) In the destitute state of sin, the use of the law cannot be "justification" because it was weak in the flesh. ...Still there is a threefold use of the law [in man's destitute state of sin]. (a) For conviction... (b) For restraint... (c) For condemnation...

---

[102] Ursinus, *Heidelberg Catechism*, 495.

[103] Ibid., 496.

[104] Turretin, *Institutes*, II:137.

[105] Ibid., II:6-7.

(3) In the restored state of grace, it has a varied use with respect to the elect, both before and after their conversions. Antecedently, it serves (a) to convince and humble man... (b) To lead men to Christ...
It not only antecedently prepares the elect man for Christ, but consequently also directs him already renewed through Christ in the ways of the Lord; serving him as a standard and rule of the most perfect life...[106]

Relatively, or considering the law in its relation "to the different states of man," the law has various functions as it pertains to the lost and the saved throughout all ages. In other words, there is a multi-functional utility to the law. Its utility transcends covenantal bounds. Due to the nature of the Decalogue, it cannot be eliminated from any era of redemptive history, which includes the New Covenant era.

Turretin's view is that of Owen, Calvin, and Ursinus.

5. Protestant Scholasticism and the multi-functional utility of the Decalogue

Richard Muller defines Moral Law in Protestant scholastic thought as follows:

[S]pecifically and predominantly, the *Decalogus*, or Ten Commandments; also called the *lex Mosaica* ..., as distinct from the *lex ceremonialis* ...and the *lex civilis*, or civil law. The *lex moralis,* which is primarily intended to regulate morals, is known to the [innate habit of understanding basic principles of moral law] and is the basis of the acts of [conscience–the application of the innate habit above]. In substance, the *lex moralis* is identical with the *lex naturalis* ...but, unlike the natural law, it is given by revelation in a form which is clearer and fuller than that otherwise known to the reason.[107]

While defining the Mosaic Law, he says:

...the moral law or *lex moralis* (q.v.) given to Israel by God in a special revelation to Moses on Mount Sinai. In contrast to the moral law known in an obscure way to all rational creatures, the *lex Mosaica* is the clear, complete, and perfect rule of human conduct. The Protestant scholastics argue its completeness and perfection from its fulfillment, without addition, by Christ. Since the law does promise life in return

---

[106] Ibid., II:138-140.
[107] Muller, *Dictionary*, 173-174.

for obedience, the Reformed argue that in one sense it holds forth the abrogated *foedus operum* q.v.), or covenant of works, if only as the unattainable promise of the righteous God and the now humanly unattainable requirement for salvation apart from grace. In addition, the Reformed can argue that Christ's perfect obedience did fulfill the covenant of works and render Christ capable of replacing Adam as federal head of humanity. Primarily, however, the Reformed view the law as belonging to the Old Testament *dispensatio* (q.v.) of the *foedus gratiae* (q.v.), or covenant of grace. It is the norm of obedience given to God's faithful people to be followed by them with the help of grace. As a norm of obedience belonging to the *foedus gratiae*, the law remains in force under the economy of the New Testament. Lutheran orthodoxy, which does not follow the covenant schema typical of the Reformed, also views the law as the perfect standard of righteousness and the absolute norm of morals, which requires conformity both in outward conduct and inward obedience of mind, will, and affections.[108]

These definitions of key theological terms and concepts used by Protestant Scholasticism amply display that it held to the multi-functional utility of the Decalogue.

6. Conclusion

Owen's view of the multi-functional utility of the Decalogue comports with his view of abrogation, Jer. 31:33, 2 Co. 3:3, and Matt. 5:17, and also with many of his theological contemporaries. There is a way to understand Owen on abrogation which both eliminates the Decalogue from the New Covenant and preserves it. Relatively speaking, as the Decalogue functioned under the Old Covenant, it has been abrogated. Absolutely speaking, as the Decalogue represents and summarily comprehends the Moral Law as to its substance, it has not and cannot be abrogated. It has more than one function.

Wells' theory that John G. Reisinger and NCT have adopted Owen's view of the Mosaic and New Covenants becomes more and more suspect as the evidence mounts.

Some Concluding Thoughts

Tom Wells has made two claims that gave rise to this discussion. Those two claims are: (1) that John G. Reisinger "has adopted John Owen's

---

[108] Muller, *Dictionary*, 174.

view of the Mosaic and New covenants, without adding Owen's 'creation ordinance' view of the Sabbath"[109] and (2) that Owen held a mediating position on the relationship between the Mosaic and New Covenants, a position substantially that of Reisinger and NCT.[110] What can we conclude in light of the evidence presented?

1. Owen and the Importance of Historical/Theological Context

Owen in the context of his own writings
Primary source documentation of Owen has been presented on (1) abrogation, (2) the perpetuity of the entire Decalogue from Jer. 31:33 and 2 Co. 3:3, (3) Matt. 5:17 as it relates to the perpetuity of the Decalogue under the New Covenant, and (4) the multi-functional utility of the Decalogue. Examining Owen on these subjects both put us into the primary documents themselves and within Owen's systematic thought on relevant theological issues. This was necessary in order to understand him on the primary issue under investigation–whether or not Tom Wells' two claims can be justified from Owen.

Ample evidence was supplied above to make the following conclusions concerning Owen and NCT. His view of abrogation must be carefully qualified, especially as it relates to the Decalogue and the New Covenant. On the one hand, he did view the Decalogue as abrogated under the New Covenant, something properly and emphatically affirmed by NCT. But he viewed it abrogated in terms of its function under the Old Covenant and along with the rest of the Old Covenant's law. His view of the abrogation of the Decalogue was not absolute, contrary to NCT, but relative. It concerned a specific redemptive-historical function of the Decalogue and not all redemptive-historical functions.

On the other hand, Owen did not view the Decalogue as abrogated under the New Covenant, something emphatically denied by NCT. He viewed it as perpetual because it contains "the sum and substance of that obedience which is due unto God from all rational creatures made in his image."[111]

These distinctions in his views on abrogation and the various redemptive-historical functions of the Decalogue are in his early and later statements in the Hebrews commentary. It may be difficult for us to

---

[109] Wells, *Reisinger*, 6.
[110] Ibid.
[111] Owen, *Works*, XXII:215.

understand them, taking them at face value, but once his careful qualifications are taken into account, along with his other clear assertions concerning the perpetuity of the Decalogue under the New Covenant and the grounds for it, his meaning comes clearly into focus. But if we import into Owen our understanding of what certain statements mean or fail to understand his systematic thought, we are apt to misread him and either force upon him something he never intended or force him to contradict himself.

It appears that Wells misunderstood Owen. Wells' claims give the impression that he may not have taken all of the relevant data into consideration. This caused him to claim that the mediating position of Owen was that of Reisinger and NCT, without Owen's creation ordinance view of the Sabbath. We have seen, however, that this is an overstatement in need of numerous crucial qualifications. And these qualifications would actually reveal the fact that Owen and NCT are farther apart on these matters than a *prima facie* approach may indicate.

The historical/theological context in which Owen wrote
Primary source documentation has been presented from Calvin, Ursinus, Witsius, Turretin, Protestant Scholastic thought, and Boston. In doing so, the attempt was made to put Owen in historical and theological context. We found that his views on the subject matters examined were not novel and fit within the theological nomenclature of his contemporaries. Though what he said may be hard for us to understand and even appear novel, it was not so in his day. Owen's statements, put under the microscope of his theological peers, do not warrant Wells' assessment of him–that his mediating position is substantially that of John G. Reisinger and NCT.

2. The Contemporary/Theological Issues which gave rise to this Discussion

When understood in context, with Owen's own qualifications, and in light of other pertinent statements of his on related matters, and in light of the historical/theological nomenclature of his day, Owen can be understood to teach the same thing throughout the Hebrews commentary about the perpetuity of the Decalogue under the New Covenant. His views were somewhat standard in his day, though with their own nuances. They were neither novel nor those of NCT.

Tom Wells' claims have been referenced throughout this discussion and proven wrong for several reasons and in need of some crucial qualifications. What are those crucial and necessary qualifications? Here is a suggested list of agreements between John Owen and NCT and some necessary qualifications:

(1) Both John Owen and NCT believe that 'the first covenant' in the book of Hebrews is a reference to the Old or Mosaic Covenant.

(2) Both John Owen and NCT believe that the Old Covenant was a distinct and temporary covenant for Israel in the land of Canaan, abolished by Christ and replaced by the New Covenant. But Owen did not believe that Christ fulfilled the terms of the Old Covenant *in itself* for believers; NCT, at least John G. Reisinger, does.

(3) Both John Owen and NCT believe that the Old Covenant was not an administration of the covenant of grace. But Owen believes it was not a covenant of works *in itself* but revived the original Adamic covenant of works; NCT, at least John G. Reisinger, believes it was a covenant of works *in itself*.

(4) Both John Owen and NCT believe that the Bible contains a legal covenant or covenant of works. But Owen equates this covenant with the Adamic economy; NCT, at least John G. Reisinger, with the Old Covenant.

(5) Both John Owen and NCT believe that the New Covenant is an effectual covenant, securing all of the promised blessings of it for all in the covenant.[112]

(6) Both John Owen and NCT believe in the abrogation of the Decalogue under the New Covenant. But Owen believes in it

---

[112] In Owen, *Works*, XXII:116, Owen says: "There is ascribed unto this covenant such an *efficacy of grace*, as nothing but almighty power can make good and accomplish. ...But this covenant is of that nature, as that the grace administered in it shall effectually preserve all the covenanters unto the end, and secure unto them all the benefits of it." In Owen, *Works*, XXII:118, Owen says: "For all those with whom this covenant is made shall as really have the law of God written in their hearts, and their sins pardoned, according unto the promise of it, as the people of old were brought into the land of Canaan by virtue of the covenant made with Abraham. ...The covenant of grace in Christ is made only with the Israel of God, the church of the elect.–For by the making of this covenant with any, the effectual communication of the grace of it unto them is principally intended. Nor can that covenant be said to be made absolutely with any but those whose sins are pardoned by virtue thereof, and in whose hearts the law of God is written; which are the express promises of it." In Owen, *Works*, XXII:147, he says: "And therefore all with whom this covenant is made are effectually sanctified, justified, and saved." See also Owen *Works*, XXII:127, 131, 132, 133, 135, 138, 150, 167, 168, 169, and 170.

relatively, as it was "compacted" with the rest of the Old Covenant's law; NCT absolutely.

(7) John Owen believes in the multi-functional utility of the entire Decalogue; NCT does not.

(8) John Owen believes that the New Covenant includes the perpetuity of the Sabbath and not only because the Sabbath is a creation ordinance; NCT does not. In fact, as we have seen above, Tom Wells claims that the only difference between John Owen and John G. Reisinger (and NCT) on the Mosaic and New Covenants is Owen's creation ordinance view of the Sabbath. This, indeed, is not the case and an oversimplification of Owen's view.

This list reflects something mentioned above. When Owen and NCT are examined side by side, they appear to be farther apart on these matters than a surface approach may reveal.

In the section in *Reisinger* which presents Wells' understanding of Owen's mediating position, he says:

> Why, then, has the negative term antinomian stuck to so many who take this to be the best explanation of the presence of OT laws under the New Covenant? [I take "this" to refer to Wells' previous statement concerning his understanding of Owen's mediating position: "a law of any kind may be the property of more than one covenant, but no covenant is still in force in any way after it has reached its end."]
>
> If the answer is that this is essentially an antinomian explanation two replies seem obvious. First, if it is antinomianism in John Reisinger it is also antinomianism in John Owen. Second, it does not fall under the strictures against antinomianism in the latest volume to deal extensively with that issue, *The Weakness of the Law* by Jonathan Bayes, though Mr. Bayes himself holds the "orthodox" Puritan position.[113]

Understanding Owen's mediating position as he does, Wells argues that if one wants to label John G. Reisinger an antinomian[114], then John Owen must be also. We have, however, seen that Owen's views are somewhat standard concerning abrogation, Jer. 31:33, 2 Co. 3:3, Matt. 5:17, and the multi-functional utility of the Decalogue. Assuming Wells' interpretation of Owen and that Owen's views were somewhat standard (something proved above), we would then be forced to label Calvin, Ursinus, Witsius, Turretin, and Boston as antinomians, since they held substantially what Owen did. This would be interesting, especially since those men wrote against

---

[113] Wells, *Reisinger*, 9.
[114] I prefer the phrase "doctrinal antinomian" which I define below.

antinomianism in its various forms. This would mean either they all changed their views or they contradicted themselves.

The evidence above, however, provides a better solution. Owen cannot be labeled as an antinomian in any sense because he did not abrogate the Moral Law (Decalogue as a unit) in all senses from the New Covenant. In other words, he did not deny the third use of the law (as a rule of life for believers) as traditionally understood in Reformed theology. NCT does and hence, is doctrinally antinomian.[115]

Owen's "each covenant has its own positive law" motif (i.e., Wells' understanding of Owen's mediating position) is adhered to by NCT, though applied differently. It appears that NCT uses this motif to eliminate the Decalogue as a unit, especially the fourth commandment, under the New Covenant, among other things. Owen's understanding and application of "each covenant has its own positive law" did not. It may well be that this motif is one reason why the seventeenth century Particular Baptist Nehemiah Coxe was endeared to Owen on the Mosaic and New Covenants. If applied consistently, it eliminated *infant baptism* from the New Covenant, not the Decalogue or only its Sabbath. Coxe deals with the covenants from the covenant of works through the Covenant of Circumcision. Owen deals with the Mosaic and New Covenants in his Hebrews commentary. Both may[116] have held to the "each covenant has its own positive law" motif,

---

[115] Historically, antinomians have been labeled differently, depending on the type of antinomianism adhered to. Practical antinomians not only teach against law in the Christian life, they also advocate lawless living. Doctrinal antinomians, however, do not advocate lawless living, but they deny the third use of the law or, at best, advocate it but redefine what law means. See Turretin, *Institutes*, II:141ff. where he discusses the fact that antinomians deny the third use of the law. See Ernest F. Kevan, *The Grace of Law* (Grand Rapids: Baker Book House, 1976, second printing, February 1983), 22 (n.32), 24-25, for evidence that those who denied the perpetuity of the Decalogue and hence, the third use of the law, were labeled as moderately antinomian or doctrinally antinomian, even though considered otherwise virtuous. See also Jonathan F. Bayes, *The Weakness of the Law* (Carlisle, Cumbria, UK: Paternoster Press, 2000), 44-46, where he discusses John G. Reisinger in the context of doctrinal antinomianism, my article "The Death of the Decalogue," *Tabletalk*, September 2002, which is a brief discussion of the doctrinal antinomianism of NCT, my review of *New Covenant Theology* by Tom Wells and Fred Zaspel in *Reformed Baptist Theological Review*, I:1, January 2004, and Ian McNaughton, "Antinomianism in Historical Perspective" and James M. Renihan, "Caterpillars and Butterflies," which is a book review of *New Covenant Theology* in *Reformation Today*, September-October 2003, No. 195, 9-16 and 23-26. NCT, as a movement, abominates practical antinomianism, and rightly so.

[116] Coxe does not say if this motif endeared him to Owen's treatment of the Old and New Covenants. In Coxe's preface to the reader, he does say that Owen's recently published argument "That the Old Covenant and the New do differ in substance, and not

though if so, they applied it differently when it came to the subjects of baptism. But, if held to by both, neither used it to eliminate the Decalogue from the New Covenant. Hence, using Owen as a precursor to John G. Reisinger or NCT simply does not fit the evidence.

3. Closing Comments

We have examined Owen in light of Owen, his historical and theological context, and Tom Wells' claims that align him with John G. Reisinger and NCT. In light of the discussion above, it is safe to say that Owen cannot be claimed by NCT on the grounds Wells claims him. He held views with which NCT is sympathetic. But his views did not change, at least as far as the perpetuity of the Decalogue under the New Covenant goes, nor were they contradictory or novel. The novelty in all of this appears to be NCT's method of abrogating the Decalogue from the New Covenant. It does this upon the grounds of it being a unit of law applicable to Old Covenant Israel as a body politic and applicable to them alone. This leads NCT to view the Old Covenant as a covenant of works in itself and unrelated to the Edenic covenant of works. Radical antinomians eliminate the Decalogue because it is law. Doctrinal antinomians eliminate it because it is Moses' Law and not Christ's. This has detrimental implications for the identity of the Natural Law, the basis of the covenant of works, the perpetuity of the Moral Law, the Sabbath, the active obedience of Christ, and the imputation of righteousness–indeed, the gospel itself. The issues are far-reaching and have very practical relevance.

In closing, it is important to remember what was said at the outset. Owen can be easily misunderstood if not followed very carefully and if his statements are not examined in light of his systematic thought and the historical and theological context in which he wrote. It appears that both John G. Reisinger and Tom Wells did just that.[117] May we all learn from this to be careful when making claims about another's position, especially someone who carries as much theological weight as John Owen. In making such claims, we may be making sweeping generalizations unawares and leading others to believe that which is simply not true.

---

in the manner of their Administration only ..." prevented him from writing on this subject since he viewed his treatment as satisfactory on this point. Coxe is referring to Owen's Hebrews commentary on Hebrews 8.

[117] The author confesses that he has done this before and, most likely will again, though without malicious intent. We must assume the same in our NCT brothers.

Scripture Index

Name and Subject Index

Lightning Source UK Ltd.
Milton Keynes UK
UKHW010247021021
391524UK00001B/12